WHEN BRER RABBIT MEETS COYOTE

EDITED BY

JONATHAN BRENNAN

# When Brer Rabbit
# Meets Coyote

*African–Native American*

*Literature*

UNIVERSITY OF ILLINOIS PRESS

URBANA AND CHICAGO

Library of Congress Cataloging-in-Publication Data
When Brer Rabbit meets Coyote : African-Native American
literature / edited by Jonathan Brennan.
p.   cm.
Includes bibliographical references and index.
ISBN 0-252-02819-8 (alk. paper)
1. American literature—African American authors—History
and criticism.
2. American literature—Indian authors—History and criticism.
3. Literature, Comparative—African American and Indian.
4. Literature, Comparative—Indian and African American.
5. Literature and folklore—United States.
6. Indians of North America—Folklore.
7. African Americans in literature.
8. African Americans—Folklore.
9. Folklore in literature.
10. Indians in literature.
I. Brennan, Jonathan.
PS153.N5W43     2003
810.9'896073—dc21     2002014265

*A mi esposa, Natalia,*

*y mis hijos, Carmen Alicia y Liam Rafael:*

*Que nos quiten lo bailao*

I was a red man one time,
But the white man came.
I was a black man, too,
But the white men came.

They drove me out of the forest.
They took me away from the jungles.
I lost my trees.
I lost my silver moons . . .

—Langston Hughes, "Lament for Dark Peoples"


Jazz music is proving too much
for the American Indian
says Dr. Henry Beets, secretary of the
Christian Reform Church Missions.
He declares that jazz and the shimmy
are driving the redskin back to the war dance.

—Sherman Alexie, "Harmful Jazz"

# Contents

# *Preface*

## The Call

In 1891, the folklorist Alexander F. Chamberlain called for "an investigation of the influence of the Indian upon Negro folklore and the influence of the Negro upon Indian folklore."[1] This call appeared unanswered several decades later, when an article in the *Journal of Negro History* in 1920 insisted that African–Native American relations remained one of the "longest unwritten chapters of the history of the United States."[2]

## The Response

In the summer of 1989, while browsing through the Native American literature section of a San Francisco bookstore, I reached for one title only to find another book falling into my hands. This book, *The Life of Okah Tubbee,* a collaborative autobiography spoken by an African Choctaw, Okah Tubbee, and written and edited by his Mohawk Delaware wife, Laah Ceil, became the focus of my work for the next several years, yet with each successive reading its categorization proved more elusive. Was this a Native American text, shelved appropriately at the bookstore? Or, as it became clearer that Tubbee was at least part African American, was this an African American text? Because Tubbee was a slave in Natchez, Mississippi, I began to lean toward identifying their autobiography as an African American slave narrative, yet the majority of the text deals not with his enslavement but with his discovery and promotion of his Choctaw identity, thus demanding that the reader view it as a Choctaw autobiography. Tubbee was not an active participant in the Choctaw nation, however, and in the early part of his life he was raised in a community that was likely more African American than Choctaw, although he certainly may have had interactions with the many Choctaws (and African Choctaws) in the area.

As I searched for answers, I wondered if there were other African–Native American (Black Indian) texts that might help to answer my many questions. Despite the fact that much work remained to be done almost a century after Chamberlain's call for an investigation of African–Native American cross-influences, there had been some research on African–Native American relations. I examined existing research, uncovered a growing number of sources, and ultimately discovered that there is indeed a significant body of African–Native American literature. This tradition includes mythology and folklore, interweaving African and Native American storytelling, the work of an early African American dramatist (Brown) whose subject is the Black Carib Indian nation of eighteenth-century St. Vincent, and the novels of contemporary writers such as Clarence Major and Alice Walker. By gathering the essays in this collection, I intend to answer the call of earlier critics, to confirm the existence and significance of African–Native American literature, and to listen carefully to what this literature has to teach us.

Chamberlain's call to explicate African–Native American folklore and mythology leaves the respondent at a crossroads. One might choose to proceed, ignoring the well-worn paths of African and Native American traditions to either side. One might decide to turn back, returning to a road of familiarity. One might choose to follow only one path, either African or Native American, turning one's back on the tradition that lies across the way. Yet one might instead choose to linger at the crossroads, sitting down for a drink brimming with the salt water of the Middle Passage and the Trail of Tears, pouring a libation and offering tobacco, and listening carefully to the interwoven strands of storytelling from African and Native American literary traditions.

As meeting places for travelers from different lands, crossroads are ripe with the possibilities of exchange, negotiation, and collaboration. In *Africans and Native Americans*, Jack D. Forbes relates a story from Guyana in which Anancy, the spider-trickster, Nyan, an African sky-spirit, and the African earth- and river-mothers "met the Great Spirit, the Father Sun, and other spirit-powers of the Americans: 'The next day, all the peoples of the earth complained to Father Sun and for the first time, the ebony people, who were neighbors of Tihona, made themselves heard. . . . The Great Spirit invited Nyan, the anthracite-coloured Sky God . . . to share his domains. . . . They [the African spirits] agreed on condition the Great Spirit, in turn, shared the distant kingdoms of earth and sky that Nyan ruled."[3] These spiritual collaborations, much like the fusion of Arawak, Carib, and West African spiritual traditions in Haitian Voudoun noted by the anthropologist Maya Deren,[4] create a new mythological space, a New World formed from the merging of African and Native American traditions. This new world parallels the transformation Henry Louis Gates Jr. argues was made by the *jigue* (Cuban) trickster crossing the Atlantic to the New World, a journey from African to African American, an identity that was also created by negotiations between African and Native American cultural traditions.[5] Gates notes the close relationship between the *jigue* and Esu Elegbara, the Yoruban trickster. Elegbara serves many roles, especially as linguist, interpreter, and translator between worlds—in fact, Gates argues, "Legba is the indeterminacy of the interpretation of writing, and his traditional dwelling place, at the crossroads, for the critic, is the crossroads of understanding and truth."[6] At the crossroads, the meeting place of runaway African slaves and displaced Indians, of oral and written traditions, of the human and the divine, of meaning and indeterminacy, of the past and the future, we find a liminal space of mixed-race Black Indian identity and culture where the longest unwritten chapter in American history is written (and spoken). African–Native American literature becomes a possibility when the trickster interprets between worlds, when understanding meets truth, when Brer Rabbit meets Coyote.

## Notes

1. Alexander F. Chamberlain, "African and American: The Contact of Negro and Indian," *Science* 17 (1891): 90.

2. Carter G. Woodson, "Relations of Indians and Negroes in Massachusetts," *Journal of Negro History* 5 (Jan. 1920): 45.

3. Jack D. Forbes, *Africans and Native Americans: The Language of Race and the Evolution of Red-Black Peoples*, 2d ed. (Urbana: University of Illinois Press, 1993), 6.

4. Maya Deren, "Some Elements of Arawakan, Carib, and Other Indian Cultures in Haitian Voudoun" (appendix B), in *The Divine Horsemen: The Voodoo Gods of Haiti* (New York: Dell Publishing, 1970), 271–86.

5. Henry Louis Gates Jr., *The Signifying Monkey: A Theory of Afro-American Literary Criticism* (New York: Oxford University Press, 1988), 18.

6. Ibid., 25.

# Acknowledgments

Permission to reprint the following material is gratefully acknowledged:

Epigraphs (p. vii): Sherman Alexie, "Harmful Jazz," reprinted from *The Summer of Black Widows,* © 1996 by Sherman Alexie, used by permission of Hanging Loose Press; Langston Hughes, excerpt from "Lament for Dark Peoples," from *The Collected Poems of Langston Hughes,* © 1994 by the Estate of Langston Hughes, used by permission of Alfred A. Knopf, a division of Random House, Inc.

Chapter 2: "Brer Rabbit and His Cherokee Cousin: Moving Beyond the Appropriation Paradigm," by Sandra K. Baringer, in *Trickster Lives: Culture and Myth in American Fiction,* ed. Jeanne Campbell Reesman (Athens: University of Georgia Press, 1999), © 1999 by the University of Georgia Press, reprinted with minor editorial changes by permission of the University of Georgia Press.

Chapter 3: "Red, White and Black," by John Sekora, in *A Mixed Race: Ethnicity in Early America,* ed. Frank Shuffelton (New York: Oxford University Press, 1993), © 1993 by Frank Shuffelton, reprinted with substantial editorial changes by permission of Oxford University Press, Inc.

Chapter 4: "Recapturing John Marrant," by Benilde Montgomery, in *A Mixed Race: Ethnicity in Early America,* ed. Frank Shuffelton (New York: Oxford University Press, 1993), © 1993 by Frank Shuffelton, reprinted with minor editorial changes by permission of Oxford University Press, Inc.

Chapter 5: "Speaking Cross Boundaries: A Nineteenth-Century African–Native American Autobiography," by Jonathan Brennan, in *a/b: Auto/Biography Studies* 7.2 (Fall 1992): 219–38, reprinted with substantial editorial changes by permission of *a/b: Auto/Biography Studies.*

Chapter 6: "In Search of the Mardi Gras Indians," by Jason Berry, Jonathan Foose, and Tad Jones in *Up from the Cradle of Jazz: New Orleans Music since World War II*, by Jason Berry, Jonathan Foose, and Tad Jones (Athens: University of Georgia Press, 1986), 203–19, © 1986 by Jason Berry, Jonathan Foose, and Tad Jones, reprinted with minor editorial changes by permission of the authors.

Chapter 7: "Mardi Gras Indians: Carnival and Counternarrative in Black New Orleans," by George Lipsitz, in *Cultural Critique* 10 (Fall 1988): 99–121, reprinted with minor editorial changes by permission of *Cultural Critique* and the University of Minnesota Press.

Chapter 9: "'If You Know I Have a History, You Will Respect Me': A Perspective on Afro–Native American Literature," by Sharon P. Holland, in *Callaloo* 17.1 (1994): 334–50, © 1994 by Charles H. Rowell, reprinted with minor editorial changes by permission of Johns Hopkins University Press.

---

I am grateful to many people for the opportunity to teach and learn about African–Native American history, culture, and literature. First and foremost I would like to thank mi esposa, Natalia, por los años de amor, de fuerza, y de pasion, y por las habichuelas tan ricas. I am grateful for all that we do together, especially for the cha-cha, las plenas de noche buena, long walks, and the vision we share. I would also like to thank Carmen Alicia, my daughter, for her paintings, her funny jokes, and everything she continues to teach me about being a father. I thank Liam Rafael, my son, for his gentle spirit, his songs, and his patience.

I am also grateful for the support of my parents and family, especially for all that my brother Peter and my sister-in-law Mandy have done. Gracias a Carmen y Fernando, dos personas con corazones d'oro y espiritus de viento y sol.

I am thankful for the contributions of my students, who always teach me something new. Thank you also to the contributors to this volume, who have worked so hard to bring African–Native American literature into the light. I deeply appreciate the support of my colleagues and friends, especially Donnelle McGee and Yolanda Coleman, Manouso and Rita Manos, JoeSam., the Karimabadi family, and Skip Downing. A special thanks to Hertha Dawn Sweet Wong and the late Barbara Christian for all their support, encouragement, and guidance. Thanks as well to the many Mardi Gras Indian tribes who carry the Black Indian tradition, singing:

> Hey, hey, Indian's coming
> Hey, hey, Indian's coming
> Hey, hey, Indian's coming . . .
> Indians, here they come
> Get out the way.

# WHEN BRER RABBIT MEETS COYOTE

JONATHAN BRENNAN

# Introduction: Recognition of the African–Native American Literary Tradition

Here we are, all living as in one house.
—John Horse (African Seminole)

**recognize:** to acknowledge formally . . . to admit as one
being entitled to be heard . . . to acknowledge the de fac-
to existence or the independence of . . . to perceive to be
something or someone previously known . . . to perceive
clearly . . .
—*Webster's Ninth New Collegiate Dictionary*

In 1526, long before English colonies were established in
North America, Lucas Vásquez de Ayllón, a Spaniard living on Haiti,
brought a ship carrying Spanish colonists accompanied by one hundred
African slaves to land in North America near what would later become
South Carolina: "Determined to succeed, Ayllón drove his people until
they came to a great river, which was probably the Pee Dee. Selecting a
location in a low, marshy area, Ayllón ordered his band to set up camp.
He paused to name his settlement 'San Miguel de Gualdape.' When he
ordered the Africans to begin building homes, he launched black slavery
in the United States."[1] The colony disbanded when Ayllón died after four
months; the Spanish colonists returned to Haiti after the rebellion of the
African slaves, who joined a Native American nation.[2]

The new African–Native American community was likely one of the
earliest in a long series of racial, cultural, and territorial collaborations

and negotiations between Africans and Native Americans. One of the many cultural productions of these new African–Native American communities was a body of literature drawing from both African and Native American literary traditions. This literary body, composed of writers and speakers in nearly every genre, extends from myths and folklore of the sixteenth century to numerous contemporary African–Native American writers, yet it has been given little recognition or critical attention by literary scholars. Through an examination of the historical interactions that resulted in the creation of African–Native American cultures, through a discussion of the literatures of African–Native American authors, and through an articulation of the distinct features of African–Native American literatures, I hope to reveal the depth, breadth, and significance of the African–Native American literary tradition and to recognize the importance of literary expressions by African-Native Americans. I will argue that a number of common features bind these texts together in a distinct literary tradition, including the narration of African–Native American subjectivity, strategic discourses and situational identities, a literary hybridization of elements derived from both African American and Native American literary traditions, a sustained focus on African, Native, and African–Native American history and politics, and finally a textual state of rootlessness often answered by the engagement of dual histories that attempt to repair the narrative site of rootlessness.

## African–Native American History

The creation of African–Native American cultures (and literatures) might well have begun before the European colonization of Africa and the Americas. In *They Came Before Columbus* and *African Presence in Early America,* Ivan Van Sertima and other scholars discuss a body of historical and archaeological evidence that suggests that Native Americans may have been traveling to Africa and interacting with Africans and that Africans may have been traveling to the Americas and interacting with Native Americans for centuries before European "discovery" and colonization.[3] In *Africans and Native Americans,* Jack D. Forbes cites Van Sertima's argument that the two Atlantic ocean currents, one in the North Atlantic and the other in the South Atlantic, form "two great circular rivers in the ocean"[4] by way of which Native Americans and Africans could have traveled to each other's continents and returned home again. Forbes also notes archaeological evidence suggesting that Native Americans had traveled to Africa for centuries before European colonization and discusses the documented navigational expertise of Native

Americans as well as Columbus's use of the southerly ocean current crossing after he was told by the Portuguese that it had been used by African traders from Guinea traveling to the west with their goods.[5] Early contacts and trading, suggestive of a long-standing pattern of cultural interaction and exchange between Africans and Native Americans, may have produced racial and cultural mixing on both sides of the Atlantic. Thus, some Africans may have brought an existing African–Native American culture to the Americas as slaves, and the Native American cultures to which they arrived may, in some instances, have already been an African–Native American culture.

After the start of the European colonization of Africa and the Americas, contacts between Africans and Native Americans increased considerably. Columbus captured Native Americans in his first voyage to the Caribbean and eventually "proposed that American slavery be used to finance the conquest"[6] of the Americas. The Portuguese and the Spaniards would eventually ship thousands of Native Americans to European cities as well as to their colonies in African nations. These Native Americans worked as slaves alongside the Africans captured by the Portuguese and Spaniards. As Forbes notes, "it will perhaps be surprising to some readers to learn that the greatest degree of intensive contact between Americans and Africans did not occur initially in either the Americas or Africa, but rather in European cities such as Lisbon, Seville, and Valencia."[7] Thus African–Native American cultures may have formed in any number of European communities as well as in African nations and the Americas.

The largest concentration of African-Native communities, however, stems from the massive plantation system created by European colonists, which first relied on Native American slaves and subsequently a combination of African and Native American slaves for labor. In the colonies of what would become the United States, the Spanish, French, and English enslaved Native Americans as part of the colonization process. Millions of Native Americans were enslaved throughout the Americas and the Caribbean; this enslavement continued in most colonies alongside the enslavement of Africans, and the eventual result in many slave communities was a racial and cultural mixture of Africans and Native Americans. Because most historians ignore or downplay the substantial enslavement of Native Americans, and because the widespread enslavement of Native Americans was a critical factor in the creation of numerous African–Native American communities, it is essential to further examine the institution that enslaved Native Americans.

In a study published in 1913, "Indian Slavery in Colonial Times within the Present Limits of the United States," Almon Lauber, relying on colonial European and American documents, establishes the existence of a substantial and widespread policy of enslaving Native Americans. The enslavement of Native Americans is also well represented in colonial documents such as plantation records and advertisements for runaway slaves, and any serious inquiry into the enslavement of Native Americans demonstrates that such a policy was not incidental nor sporadic but rather deliberate and widespread. For instance, the Spaniard Hernando de Escalante Fontanedo insisted that Native Americans in Florida "can never be made submissive and become Christians . . . [and should be] placed on ships, and scattered throughout the various islands, and even on the Spanish Main, where they might be sold as His Majesty sells his vessels to the grandees in Spain."[8] This was, in fact, the policy pursued by the Spanish colonizers. Hernando de Soto carried "bloodhounds, chains and iron collars for the catching and holding of Indian slaves"; Francisco Vasquez de Coronado "imprisoned and made servants of all the people, one hundred and fifty men, women and children" in Tiguex; and Cabeza de Vaca traveled with a Spanish expedition "in the company, among others, of six Christians and five hundred Indian slaves."[9]

In California, Spanish colonists raided Native American rancherias to "secure agricultural workers, herdsmen, and domestic servants,"[10] and the Spanish mission system enslaved Native Americans for more than six decades, from 1769 until 1834: "The Indians constructed the buildings, planted and cultivated the fruit trees and vineyards, tended the cattle, made pottery, wove cloths, and performed, in fact, all the manual labor that was necessarily required in an extensive colony."[11]

In the French colonies in North America, French missionaries also held Native American slaves. From the time of the earliest French expeditions to North America, Native slaves were captured and interrogated, displayed as captives and utilized as interpreters. In 1534 Cartier "seized some of the natives and carried them aboard his ships," and in 1562 the "queen of France commanded Ribaut to bring back some of the natives"[12] from his colonizing expedition. In Louisiana, the French colonists responded to a counterattack by the Natchez Indians by capturing and enslaving them: "Four hundred and fifty of the tribe, including the Great Sun, the Little Sun, and several of the principal war chiefs . . . were . . . carried to New Orleans. The women and children were retained as slaves on the plantations. Some of the prisoners were burned in New Orleans. The Great Sun, the Little Sun, their families and more than four hundred of the captives, were sent at once to Cape Francois, Haiti, and most of them sold to the planters as slaves."[13]

Like the Spanish and French colonizers, the earliest English explorers often seized Native Americans and brought them back to England to be displayed or to Spain to be sold. Sebastian Cabot brought "three natives from the New World"[14] back to England in 1498. Martin Frobisher captured several Native Americans on his three voyages, and Thomas Hunt captured twenty-seven Native Americans in present-day Massachusetts and sold some of them as slaves in Spain.[15] The English colonists responded to perceived threats and to actual attacks by Native Americans on European colonies by invading Native nations and selling the captives as slaves within the mainland colonies and to the Caribbean colonies. After an attack on the colonists by Native Americans in 1622, a tract was published in London that railed against the "Barbarous Massacre" and suggested the potential profit that might be realized as a result of a policy of enslavement: "Because the Indians, who before were used as friends, may now most justly be compelled to servitude in the mines, and the like, of whom some may be sent for the use of the Summer Islands."[16]

In the Carolinas, the colonists attacked the Kussoe in 1671, the Stono in 1680, and the Spanish missions, Spanish-aligned Native nations, and the Spanish city of Saint Augustine numerous times in the early 1700s. Thousands of Native Americans were captured and sold as slaves; in the Carolina colonists' wars against the Yamasee, Apalachee, and Timucua (1702–8), "there was carried back to Charleston, for sale as slaves, almost the entire population of seven towns, in all, some 1,400 persons."[17]

In the New England colonies, the captives of the colonists' war against the Pequot nation (1637) were given to the English soldiers as slaves, to the Narraganset as "allies," to the colonists in the Massachusetts and Connecticut colonies, and sold to slave traders in the West Indies.[18] During King Philip's War (1675–76), Pequot captives were sold to "the Spanish West Indies, Spain, Portugal, Bermuda, Virginia, and the Azores."[19]

Native Americans were also enslaved by the criminal courts, by kidnapping, by birth to an enslaved mother, by straying from reservation boundaries imposed by the colonists, and through the colonial "education" system set up for Native Americans. In South Carolina, Massachusetts, Virginia, Rhode Island, and Connecticut there is ample evidence in the legislative and judicial records of Native Americans accused of theft being sold into slavery and shipped to plantations in the mainland or Caribbean colonies.[20] Sometimes they were traded for African slaves, since the colonists believed the African slaves less inclined to run away because they were so far removed from their nations.[21] Other Native Americans, like African Americans, were kidnapped into slavery by slave traders. In many colonies the legislature formalized the already informal

practice of enslaving the children born of enslaved mothers, even if the
term of slavery for the mother was not for life:

> South Carolina, for example, by an act of 1712, repeated in 1722 and
> 1735, declared that, with the exception of certain individuals freed by the
> government, 'all negroes, mulattoes, mustizos, or Indians which at any
> time heretofore have been sold, or now are held or taken to be, or hereaf-
> ter shall be bought and sold as slaves, are hereby declared slaves: and they
> and their children, are hereby made and declared slaves to all intents and
> purposes.' . . . In 1705, Virginia similarly declared all children bond or free
> according to the condition of their mothers . . . [a] Maryland act, June 2,
> 1692, provided that all children born or thereafter to be born of slaves
> within the province were to be slaves for the term of their natural lives. . . .
> New York, on its own part, in 1706, decreed that any negro, Indian, mu-
> latto or mustee child should follow the condition of the mother.[22]

Finally, Native American children were often enslaved when they
were given up to the European colonists for "education." In North Carolina, European settlers left their colony at Old Town Creek because of the
angry reactions from neighboring Native nations whose "children had
been entrusted to their care, under the pretext of sending them north to
be educated," when in fact they were "shipped off as slaves."[23] The Tuscarora nation was similarly outraged when "their children who had been
bound out for a limited time in English families were, contrary to the spirit
of the agreement, transported to other plantations and sold as slaves."[24]

Partial steps toward abolishing the enslavement of Native Americans
were taken by only four of the thirteen colonies. In Virginia, the legislature passed an act in 1691 that was later interpreted by the Supreme Court
to mean that no more Native American slaves could be brought into the
colony; it appears to have been ignored for at least one hundred years. In
South Carolina, the legislature passed an act in 1740 declaring that those
Natives who were not already enslaved, as long as they were "in amity
with this government,"[25] were exempted from slavery. In Rhode Island
the legislature passed an act declaring that "no Indian in this colony be
a slave but only to pay their debts, or for their bringing up, or courtesy
they have received, or to perform covenant as if they had been country-
men not in war."[26] The New York legislature addressed the issue several
times, primarily noting the differences between those Natives enslaved
from within the colony and those brought from outside the colony and
ruling that those from Spanish colonies should be sent back.[27] The many
exemptions to these legislative decrees and the fact that many European
colonists simply ignored them hampered whatever benefit Native Americans might have received from the legislation.

## African–Native American Communities

Most of the colonies, however, never abolished Native enslavement. As more Native nations were pushed from their lands by warfare, disease, removal, and a series of broken treaties, as the population of Natives began to diminish, as the number of European colonists grew, and as the number of African slaves began to grow dramatically in proportion to the Native slaves, many Native slaves began to be incorporated into an enslaved body of African-Native Americans. The result was the creation of culturally and racially mixed communities. They were often classified as "colored," "black," or "mulatto," whether racially mixed or not, and the distinctions between African and Native began to blur, especially as the term "mulatto" was widely used to describe both African-European and African–Native American people. There is substantial evidence that slaves were commonly Native Americans and African-Native Americans, for example Jack D. Forbes's citations of Virginia, North Carolina, and South Carolina runaway slave advertisements:[28]

> 1752 Ran away from Somerset County, Maryland, "a tall Slim Mulatto Man Slave, . . . looks much like unto an Indian and will endeavour to pass for such; had with him a strip'd Indian Match-coat."

> 1772 Ran away from Cumberland a "Mulatto Man named Jim, who is a Slave, but pretends to have a Right to his Freedom. His father was an Indian, of the name of Cheshire, and very likely will call himself James Cheshire, or Chink." He has "long black hair resembling an Indian's."

> 1773 Ran away from Amelia County "a Negro man of the name of Tom . . . of a yellowish complexion, much the appearance of an Indian. . . . His hair is of a different kind from that of a Negro's, rather more of the Indian's, but partaking of both, which though short, he frequently ties behind."

> 1746 Ran away "a tall lusty young Wench, can speak good English, Chickesaw, and perhaps French, the Chickesaws having taken her from the French settlements on Mississippi." She fled with her negro husband.

Runaway slave advertisements also described African-Native Americans as "mustees," a term that could refer to a variety of racial mixtures but most often described African-Native Americans:[29]

> 1743 "A Mustee Fellow named Nedd . . . short curl'd Hair, but not woolly, thick lip'd, small eyes."

> 1759 "a Negro woman named HAGAR, with her child Fanny, a Mustee."

> 1772 a "slim Negro wench, named CATHARINA . . . and carried away with her a Mustee Child (her Daughter) about Six Years old."

1775 "Jemmy, a Mustee Fellow . . . sharp visaged, not flat nosed, which shews the Indian blood more than the negro."

There is substantial documentation showing that large numbers of Native Americans were not exempted nor released from slavery but instead merged into a mixed African–Native American slave community and were not emancipated until 1865 at the end of the Civil War. There have been studies of these African–Native American slave communities, but inevitably they are theorized as only African American and not also African–Native American communities, which is misleading for scholars who rely on such research to set cultural parameters for their studies. Forbes argues, and I strongly agree, that anyone studying "colored" Americans in early American history should rely primarily on original source material and careful readings of racial terminology rather than research predicated on racial and cultural assumptions.

The conditions for the creation of African–Native American communities also existed outside the parameters of plantation slavery. African–Native American communities resulted from runaway African American or African–Native American slaves. Many slaves bolted from the plantations to create separate maroon communities and nations that were often African-Native American; they also joined and were incorporated into existing Native American nations. They married, had children, and often became effective leaders, negotiating treaties and serving as valued interpreters within the Native nation. The historian Rhett Jones argues that the Senecas, Onodagas, Minisinks, and many other northeastern Native American nations aided and abetted fugitive African American slaves, even incorporating them into their nations, that African–Native American maroon nations in the southeastern United States often defended themselves against European American colonists' attacks, and that there are many recorded instances of African–Native American collaboration and rebellion against European American colonial rule.[30] Some of these new maroon nations assumed names that declared their independence and purpose: "God Knows Me and None Else," "Disturb Me If You Dare," "Come Try Me If You Be Men," "I Shall Moulder Before I Shall Be Taken,"[31] "Hide Me," and "The Woods Lament for Me."[32] Herbert Aptheker points to the "evidence of the existence of at least fifty such communities . . . from 1672 to 1864"[33] in the current states of South Carolina, North Carolina, Virginia, Louisiana, Florida, Georgia, Mississippi, and Alabama. The maroon nations faced attacks from European American colonists as well as from militias composed of either African American slaves or Native American bounty hunters who were paid to recapture the maroons. They often attacked local plantations to retrieve family members from slavery or to secure food or other provisions. Some of these maroon nations grew to considerable size and played an important role in influencing local and state politics. The Dismal Swamp Maroon nation of Virginia and North Carolina and the Seminole nation of Florida were two of the largest and most influential.

The Dismal Swamp, a one-thousand-square-mile freshwater swamp running through the Tidewater regions of Virginia and North Carolina, became the center of a powerful maroon nation. Hugo Prosper Leaming believes that the earliest inhabitants were the "survivors of the small [Native American] nations of the east coast which had been destroyed by English colonists, or fugitives from slavery."[34] These maroons were later joined by members of the Susquehanna, Powhatan, and Chowan nations as well as escaped Irish "indentured servants" whose Gaelic survives in trail names and local dialect.[35] As African slaves arrived in greater numbers to the colonies, they too escaped to the Dismal Swamp nation. The nation survived for at least two centuries, playing a key role in slave revolts and creating a distinctive African–Native American maroon culture that eventually merged into "the general African American community."[36]

The Seminole nation, a branch of the Creek nation that had split away and moved further south to Florida (Seminole in Creek translates as "runaway"), was joined by runaway Native, African, and African–Native American slaves whose escape was also encouraged by the Spanish colonists, who wished to maintain a foothold against the expanding English colonies. The relationships between former Creek Seminoles and African Seminoles were always complex; sometimes the Creek Seminoles held the African Seminoles as slaves, although most often this was a very different type of slavery than that practiced by the English colonists. African Seminoles had a great deal of autonomy within the nation and often a great deal of political influence as well, particularly as the maroon nation grew in size and strength. There was substantial intermarriage and cultural exchange among the various Seminole communities, leading to an African–Native Seminole culture. Richard Price argues that the exchange of technology between African and Native American cultures was essential to their survival:

> A great many of these techniques for dealing with the environment clearly were learned, directly or indirectly, from American Indians. It is not yet possible to say how many had some sort of antecedents in the African homeland as well. . . . I would suggest, however, that a good deal of maroon technology must have been developed on the plantations

during slavery. Throughout Afro-America, Indians interacted with slaves, whether as fellow sufferers, as trading partners, or in other capacities. Indian technologies—from pottery making and hammock weaving to fish drugging and manioc processing—were taken over and, often, further developed by the slaves, who were so often responsible for supplying the bulk of their own daily needs. Life as maroons meant numerous new challenges to daily survival, but it was on a base of technical knowledge developed in the interaction between Indians and blacks on plantations that most of the remarkable maroon adaptations were built.[37]

Price's argument also reveals that African–Native American culture was an important issue to examine on the plantations and not only in the maroon nations; what many scholars discuss as "African American" culture on the slave plantations was, in fact, often African–Native American culture.

Some members of Native nations, especially the Choctaw, Chickasaw, Cherokee, Creek, and Seminole, also held African Americans as slaves.[38] Some scholars argue that this was most often the result of European Americans marrying into the Native nation and creating a more assimilated cadre who espoused European American cultural values, including the holding of slaves. Others argue that the slavery was an adaptation of traditional Native American forms of slavery, which resulted from the necessity of incorporating captives from warfare into the nation and were generally radically different than the form practiced by European Americans. Those enslaved in Native nations often had substantial rights within the nation, were enslaved for a limited period of cultural adaptation, and could marry and have children who would be free citizens of the nation. The conditions of enslavement varied from nation to nation, and the Seminole nation created an African–Native American culture more rapidly and readily than the others. Certainly each of these nations experienced a significant degree of cultural exchange and created African-Native subcultures within the nation.

In other communities, such as the Lumbee of North Carolina, Mattaponies and Gingaskin of Virginia, Nanticoke of Maryland, or many of the Native nations in the northeastern United States, including the Pequot and Montauk, free or indentured Natives intermarried with free or indentured African Americans and created African–Native American communities. This was especially common throughout New England.[39] Similarly, African Americans and Native Americans had innumerable contacts in the western United States. Spanish and French colonists utilized Africans as trappers, hunters, traders, and interpreters in their contacts with numerous Native nations. Many of these Africans rapidly developed a linguistic and cultural fluency within Native nations, and some joined these nations as citizens and leaders.[40]

Despite the significant numbers of African–Native American communities established in the United States, scholars tend to collapse these sites of multiple identity into a singular identity more closely aligned with prevailing racial categories. In an analysis of the African Montauk writer Olivia Ward Bush-Banks's unpublished play *Indian Trails*, Bernice F. Guillaume argues that the three-act play contains "names and terms . . . which reveal that Bush-Banks was privy to knowledge of Algonquian socio-political structure, language, and material culture that the scientific community presumed had been lost by the early nineteen-hundreds."[41] One of the major reasons, Guillaume notes, that the "scientific community" presumed the loss of culture was because African–Native American communities, such as the Shinnecock Reservation, were generally characterized as "degraded" and thus not regarded as legitimate Native American communities by many researchers.[42] The argument that African-Native Americans, unlike European-Native Americans, could not or should not be classified as Native Americans was extended to most African-Native communities, and in 1843 European Americans in Virginia attempted to "dispossess the Pamunky of their lands," insisting that "the claim of the Indians no longer exists. . . . His blood has so largely mingled with that of the Negro race as to have obliterated all striking features of Indian extraction."[43] It is clear that European Americans feared the alliance of African and Native American communities, for in this instance the European American petitioners claimed that the Pamunky nation had "'assumed all the features of a legally established body of free Negroes, the resort of free Negroes from all parts of the country . . . the harbour for runaway slaves.'"[44] For centuries, African–Native American communities and nations have struggled to retain their Native identity in the face of hostile attacks from surrounding communities, local, state, and federal government bodies, and even from federally "recognized" Native American nations who have attempted to define away the Native identity of African-Native Americans. Many scholars have followed the same master narrative of race, basing their research on the assumption that the racial categories of black and white created to support enslavement provide a valid basis for what are essentially cultural (not racial) interrogations.

One scholar who has not operated on assumptions of impermeable racial identity, Jack D. Forbes, argues that the language of racial terminology reveals the widespread existence of African-Native Americans as well as the obscuring of their identities. Forbes cites a wealth of racial terminology in multiple languages that has been used to describe African-Native Americans: *griffon, half-blood, half-breed, mulatto, mustee, mamaluco, mestizo, branco,* and *Indian-Negro.* There are, of course, others in use, *Black Indian* being one of the most popular, but ultimately Forbes's research demonstrates that while we must acknowledge the shifting terminologies that are chronologically, geographically, and linguistically distinct (although they attempt to encompass a similar concept), we cannot rely on any single African–Native American experience to embody the entirety of African–Native American identity. Instead, we must ground any inquiry into African–Native American experience in the particular subject's historical circumstances.

Because these historical circumstances are considerably complex, the resulting African–Native American identities are equally complex. It would perhaps be useful to begin to make distinctions based on region, with the historical period as a controlling variable. Thus one might be tempted to conclude that the experience of the western, the southeastern, and northeastern regions of the United States might create distinct African–Native American groupings to examine. In fact, they do, but with limitations. There were indeed experiences in common between African Americans and western Native American nations, especially Plains Indian nations, for in the western United States, African Americans and Native Americans had innumerable contacts, especially through the fur trapping industry. In "Blacks in the American West: An Overview," Quintard Taylor argues that European American homesteaders arriving in Oklahoma in the late nineteenth century found African-Native farmers working their small farms.[45] The African Mexican Estevanico came northward with Spanish explorers in the sixteenth century and interacted with the Pueblo nations. Pierre Bonga, the son of Africans enslaved in Minnesota in the late eighteenth century, was a trapper and interpreter who married a Chippewa woman. George Bonga, Pierre's son, also married a Chippewa woman and worked for a fur company.[46] Edward Rose, a Cherokee-African-European American, was also a guide, trapper, and interpreter who was fluent in many Native American languages, and he served as a Crow chief.[47] James P. Beckwourth, an escaped African–European American slave from Virginia and also a guide, fur trader, and interpreter, married into the Crow nation and eventually served as a chief for many years. Other African Americans, such as "Bass Reaves, Grant Johnson, and Isaac Rogers were raised in Oklahoma, knew Indian languages, and often were more trusted by the Native Americans than were white marshals."[48] Kenneth Wiggins Porter cites a case of a "Negro woman who had been stolen from near Dardanelle, Arkansas, [brought to Texas by Comanches,] and was the mother of four part-Indian daughters."[49] In spite of the breadth of African–Native American interactions represented here, and in spite of the temptation to fashion an African–Native American identity that is characteristic of the western United States from some parallel experiences, when examining the cultural traditions that arose from these interactions the most accurate assessment of any literary tradition will be drawn from specific interactions (Comanche–African American, or Crow–African American, or African American–Chippewa) taking place during specific time periods.

This regional approach is also relevant in the Southeast, for especially among the Choctaw, Chickasaw, Cherokee, Creek, and Seminole nations there was substantial interaction between African and Native Americans, interactions that reveal interesting parallels and unique variations. There were also cultural collaborations between African Americans and Natchez, Hitchiti, Seminole, Potowatomi, Alabama, and Koasati Indian nations, among others. In *Africans and Creeks,* Daniel F. Littlefield Jr. notes that racial prejudice by Creeks toward African Creeks grew in severity as the Civil War approached, yet it is still clear that portions of the Creek nation underwent a transformation to an African-Creek nation, as "persons of not more than half African blood, if their mothers were Creeks, were considered Creek citizens . . . 'and intermarriages between the negroes and Indians was rather common. The half-breeds resulting from such unions were accepted as bonafide members of the tribe by the Indians in the distribution of annuities, but not by the United States courts.' . . . [I]n 1915, the Creeks presented 'a very curious spectacle of an almost complete mixture.'"[50] Members of the Cherokee nation held slaves as well (2,511 by 1860), more than any other Native American nation, and Littlefield cites historians who believe that the treatment of their slaves was not significantly different than that of European American slaveholders.[51] Numerous regulations were enacted restricting the freedom of African Americans in the Cherokee nation, including prohibitions against teaching reading and writing to African Americans and intermarriage between Cherokee and African Americans. The latter law did not eliminate substantial intermarriage and cultural interactions among Cherokees and African Americans, however, and in their written constitution of 1839 the "Cherokees admitted to citizenship the African offspring of Cherokee women but excluded the African offspring of African women and Cherokee men";[52] legal citizens or not, African Cherokees were a part of the Cherokee nation.

The Choctaw held nearly as many African American and African–Native American slaves as the Cherokee (2,349 in 1860), and the Chickasaw held nearly a thousand slaves in 1860,[53] but it was likely within the

Seminole nation that the most substantial acculturation process took place. In *Africans and Seminoles*, Littlefield argues that African Seminoles "lived like their masters and allies . . . dressed Seminole fashion," and spoke "Spanish and English as well as the Indian languages. As a result, they were called upon more and more as interpreters and go-betweens when the Indians dealt with the whites."[54] This led to the development of a system of slavery significantly different than that developing on the plantations of European Americans to the north:

> One scholar has postulated that the Seminoles were at first simply impressed enough with the prestige attached to the ownership of Africans to exchange livestock for them but, not subscribing to the whites' system of economics, were at a loss as to what to do with them. The Indians therefore gave them tools with which to build houses of their own and set them to work cultivating crops and raising livestock of their own, a small portion of which the master took as tribute. However, this assessment appears to have been based on descriptions of Seminole slavery written a generation after it began among the Seminoles.[55]

Littlefield notes that although there were historical periods in which the majority of Africans among the Native Seminoles were free, some of the Native Seminoles, after Removal to the West and under pressure from the government and the neighboring slaveholders, found it "politically inexpedient" to continue their amicable relations with the African Seminoles.[56] Certainly some Native or African-Native Seminoles were cruel slaveowners, and others much less so, yet there had already been and continued to be cultural interaction and intermarriage; the large number of African Seminoles ensured a continuing African Seminole culture. This African-Native culture was particularly threatening to Cherokee slaveholders, and the interaction of their African or African Cherokee slaves with the African Seminoles would contribute to the Cherokee Slave Revolt of 1842.[57]

While there are parallels among the African–Native American nations in the southeast, such as the acquisition of African–Native American community members through enslavement, social conditions for African-Native Americans differed from nation to nation. These social conditions changed through time, making it essential to understand the contemporary political and social issues surrounding any African–Native American community in order to theorize the ways in which they formulated identity. Yet African–Native American community members were acquired by southeastern Native American nations through other means, especially through harboring escaped slaves or developing political alliances between African Americans and Native Americans, like those demonstrated by Gwendolyn Midlo Hall in *Africans in Colonial Louisiana*,[58] so such communities cannot be accounted for by the prevailing model of acquisition through slavery.

Just as African–Native American communities arose both during enslavement and in "freedom" in the southeast, so too did many free or formerly enslaved African Americans and Native Americans create African-Native families and communities in the mid-Atlantic, southern Atlantic and northeastern regions. In nations such as the Lumbee of North Carolina, Mattaponies and Gingaskin of Virginia, Nanticoke of Maryland, or many of the Native nations in the northeastern United States, including the Pequot, Wampanoag, and Montauk, free or indentured Native Americans intermarried with free or indentured African Americans and created African–Native American communities. In Lorenzo Greene's study of African Americans in New England, the connections between Africans and Native Americans are extensive. Greene asserts that "considerable intermixture went on between Negroes and other racial groups, especially between Indians and Negroes,"[59] and notes extensive African-Native amalgamation in Connecticut, Rhode Island, and Massachusetts and records of marriages between African American and Native American slaves and "free" African Americans and Native Americans. He argues that there was substantial intermarriage between African American men and Native American women because of the lack of "legal obstacles," "social differences," and African American women.[60] Greene also notes that "Indians and Negroes were grouped together in the slave codes of all the New England provinces,"[61] and, in fact, much of the legislation enacted by colonial legislatures continually addresses both African and Native American slaves as well as "mulattoes" (African-Native or European-Native Americans). Both African and Native Americans, free and enslaved, were excluded from militia duty, punished for violations of curfews and boundaries, prohibited from selling goods, lighting bonfires, begging for money, drinking in public taverns, dancing, gambling, defaming any European American, carrying sticks, keeping hogs, or holding social gatherings.[62] It becomes increasingly clear that social conditions for "free" African and Native Americans (and African-Native Americans) as well as for slaves (African, Native, and African-Native American) were strikingly similar in New England and that both "free" and slave communities were, in many instances, African–Native American communities.

Another example of an African–Native American community is the significant Garífuna population in New York and Los Angeles. Formerly in St. Vincent, the Garífuna nation (or Garinágu, plural), also called Black

Caribs, began as a seventeenth-century maroon society composed of Island Caribs and Africans brought to the island by Carib attacks on European colonies and as a result of a Spanish slave shipwreck in 1635, from
which escaped Ebo and Efik African slaves made their way to St. Vincent.
Other enslaved Africans, likely from the Yoruba, Fon, Fanti-Ashanti, and
Congo nations,[63] later escaped from surrounding islands and made their
way to join them.[64] The Garinágu were eventually removed to the island
of Roatan near the coast of Honduras; they can be found in British Honduras, Honduras, Nicaragua, and the United States. The Garífuna nation,
although predominantly phenotypically African, adopted a substantial
part of their culture from the Island Caribs, including dress, ritual and
ceremonial practices, and social organization, and currently "speak the
language of the Island Carib in a form which has remained relatively
unchanged lexically since their original contact with these Indians almost
three and a half centuries ago."[65] The sizeable Garífuna population that
has emigrated to Los Angeles and New York continues to celebrate traditional Settlement Day festivities and has produced literary works such
as the novel *Tumba Le,* by Don Justo.[66]

Taken together, these examples of African–Native American individuals, communities, and nations demonstrate sets of parallel and differing conditions that allow us to recognize a common ground in terms of
political, social, and legal conditions as well as to articulate distinct cultural and historical characteristics of these multiple, parallel traditions.
For example, some African–Native American communities are relative
newcomers to the United States, such as the Garífuna and other Latin
American immigrant populations, and thus did not share the same historical circumstances of those African-Native communities in the North
American colonies and the United States, yet they have shared experiences in the wider colonial history and in the contemporary United
States. Other African-Native Americans, especially those affiliated with
the Choctaw, Chickasaw, Cherokee, Creek, and Seminole nations, share
a history of forced relocation and enslavement by Native American owners. Yet many Native American nations, in conjunction with African-
Native members, share a history of relocation, and Littlefield and other
researchers have made it clear that there were many disparities in social
and legal conditions for members of these five nations.

It is also apparent that in the Northeast, a body of legislation and
social conditions for African-Native Americans as slaves and in "free
colored" communities produced common experiences for African-Native
Americans in Rhode Island, New York, Massachusetts, and other colonies and states. Still, the experiences of Olivia Ward Bush-Banks, an Af-

rican Montauk tribal historian who lived in Harlem during the Harlem Renaissance, were quite different from those of William Apess, an early nineteenth-century Methodist minister and civil rights activist for African and Native American rights who was raised as part of an African Pequot community in Connecticut, or Elleanor Eldridge, a struggling African Narragansett woman who sold her autobiography in the early nineteenth century in Rhode Island to raise money for the relief of her own debts, or Paul Cuffe, a successful ship captain raised in an African–Native American Wampanoag community near Martha's Vineyard in the mid-eighteenth century who employed both Africans and Indians to crew his several trading vessels. There has clearly been a vast array of African–Native American identities and communities.

## African–Native American Folklore and Mythology

One of the results of the creation of these African-Native communities was the development of a literature that was an expression of both African American and Native American traditional literatures. The earliest literatures combined folktales and mythologies. Scholars of southeastern folklore have discovered that African Americans have borrowed from Native American folktales and that Native Americans have borrowed from African folktales. Subsequently, some of these scholars have focused their efforts on discovering the African or Native American roots of particular folktales and arguing vociferously the inability of either Africans or Native Americans to have created such tales. Some ascribe the folktales to European origins, while others, depending upon whether they are scholars in the field of African American or Native American folklore, have insisted that the folktales are absolutely the property of either African Americans or Native Americans.[67] Most of these scholars have not analyzed these folktales in the light of overwhelming evidence that African Americans and Native Americans have exchanged traditional literatures and that African American, Native American, and African–Native American folktales are not the result of theft but rather of cultural and literary interaction and collaboration.

Folklorists and anthropologists appear to agree, however, that among the Native American nations that exhibit an African-Native folkloric and mythological tradition are the Cherokee, Creek, Natchez, Hitchiti, Seminole, Potowatomi, Alabama, and Koasati.[68] As the surrounding world changes, a community's mythological framework must change. Some nations adapted Native American and African myths to explain the origins of Africans, Native Americans, and Europeans, for example Seminole and Creek versions of a creation myth that, although it reflects an awareness of the social conditions of African Americans, merges Seminole and Creek cultural perspectives with an African creation myth:

> . . . some people once came to a very small pool of water to bathe. The man who entered this first came out clean and his descendants, the white people, have the same appearance. He had, however, dirtied the water a little and so the next man was not quite so clean, and his descendants are the Indians. By this time the water was very dirty and so the last man came out black and his people are the negroes.[69]

> Listen father, and I will tell you how the Great Spirit made man, and how he gave to men of different colours the different employments that we find them engaged in. After the world was made it was solitary. It was very beautiful; the forests abounded in game and fruit; the great plains were covered with deer and elk, and buffalo, and the rivers were full of fish; there were many bears and beaver and other fat animals, but there was no being to enjoy these good things. Then the Master of Life said, we will make man. Man was made, but when he stood up before his maker, he was *white*! The Great Spirit was sorry; he saw that the being he had made was pale and weak; he took pity on him and therefore did not unmake him, but let him live. He tried again, for he was determined to make a perfect man, but in his endeavour to avoid making another white man, he went in the opposite extreme, and when the second being rose up, and stood before him he was *black*! The Great Spirit liked the black man less than the white and he shoved him aside to make room for another trial. Then it was that he made the *red man;* and the red man pleased him.[70]

The first creation myth, embodied in both Seminole and Creek traditions, has its origins, according to the folklorist Alan Dundes, in an African creation myth,[71] and the second, he suggests, has its roots in a Seminole oral tradition.[72]

More recently, William Sturtevant has responded to Dundes's essay by discussing a series of myths: an 1824 version of the creation myth, a 1913 report by Lucien Spencer that contains an entirely different Seminole creation myth, several Seminole creation myths collected by Sturtevant between 1950 and 1952, and one version of a Creek creation myth collected by John Swanton between 1908 and 1914. These myths portray the creation process as bathing, as does the first myth, and Sturtevant, like Dundes, focuses on the order of creation of Africans, Native Americans, and Europeans. Sturtevant concludes with his analysis of the "rankings" of Africans, Native Americans, and Europeans as indicated by gifts given by the Great Spirit, "cleanliness" after bathing, favoritism by the Great Spirit, and so forth: "more acculturated . . . Oklahoma and Florida

Seminole . . . reflect awareness of the actual ranking of Whites, Indians, and Negroes, whereas the older and less acculturated Florida versions reflect the expected Seminole ethnocentrism, as does the other Seminole myth of the origin of races reported by Dundes."[73]

Yet the work of Dundes and Sturtevant alone may not initially appear to further an exploration of African–Native American myths. After all, aren't these simply Native American myths that have been modified to account for the creation of Africans and Europeans as well as Native Americans? In a word, no. In "A Note on the African Sources of American Indian Racial Myths," William Gerald McLoughlin insists that some of these racial origin creation myths originated in African creation myths, which merged with Native American mythologies with an adaptation of "the explanation that Africans had already established after they came in close contact with white Europeans."[74] The vocation creation myths, according to McLoughlin, some of which were recorded by Europeans in the seventeenth century, were told by Ashanti and Fanti storytellers and accounted for European skill in reading and writing and Ashanti skill in goldsmithing. They would be adapted to account for Seminole, Creek, or Cherokee skills in wartime and hunting, retaining an explanation of European literacy.

Dundes also discusses the creation myths in "African Tales among North American Indians," in particular the successive bathing creation myth. Dundes notes that the myth, "one of the most widely diffused African elements in American Indian oral tradition,"[75] comes from the tale-type A 1614.2, Races Dark-skinned from Bathing after White Men.[76] Some readers may be disturbed by the myth's association of African and Native American skin color with dirty water, although it is difficult to speculate as to the context in which an eighteenth- or nineteenth-century Ashanti, Fanti, or Seminole audience may have understood such a myth. It must also be true that the myth would have been used for different purposes depending upon audience and inclination. A Native Seminole or Cherokee who was prejudiced against Africans might have assigned a negative characteristic (i.e. "laziness")[77] to the Africans in the myth, or perhaps alternately, as in the earlier African myth, they were hoping to explain both skin color variations and the social order created and enforced by Europeans and European Americans, and as Sturtevant explains, the myth that places the African last in creation may have reflected the reality of their standing in American society. Many of the myths do not assign negative characteristics but simply account for color differences, in particular one recorded by Sturtevant from the Mikasuki Seminole Josie Billie: "On another occasion this informant inserted a reference to the motif in a telling of the standard Florida Seminole sib origin myth: after the sib ancestors, led by Wind and Puma, emerged from a mountain (in a significant order), these two leaders decided that the ancestors should bathe in a nearby river—'but the water got stirred up and the colored man came in behind and got black.'"[78] This myth is especially relevant to the tradition because it accounts for the origins and differences of two ancestors of the Seminole nation, Africans and Native Americans, and as Sturtevant notes,[79] it leaves out Europeans entirely. In this instance, the creation myth serves not to account for the existence of different peoples known to Native Americans but to recall the creation of the Seminoles in an African–Native American creation myth.

Dundes also raises the arguments over the African, Native, or European origins of these folktales and asserts that "previous scholarship devoted to the question was often subjective and frankly racist in denying [their] African origin."[80] He also notes Alexander Chamberlain's call in 1891 for "an investigation of the influence of the Indian upon Negro folklore and the influence of the Negro upon Indian folklore,"[81] a call that unfortunately has yet to be acted on in any comprehensive manner by folklore scholars. In his 1987 collection of southeastern Native American folklore, the folklore scholar George Lankford notes that there is a large body of African–Native American folktales, and he includes mixed Ashanti-Creek, Fan-Creek, Bakongo-Biloxi, and Ibo-Creek trickster tales but concludes, nearly one hundred years after Chamberlain, that although "the amalgamation of African and Native American folklore is one of the more interesting topics in Southeastern studies . . . the subject awaits careful study by a student of all three culture groups: African, Afro-American, and Native American."[82]

Finally, although Dundes argues that the tale type index proves the African origins of numerous folktales told in Native American communities, he does not explore what transformations might have taken place in the folktales from the African–Native American cultural exchanges. There are also numerous folktales told in African American or African–Native American communities that have as their basis a Native American folktale (such as Rabbit trickster tales), but these still need more exploration as well. The tale type (if accurate) may account for the basic form in the originating tradition, but it does not explore its variations and uses among African Americans, Native Americans, and African-Native Americans. It is also crucial to explore other features of the folktale's performance, not only its original form, for clues as to its function and importance in the communities in which it is told. In what order and manner are particular folktales related? Which audiences are told which folktales? In what ways do African and Native American folktale traditions combine?

If we were to focus on the transformation and merging process rather than simply identifying the originating folklore tradition, we might understand the functions of these new myths in new ways. In an essay entitled "Black Perceptions and Red Images: Indian and Black Literary Links," Mary Ellison argues that it is "specifically within the area of folktales and myths that the culture of blacks and Indians seems to mingle most powerfully and most inextricably."[83] She discusses the various arguments as to the origins of African–Native American myths and notes that "whether their origin was black or Indian is ultimately less important than that they had become a shared element in cultures that had much in common."[84] Ellison focuses on the exchange of literary traditions between African Americans and Native Americans and on the parallel concerns of the two literatures, for the continued emphasis on proprietary oratures overwrites the true origins of these New World myths and folktales in African–Native American cultural collaborations as well as their importance in defining and negotiating a New World in which the adaptation of traditional mythology and folklore offers African and Native Americans the best opportunity for the survival and maintenance of cultural integrity.

## African–Native American Writers

The lengthy history of African–Native American literary collaboration produced not only a syncretic oral tradition but also a literary trail. One of the earliest writers of African–Native American literature was Paul Cuffe (1759–1817), best known as a founder and advocate of the back-to-Africa movement. Cuffe's father, Cuffe Slocum, was an African slave in Massachusetts who eventually earned enough money to purchase his freedom and promptly married Ruth Moses, a member of the Gay Head Wampanoag nation; they lived in the Wampanoag community on the island of Cuttyhunk. Paul Cuffe, the youngest of the sons, signed on to a whaling ship, a common occupation for Wampanoag men. He learned his trade well, purchased his own small boat, drew his crews from African Americans, Native Americans, and African-Native Americans, and eventually built himself a thriving maritime business of whaling, hauling cargo, and trading. He married Alice Pequit of the Wampanoag nation in 1783, began a racially integrated school to educate his children, struggled repeatedly with the Massachusetts legislature over his rights as an African American and a Native American, and worked to further his plans to develop a colony in Sierra Leone for African Americans to return to their homeland. From 1811 to 1812, Paul Cuffe wrote an autobiographical travel narrative in a ship's journal that details his trading practices, travel to Sierra Leone, and political dealings. Although the journal discusses navigation and trade in great detail, Cuffe also argues for the abolition of the English slave trade. Interspersed with his notations of the price per barrel of flour are his notations on the Portuguese slave trade. His journals are filled with his plans for a back-to-Africa movement as well as his personal letters to family and friends.[85]

Another early African–Native American writer was William Apess (also Apes; 1798–?).[86] A member of the Pequot nation, he was the son of William and Candace Apes. His father was Pequot and European American, and his mother was apparently Pequot and African American. Although born in Massachusetts, he was raised as part of an African-Pequot community in Connecticut. His wife, Mary, was the daughter of a poor English American mother and likely a Cuban or Puerto Rican father. William Apess was brutally treated as a child, both by family members and by a number of masters who owned him as an indentured servant. He ran away, joined the army, drank to excess, and finally underwent a spiritual conversion before becoming a Methodist minister. Apess published five works between 1829 and 1836, *A Son of the Forest: The Experience of William Apes, a Native of the Forest, Written by Himself* (1829, rev. ed. 1831), *The Increase of the Kingdom of Christ: A Sermon* and *The Indians: The Ten Lost Tribes* (1831), *The Experiences of Five Christian Indians of the Pequot Tribe* (1833), *Indian Nullification of the Unconstitutional Laws of Massachusetts Relative to the Marshpee Tribe; or, The Pretended Riot Explained* (1835), and a *Eulogy on King Philip, as Pronounced at the Odeon, in Federal Street, Boston* (1836).[87] In his autobiography, *A Son of the Forest*, he includes his conversion narrative and, common to many Native American autobiographies, a sociological/historical essay aimed at a European American audience, yet most striking are his analyses and indictments of European American racism and his linguistic and cultural explorations of the meaning of "Indian." He details a wretched and impoverished upbringing and includes a story in which, as a young boy, he flees a party of "Indians" in the woods because he fears for his safety. The Indians turn out to be European American women picking berries, and Apess uses the opportunity to provide his reader with an analysis of the effects of European American stereotyping. *The Increase of the Kingdom of Christ* is a sermon that was published with a short essay, *The Indians: The Ten Lost Tribes*. The evangelistic language of the sermon is answered by Apess's arguments in his essay that eloquence is not confined to European Americans and that Native Americans are as deserving of justice as European Americans. Apess demonstrates his ability to preach and cite scripture in his counterarguments to those posed by European Americans, a privilege generally reserved for European Americans. *The Experiences of Five Christian Indians of the Pequot Tribe* includes a version of his autobiography and an autobiography of his wife, among others. Mary Apess's short autobiography is a conversion narrative that details her loneliness as an orphan, her struggles to live a Christian life, the vision that appeared to her, and the power she obtains through sanctification. William Apess's autobiography, again a conversion narrative, develops a critique of the racism he endures from surrounding European Americans and from the Methodist church, a far more scathing critique than that published in *A Son of the Forest*. These criticisms are elaborated in the concluding essay in the collection, "An Indian's Looking Glass for the White Man," in which Apess examines the behavior of European Americans toward African Americans and Native Americans.

Apess's turning of the lens toward European Americans culminates in his development of a strong political voice in *Indian Nullification* and *Eulogy. Indian Nullification of the Unconstitutional Laws of Massachusetts, Relative to the Marshpee Tribe* is a collection of documents related to Apess's involvement in the Marshpee (Mashpee) nation's successful attempts to require the legislature to redress long-standing grievances from their treatment by European Americans. Apess played an essential role in the petitions to the legislature, from his imprisonment for preventing the theft of Mashpee timber to his representation of the Mashpee nation in the state legislature; his oratory invoked such revolutionary rhetoric as "no taxation without representation." Finally, in his *Eulogy on King Philip*, Apess compares Philip (Metacomet), the leader of an alliance of New England Native nations, to George Washington with a political rhetoric that notes, as would Frederick Douglass in his famous Fifth of July speech, the shame of the American Independence Day for European Americans while people of color remain in bondage.

In the following decade, in 1841, Ann Plato published her *Essays; Including Biographies and Miscellaneous Pieces, in Prose and Poetry*.[88] A resident of Hartford, Connecticut, perhaps African Pequot like William Apess (but apparently not indentured), a member of James W. C. Pennington's Colored Congregational church, and apparently a teacher, very little is known or has been written about this writer and her life. Until more research is done, we must garner what we can from her own writing. "The Natives of America" includes a conversation between Plato and her father in which he relates his grief at the history of European colonization that has left him "roaming" without a nation. In the "Daughter's Inquiry," Plato writes to her father to implore him to return from this "roaming" to his family. It was typical for Pequot men to earn a living at whaling or shipping out for long periods of time because of the poor prospects of employment on the reservation or in the community. Many of Plato's poems speak to family and loved ones, while others address her spiritual life. "To the First of August" celebrates the end of slavery in the British Caribbean colonies and, in the rhetorical style of many African American slave narrators, juxtaposes England's policies with those of the United States. Plato also published a series of essays in the same book. Her essays address character and values in such issues as "Education," "Religion," "Diligence and Negligence," and, in an obvious response to the autobiography of Benjamin Franklin, "Employment of Time" and "Eminence from Obscurity." A series of biographical writings (extended obituaries) follow her essays. These pieces eulogize young women in her community who have died and, like many of her poems, demonstrate the continued importance of her inclusion of family and friends in her writing.

The inclusion of community in African–Native American writing was also accomplished through historical writing. Many African American and Native American writers published historical work in conjunction with their literature, particularly in conjunction with their autobiographies. Their inclusion of "race histories" in their autobiographies satisfied the curiosities of a substantially European American audience regarding the African or Native American "races," yet it also allowed writers to construct the historical and cultural traditions of their nation, a privilege denied to African Americans and Native Americans. From this historical reconstruction, writers could contextualize the self they were inscribing within their autobiographies and relate that self to a wider community embodied in the text. Many writers, such as James W. C. Pennington, William Wells Brown, Charles Alexander Eastman, and Robert Benjamin Lewis, also included a more extensive "race history."[89] Lewis, an African–Native American writer, constructs a history of both African Americans and Native Americans in his *Light and Truth, Collected from the Bible and Ancient and Modern History, Containing the Universal History of the Coloured and Indian Races, from the Creation of the World to the Present Time* (1844). Among other issues, his four-hundred-page world history discusses the Haitian revolution, prominent "colored" leaders, the importance of Africans to the development of Christianity, the origins of Native Americans, and the categories assigned to those of mixed race.

In 1848 the first of three editions of the life of Okah Tubbee (1810–?), an African Choctaw escaped slave, and Laah Ceil (1817–?), a Mohawk Delaware, was published.[90] Okah Tubbee, a brilliant traveling musician, was born as Warner McCary in Natchez, Mississippi. Warner was the son of Franky, an African American woman enslaved by James McCary. The identity of his father remains unclear, but it seems that Okah Tubbee was either African-European American or African-Native American. In any case, as Warner believed that if he asserted a Native American identity he might escape the bonds of slavery, he began to claim that his father was the Choctaw leader Moshulatubbee. It seems unlikely that his father was Moshulatubbee, but he certainly could have been Choctaw. Tubbee's brother and sister were freed by James McCary at the time of his death and given substantial estates—it is likely that these mixed children were the offspring of Franky and the master. But Tubbee was left as a slave to McCary's estate, and it could well be that he was the child of Franky and any one of the Choctaw who lived around Natchez. For the remainder of his life, Tubbee identified as Choctaw and was accepted as Choctaw by many communities, including Choctaw and other Native American nations. *A Thrilling Sketch of the Life of the Distinguished Chief Okah Tubbee* was spoken by Tubbee and written by Laah Ceil. The text includes a narrative of Tubbee and Ceil's lives as they traveled the country playing music and speaking on the Christian temperance movement and Native American rights.

Like Okah Tubbee, James P. Beckwourth (1798–1866), an African-European American from Fredericksburg, Virginia, was apprenticed as a town slave to a blacksmith. Like Tubbee and Frederick Douglass, Beckwourth narrates a struggle in which he bests his master and determines to seek his manhood. Beckwourth finds himself first working with the U.S. military and subsequently for fur companies hunting, trapping, and negotiating with a variety of Native nations. He eventually marries into the Crow nation and lives as an African Crow for many years, earning war honors and increasing responsibilities as a leader in the nation. Beckwourth's autobiography, *The Life and Adventures of James P. Beckwourth, Mountaineer, Scout, and Pioneer, and Chief of the Crow Nation of Indians* (1856), was spoken to T. D. Bonner, who transcribed and then edited it.[91] Beckwourth narrates a considerable portion in the form of traditional Crow coup tales, dictating the theft of horses and attacks on other Native nations, counting coup, and reciting the number of dead, number of horses stolen, and celebratory Crow rituals performed to honor the warriors.[92] Like other African-Native autobiographers, he negotiates his racial and cultural identity depending upon his audience and circum-

stances, and he alternates between his use of rhetorical styles and discourses. At times he speaks as a Crow, defending the Crow nation and
lauding the virtues of Native American culture; at other times he utilizes
the European American discourse of the noble savage, lamenting a passing race that has such dignity. He also aligns himself on occasion with a
European American racist "savage" discourse, particularly when he might
be seen by his audience as becoming more "Crow" than "American." For
many African-Native autobiographers, the development of strategic discourses was a defense against racism or enslavement, particularly when
as both African Americans and Native Americans they were vulnerable
to a variety of attacks.

In the early twentieth century, Joseph Seamon Cotter Jr. (1895–1919)
published one volume of poetry, *The Band of Gideon* (1918), before dying of tuberculosis at the age of twenty-four. He also published numerous poems in the *A.M.E. Zion Quarterly Review,* and he left a number
of unpublished poems at the time of his death. He was a student at Fisk
University and wrote many of the poems in *Band of Gideon* while seriously ill in bed.[93] Cotter's poetry showed great talent and enormous promise. He wrote spiritual poetry, love poems, poems on death, a series of
sonnets, including one in honor of African American soldiers, and a number of poems addressing racism and his mixed identity. In "The Mulatto
to His Critics," Cotter dismantles racial hierarchies by claiming his
Native, African, Anglo, and Celtic identities but notes that it is the "colored" race from which he draws cultural inspiration. Like William Apess
and many African American slave narrators, he challenges European
Americans to stand before God and admit their sins in "And What Shall
You Say?" Cotter has plenty to say as he accuses European Americans of
hatred, beatings, and stealing land, political issues that are often addressed
by African Americans and Native Americans. Cotter's poetry uses a wide
variety of forms, voices, and rhetorical strategies, including sonnets, dialect poetry, and oratory.

Another early twentieth-century writer, Olivia Ward Bush-Banks
(1869–1944), an African Montauk from New York, celebrated her African American and Native American identity. She was born the child of
Eliza and Abraham Ward. Her mother died the same year she was born,
and she was raised by her aunt in Providence, Rhode Island. She married, had two children, and then divorced Frank Bush. Bush-Banks maintained close ties to both her Native American and African American
identities. She wore traditional Montauk dress at pow-wows and maintained the Montauk tribal history; she also wrote poems that displayed
her pride at being African American, celebrating Frederick Douglass and

Paul Laurence Dunbar, and wrote a series of sketches in the black dialect of her Harlem community. Bush-Banks published two volumes of poetry, *Original Poems* (1899) and *Driftwood* (1914), a play, *Memories of Calvary: An Easter Sketch* (1917), and three essays in *Colored American* magazine and the *Westchester Record-Courier*.[94] She was also the author of several dozen unpublished poems and a significant number of unpublished plays, vignettes, essays, and sketches as well as an unpublished autobiography, *The Lure of the Distances* (1935–44). Her first published work, *Original Poems*, explores her Christian spirituality, nature's beauty, life transitions, and heroes of the colored races. Her work is both introspective and loudly celebratory; her poem "A Hero of San Juan" challenges African Americans to charge life like the soldiers charged San Juan Hill and to fight hard for equality, yet at the same time she sees the dying soldier with a mother's eyes. In the following poem, "Crispus Attucks," the first man to die in the American Revolution demands his place of honor as an American hero. Although she identifies Attucks as a "Negro" in the poem, she may well have known that he was both African American and Native American (Natick), and her poem may be a corrective on the writing of nineteenth-century European American historians that excluded Attucks's African American identity and rewrote him as a Nantucket Indian. *Driftwood*, Bush-Banks's second published volume, is divided into nine sections, including the "driftwood" trilogy in iambic pentameter, which early establishes the central motif in this collection: life drawn from death "cheers up Earth's dreary places." Bush-Banks writes about the loss of love and the literary creation that follows; her work includes a series of dream poems (including dreams deferred), elegies on Wendell Phillips, William Lloyd Garrison, Frederick Douglass, and Paul Laurence Dunbar, and two prose pieces, "A Christmas Legend" and "Hope."

Bush-Banks also published a one-act play entitled *Memories of Calvary: An Easter Sketch* (1917). Her unpublished work includes *Indian Trails; or, Trail of the Montauk* in which, unlike the writers of the popular Indian plays that were enacted from the seventeenth century on, she utilizes several Native languages and Native cultural mythologies in naming characters and structuring the play rather than fictionalizing a presumed Native culture whose "heaps" and "hows" stood in as European American linguistic and cultural substitutions for the realities of Native cultures.[95] Bush-Banks also wrote an important series entitled *Aunt Viney's Sketches* (1920–32). Aunt Viney, a character who speaks in black dialect, is a sharp and observant woman whose conversations with Miss Ollie, the proprietor at a gift shop she visits, raise provocative cultural, gender, economic, religious, and political issues while poking fun at white and colored cultures.

In her introduction to Bush-Banks's collected work, Bernice F. Guillaume asks, "how would one characterize an African Indian?" In her critique of Bush-Banks's work Guillaume reflects the same bicultural awareness that she attributes to Bush-Banks during the writer's lifetime: "Bush-Banks embraced and consciously cultivated her dual sensibility."[96] Guillaume notes Bush-Banks's role as Montauk tribal historian, her attendance at "pow-wows and other native gatherings on Long Island," and her use of Algonquian "names . . . social and cultural patterns" in *Indian Trails*.[97] She positions Bush-Banks as a "patron of the New Negro movement" and a "minor but viable elder of the Negro Renaissance movement"[98] who performed dramatic works in her studios in Chicago and New York, reviewed the works of Langston Hughes, and wrote racial uplift poetry for an African American audience, elegies on Frederick Douglass and Paul Laurence Dunbar, and a series of black dialect sketches that "precede[d] the appearance of Langston Hughes's 'Jesse B. Simple' character by at least six years."[99] Guillaume notes that regarding Bush-Banks's African–Native American identity, "a clearly extant cultural niche in Banks's time is not necessarily comprehensible to contemporary critics, especially those standing outside the African-Indian's world,"[100] and fashions a critical perspective whose underlying understanding of Bush-Banks's dual identity (and use of both Montauk and African American comparative historical research) allows her to fully assess her literary and historical importance.

An African–Native American contemporary of Bush-Banks was Chief Buffalo Child Long Lance, born Sylvester Long in 1890 in North Carolina. His father, Joe Long, was enslaved as a boy and was apparently an African-European-Native American. Joe Long's obituary indicates Catawba ancestry, and when enrolling his son at Carlisle Indian school he identified as Eastern Cherokee, but Donald B. Smith suggests that Joe Long may not have known exactly from which Native American nation he was descended, since he had never known his own parents.[101] Long Lance's mother, Sallie Long, was considered Lumbee (then Croatan—a mixed African-European-Native American community in North Carolina near the border with South Carolina), as was her mother, but the family was actually from a Native American community in South Carolina.[102]

Smith traces Long Lance's career from his treatment as "colored" under Jim Crow laws in Winston-Salem, his three years performing in a Wild West show, his education at Carlisle Indian school, and his enlistment in the Canadian military to his career as a journalist writing on

Native American affairs in Canada. Long Lance covered numerous issues as a journalist for newspapers such as the *Calgary Herald, Vancouver Sun,* and *Winnipeg Tribune,* from boxing to the political arena, but perhaps his most important journalistic work was his promotion of Native American civil rights. He wrote a series of articles, beginning in 1921, covering the Blackfoot, Sarcee, Bloods, Squamish, and many other Native American nations in Alberta, Manitoba, and British Columbia:

> He defended their customs, and their right to hold to their traditions. Why, he asked, did the Department of Indian Affairs and the Christian missionaries try to destroy Indian society, to do away with totem poles and traditional carvings, to end important Native ceremonies like the Potlatch? To a non-Indian audience, he also explained the Indians' requests for "full title to their reserve lands, as enjoyed by the other tribes of the Dominion, and for better education facilities and medical attention . . . instead of asking for financial renumeration for the reserve lands that have been taken over and sold by the province in the past, they are asking for extensions where they are most needed."[103]

Long Lance also published a highly controversial article after "interviewing several old Sioux warriors living in Canadian exile,"[104] "The Secret of the Sioux," which argued that the famous General George Armstrong Custer had actually committed suicide rather than holding out for the renowned "last stand." This would lead to an assignment from *Cosmopolitan* to write a story for young readers of traditional prereservation Blackfoot life, which Long Lance completed in 1927. *Cosmopolitan* "thought it was too good for a boy's book, and forthwith decided to run it as my autobiography,"[105] Long Lance declared.

Much of the controversy surrounding Long Lance lies in this published "autobiography," a work of historical fiction that he researched in interviews with Mike Eagle Speaker, "a young Blood student then studying at the agricultural college at Claresholm, south of Calgary,"[106] but did not intend to publish as his own autobiography. Yet due to his adoption by the Bloods in 1923 and their gift of a new name, Buffalo Child, Long Lance was identified with the Blood nation, and he apparently accepted *Cosmopolitan*'s insistence on publishing the fictional work as his own autobiography. Certainly many Native nations adopt new members, and a new name taken at a key moment of transition, also a Native tradition, indicates a constantly evolving identity, but perhaps Long Lance was also a bit of a trickster, as evidenced by his planting a fake "bomb" at the Calgary City Hall when there was a dearth of interesting news to report.[107]

It is crucial to examine Long Lance's surroundings as a boy to understand his shifting identity. Because he was of mixed race, and because

European Americans in North Carolina assumed that African-Native Americans were Lumbee, Long Lance was treated as a Lumbee, which meant that he was oppressed under the same Jim Crow laws that applied to every person of color in his community. Because of their intermarriage with African Americans, the Lumbee were classified as "'free persons of color' and later as 'free Negroes,'"[108] and the Lumbee nation always struggled to maintain their Native American identity. Some Lumbee still identify with one of the nearest Native nations that receives official recognition, the Eastern Cherokee,[109] so Long Lance's identification as Cherokee would not have been unusual for a Lumbee; he may well have had Cherokee ancestry on both his mother's and father's side and, while traveling and performing with a Cherokee named Whipporwill, he learned to speak "some of the [Cherokee] language."[110] Thus his identification as Cherokee may not have been, as Smith argues, "racial passing,"[111] since he had numerous Indian ancestors on both sides of the family, but rather a deliberate shift in cultural or political affiliation perhaps due in part to his heritage and in part to the prevailing argument that Black Indians were "degraded" Indians or not Indians at all. It is no indictment of Long Lance's "Indianness" that the Indian agent George Gooderham believed that he "didn't know much about Indian life,"[112] because life on a Canadian Blackfoot reservation was quite different than that of the North Carolina African–Native American community in which he had grown up. The epithet expressed by one of the Oklahoma Cherokee students who objected to his Cherokee identification—"Cherokee nigger"[113]—is telling, in that Long Lance faced the accusation of being a "black" Cherokee rather than the accusation of not being a Cherokee at all. The implication must have been that an African Cherokee could not be a "real" Cherokee (even though this student must have encountered African Cherokees in Oklahoma as well),[114] but this is a very different issue than a non-Indian attempting to pass as an Indian. Long Lance *was* a Native American, and certainly his racial and cultural heritage were complex. But although his family and community provided his African–Native American cultural background, as a nonreservation, displaced African-Native American, his political affiliations were based on his immediate circumstances, and he was always under the obligation to create and defend his identity. He perhaps represented what Karen Blu, in her study of Lumbee culture, discusses as Lumbee "situational identity:"

> Because it is not a fully conscious, fully articulated notion, Lumbee group identity can, for them, spontaneously and genuinely "come from the heart" rather than coldly and calculatingly from the head (which is not to be confused with state of mind), even if some parts of that identi-

ty are deliberately manipulated from time to time. Such a "tangled form" of identity can, then, encompass contradictions, ambiguities and fuzziness. New aspects can be added without apparent difficulty, just as alterations in the ideas about origins have been rather readily absorbed into the tangle, whereas they might have challenged or even destroyed the fabric of a tightly structured and explicitly defined identity. So too various tactics developed through the years are added to their storehouse of possibilities without threatening Lumbee notions of who they are and how they ought to behave. This flexibility in their identity allows Lumbees a wide latitude in innovating or selecting from an already established repertoire when they express that identity in various situations.[115]

The grappling with African–Native American identity continues today, and among the many contemporary African–Native American writers are Alice Walker (b.1944) and Clarence Major (b.1936). The Pulitzer Prize–winning author of *The Color Purple,* Walker is also the author of numerous volumes of poetry, novels, essays, and other writings.  In much of her published work, she has developed an African Cherokee identity (her great-grandmother Tallulah was African Cherokee) to which several critics have taken offense. Daniel E. Turner goes so far as to attempt to "prove" that because some Cherokees held African slaves and because European colonists pitted Cherokees against African Americans as part of their colonization strategy, what Alice Walker wrote about the creation of Cherokee African culture was not true.[116] Of course, this does not take into account the fact that it was precisely the adoption of slavery by some Cherokees that helped to create African Cherokee cultures (along with earlier mixing between Cherokee and escaped African slaves as well as between Cherokee slaves and African slaves). Another critic, K. T. H. Cheatwood, lambasts Walker's dedication of her book of poetry, *Horses Make a Landscape More Beautiful,* to both her European American ancestor and her Cherokee ancestor, insisting that if she claims Cherokee identity, she is rejecting African American identity.[117]

It is clear that the reason Walker can claim both Cherokee and African American identity is because she is both, as are many writers who claim African American, Native American, or African–Native American identity. Although the former English colonies have structured racial and cultural categories in such a way as to make it difficult for writers to claim their African-Native identity (in contrast to the more permeable policies of former French and Spanish colonies), African-Native Americans are not obligated to choose one community over the other. When they do choose to assume both identities, they sometimes alternate between identities and sometimes assume them simultaneously.

In *The Color Purple, Meridian,* and her collection of essays entitled *Living by the Word,* Walker consciously creates space for and develops an African Cherokee identity as well as a relationship to a pan-Indian identity.[118] In *The Color Purple,* Walker writes about Spelman Seminary and the African Cherokee students, including Corrine, and she discusses the existence of African Cherokee culture as well as the reasons for its denial. She opens the novel *Meridian* with a quotation from the final pages of Black Elk and John G. Neihardt's collaborative autobiography *Black Elk Speaks,*[119] and she discusses Meridian's father's relationship to Cherokee and pan-Indian culture, his "sale" of a traditional Cherokee burying ground to Walter Longknife, a removed Cherokee who returns from Oklahoma, and the curving Sacred Serpent that runs across their farmland. In *Living by the Word,* Walker discusses African–Native American identity in three of her essays. In "My Big Brother Bill," she introduces the anthropologist James Mooney's argument that the European American institution of slavery began with the enslavement of Native Americans who eventually mixed with the Africans enslaved in the same institution. She also discusses African Cherokee folklore, her relationship with Bill Wahpepah, and her growing understanding of the spiritual and political connections between Africans and Native Americans. In "The Closet of the Soul," she argues that the acceptance of our mixed heritages, including the acceptance by European Americans of the fact that many of them are not "white" but genetically mixed with "colored" people, is a necessary precursor to freedom and development; she insists that to identify with only one of our racial or cultural identities must lead to "psychic illness" rather than the psychic integration and wholeness of accepting all of our identities. In "Everything Is a Human Being," Walker again cites *Black Elk Speaks,* this time relating the European American slaughter of the bison and continuing devastation of the earth to the oppression of African Americans and Native Americans. She also engages in storytelling and analysis, relating a snake story to both Cherokee and Chippewa traditions.

Clarence Major, a painter and author of seven novels, twelve books of poetry, and numerous nonfiction works including the *Dictionary of Afro-American Slang,* was born into an African Cherokee family and community in Atlanta and grew up in Chicago, still making frequent visits to his grandparents in Georgia.[120] His family stories about Cherokee identity circulate in the oral tradition, according to Major, and the issues of African Cherokee or African–Native American identity arise in several of his written texts. Major's sixth novel, *Such Was the Season* (1987), describes children gathering at their Momma and Poppa's for the customary feasting, drinking, and singing. Poppa, whose name is Olaudah Equiano Sommer, speaks Cherokee and proudly discusses his African Cherokee identity; his father was a leader in the Cherokee nation who had helped African Americans raise money to return to Africa. Annie Eliza, the narrator, recalls Poppa's story of the bird his father carved and painted to bring luck to the Cherokee nation. She dreams about this bird again and again. It is clear that there are many other African Cherokees in the community, including Cherokee Jimmy and Selu, and the issue of African Cherokee identity arises numerous times throughout the novel, informally in conversations about ancestry and culture and more formally in the appearance of a scholar discussing his historical research on the interactions between the Cherokee and African Americans in Georgia.[121]

Major has also lived in the southwestern United States, and his novel, *Painted Turtle: Woman with Guitar* (1988), and book of poetry, *Some Observations of a Stranger at Zuni in the Latter Part of the Century* (1989), raise issues of Zuni and African Zuni culture.[122] Painted Turtle struggles with the attempts of some members of the Zuni nation to prevent her from returning to the nation after she travels outside of the reservation playing her guitar and singing. The narrator, who is both Hopi and Navajo, discusses his struggles as the child of two cultures and nations. *Painted Turtle* focuses on the struggle for cultural definition and the oscillations between insider and outsider. In an essay entitled "Against Commodification: Zuni Culture in Clarence Major's Native American Texts," Steve Heyward argues that *Some Observations of a Stranger at Zuni in the Latter Part of the Century* and *Painted Turtle* "resist commodification and . . . dioramification"[123] and "sit in opposition"[124] to the dioramic museum representation and cultural commodification of Native Americans. Heyward relies on Walter Benjamin's analysis of Brechtian theater and draws a parallel between Brecht's exposure "at all turns [of] the theatricality of the theater itself" and Major's "foregrounding the textual-ness"[125] of his Zuni texts. Major destabilizes the notion of the author and explores subjective perspectives through what Heyward labels "mudhead subjectivity/perspectivalism."[126] The mudheads, incestuous offspring marginalized by clan rules, operate on the periphery of Major's writing and "serve the role of metaphoric personification of the perspectival outsiderness which characterizes Major's speakers and narrators,"[127] perhaps commenting on Major's own relationship to Native American culture. Major also includes a character named Baldwin Saiyataca (Baldy), whose mother was Hopi and father Navajo: "Having a Navajo father in Hopi land wasn't exactly a picnic. Hopis had nothing but a history of trouble with them Navajos. My mom had trouble with my dad. So it goes."[128] Heyward suggests that Baldy's mixed background combined with an historic "ancestral division renders Baldy into a parallel of a mudhead on his own reservation,"[129] and perhaps Major also comments on the historic divisions between two other tribes, African American and Cherokee, which would in some instances render Major's mixed heritage equally problematic in that an assertion of both identities would raise questions on both "reservations" about his appropriate identity and social status.

## Theorizing an African–Native American Literary Tradition

In spite of the lengthy and continuing history of African–Native American literature, the verification of an established African–Native American literary tradition requires theorizing a web of connected texts. We must begin by noting that within both African American and Native American literary traditions there are numerous distinct traditions defined by genre, historical period, and region. There are also distinct cultural and literary traditions from which these greater literary traditions originated, and although African American literature is generally discussed as a distinct and unified tradition, it evolved into a New World tradition from the preexisting oral and written traditions of such diverse African peoples such as the Ibo, Hausa, Yoruba, and Mandingo. As Lawrence W. Levine argues in *Black Culture and Black Consciousness*, "Africans brought to the English colonies as slaves in the seventeenth, eighteenth, and nineteenth centuries did not carry with them a network of beliefs, customs, institutions, and practices constituting what might be called with accuracy a unified 'African' culture. No such monolithic culture existed."[130] These divisions are even more apparent within the numerous independent Native American cultural and literary traditions that make up the wider body of Native American literature. A. LaVonne Brown Ruoff notes that in the fifteenth century, Native Americans "were divided into more than three hundred cultural groups and spoke two hundred different languages, plus many dialects. . . . By 1940, 149 of these languages were still in use."[131] Ruoff argues that Native American literatures should be examined in their particular cultural and linguistic framework as well as understood to be a connected literary tradition. I would argue that the proposition of an African–Native American literary tradition should be approached in a similar fashion, and because of its inextricable literary links to Native American literatures, African–Native American literature should be discussed in much the same way as Native American literature, the existence of which is widely accepted today among literary scholars.

Thus the widely diverse experiences of African Choctaws, African Senecas, or African Athabaskans should be examined as individually articulated traditions as well as a literary tradition that, much like African American and Native American literary traditions, shares distinct features and themes despite the differences embodied within its various components. There have been five centuries of African–Native American literature, and these oral and written expressions have included autobiographies, published sermons, histories, poetry, short stories, slave narratives, folktales, myths, novels, plays, essays, travel narratives, eulogies, dictionaries, legal writing and petitions, and speeches. Within the context of each of these genres, particular features are self-contained while others cross literary genres to link African–Native American texts in a unified tradition. The shared features and themes of African–Native American literature include the narration of African–Native American subjectivity; strategic discourses and situational identities; a literary hybridization of elements derived from both African American and Native American literary traditions; newly acknowledged identities accompanied by linguistic transformations; a sustained focus on African and Native American politics and history; and the engagement of dual histories in an attempt to repair a state of narrative rootlessness.

By what criteria should we posit a literary tradition? In his foreword to the *Oxford Companion to African American Literature,* Henry Louis Gates Jr. argues that "only a body of shared information can end the curse on scholars of African and African American studies: that each generation must reinvent the proverbial wheel, must, that is, reestablish even the most basic facts about the tradition before deeper interpretation and analysis can begin to occur."[132] Set alongside his observations that only the creation of reference works for African American literature would overcome the reluctance of American scholars to acknowledge an African American literary tradition of sufficient importance to incorporate it into a "standard curriculum in any respectable faculty of arts and sciences,"[133] Gates argues that the creation of research tools to examine a literary tradition is one way for such a tradition to be established. Yet Gates also acknowledges that his first proposal to Oxford University Press (in 1977) of a companion to African American literature fell flat, stymied by fears that sales in a field not yet widely acknowledged would not support such an undertaking. Read through this lens, one must ask, when does a tradition become a tradition? Certainly a sizeable body of interconnected texts by African American writers and speakers, an African

American literary tradition, existed in 1977, yet the *Companion* was not published until 1997. A literary tradition can exist, however, regardless of whether it is acknowledged or whether it generates academic sales. In fact, despite centuries of the production of African American and Native American texts, only since the 1970s has either tradition received formal and widespread acknowledgment, and African American and Native American literary works have previously languished on the shelves alongside anthropological or historical works.

Another perspective on the question of tradition is provided by the Native American literature scholar A. LaVonne Brown Ruoff, who argues that scholars of American literature have often failed to hear the sounds of Native American literature. One of the foundational critical resources for the Native American literary tradition, Ruoff's *American Indian Literatures*, raises issues that resonate with those raised by Gates. Despite the existence of a large body of written work by Native American authors since 1772 as well as a massive body of orature (literature from the oral tradition), Ruoff argues that "they have not generally been included in American literature courses. In 1917, Mary Hunter Austin, in her chapter entitled "Aboriginal" in *The Cambridge History of American Literature,* decried this exclusion: 'Probably never before has a people risen to need a history of its national literature with so little conscious relation to its own aboriginal literature. Yet if we extend the term American to include the geographical and racial continuity of the continent, unbroken at its discovery, we have here the richest field of unexploited aboriginal literature it is possible to discover anywhere in the world.'"[134]

Much like Gates, Ruoff insists upon the necessity of establishing formal and widespread scholarship in the field of Native American literary studies in order to educate emerging and established scholars as to the existence and importance of a Native American literary tradition. Once again (as was the case with African–Native American folklore), an early scholar (in *The Cambridge History of America Literature,* no less) arguing for a literary exploration went essentially unheeded for decades. Yet in spite of the importance of the approval and participation of the academic community, a literary tradition (the call) must already exist for it to be acknowledged and theorized by scholars (the response). African American literature was popularized by American readers long before scholars took up the claim, as evidenced by the dramatic sales of mid-nineteenth-century slave narratives or the popularity of writers from the Harlem Renaissance. When Black Hawk, the Sauk and Fox warrior and autobiographer, traveled the eastern seaboard, he drew a crowd in Philadelphia nearly equal to that of his contemporary, President Andrew Jackson.[135] The autobiography *Black Elk Speaks,* narrated by Black Elk to John Neihardt, remains a strong seller nearly seven decades after it was first published. The writings of Long Lance or Alice Walker demonstrate an equivalent trend in African–Native American literature.

Despite such claims of recognition and tradition outside of the academy, the collection of essays I am introducing attempts to do for African–Native American literature what scholars have done for African American and Native American literature: to present a unified body of texts with tools for literature scholars to assess them. Although the road to an African–Native American literary tradition has not been founded upon a bedrock of preexisting scholarship, at least not a foundation as extensive as those created for Native American and African American literature, the sense that a body of literature should have scholarly engagement to be considered a literary tradition is worth pursuing in the case of African–Native American literature as well, and in fact this tradition has received scholarly attention long before the more recent work in this collection. Scholarly research in the field of African–Native American studies began at least as early as the essays published by historians such as Carter G. Woodson in the *Journal of Negro History* in the 1920s and primarily with the research of Kenneth Wiggins Porter.[136] Porter published a number of articles in the *Journal of Negro History* and the *Southwestern Historical Quarterly* in the 1940s that would later be collected in *The Negro on the American Frontier,* a documentation of the numerous interactions between Native Americans and African Americans throughout the United States that uncovers politicians, authors, traders, and many others of African–Native American descent.[137] Porter was particularly interested in researching the African Seminole nation.

At the same time as Porter conducted and published his research, and in some cases even earlier, other scholars pursued African–Native American studies, including the well-known historians Carter Woodson and Herbert Aptheker. Woodson and Aptheker published in the *Journal of Negro History,* Woodson in the 1920s, and Aptheker in the 1930s.[138] James H. Johnston and Wyatt F. Jeltz published articles on the interactions between Native Americans and African Americans in the *Journal of Negro History* as well, Johnston in the late 1920s, and Jeltz in the late 1940s. In the 1930s Laurence Foster completed a dissertation at the University of Pennsylvania entitled "Negro-Indian Relationships in the Southeast."[139]

Since the early research into African–Native American studies published in the *Journal of Negro History* and elsewhere, there has been much more work done in this field. A 1963 contribution to the *Journal of Negro History* by William L. Willis, "Divide and Rule: Red, White and Black in the Southeast," explores attempts on the part of European Americans to erase or derail African–Native American relations, beginning in the colonial period.[140] The historian and literary scholar Daniel F. Littlefield Jr. has published studies on the relations between African Americans and Native Americans, including *Africans and Seminoles: From Removal to Emancipation* (1977), *The Cherokee Freedmen: From Emancipation to American Citizenship* (1978), *Africans and Creeks: From the Colonial Period to the Civil War* (1979), and *The Chickasaw Freedmen: A People without a Country* (1980). Karen Blu discusses the complex issue of the construction and maintenance of identity in the African–Native American North Carolina Lumbee Indian nation. The historian Rhett S. Jones has published a number of essays on interactions between African Americans and Native Americans, in particular discussions of identity in maroon nations ("Identity, Self-Concept, and Shifting Political Allegiances of Blacks in the Colonial Americas: Maroons against Black Shot"), early African–Native American history ("Black and Native American Relations before 1800"), and the representation of Native Americans by African American scholars ("Black over Red: The Image of Native Americans in Black History").[141] Jack D. Forbes has published articles in *American Indian Quarterly* as well as a thorough study of the creation of African–Native American nations and the racial classification process and terminology that obscured Native American identity in the colonial Americas. William Loren Katz published *Black Indians: A Hidden Heritage* in 1986, a popular work that has fueled responses from newer scholars working in this field. New work and scholarly interest are being generated at an increasing pace, as evidenced by the April 2000 conference at Dartmouth University, "Eating Out of the Same Pot: Relating Black and Indian (Hi)stories."

Within the larger body of research published on African–Native American history and culture there has also been research on African–Native American literatures. Alan Dundes and other senior folklore scholars have been addressing African–Native American folklore for decades. It has been taken up again more recently by Forbes, who introduces a story from Guyana in which African and Native American spirits meet to negotiate a power-sharing relationship between the Africans and Native Americans, and the folklore scholar George Lankford has written on mixed African and southeastern Indian traditions. Many African–Native American writers were included in the earliest literature anthologies devoted to writers of color, including Julia Griffiths's *Autographs for Freedom* (1853), Sterling Brown, Arthur Davis, and Ulysses Lee's *The Negro Caravan* (1941), and Vernon Loggins's *The Negro Author, His*

*Development in America* (1931).[142] More recent anthologies and scholarly handbooks have discussed such writers as Ann Plato and Olivia Ward Bush-Banks (*The Oxford Companion to African American Literature*, which includes a separate entry on African–Native American literature), John Marrant (*Call and Response: The Riverside Anthology of the African American Literary Tradition*), and Nancy Prince and H. Cordelia Ray (*Afro-American Women Writers, 1765–1933*).[143] There have also been articles on African–Native American writers and writing published in academic journals, including Mary Ellison's "Black Perceptions and Red Images: Indian and Black Literary Links" (1983) and Bernice F. Guillaume's "Character Names in *Indian Trails* by Olivia Ward Bush (Banks): Clues to Afro Assimilation into Long Island's Native Americans" (1986). At least six edited collections of writing by African-Native Americans have appeared, including work by William Apess, Paul Cuffe, Ann Plato, Long Lance, Olivia Ward Bush-Banks, and Okah Tubbee and Laah Ceil. Barry O'Connell has written a fascinating introduction intertwining the African and Native American cultural and literary aspects of William Apess's life and writing. Guillaume's introduction to the Oxford Black Women Writers series publication of *The Collected Works of Olivia Ward Bush-Banks* weaves Bush-Banks's African and Montauk aspects together in a reading squarely in the tradition of African–Native American scholarly criticism. The writing of Ann Plato was published in the same series (*Essays; Including Biographies and Miscellaneous Pieces, in Prose and Poetry* [1988]), and Rosalind Cobb Wiggins has edited the collection of letters and journals by Paul Cuffe. Daniel F. Littlefield Jr. has done meticulous research on the lives and autobiographies of Okah Tubbee and Laah Ceil in *The Life of Okah Tubbee* (1988), and Long Lance's autobiography has been published with an introduction by Donald Smith. Independent studies or essay collections have also examined African–Native American literatures. The African–Native American scholar bell hooks has written on African–Native American women in her essays.[144] Alice Walker has focused on African Cherokee issues. The New Orleans writer Jason Berry discusses the Mardi Gras Indian tradition as well as spiritual mergings between African American and Native American ceremonial traditions in *The Spirit of Black Hawk: A Mystery of Africans and Indians*.[145]

Despite this significant body of work on the history, culture, and literature of African-Native Americans, a scholarly myopia remains, clouding African–Native American studies in an often impenetrable fog. The historian Gary B. Nash argues in *Red, White, and Black: The Peoples of Early America* (1982) that "the convergence of African and Indian peoples is the least studied chapter in the history of race relations in early America,"[146] which echoes the claim made by an article in the *Journal of Negro History* in 1920 that African–Native American relations represent one of the "longest unwritten chapters of the history of the United States."[147] This situation is mirrored by Alexander Chamberlain's 1891 call for "an investigation of the influence of the Indian upon Negro folklore and the influence of the Negro upon Indian folklore"[148] and echoed again by the folklore scholar George Lankford's more recent conclusion that although there are numerous African–Native American folktales, "the amalgamation of African and Native American folklore . . . awaits careful study by a student of all three culture groups: African, Afro-American, and Native American."[149] While these scholars make several important points—the interaction between African Americans and Native Americans is critical to understanding American history and literature, and there remains a great deal of work to be done in the field of African–Native American studies—such arguments also tend to undermine and to ignore the existing research. Much work remains to be done, but the path seems more remote without an acknowledgment of the work that has already been accomplished.

Alongside a scholarly myopia lies a more deeply ingrained resistance to African–Native American literature. Despite the substantial body of African–Native American literature and the growing number of scholars addressing it, there is still resistance to the acknowledgment of African–Native American identity and authorship. Much of the existing scholarship fails to discuss these writers' mixed heritage or concurrent literary traditions, instead portraying them strictly as one or the other of their dual heritages, while other writers have been almost entirely ignored. One explanation for the lack of critical attention must be that until recently there has been only a limited pool of scholars pursuing the serious study of either African American or Native American literatures, much less African–Native American literature, and this has hampered the development of the field. For those scholars who pursue African–Native American literature, the analysis of mixed-race writing requires cross-disciplinary specialities and often the development of a new critical lens through which to view it, a daunting task, especially when the majority of established critical apparati do not lend themselves to the unfolding of mixed-race writing.

Yet it has also been difficult for African-Native Americans themselves to acknowledge and celebrate their mixed heritage. The construction of racial categories in the United States, although sometimes acknowledging the various racial mixtures (even measuring to a one-sixteenth percentage), has functioned primarily to create a divide between "white" and "colored." Such racialized political divisions have resulted in an unfortunate reliance on a dichotomous racial system that excludes mixed-race identities as well as in the creation of enclosures of identity used as protection by both African American and Native American communities. Unfortunately, many of the definitions that are used within the communities to define community members are remnants of archaic and divisive European American creations of racist legislation and policies, a systematic continuation of "the master's tools"[150] that serve to divide communities. These categories of identity have been based on the perception of "race" and are intended to create caste divisions, not to define and acknowledge the numerous cultural mixes occurring in the United States. The establishment of a monolithic system of dichotomous racial identity, a system that still cannot and will not acknowledge mixed heritage, continues to foster the subordination and exclusion of African-Native (and other mixed-heritage) Americans. Many mixed-race writers find themselves enveloped in a category of singular identity, while others resist such categorizations altogether. When encountering those African-Native Americans who declare themselves both African American and Native American, most scholars rely on these monolithic categories, following the racial codings of the master discourse and reading mixed-race writers as one-raced writers. Furthermore, most historians, if they discuss interactions between "white" and "colored," limit their explorations to the interactions between European Americans and African Americans, or between European Americans and Native Americans. Because until recently most historians and literary critics have been European Americans (or if not, they respond to the academic racial parameters initially set up by European Americans), their primary interest in exploring these cultural interactions has always been in relation to themselves. The relations between African Americans and Native Americans clearly did not involve European Americans and thus were denied serious inquiry.

It has also been difficult for African-Native Americans to choose both identities because for centuries there has been substantial pressure not to do so and because political pressure has divided the allied interests of African Americans and Native Americans. From the start of the European colonization of the Americas, plantation owners believed that it was in their best interest to prevent interactions between African Americans and Native Americans. The official policy of European governments and European American colonial governments often entailed a "divide and conquer" strategy when it came to Native Americans and African Americans. A French colonial document states that "between the races we cannot dig too deep a gulf,"[151] and this policy was pursued in nearly every colony in the Americas.[152] Colonial authorities were fearful of alliances between African Americans and Native Americans, and this fear led the British Indian Service to proclaim that "Negroes infused many very bad notions in their [Indian] minds."[153]

Because of centuries of legislation and divisive tactics on the part of colonial authorities, African-Native Americans must overcome the deep distrust that sometimes marks relations between African Americans and Native Americans in order to allow both cultures to peacefully coexist, if not thrive. Although there are many instances of cooperation and coexistence between African American and Native American communities, there are also lingering "racial" animosities fueled by centuries of intentional deception and division.[154] Those who belong to both cultures, African-Native Americans, must constantly negotiate the boundaries of these historical minefields to retain their membership in both communities.

Yet substantial pressure is often exerted by African American and Native American communities on those who would opt "out" of the community by claiming both identities. As demonstrated by Cheatwood's comment on Walker's claim to African Cherokee identity ("So again, here we go with the old Negro refrain of: 'me ain't really a nigger . . . no, no, me really an injin,'") this pressure can be hostile and threatening.[155] There are certainly legitimate concerns on the part of both communities. African Americans and Native Americans have experienced a genocide that threatens the existence of both communities, and the redefinition of members of the community as something other than African American or Native American is viewed by some as potentially destructive. Yet it is clear from Cheatwood's comment that this threat comes from the belief that one must choose one or the other identity, that one may not be both. An African-Native American, however, is both at once, and choosing to assert a mixed heritage does not demand the negation of one of the cultures. To continue to insist that one must choose one or the other community only perpetuates a racial categorization that was created outside of and imposed onto the communities. This categorization has never reflected the reality of the lives of African Americans, Native Americans, or African-Native Americans, and it is counterproductive to retain a system of racial categorization that has always been patently false and divisive.

Like many others, Clarence Major must negotiate these fixed racial and cultural boundaries. In *Some Observations,* Major explores the tension between assimilation and the retention of "traditional" culture in his decision to use a mixture of Zuni and English in his poetry. In one poem, Major writes about a "liberal" who wants to make a film about Gatumlati until he discovers that she was African Cherokee rather than the "pure" Cherokee on which the filmmaker's representation of Cherokee identity insists; Major clearly struggles with the same issues while fashioning subjectivities in his writing. Yet his writing speaks for itself, and it is an articulation of the cultural negotiations that take place within an African-Native American, and, although critics have generally interpreted his writing only within an African American literary discourse, he, like many in a long African-Native literary tradition, has written an African–Native American literature. In spite of the limitations imposed from outside of the African–Native American communities, and in spite of the limitations that threaten from within, many African-Native Americans have written across this "deep gulf" created by the European colonial authorities. This literary tradition demands recognition and a critical analysis that acknowledges both the African American and Native American cultural and literary influences and the unique features of mixed-race and African–Native American writing.

Because African–Native American literature represents an amalgamation of Native American and African American writing traditions, these literatures can be critically examined within at least four different frameworks: as mixed-race literatures, Native American literatures, African American literatures, and African–Native American literatures. As texts representing the work of writers who are racially and culturally mixed, African–Native American literatures share a number of features of a wider genre of mixed-race writing that draws from the writings of Eurasian Americans, European-Native Americans, African-European Americans, and many others. As I have argued in the introduction to *Mixed Race Literature,* "there are themes and literary strategies that often inform mixed race texts, including narratives of passing, formations of new racial space, multiple naming, redefining and challenging racial categories, gendered racial crossings, grappling with the tragic mulatto, and the appearance of the tragic trickster."[156] Such themes also resonate in many African–Native American texts. The autobiographies of John Marrant, Okah Tubbee and Laah Ceil, and James P. Beckwourth all grapple with narratives of passing, multiple racial crossings, and politically strategic (and shifting) alliances made possible by their affiliations with both African Americans and Native Americans, and in this they share common themes with the work of the English-Chinese writer Sui Sin Far, the African-European American Charles Chestnutt, and the African-Danish American Nella Larsen. Successive naming, the adoption of new names at a critical juncture in life, and multiple naming, the acquisition and use of successive, multiple parallel, or shifting names, occur in the African–Native American texts of Long Lance and Okah Tubbee as well as in the mixed-race texts of Sui Sin Far, her sister Onoto Watanna (who adopted a "Japanese" writing identity with her pen name), and the African-European American slave narrator William Wells Brown.[157] Gendered racial crossings can be found in Alice Walker's transformation of the Cherokee Wild Boy into an African American female "Wile Chile" in *Meridian*, the novel *Clotel* by William Wells Brown, the slave narratives of Harriet Jacobs and William and Ellen Craft (who transformed her gender and assigned race [black] during the Crafts' escape from slavery), the short stories of Sui Sin Far, and William Apess's *A Son of The Forest*, in which he narrates a trip to the woods where he mistakes a group of white female berry pickers for Native American warriors in search of scalps.[158]

Mixed-race texts share a number of other characteristics. Carol Roh Spaulding argues that repetitive notions of mixed identity are presented by a number of mixed-race writers: "First, mixed race is founded in the experience of marginality; second, mixed race characters are always negatively defined (neither 'white' nor 'raced'); third, the characters serve a kind of barometric function, revealing the racial tensions embedded in the text; and last, mixed race protagonists come to a crisis point in the narrative when they are forced to confront in some manner their indeterminate racial status."[159] These features are equally present in African–Native American writing, marking African–Native American texts as part of a wider tradition of mixed-race writing in the United States, yet there are also crucial differences. The barometric function can be seen in the work of Nettie Jones, whose African-Native subjects in *Mischief Makers* are part of "'a true ethnic melting pot whose temperature is perpetually near the boiling point'"[160] and whose African–Native American characters, Raphael and Lilly, serve as a focal point for racial tensions between African American, Native American, and mixed-race subjects negotiating identity in the larger American society. In the autobiography of Okah Tubbee and Laah Ceil, the narration of a tornado and Laah Ceil's editorial manipulations of the text disrupt a focus on African identity (during which Tubbee's status as a slave is argued) and eclipse it with a Choctaw focus, thus reenacting the primary racial tension embedded in this autobiography. The confrontation of indeterminate racial status occurs in many African–Native American texts, including the autobiographies of John Marrant and Okah Tubbee/Laah Ceil, Michael Dorris's *A Yellow Raft in Blue Water*, and the poetry of Joseph Seamon Cotter Jr.[161]

Yet the first two features Spaulding posits, the experience of marginality and characters defined as "neither white nor raced," mark a key difference between African–Native American texts and other mixed-race texts. While there is an experience of marginality in African–Native American texts, it is not predicated on a dichotomy between "raced" and "white." African–Native American subjects may oscillate between identities or claim both simultaneously, yet they generally do not have the "privilege" of rewriting themselves as European American. Thus there is not an inherent tension as to whether a character will ally him- or herself with either a marginalized or empowered community—the choice is between two marginalized communities, and thus the fear of the "colored" passing into "whiteness" is much less prevalent in African–Native American texts.

Although the African–Native American text is not marked by the dichotomy of marginality between "colored" and "white," the African–Native American subject often finds him- or herself marginalized from either of their potential communities. In the majority of cases, the subject is relegated by European Americans to a state of fixed "blackness" that erases "Indianness," following the theory of hypodescent, which assigns one's identity to the most marginalized position. But African–Native American subjects who wish to assert their "Indianness" are also restricted by Native American individuals or communities reluctant to acknowledge African ancestry or accept African–Native community members and by African Americans who do not wish to lose community members to other racial or cultural communities. The middle ground of "neither/nor" occupied by the mixed-race subject is common in African–Native American writing and the wider tradition of mixed-race writing, but African–Native American identities, whether in conjunction with European or standing alone, often provoke little of the sympathy engendered for the "tragic" African-European mulatto and instead a strong invective against combining the two oppressed peoples.

Jack D. Forbes discusses a "marker erected to commemorate a woman who had testified that the Nanticoke people of Delaware had African ancestry. The Indians were referred to on the marker as 'arrogant negroes that assumed to be what they were not.'"[162] Langston Hughes records a similar hostile response. Widely known as an African American writer, Hughes was raised primarily by his Native American maternal grandmother: "I was born in Joplin, Missouri, in 1902, but I grew up mostly in Lawrence, Kansas. My grandmother raised me until I was twelve years old. Sometimes I was with my mother, but not often."[163] His grandmother, Mary Sampson Patterson, was French Cherokee or African-French-Cherokee.[164] She had a marked influence on Hughes's development as a writer, for he recalls her storytelling ("long, beautiful stories") as an important part of his childhood,[165] but his part-Indian identity provoked a strong reaction from his seventh-grade teacher, who claimed that "'he was a bad combination—Part Indian, part Nigra and part white.'"[166] Perhaps these negative reactions stemmed from European American fears of collaboration and cooperation between Africans Americans and Native Americans, embodied in African–Native American subjects, and certainly such alliances had previously posed threats to European American sovereignty, for example in the Seminole nation's defeats of European American colonists in Florida. In any case, they would lead to a literary depiction of mixed-race African–Native American subjects that differs significantly from that of African-European subjects and to a subjectivity that, rather than being "neither white nor raced" (and thus tragic), was racialized with a hostility by European American narrators that paralleled the narration of the Native-European "half-breed" subject in nineteenth- and twentieth-century American literature.

African–Native American and Native American writers have struggled with the "half-breed" subjectivity imposed on them, but because African–Native American literatures are also Native American literatures, they share a wide-ranging set of common features. Among the African–Native American folktales discussed by George Lankford are mixed Ashanti-Creek, Fan-Creek, Bakongo-Biloxi, and Ibo-Creek trickster tales, all of which are immersed in the Creek or Biloxi oral traditions alongside their West African traditions. Paul Cuffe's autobiographical travel narrative resembles that of the Ojibwa writer George Copway, incorporating Christian missionary writing, spiritual confessional writing, and protest writing typical of eighteenth- and nineteenth-century Native American writers such as Samson Occom, George Henry, George Copway, and William Apess.[167] Apess's autobiography, *A Son of the Forest,* contains his conversion narrative and a tribal history essay, which is a key component of nearly every nineteenth-century Native American autobiography and served as an authentication of the author's identity, and permitted him or her to document mistreatment at the hands of European Americans and to express a communal identity. Such histories can also be found in the works of the African–Native American writers Okah Tubbee and Laah Ceil, James P. Beckwourth, Long Lance, Robert Benjamin Lewis, and Olivia Ward Bush-Banks. Bush-Banks's 1920 play, *Indian Trails; or, Trail of the Montauk,* utilizes "character roles matching Algonquian social and cultural patterns and names that correspond to the r Algonquian dialect traditionally existing between eastern Long Island and southeastern New England."[168] Although Bush-Banks also works in an African American tradition, the play requires an analysis grounded in Algonquian scholarship. James P. Beckwourth, an African European who was adopted and married into the Crow nation, also drew from Native American traditional literatures when he utilized the form of traditional Crow coup tales in his autobiography.

Many Native American autobiographies are also marked by dreams and visions, for example those of George Copway, Black Hawk, and Black Elk, whose vision forms the fundamental framework of his autobiography. Black Elk's autobiography includes the enactment that must follow his powerful vision in order to bring it to fruition for his nation. In Okah Tubbee and Laah Ceil's narrative, numerous dreams are used to prophesize and explain events, and these explanations insist that enactment follow the appearance of a powerful dream. James P. Beckwourth narrates numerous instances of prophesy and enactment, including an explanation of the role of the Snake Indian Barchk-Parchk (prophet or dreamer), a vision narrated by the Snake O-mo-gua, which is fulfilled in the following chapter,[169] the prediction and fulfillment of A-ra-poo-ash's death,[170] and the dreamers of the medicine lodge and their role in the Crow nation:

> All kinds of meats and dried berries, variously cooked, are spread before the partakers, which includes all who can obtain seats, except the medicine men, prophets, and dreamers. Their fast continues for seven days, during which time their inspiration is continually moving them. There are plenty of warriors in attendance to convey messages and execute orders, like deputy sheriffs in a justice's court; and as fast as an ordinance is dreamed out, prophesied on, and medicined, the instructions are delivered to the messengers, and away they start, one party in this direction, and one party in another, to communicate the instructions and execute orders.[171]

Beckwourth succinctly relates the importance of dreaming and visions in Crow society and especially the enactment that must follow. After his departure and triumphant return, the old men of the Crow nation bring the drums to Medicine Calf (Beckwourth) to accompany the songs and celebratory performance that bring the nation out of mourning. In a manner strikingly similar to the narration of the enactment of Black Elk's vision, the nation gains power when it joins in the performance of the vision because the cyclical renewal of the nation depends on the dreamers and the embodiment of their dreams.

Many early Native American and African–Native American autobiographers made their conversion to Christianity the occasion for their autobiography, and their narratives followed the tradition of European American conversion narratives. This Christian discourse meshed with

Native and African traditions in which contacts with gods, spirits, and the sacred were often made through a vision or dream. In one portion of Tubbee and Ceil's autobiography, Ceil includes a dream describing a spiritual contact, using the nineteenth-century Christian conversion narrative as well as a traditional Delaware form: "discussions with Delaware traditionalists made both ethnologists aware that the most vital and intimate phase of Delaware religion was a belief in dreams and visions . . . the vision was the point of contact, a line of communication between the supernatural world and the sphere of everyday life."[172] Drawing from these Native American cultural traditions, William Apess includes in his first autobiography (1831) "frightful visions" and a fiery dream of an "awful lake" juxtaposed with the "happy company"[173] of heaven that precede his conversion to Christianity.

Although African–Native American literatures draw extensively from Native American literary traditions, they are also part of the African American literary tradition, and thus they share a second set of common features. William Apess, Paul Cuffe, and Olivia Ward Bush-Banks, among others, all advocate African American civil rights and equality in their writing. Bush-Banks's work can be situated in the tradition of the Harlem Renaissance just as easily as in a Native American literary tradition. Okah Tubbee's slave narrative shares features of eighteenth- and nineteenth-century African American slave narratives, including the account of the kidnapping and enslavement of the narrator,[174] prefatory and appendatory authenticating documentation supplied by editors of these narratives, the use of Christianity as a political tool to sway northern Christian audiences, and the invocation of American constitutional rhetoric to undermine the claims of slaveholders. Clarence Major's work is clearly embedded in the African American literary tradition and includes representations of Black English in his editing of the *Dictionary of Afro-American Slang* and in his fiction. Ann Plato's essays in many ways exemplify the tradition of nineteenth-century African American religious and didactic writing, "using literature as a vehicle for moral suasion,"[175] and appear to be a response to Phillis Wheatley's poetry in the same tradition.[176] Paul Cuffe wrote extensively on the subject of abolition, advocating an end to the slave trade, which links him with such notable African American writers as Frederick Douglass, Harriet Jacobs, William Wells Brown, and David Walker. Alice Walker's essays, poetry, novels, and other writing are also clearly linked to many segments of African American writing, as she "join[s] Toni Morrison in . . . a Renaissance of African American women writers."[177]

## Subjectivity, Strategic Discourses, and Situational Identity

Alongside links to existing African American and Native American literary traditions, distinctive features characterize African–Native American texts. African–Native American subjects have been represented in works by African–Native American writers and by writers from outside of these communities, beginning as early as the seventeenth century and continuing with contemporary writers such as Michael Dorris and Nettie Jones. Such textualization of African–Native American subjectivity may have begun with William Shakespeare's *The Tempest*, which reflects Shakespeare's attempts to compound African and Native American (Carib) identities in the character of Caliban. In fact, the representation of African–Native American subjectivity also marks the beginnings of African American drama. The earliest African American dramatist, according to the *Oxford Companion to African American Literature*, went by the last name of Brown and his play, *The Drama of King Shotaway*, focuses on Joseph Chatoyer (King Shotaway), the leader of the Black Carib (Garífuna) nation on St. Vincent in the late eighteenth century. The play was performed by the African Company in 1823 at the African Grove Theatre in New York.[178]

Edward Rose, an African Cherokee who, like James P. Beckwourth, worked for fur and trading companies and served as a Crow chief, was fictionalized in the 1848 book *Five Scalps*.[179] Beckwourth was fictionalized on film (in *Tomahawk*, where his African-Native identity was erased when he was portrayed by a European American actor). Bill Pickett, the African Cherokee rodeo star, was also captured on film in two silent movies in the early 1900s.[180] William Faulkner includes African Chickasaw characters (Sam Fathers and Moketubbe) in "The Old People" in *Go Down, Moses*, representing what he believes to be their consideration and negotiation of their dual identities. Martin R. Delany, a well-known political activist during the mid-nineteenth century and into the Reconstruction period, published numerous articles in newspapers such as Frederick Douglass's *North Star*, and he also published one novel, *Blake; or, The Huts of America: A Tale of the Mississippi Valley, the Southern United States, and Cuba*. *Blake* was first published serially in the *Anglo-African Magazine* (1859) and features African American, Native American, and African–Native American characters plotting an African–Native American rebellion in the United States. Also during the Reconstruction era, Albery Whitman wrote an epic poem in Spenserian stanzas entitled

*Twasinta's Seminoles* that narrates the events of the Seminole Black Indian struggle against the U.S. military. First published in 1884 as *The Rape of Florida, Twasinta's Seminoles* uses the African–Native American Seminoles to raise issues of racial solidarity and common bonds between African Americans and Native Americans. Finally, a collection of folklore published in the late nineteenth century utilized an African–Native American subject as the narrator.

In an essay on African American and Native American literary parallels, Mary Ellison discusses the various arguments as to the origins of African–Native American myths and notes that one nineteenth-century folklorist acknowledges the origins of the trickster in both African American and Native American traditions: "Mary Alicia Owen in 1893 neatly claimed joint origins for the tales by using a freed black-Indian woman as her narrator. She takes great pride in her Indian ancestry and draws on her Indian myths as well as slave tales, experiences, and dialect to create rich trickster stories."[181] Ellison also argues that African–Native American subjects have been represented in *All Shot Up* by Chester Himes, whose Native American grandmother served as a model for his character Mammy Louise, "a 'geechie' descended from runaway slaves and Seminole Indians," by Jesse Hill Ford, who writes of African Chickasaws in *The Liberation of Lord Byron Jones*, by Toni Morrison (Pilate in *Song of Solomon*), and by James Baldwin, whose Hall Montana in *Just Above My Head* comes from "the Indian-stained Africa of California."[182]

The tradition of exploring the Black Indian subject extends into the literature of contemporary writers such as Michael Dorris, Alice Walker, Nettie Jones, and Leslie Marmon Silko. In the novel by Michael Dorris, *A Yellow Raft in Blue Water*, the central character, Rayona, is an African Chippewa who presents herself as an African-Native American, which makes an interesting parallel to the well-established mixed-blood European-Native American tradition engaged by many works of Native American literature. Alice Walker's *Meridian* is an African Cherokee text that "firmly links together the collective struggle for freedom undertaken historically by Native American and African American peoples," according to Patricia Riley's essay in this collection. There are also representations of African–Native American literary subjectivity in Nettie Jones's *Mischief Makers* and Leslie Marmon Silko's *Almanac of the Dead*, which will be delineated by Sharon P. Holland's essay.

Representations of Black Indian subjectivity are often accompanied by strategic discourses, an attempt to create a textual apparatus flexible enough to represent multiple or shifting identities. The autobiographies of John Marrant, Okah Tubbee, James P. Beckwourth, and Sylvester Long

Lance all grapple with narratives of passing, multiple racial crossings and politically strategic (and shifting) alliances made possible by their affiliations with both African Americans and Native Americans. For many African-Native autobiographers, the development of strategic discourses to promote, obscure, or manipulate these alliances were a defense against racism or enslavement, particularly when as African Americans and Native Americans they were vulnerable to a variety of attacks. Among the techniques adopted by these African–Native American autobiographers were sudden identity shifts, persistent scenes of misrecognition, a discourse of distancing, linguistic reversals, and sudden assumptions of fluency.

Misrecognition is a defining feature of African–Native American literature. William Apess narrates a scene in *A Son of the Forest* in which he misrecognizes a group of European American women, out picking berries, as a group of Native American warriors.[183] In his Blood Indian "autobiography," Long Lance narrates a similar berry-picking scene in which he and several other Blood Indian boys pass themselves off as Blood warriors, threatening to kill four Crow Indian boys.[184] He also narrates a ruse played on a group of Gros Ventres and Assiniboines by Blood Indians who pretend to come from a tribe of Blackfeet Indians that did not exist.[185] James P. Beckwourth presents numerous accounts of mistaken identity: he mistakes a buffalo for a bear[186] and European American trappers for Native American warriors,[187] and he relates the story of a Snake Indian who, disguised as an antelope, is mistaken for a real antelope and shot by a hunter.[188] Beckwourth is assumed dead numerous times and is mistaken for a dead Native American warrior by a fellow trader.

These scenes of misrecognition allow the narrators to reenact and negotiate the representation of identity; when we're not certain of anyone's identity, when our assumptions of identity are supported and then undercut by the narrator, we begin to develop a suspicion of any fixed identity. The result of such a suspicion is that the reader begins to allow the narrated subjects a textual space for creating and revising identity. Such a perspective permits Beckwourth to become Native American rather than African American to European American traders who are constantly taken in by his assumptions of a complete Crow identity rather than assuming his African roots. During his interaction with European American traders, traders who already "knew" James P. Beckwourth, he "waited until the Indians had nearly completed their exchanges, speaking nothing but Crow language, dressed like a Crow, my hair as long as a Crow's, and myself as black as a crow"[189] before revealing his identity. In another interaction, once Beckwourth reveals his other identity, a trader exclaims, "'I certainly should never have dis-

tinguished you from any other Indian.'"[190] Misrecognitions often occur during homecomings, scenes of return from one "home" to another "home" in which the easy assumption of multiple identities is accompanied by the tension of potential misrecognition and rejection.
Beckwourth is not only misrecognized when returning from the Crow
to the European American trading posts but also when he returns to
the Crow nation. One of his Crow wives initially fails to recognize him
when he appears after a lengthy time.[191] In his captivity narrative, John
Marrant asserts that "he would rather die than go home,"[192] rejecting
his former home for his new Cherokee home, and he undergoes a transformation in identity, the death he prophesies, when he does arrive
home: "My dress was purely in the Indian style; the skins of wild beasts
composed my garments, my head was set out in the savage manner,
with a long pendant down my back, a sash around my middle, without breeches, and a tomahawk by my side."[193] Marrant's family also
fails to recognize him when he returns, and they reject his assumption
of a second home when he reveals his African identity while retaining
his Cherokee clothing and language. Marrant struggles with both African American and European American cultural rejection, and his linguistic transformation, rejection of "home," and adoption of Cherokee
clothing are all markers of his new alliance with Cherokee identity.

Marrant's return and identity change are also marked by a significant
linguistic shift. During the period of his captivity, he experiences some
degree of acculturation and a new proficiency in the Cherokee language,
and early in his captivity narrative Marrant narrates a critical linguistic
shift that parallels Beckwourth's assumption of the Crow language. These
linguistic shifts allow the narrators to negotiate a Native American identity when they assume a fluency in a Native American language. Marrant's
fluency mirrors Beckwourth's retreats to Crow fluency when among the
European American traders and a similar shift narrated by Tubbee and
Ceil (when Tubbee meets with a group of Choctaw):

> I appeared nailed to the spot, my heart leaped with joy, yet a choking
> sensation amounting to pain seized me; confused ideas crowded upon my
> mind; they were near me, yet I moved not, until the keen eyes of one of
> them rested upon me; he spoke, the eyes of the whole company turned
> upon me, and then upon each other, while as it seemed to me they uttered
> an exclamation of surprise; they came towards me; I was wild with delight,
> I thought I was their child, that they were seeking for me; I started and
> held out my hands, tears gushed from my eyes, I addressed them in a lan-
> guage to me unknown before; it was neither English, Spanish or French;
> astonished, they spoke kind to me, smoothing my hair with their hands;
> an explanation now took place, as one could speak English; he said I had

asked in Choctaw for my father, saying he had gone and left me, and I was with bad people; that I begged to know if he was not with them.[194]

Tubbee, Beckwourth, and Marrant narrate a critical moment of cultural identification marked by a sudden linguistic fluency. Regardless of their actual fluency in the Cherokee, Crow, or Choctaw languages, their linguistic transformation serves to define them as Native American (rooted in a Native language) in opposition to European American (rooted in the English language), to create a textual alliance between African American or part–African American men and the Native American culture that better represents their social, personal, and political condition. Within an originally European literary tradition (written autobiography), this linguistic shift permits them to utilize a tradition (European American Christian confessional autobiography) that arises from a culture inherently antagonistic to their own while simultaneously allowing a textual representation that repudiates this tradition, linking them instead with a body of Native American oral traditions.

The autobiography of the Native American writer George Copway also reveals a linguistic shift when he narrates his Christian conversion vision in his autobiography. His vision happens within a church setting: "The small brilliant light came near to me, and fell upon my head, and then ran all over and through me. . . . I arose; and O! how happy I was! I felt light as a feather. I clapped my hands, and exclaimed in English, '*Glory to Jesus.*'"[195] Copway's experience is marked by a reverse linguistic transformation—his vision and conversion lead to a fluency in English. This fluency, noted by so many slave narrators, is theorized by Frederick Douglass to be a crucial step toward freedom. Rather than being controlled by the language of the master, the narrator can shape and present his or her own life. There is a shift when language moves from being a fetter for the tongue and a mark of difference to a vehicle for expression and self-definition. Copway connects the English language with Christianity—fluency in Christian cultural discourse was as important a strategy as fluency in the English language. Unlike Copway and Douglass, these African–Native American autobiographers present not English but Native American language shifts, but they articulate these sudden assumptions of fluency as the opportunity for expression and self-definition and as key moments in the shaping and narrative presentation of their lives.

## Merging of African–Native American Literary Elements

The linguistic fluency represented by African–Native American writers is mirrored by another feature of African–Native American writing, a fluency in multiple cultural and literary traditions that allows the writer to draw from both African American and Native American literary tools to fashion a merged African–Native American writing. In her essay on the interconnections between African American and Native American literatures, Mary Ellison argues that African American and Native American folktales reflect their cultural mergings and notes the lengthy history of cross-pollination between African American and Native American literatures, based not only on substantial interaction and intermarriage but also on deep and pervasive shared cultural practices, particularly spiritual practices, and a common history of colonization that has led to literary hybridization of trickster tales. The trickster tales provide an opportunity to best European American oppressive practices through the engagement of trickster deception, a shared African–Native American strategy that is a "triumph of affinity over alienation."[196] Ellison goes on to argue that the "literary links" run much deeper than the folktales, marking both African American and Native American literary practice, with African–Native American literary roots appearing in work by writers such as Ishmael Reed, Thomas Sanchez, and Marnie Walsh and often manifesting themselves in the work of writers who share an African American and Native American heritage, such as Langston Hughes, Clarence Major, Chester Himes, and Melvin Tolson.

There has been a substantial call and response between and among African American and Native American writers and within the work of African–Native American writers. Perhaps these literary traditions engage in what Henry Louis Gates Jr. describes as "signifying,"[197] or perhaps they are a form of cross-signification when voiced through an African–Native American mediator. A particular and distinctive version of signifying takes place between African American and Native American literature. If African American literature is characterized by a continuous dialogue with African American literary ancestors, in African–Native American literatures there is a dialogue with African American and Native American literary ancestors, and the process that generates and maintains this responsive dialogue is "free of the white person's gaze," as Gates describes African American signifying.[198] The tradition of the Signifying Monkey, as described by Gates, comes from the Yoruba trickster Esu-Elegbara, but this tradition merged with Native American trickster traditions during the period of colonization, as did many other African and Native American mythological traditions (see the essays by Baringer and Gay in this collection). If the mythologies of African and Native Americans merged to become African–Native American mythologies, what Gates identifies as an African tradition of signifying is sometimes an African–Native

American tradition. If the trickster is an essential element in the process of signification, the confluence of African and Native American trickster traditions in the African–Native American folkloric tradition is an important site to investigate the origins or transformations of signification. If, as Gates suggests, the *jigue* (Cuban trickster figure) "underwent a transformation of the most profound sort in his passage from Africa to the New World,"[199] one key element of his transformation was a merging with Native American traditions, as the anthropologist Maya Deren has shown in the creolization of African, Arawakan, Carib, and other Native American spiritual traditions in Haitian Vodoun.[200]

African–Native American writers also draw from their dual heritages to fashion their literary works. Paul Cuffe's autobiographical travel narrative documents his navigation, trade, and travel to Sierra Leone, England, and Washington, D.C., where he met with President James Madison. Portions of his journals were originally published in Sheldon Harris's biography of Cuffe, and the journal in its entirety was finally published in Rosalind Cobb Wiggins's edition of Cuffe's ship logs and correspondence.[201] The mostly self-taught sea captain and civil rights advocate transforms the ship's log into an elaborate travel narrative as well as a spiritual narrative grounded in Quaker values and African and Wampanoag traditions.

Cuffe's writing is related to the autobiographical narratives of two writers of the African Diaspora, the African American autobiographer Briton Hammon and the Anglo-African autobiographer Olaudah Equiano.[202] Hammon's narrative, written in 1760 by an enslaved African American New Englander, is as much a travel narrative as a captivity narrative, covering his sea voyages to Cuba and England and his captivity in Florida. Cuffe and Hammon's travel narratives share the characteristics of travel writing, the features of the mariner's tale, and the significance of the captivity tale, which, when written by an American of African descent, create a bridge to the slave narrative. The writing of Equiano, an African English seaman in the 1760s, merges a travel narrative and a spiritual narrative, much like Cuffe's work, evaluating his life's experiences through the lens of Christianity while relating voyages at sea and arguing against the institution of slavery.

Cuffe's writing holds much in common with the work of his African American contemporaries, but it also demonstrates the influences of his Wampanoag cultural background. According to William Simmons's study of New England Indian folklore and history, for centuries the Wampanoag have recorded any important historical incident by creating a memory hole, as noted by Edward Winslow in 1624:

"Instead of chronicles and records, they take this course. Where any remarkable act is done, in memory of it, either in the place, or by some pathway near adjoining, they make a round hole in the ground, about a foot deep, which when others passing by behold, they inquire the cause and occasion of the same, which being once known, they are careful to acquaint all men, as occasion serveth, therewith; and lest such holes should be filled or grown up by any accident, as men pass by, they will oft renew the same, by which means many things of great antiquity are fresh in memory."[203]

Cuffe's impulse to record history, to pass regularly by his memory hole to add another entry, represents a new form of a Wampanoag tradition of storytelling. He was compelled to record "remarkable acts" in his travel journal. There are several unique features of the Wampanoag memory hole storytelling tradition that Cuffe observes in his autobiographical journal. First, the memory holes served to honor one's ancestors, as Cuffe does in an 1815 journal entry drafting a letter to the African American minister Daniel Coker in which he invokes the ancestors' memory as a spur to renewed political action. Second, the memory holes were an occasion for Wampanoag storytelling, and Cuffe's shorter log entries and lengthier remarks and commentary often served as an impetus for revisiting and narrating these events in longer letters to family and friends, "renew[ing] the same" by acquainting family and friends with the more important events he logged in his travel journal.

As a travel journal, Cuffe's work is also a forerunner to two mid-nineteenth century Native American travel narratives, George Henry's 1848 pamphlet entitled *An Account of the Chippewa Indians*, which discusses a traveling band of Indian performers, and George Copway's *Running Sketches of Men and Places in England, France, Germany, Belgium, and Scotland*, which Copway wrote while attending the Third General Peace Congress in August 1850.[204] Copway maintains a journal of his travels through Europe and speeches before church congregations and temperance meetings, and like Cuffe he discusses his meetings with well-known politicians and businessmen.

The autobiography of Okah Tubbee and Laah Ceil demonstrates a fascinating merging of African American and Native American traditions. Tubbee narrates his enslavement in terms that parallel eighteenth- and nineteenth-century African American slave narratives, including stories of kidnapping, documentation of abuses, an initial awareness of being a slave, condemnation of slavery, a turning point into manhood, and finally the use of Christian and Constitutional rhetoric as a strategic tool.[205] Their autobiography shares with Native American collaborative autobiographies the use of prefatory and appendatory documentation, the inclusion of tribal histories, the narration of spiritual awakenings, conversion, dreams, and visions, especially through the Delaware cultural traditions with which Laah Ceil was familiar. Tubbee also narrates a pivotal moment in which he bests his captor and gains his freedom, a moment that mirrors a similar transition into manhood in slave narratives like Frederick Douglass's description of the fight with his overseer, Edward Covey, and in Native American autobiographies like Black Elk's account of his passage into manhood through a powerful dream.

Much like Tubbee, James P. Beckwourth, also apprenticed as a town slave to a blacksmith, narrates a turning point at which he finds his manhood and his freedom. His narrative is marked by characteristics of both slave narratives and Crow autobiographies and makes substantial use of the trickster motif from African American slave narratives, like those of Jacob D. Green or William Wells Brown,[206] and in Native American narratives such as Sam Blowsnake's Winnebago narrative *Crashing Thunder*. Beckwourth eagerly assumes the role of trickster, relishing the many times his fellow European, African, or Native Americans fail to recognize him and eagerly manipulating their ignorance. In fact, such a role reflects the traditional elements associated with the African American trickster[207] as well as the roles associated with the Native American trickster figures, who trick the master to gain the upper hand and defy the sacred or traditional cultural roles to challenge a fixed society.

## African–Native American Politics and History

The challenges posed by James P. Beckwourth in his trickster role are much like the challenges presented to European Americans by African–Native Americans who demonstrate an interest in and commitment to an African–Native American politics. An African–Native American politics is generated from the civil rights interests of both African Americans and Native Americans. It can alternate between a focus on African American and Native American politics within the same text, on African American and Native American issues simultaneously, or on the interests of distinct African–Native American communities. African–Native American texts also demonstrate a sustained focus on redressing African–Native American rights lost in the process of the colonization of Native Americans and Africans.

The journal and collected letters of Paul Cuffe contain important examples of this type of writing. While at sea, Cuffe's journal initially consists of brief log entries written during the four-hour watch. He also includes drafts of numerous letters, some inserted into the text and others copied into the back of the journal. The short entries typically note weather, longitude and latitude, and any unusual events: "Remarks onboard, second day of the second month, 1811: 'High wind South South-east and stormy at three A.M. Wind and sea struck us down on our beam end. Washed John Masterns overboard but by the help of some loose rigging he regained the ship again. Latitude per observation 34/26 and longitude 34/09.'"[208] Eventually Cuffe begins to expand on these short entries while anchored offshore, developing a distinct voice and a fascinating hybrid of the traditional ship's log, the American travel narrative, and African and Native American political rhetorical strategies, moving quickly from the prevailing trade winds to the prevailing political winds, from the lack of sea biscuit to the hunger for racial justice: "Remarks, 1st watch, fourth Month, day 22, 1812: 'This day commences with the wind in from the seaboard at West South-west. At 9 o'clock this morning arrived a fine pilot boat like a built schooner taken by his Majesty's ship and sent into this port with slaves in it. She was taken in Gambia. I do long to see the slave trade discouraged and wish that men could feel their causes to be put into the slaves stead. I believe they would feel themselves condemned by their own consciences.'"[209] Cuffe's entries become increasingly elaborate as he engages a wide variety of political, social, and ethical issues. As he writes about his consideration of the slave trade while noting the swells from the northwest, he notes the pain that strikes him like the waves strike the ship. While he trades for pottery, he discusses the abolition of the slave trade and political strategies that might convince two warring nations, the United States and England, to end the slave trade in favor of establishing a profitable trading coalition with African nations.

In his letters, Cuffe focuses on Native American and African American rights. He inquires about two "Mollato Children" who need to be educated away from the "prejudice of Coulor" they had experienced in the North.[210] Cuffe founded his own school for the education of African American and Native American children. The difficulties he encountered in maintaining and defending both identities are revealed in a series of legal struggles with the Massachusetts legislature over his rights as an African American and as a Native American. In 1778, the state legislators of Massachusetts began arguments over a constitution that would exclude women, Native Americans, African Americans, and mixed-race people from voting: "'every male inhabitant of any town in this state, being free and twenty-one years of age excepting Negroes, Indians, and mulattoes, shall be entitled to vote.'"[211] Paul Cuffe and others petitioned for relief from paying poll and property taxes, identifying themselves in their written petitions as "several poor Negroes and mulattoes." When they were discussing slavery, they identified themselves as "chiefly of the African extraction," and when they were turned down by the state legislature, they petitioned the county for relief as "Indian men and by law not the subjects of taxation for any estate."[212] Cuffe's writings reveal a deliberate attempt to obtain justice both as an African and as a Native American, since Africans, Native Americans, and mixed-race people had been targeted in the legislation. Because one set of laws was aimed at "colored" citizens (including African, Native-African and non-recognized Native Americans) while another body of laws (often derived from treaties or separate legislation) was aimed at Native Americans, and because multiple restrictions impeded their lives as African Americans and as Native Americans, their response as African-Native Americans necessitates multiple legal arguments in their writing.

William Apess was also a staunch advocate for the rights of Native Americans and Africans. In 1833, in *The Experiences of Five Christian Indians of the Pequot Tribe,* he asserts that God created far more people of color than white people and to condemn people with colored skin is to condemn God's creation. He engages in a scathing critical reading of European American racism by examining the skins of European Americans to find their crimes against African Americans and Native Americans written on their very selves:

> Now let me ask you, white man, if it is a disgrace for to eat, drink, and sleep with the image of God, or sit, or walk and talk with them. Or have you the folly to think that the white man, being one in fifteen or sixteen, are the only beloved images of God? Assemble all nations together in your imagination, and then let the whites be seated among them, and then let us look for the whites, and I doubt not it would be hard finding them: for to the rest of the nations they are still but a handful. Now suppose these skins were put together, and each skin had its national crimes written upon it—which skin do you think would have the greatest? I will ask one question more. Can you charge the Indians with robbing a nation almost of their whole continent, and murdering their women and children, and then depriving the remainder of their lawful rights, that nature and God require them to have? And to cap the climax, rob another nation to till their grounds and welter out their days under the lash with hunger and fatigue under the scorching rays of the burning sun? I should look at all the skins, and I know that when I cast my eye upon that white skin, and if I saw those crimes written upon it, I should enter my protest against it immediately and cleave to that which is more honorable. And I can tell you that I am satisfied with the manner of my creation, fully—whether others are or not.[213]

Like Cuffe, Apess has often been seen by scholars as belonging exclusively to one race, in his case Native American rather than African American. Yet Apess, like Cuffe, was a member of an African–Native American family and community, and like other African-Native Americans he addresses the oppression of Native Americans and African Americans. The concluding essay in his autobiography links African American abolitionist discourse with Native American political and legal arguments, especially those surrounding land retention, sovereignty, and constitutional rights. Cuffe recognized that the African slave trade paralleled and supported justifications for the enslavement and oppression of Native Americans. Much like the African–Native American historian Robert Benjamin Lewis, who quotes De Las Casas as saying, "'Thus we see the Island of Hispaniola, or St. Domingo was taken from the white Spaniards, or French, and given to the blacks and Indians of the island,'"[214] Cuffe and Apess advocate redressing African and Native American losses, and all three draw from a merged African American and Native American consciousness to align their political and moral visions with the future of both African Americans and Native Americans, a complexity that should be acknowledged for its potential to enrich our understanding of early American literature and history.

Just as a merged African–Native American political consciousness is an important feature of African–Native American writing, another essential characteristic is the inclusion of historical narratives that draw from both African American and Native American history to present an African–Native American historical context that supports the articulation of an African–Native American politics. In 1844, Lewis published *Light and Truth, Collected from the Bible and Ancient and Modern History, Containing the Universal History of the Coloured and Indian Races, from the Creation of the World to the Present Time.* Although his work was perhaps one of the earliest histories of "colored" Americans, African American histories were published by George Washington Williams in 1883 and Booker T. Washington in 1909, among others.[215] Native American histories were published by the Tuscarora writer David Cusick in 1827 and by the Ojibwa writer George Copway in 1850, with many more histories following before the end of the nineteenth century.[216] But unlike African American or Native American writers, Lewis constructs a history of both African Americans and Native Americans in his *Light and Truth.* In his four-hundred-page world history, Lewis discusses the Haitian revolution, prominent "colored" leaders, the importance of Africans to the development of Christianity, the origins of Native Americans, and the categories assigned to mixed-race people. He compares the treatment of African and Native Americans in American history and explores the biblical roots of Africans and Native Americans, tracing African origins to Noah's son Ham and Native American origins to a tribe of Israelites coming out of Egypt, who had links to Ethiopians.[217] He also includes linguistic analyses of Carib, Creek, Hebrew, and English words to argue the Judeo-Christian origins of Native Americans, a popular argument in the early and mid-nineteenth century. Lewis's history has an interesting parallel in the history written by Martin Delany, the newspaper editor, writer, and political activist whose family was African, European, and Native American. Delany published *Origin of Races and Color* in 1879, a historical treatise that offers arguments concerning the origins of Africans, Native Americans, and other races in the Old Testament and praises the contributions made by the oppressed races to the development of world civilization.[218]

Full-length historical treatises were not the only form of African–Native American historical writing. Many African American and Native American writers also published historical work to accompany or inform their literature, particularly in conjunction with their autobiographies. The African American writers James W. C. Pennington and William Wells Brown as well as the Sioux Charles Alexander Eastman included extensive histories in their autobiographies. Their inclusion of "race histories" satisfied the curiosities of a substantially European American audience regarding the African or Native American "races," yet it also allowed the writers to reconstruct the historical and cultural traditions of their nation of origin, a privilege denied to both African Americans and Native Americans. From this historical reconstruction, the writers could contextualize the self they were inscribing within their autobiography. African–Native American writers used history to inform other genres of literature as well, including Nathan J. Cuffee, the African Montauk, who wrote an historical novel entitled *Lords of the Soil* (1909) that focuses on Montauk history during the early American period.[219] Olivia Ward Bush-Banks, another African Montauk writer, inscribed Montauk history while serving as the Montauk tribal historian and also drew from African American history in her poetry, praising African Americans such as Frederick Douglass and African–Native American historical figures such as Crispus Attucks. She also draws upon Montauk history in her play *Indian Trails; or, Trail of the Montauk*.

Other African–Native American writers held a more complex relationship to their dual histories. In response to the one-drop rule, which threatened to snatch them back into a non-Indian "colored" community to be either enslaved or restricted by Jim Crow laws, Okah Tubbee and

Long Lance refrained from utilizing their African American histories to create instead a protective perimeter of Native American history. Tubbee and Ceil included a Choctaw Indian history in their autobiography for several reasons, including the authentication of Tubbee's identity, the demonstration of abuses suffered by their nation, and as an expression of a communal identity. In the "Biography" section, they include a tribal history, which was likely performed on stage, an attempt to fix a Choctaw identity, to embed himself in Choctaw history.[220]

Long Lance engages in a similar practice. As a journalist, he wrote articles that included Blackfoot, Sarcee, Blood, Squamish, Sioux, and other Native American histories, but his historical novel, purporting to be an autobiography of a Blood Indian, used a history related to him in interviews with the Blood Indian Mike Eagle Speaker. This was not, of course, Long Lance's history, but because he came from a community of nonrecognized Native Americans and because he was denied Native American identity due to his African American identity, he created a history that would allow him to claim a Native American identity.

History and historical narrative take on an urgency in African–Native American literature because of the audience's ignorance of both African American and Native American history (which facilitated their continued oppression), because of the need to document and condemn European American mistreatment of both groups, because the inclusion of both histories allows the writer to maintain ties to both communities, and because the lack of widespread awareness and understanding of the history of African-Native Americans threatens their existence as mixed-race people. In *Black Indians*, William Loren Katz includes the story of a young African–Native American speaker appearing at a panel presentation on Black Indians who insists, "'If you know I have a history, you will respect me.'"[221] Such an argument has informed the historical efforts of African–Native American writers for generations.

## Rootlessness and Travel Narratives

As a result of the history and politics of dual colonization, "rootlessness," a condition of wandering in search of a home, is another prominent feature of African–Native American writing. African Americans and Native Americans share an historical experience of appropriation, relocation, and attempts by European Americans to sever them from cultural roots through forced assimilation or cultural misrecognition. Many African-Native Americans have experienced a condition shared by many other mixed-race Americans, an alienation brought about by rejection from both of their shared communities, a wandering rootlessness that the narrator often attempts to resolve through negotiation or the assumption of new identities. An example of this narrated rootlessness can be found in the narrative of John Marrant when he relates a story in which he was supposed dead by his family after being captured by the Cherokees; his family initially fails to recognize him upon his return and finally turns against him altogether when they believe he has rejected his roots by assuming Cherokee clothing and language. He eventually becomes a missionary, traveling to other Native American nations. William Apess's *Son of the Forest* begins with the narration of family disintegration and physical abuse, with Apess being bound out to a cooper named Furman at the age of five. Eventually, in response to the racial slurs and accusations directed at Native Americans to which he was subjected during his indenture, Apess becomes "weaned from the interests and affections of my brethren" and is frightened at the threat of being sent to the Indians.[222] His weaning from the maternal nourishment of his Pequot nation and from the political interests of a pan-Indian union are later repaired in his text, but rootlessness is a subject of deep concern to Apess and is used to further indict European Americans for their mishandling of Native American interests.

James P. Beckwourth narrates a series of shifts from nation to nation in his autobiography, oscillating between the Crows and European American traders and sometimes aligning himself with African American slaves; he changes alliances as it suits his purposes. Like Beckwourth, Sylvester Long Lance switches alliances from his African Catawba roots to Eastern Cherokee and eventually to Blood Indian when he is adopted into their nation. In his Blood Indian "autobiography," based on the experiences of a student he interviewed, Long Lance writes of "legends from other tribes . . . of 'black white men' who lived under the sun."[223] He becomes disconnected from his African roots as they become "legend" and are replaced by the "facts" of a boyhood he never experienced. Due to the rejection of Black Indians as Indians, he suffers an enforced rootlessness, forsaking both his African and Native American roots for an attempted grounding in another set of Indian roots.

Ann Plato published several poems that are marked by wandering and rootlessness, including "Alone I've Wandered," "The Natives of America," and "Daughter's Inquiry." In "The Natives of America," Plato narrates a story from her father lamenting the loss of Native American lands that left them "in foreign hands . . . Alas! It was a cruel day; we were crushed: into the dark, dark woods we rushed / to seek a refuge . . . could I tell them my grief / In its flow, that in roaming, we find no relief."[224]

The "roaming" that Plato articulates for her father is again addressed in "Daughter's Inquiry":

> I said, my father, if you please
> Do guide the ship no more,
> Some other can your place fulfill,
> And others can explore
> If not, dear father, do resign
> This ever roaming life,
> Oh, do not spend your life in this
> An ever mournful strife.[225]

Because conditions for African Americans and Native Americans were abysmal in nineteenth-century America, and because both nations suffered the appropriation of their lands, there resulted a literal wandering with no land, a wandering between cultures, and a wandering stirred by political and social conditions. For Plato, one of the answers to rootlessness lay in the Christian church. In the first essay in her collection, "Religion," she asks the reader, "where can the soul find refuge but in the bosom of religion?"[226]

Paul Cuffe sought his answer to rootlessness less in religion than in Africa. Although he was a member of the Quaker church, he was also known as the father of the back-to-Africa movement, and his journals often focus on his plans for a return to Africa. Because he contended with discriminatory legislation as a Native American and as an African American in Rhode Island, he believed that a resolution to rootlessness lay in a return to Africa. Such plans are greatly complicated by Cuffe's African Wampanoag identity and community: if one of the founders of the so-called back-to-Africa movement was a Black Indian, and if a significant number of the early colonists utilized in his voyages were Black Indian maroons from Jamaica, and if a portion of the slave community for whom Cuffe advocates was composed of Native American and African–Native American slaves, how should we view Cuffe's plans for this community? What does it mean for an African Wampanoag to propose the return of enslaved African Americans to Africa, or to create a free state for enslaved Native Americans, or for enslaved African-Native Americans? Perhaps his ideas more closely parallel the proposals made in the nineteenth century for the creation of a colored state for blacks and Indians in the western United States, a plan to repair rootlessness that never reached fruition.

In the autobiography of the African Narragansett Elleanor Eldridge, her first dislocation begins at the age of ten when her mother, Hannah Prophet, dies and Elleanor is forced to work washing clothes and doing

housework for a local family.[227] Her narrative documents a series of dis-
locations in profession and location, marked by the death of family members and the seizure of her home. Her autobiography centers around her
struggle to regain her home, which in 1832 was attached and sold for a
small debt owed by her when she was recovering from a lengthy illness.
She wrote to regain her property, offering numerous editions of her autobiography to the public to raise funds. Her autobiography represents
both the narration of rootlessness and the opportunity for its resolution,
as sales eventually raised enough money to regain her home.

In the autobiography written by Laah Ceil and Okah Tubbee, the two
performers and their children move constantly, escaping threats of enslavement, bad debts, and shifting political winds. In their attempts to support
themselves and their children, they "could well have performed a thousand times in steamboat staterooms, town and village streets, public halls,
saloons, Indian villages, and fancy theaters throughout the interior of
America from New Orleans to Cape Cod, from Natchez to Detroit, and
from St. Louis to the upper Missouri."[228] Laah Ceil was born in New York,
had removed with the Delaware nation to Missouri in 1818, was removed
again in 1829 to "lands near Fort Leavenworth,"[229] and maintained a diary of their wanderings throughout the United States and Canada. In the
narrative that was based on this diary, the first issue of rootlessness is that
of Tubbee's "scenes of sorrow"[230] from youth, in which the loss of his father severs him from his Choctaw roots and propels him into slavery. Much
of the rest of the narrative presents Okah Tubbee constantly fleeing his
tormentors, cut off even from his own mother who has him whipped, and
in search of his Choctaw roots. In his *Narrative,* Frederick Douglass discusses the root given him by Sandy Jenkins just before he seizes his own
manhood by fighting Mr. Covey; although Douglass is suspicious of the
root's power, he devotes considerable narrative space to this story, thus
endowing the root with an undeniable textual importance. Tubbee and Ceil
relate a parallel narrative in which roots as a healing and conjuring tradition acquire a critical importance in repairing rootlessness. After suffering a whipping, starvation, and a temporary escape (much like Douglass),
Tubbee acquaints himself with a Doctor Merrrill with whom he finds work.
This doctor, Tubbee claims, gives him a new lease on life by showing him
a path to his freedom through the knowledge of Native American roots for
healing purposes: "My purpose was instantly taken,"[231] and Tubbee attempts to escape his enslavement and poverty by presenting himself as a
traditional healer. Still, his lack of knowledge surrounding his family roots
remains a persistent source of anguish, and at one point, when derided for
his coloring, he "conjured heaven and earth to know where I originated."[232]

Olivia Ward Bush-Banks also raises issues of rootlessness. As she writes in a short autobiography accompanying her book *Driftwood,* "I seemed to have lost my identity regarding the distinctness of race, being of African and Indian descent. Both parents possessed some negro blood, and were also descendants of the Montauk tribe of Indians, which tribe formerly occupied the eastern end of Long Island known as Montauk."[233] Bush-Banks's play *Indian Trails* contains a scene that explores the destruction of Montauk tribal unity resulting from the 1918 New York State Supreme Court case proclaiming the Montauk people extinct.[234]

Finally, much like her predecessors Long Lance and Okah Tubbee, Rayona, an African–Native American teenage girl in Michael Dorris's *Yellow Raft in Blue Water,* attempts to narrate herself into another life.[235] With an African American father and Native American mother, and as a nonreservation Indian, Rayona is interrogated by those around her and is told she doesn't fit in either as an African American or as a Native American, being "Too big, too smart, not Black, not Indian, not friendly."[236] Responding to the displacement of African Americans and Native Americans and to the rejections she suffers from both communities when trying to assert her identities, she sometimes rejects her dis-integrated roots for more cohesive (but temporary) stories of new identity.

## The Mardi Gras Indian Tradition

Rootlessness can often be repaired through the formation of new community traditions. One of the most distinct and highly developed African–Native American community traditions, that of the Mardi Gras Indians, has a deep history and a thriving contemporary tradition. A well-established African–Native American oral performance, the Mardi Gras Indian tradition is worthy of further exploration and articulation due to its complexity, its historical roots, and its ability to integrate multiple African American and Native American traditions into a powerful ceremonial renewal.

The Mardi Gras Indians have their roots in the many interactions between African slaves and surrounding Native American nations in colonial Louisiana. Escaped African slaves joined forces with nations such as the Natchez and Chickasaw to fight against French colonial oppression, Native Americans and Africans were enslaved together on Louisiana plantations, Choctaw and African marketers exchanged goods at the French Market, and Africans and Native Americans converged for drumming and dancing at Congo Square, the Native American ceremonial site adopted by African slaves. The cultural convergence evolved into a spiritual convergence of African–Native American sensibilities, and eventually masks and costumes were displayed during Carnival season by Africans, Native Americans, and African-Native Americans who created urban tribes of Mardi Gras Indians. The Mardi Gras Indian tradition has a highly evolved set of rituals, tribal hierarchies, song cycles that accompany the hand-sewn costumes, and a richly expressive and rhythmic oral tradition that has been handed down from generation to generation.

Musical collaborations between Africans and Native Americans can be found elsewhere in the United States. In a study published in 1939, George Herzog argues that there has been a significant African influence on Native American music, especially in the southeastern and western United States. He compares African, African American, and Native American songs and asserts that African melodic elaboration (as well as solo-chorus technique) found among Native American musical traditions that had extensive contact with African slaves indicates a merging of the two traditions. He even suggests that there has been more retention of African stylistic features in some Native American musical practices than in African American musical practices, arguing that for African musical tradition, "we owe our clearest glimpses of its character and history on our soil to survivals in Indian music, which was first hospitable enough to receive a foreign idiom and then conservative enough to preserve it."[237]

Whether some Native American musical traditions retain more traditional African features than African American musical traditions is certainly controversial, but the merging of these musical forms indicates an early African–Native American musical tradition and perhaps raises an interesting question for scholars who point to African influences in American music—are these influences mediated by, moderated by, or merged with Native American musical forms? Herzog also notes that "the thematic material of the melodies" and the "Indian method of instrumental accompaniment . . . an unbroken series of evenly spaced beats"[238] are among the Native American contributions to these musical traditions. Discussing one of the standards of the Mardi Gras Indian tradition, "Iko Iko," George Lipsitz remarks on the "nonsense rhymes"[239] that mark this tune, and perhaps such a feature bears a relation to a Native American musical tradition Herzog discusses: "When there is a sizeable change upon repetition of the melody in Indian music, it is apt to produce a structural pattern. In a frequent type, found especially in the songs of the tribes of the Middle West, the melody is first sung through with meaningless syllables, which have merely an ornamental function. The second time it is sung to a text consisting of meaningful words, and the melody is changed somewhat in order to accommodate the words."[240]

Of course, the syllables are not meaningless or ornamental (as Lipsitz discusses in a linguistic analysis of the lyrics), nor are the rhymes without meaning, but perhaps scholars need to examine Native American music as carefully as they have African music in order to understand the New Orleans Mardi Gras Indian traditions, particularly in light of Arthur "Creole" Williams and Vincent Trepagnier's comments about Eugene Honore, a second chief in the Yellow Pocahontas tribe, and the origins of the Mardi Gras Indian song cycle:

> "Now Eugene Honore used to be Second Chief to Henri . . . big, tall, looked just like an Indian. Eugene is the one that mapped all them songs out—'Indian Red,' 'Take That Flag Down,' he originated those songs." . . .
> Vincent Trapagnier, another aging Creole, recalls his experiences with the Yellow Pocahontas in the 1930s. He says Eugene Honore was a Choctaw: "Eugene was seven-foot two-inches tall. He was a real Indian who came with his mama from up the country, somewhere the other side of Baton Rouge. They lived in tents. . . . And when they come in the city, they moved on Burgundy and Toulouse. Eugene was the tallest Indian I ever seen in my life. He had a high cheekbone, beautiful skin, olive complexion, and long black hair. People used to call his mama Miss Cherie, but that wasn't her name. Her name was Miss Choctaw."[241]

If Honore did map out a portion of the song cycle, there is clearly an important Choctaw contribution to the Mardi Gras Indian songs.

In *The Spirit of Black Hawk: A Mystery of Africans and Indians,* a work that examines the spiritual churches of New Orleans and their use of the Sauk and Fox leader Black Hawk as a spirit guide, Jason Berry discusses Indian Jim (Jim Alexander), a witch doctor and prominent healer in New Orleans in the late nineteenth century: "Doctor Jim was three-quarters Indian, one-quarter Negro . . . he brought much experience in the field, a reputation as a successful healer. . . . He was renowned for his dancing at Voodoo-inspired ceremonies of the late nineteenth century—a bizarre combination of the Calinda and an Indian war dance, performed in tights and with a candle balanced on his head."[242] Alexander's dancing, a merging of African[243] and Native American traditions, was not the only example of the merging of these traditions (Congo Square likely featured both forms of dancing, perhaps simultaneously), but it is representative of African–Native American traditions present in New Orleans at the time of the establishment of the earliest Mardi Gras Indian tribes.[244]

It is also clear that both African American and Native American dancing were viewed as threatening by European Americans. Berry, Foose, and Jones note that in 1751 the Calinda dances were outlawed and that in 1835 New Orleans authorities "suppressed" the drumming and dancing of Congo Square.[245] In 1890 the Ghost Dance led by Wovoka, the Paiute messiah, was a growing pan-Indian phenomenon. Wovoka promised that the dancing would bring a renewal to Native American nations, creating a new world in which European Americans would lose their power and Native Americans would regain control of their nations: "By mid-November Ghost Dancing was so prevalent on the Sioux reservations that almost all other activities came to a halt. No pupils appeared at the schoolhouses, the trading stores were empty, no work was done on the little farms. At Pine Ridge the frightened agent telegraphed Washington: 'Indians are dancing in the snow and are wild and crazy. . . . We need protection and we need it now. The leaders should be arrested and confined at some military post until the matter is quieted, and this should be done at once.'"[246] The U.S. military slaughtered hundreds of Sioux, mostly women and children, at Wounded Knee. The "emancipatory potential," as Lipsitz describes it, of both African and Native American dancing, in New Orleans or Pine Ridge, was acknowledged by all.

There is a tendency to coalesce African American, Native American, and African–Native American identity into a "black" identity with "African" roots, and this approach obscures the complexity of the African American and Native American interactions that produced the Mardi Gras Indian phenomenon. Lipsitz identifies the participants as "black males,"[247] and Kathryn VanSpanckeren identifies the community as "black working-class."[248] Some of the participants are African American ("'We're not real Indians. . . . what we're doing is just something that we copies behind the Indians really'"),[249] and it is important to articulate the meaning this tradition holds for an African American community in New Orleans. However, the fact that it emerged from an African–Native American history is an essential component in understanding its meaning for the community. The earliest African–Native American expressions at Congo Square, the African–Native American community members in New Orleans, and the African–Native American (and Native American) originators of the tribal parades and song sequence combine to mark this as an African–Native American tradition.

Several of the progenitors of the Mardi Gras Indian tradition are either Native American or African-Native American. Becate Batiste organized what was perhaps the earliest Mardi Gras tribe in the 1880s:

[H]e was soon joined by his brother, Eugene, a plasterer. The Batistes were of Indian descent, though of how much is unknown. The story of Chief Becate has come down through three generations of a Seventh Ward Creole family. Today, the linear descendant of that tribe is called the Yellow Pocahontas, and its chief, Allison "Tuddy" Montana, began leading the tribe after World War II. Trim and sturdy, Tuddy is a folk hero to thousands of blacks in the neighborhood. Born on December 17, 1922, he learned of Chief Becate Batiste—his granduncle—from his grandmother, Jeanne Durrell, who was Becate's sister. Tuddy's father, Alfred Montana Sr., led the Pocahontas in the 1930s and 1940s: "Well my grandmother, she always said that we had Indian blood. If you'd seen her, you could tell. She always were bright as you could want. We had the Indian blood mixed in. Just like on my daddy's side. I have some cousins—my daddy's sister's children—man, they look just *like* an Indian."[250]

Becate identifies both sides of his family as African-Native American, and he is an African–Native American leader of a tradition passed through generations of his family. Robert Sam Tillman (Brother Timber) and his father are associated with the founding of the Yellow Pocahontas and the Creole Wild West tribes, and, according to Paul Longpre, "the elder Tillman 'had Louisiana blood in him, and also his wife. I think they was Choctaw.'"[251] This would make their son Choctaw or African Choctaw as well, and Robert Tillman "controlled the Creole Wild West"[252] until at least the 1930s. Finally, there is Eugene Honore, the Second Chief in the Yellow Pocahontas and the originator of a portion of the Mardi Gras Indian song cycle.

When the Mardi Gras Indian tradition is not identified as African in origin, it is often identified as originating in the "Afro-Caribbean world"[253] with certain songs containing distinctive "Caribbean phrases and styles."[254] The influence of Caribbean cultures in New Orleans is uncontestable, but the question remains as to whether these are solely Afro-Caribbean and not also Indo-Caribbean influences. Berry, Foose, and Jones note that after the revolution in Haiti, "waves of [Haitians] settled in New Orleans; the largest number (ten thousand) came after expulsion from Cuba in 1809."[255] In 1730 the French colonists in Louisiana captured and enslaved nearly five hundred Natchez Indians; the women and children were enslaved in New Orleans, and over four hundred were shipped to Haiti and sold as slaves.[256] Native Americans indigenous to the Caribbean islands were enslaved or established maroon nations, and thousands of Native Americans from the many Native nations along the eastern coast of the United States were captured and sold into slavery to the Caribbean.[257] Any Caribbean influence must necessarily be an Afro-Indian Caribbean culture, and perhaps some of the slaves who returned to New Orleans were originally indigenous to Louisiana. In any case, the merging of Natchez, African, and other Native American cultures in Haiti, Cuba, and other Caribbean nations that supplied immigrant New Orleans populations (and that had parallel traditions of African–Native American Carnival masking) infused another powerful African–Native American cultural tradition into New Orleans.

In remarking on the period between the repression of Congo Square and the emergence of the Mardi Gras Indian tribes, Berry, Foose, and Jones suggest that it can be viewed as the submersion period described by the Caribbean writer Edward Kamau Brathwaite, in which the "mother culture, to survive the weight of New World domination, had to go through a submarine or tunneling stage"[258] and arises in a new form. They note Maya Deren's work on Haitain Voodoo,[259] which argues that this religion drew from both African and Native American (Petro Indian) practices and, even more importantly, that the compatibility of the worldviews of Africans and Native Americans, particularly regarding European colonization, allowed and even encouraged the African Diaspora to adopt Native American cultural practices. This New World process is captured in the narrative of John Marrant, in his emergence from "death" and transformation into Cherokee language and dress.

It was not only African cultural practices that underwent this tunneling in response to colonization but Native American cultural practices as well. The reemergence into a transformed cultural expression was (and is) a process essential to the survival of both peoples and is exemplified in a story about Brother Timber in New Orleans: "The younger Tillman, also called 'Brother Timber,' controlled the Creole Wild West in Longpre's youth and devised schemes to evade the law. In 1927 word of his death spread. Police attended his wake, says Longpre, where people wept and mourned: 'They put him in the hearse, bringed him to Holt Cemetery. He got out of the casket inside the hearse. When they got to the cemetery, they buried the casket, brought him back. On Carnival morning he had on an Indian suit—returned from the dead!'"[260] Brother Timber's return from the dead allows him to evade repression by European American authorities and reaffirms the importance of the Mardi Gras Indian rituals, a potent transformation of African and Native American cultural practices. Tillman's African and Native American cultural heritages reemerge when he masks Indian at Mardi Gras. The Native American Diaspora, those separated from their original homelands and nations, sold into slavery or driven away, now living in scattered families and small communities, converges with the African Diaspora to produce a vision that testifies to their ability to survive through the transformation and active celebration of their shared New World heritage.

## Essays on *African–Native American Literature*

Critical explorations of such African–Native American visions (captured in both oratures and literatures) can be found in this collection of essays on African–Native American literature, for in spite of the many barriers to theorizing an African–Native American tradition, fascinating work has already been accomplished. The first section in this collection is entitled "African–Native American Folklore," and in the first two essays David Elton Gay and Sandra K. Baringer explore the transformation of African and Native American folklore traditions into a merged African–Native American folklore tradition.

In an essay on southeastern American folklore, Gay argues that one of the syncretic cultural adaptations of interacting Africans and Native Americans resulted in the production of Rabbit tales. He addresses the previous scholarship, much of which advocated African origins for such tales, arguing that the existence of Rabbit tales in Native American nations that had little contact with African Americans demonstrates their previous existence among Native American nations. Gay posits instead that in the interactions between Africans and Native Americans, both traditions contributed trickster motifs and tales that, through adaptation, took shape as newly formed African–Native American Rabbit tales. Gay explores versions of the Tar Baby story, arguing that when entire stories and not only individual motifs are examined, Native American versions such as Cherokee, Hitchiti, Alabama, Natchez, and Koasati demonstrate more integrity as a group than they demonstrate individual similarities to African versions. Also as a group, they are more closely related to African American versions than to African versions, which suggests that African American and Native American cultural interaction produced such hybrid tales. Gay also examines historical conditions that promoted this cultural exchange, such as frequent intermarriage and the enslavement of both Native Americans and African Americans.

Baringer also examines cultural exchanges between African Americans and Native Americans, arguing that such practices demand "examination beyond the issue of appropriation." Baringer claims that what Henry Louis Gates Jr. theorizes as "signifyin'" is embodied in African American, Native American, and African–Native American folklore practices and that Africans and Native Americans shared cultural affinities that facilitated literary exchange and transmission. Like Gay, Baringer untangles the web of previous scholarship to establish an historical foundation for her arguments, pointing out limitations of or misreadings in previous scholarship, much of which points only to African origins for stories told by Native Americans and African Americans. For example, she provides a reading of one of the "raining fire" Rabbit stories that reflects ties to Ibo, Creek, and Cherokee stories, arguing that Native American and African American storytellers incorporated elements from each other's traditions. Baringer insists that the evolution and interaction of these traditions is far more interesting than an inquiry into simple origins and that such a complex evolution of cross-cultural folktale influence makes it nearly impossible to precisely map their origins. She compares Cherokee and Creek Rabbit tales with Brer Rabbit stories to theorize the spiritual and supernatural significance of elements such as dancing and fiddling and to argue that the existence of features one might trace back to Native American or African origins provides the careful reader a map of New World cultural interaction and development, an "historical narrative of the transmission of spiritual power" that allowed Africans and Native Americans, especially through the trickster tales, to survive European American cultural and political domination.

The essays in the second section, "African–Native American Captivity and Slave Narratives," explore eighteenth- and nineteenth-century autobiographies by Briton Hammon, John Marrant, and Okah Tubbee and Laah Ceil. John Sekora discusses Briton Hammon's African American Indian captivity narrative (1760), one of the earliest African American autobiographies and a text from which, Sekora suggests, "the intertwining of Native American and African American experience . . . would give us the slave narrative." Benilde Montgomery, in "Recapturing John Marrant," argues that Marrant's African American Indian captivity narrative (1785) is a "clear example of an emerging, polyethnic American identity, an identity that Werner Sollors would call a 'consenting' coincidence of European, African, and Native American cultures." In my study of Tubbee and Ceil's autobiography, I explore the merging of the African or African–Native American slave narrative with the Native American autobiography.

Sekora traces the printing history of the Indian captivity narrative and the African American slave narrative, arguing that the intersections of two eighteenth-century autobiographical genres would propitiate the development of the nineteenth-century African American slave narrative. He explores the earliest colonial printings recording African American voices in the Americas, such as Samuel Sewall's *The Selling of Joseph*, published in 1700.[261] Sekora examines Briton Hammon's captivity narrative, a fusion of eighteenth-century African American writing and the Indian captivity narrative, which he argues led directly to the nineteenth-century African American slave narrative. The writing published by European

Americans attempted to represent African Americans and Native Americans in similar terms, and therefore Hammon's captivity narrative represents a critical moment in literary history in which an African American writer seized the opportunity to represent himself in juxtaposition to both Native Americans and European Americans. This opportunity allows Hammon to develop the formulaic elements of the captivity narrative, in which the captivity allows the opportunity to gain "spiritual salvation," into a precursor to the slave narrative, which would argue that the degradations of captivity should be applied to no American. Sekora explores the political circumstances that allowed for the coincidence of a captivity narrative and an African American subject and concludes his essay by arguing that Hammon "expands the scope" of the captivity narrative and develops the "terms of possibility" for the slave narrative.

In the work of John Marrant and Okah Tubbee, explored in the next two essays, the two forms are brought together by an African–Native American autobiographer. Montgomery explores the Christian and culturally distinct African American and Native American elements in John Marrant's autobiography, arguing that Marrant's narrative, a "devotional" tract, carries an "almost exclusive dependence on a typology of rebirth and resurrection" that allows him to "discover his messianic identity by passing through a series of identifications with other preliminary New Testament types." His religious conversion, which prompts an angry backlash from family and friends, is accompanied by a cultural conversion, which Montgomery suggests was supported by the Cherokee response to Marrant's religious teachings; they found his ideas neither "'crazy' nor 'mad' but consistent with their own sense of a divine immanence."

Montgomery also examines the form and language of the narrative, noting the use of "cuts" that "make use of accident and rupture" in a distinctly African American cultural tradition and that disrupt "the illusion of linear progression" maintained by European Americans. Finally, Montgomery juxtaposes Mary Rowlandson's discussion of her use of the printed word to defend herself (unsuccessfully, as one of her captors "'snatched [the Bible] hastily out of [her] hand, and threw it out of doors'") with Marrant's facility in the African American oral tradition, which allows him to engage linguistically and, ultimately, to achieve freedom, perhaps in much the same way as Frederick Douglass would rely on his rhetorical abilities to engage the flawed arguments that buttressed slavery.

In the final essay in this section, "Speaking Cross Boundaries: A Nineteenth-Century African–Native American Autobiography," I explore the merging of the African American or African–Native American slave narrative with the Native American autobiography, the slave narrative influenced by the tradition of the European American and African American Indian captivity narrative, and the Native American autobiography, often a "true" version of the Indian captivity narrative, a narrative of the captivity of Native Americans by European Americans. I discuss eighteenth- and nineteenth-century Native American, African American, and European American autobiographical narratives, some of which likely served as models for Tubbee and Ceil's autobiography and others of which are useful for a comparative literary analysis. Following this discussion, the essay focuses on the prefatory and appendatory materials that often accompanied African American and Native American eighteenth- and nineteenth-century autobiographies. This documentation, provided by speakers, writers, interpreters, editors, publishers, and abolitionist societies or by prominent religious or political figures, "purports to grant them permission to speak and ascertains their 'authentic' identities."[262] Finally, the essay discusses the inclusion of dreams by Tubbee and Ceil and the convergence of African American, European American, and Native American traditions of narrating dreams. For all three traditions, dreams and visions were often the appropriate vehicle for relating interactions with gods and spirits, and thus Ceil draws from Delaware and European American Christian traditions when she includes a conversion narrative that uses a dream to narrate her interaction with God or an angel, and Tubbee draws from all three traditions when he narrates his "Ancient Shepherd" dream filled with biblical imagery.

In the next section, several scholars examine the Mardi Gras Indian tradition. Jason Berry, Jonathan Foose, and Tad Jones's "In Search of the Mardi Gras Indians" discusses the historical roots and contemporary manifestations of the Mardi Gras Indians. George Lipsitz, in "Mardi Gras Indians: Carnival and Counternarrative in Black New Orleans," explores the "emancipatory potential" of the counternarrative offered by the Mardi Gras Indians. Berry, Foose, and Jones's essay focuses on the history and development of the Mardi Gras Indian tradition, for which it is essential to establish both the African American and Native American origins in order to understand its contemporary manifestations. They discuss the early relations between African slaves and Choctaw, Chickasaw, and Natchez Indians (among others), a relationship that resulted in African–Native American maroon nations who fought against European colonists. From these many African–Native American interactions, including socializing in the marketplace and playing raquette on the fields of what would become Congo Square, arose a mixed African–Native American population, which they note was acknowledged by at least the late nineteenth century, as "the word *griffon*, which meant 'black Indian,' had entered the lexicon of the city's racial code." They also examine the spiritual dimensions of the tradition, suggesting that the African tradition of "honoring the dead" through drumming, dancing, and singing has been maintained by the Mardi Gras Indian tribes. Berry, Foose, and Jones wonder "if Indians danced at Congo Square," and one should also wonder whether Indians were drumming or playing other instruments at Congo Square. I would suggest that Congo Square, which has been discussed primarily as an African tradition, might more accurately be discussed as an African–Native American tradition, drawing from both African and Native American dancing, drumming, and singing and providing a foundation for the unfolding of the Mardi Gras Indian performances.

In the second essay on Mardi Gras Indians, George Lipsitz raises José Limon's argument that localized "cultural expressions and performances can challenge the hegemony of the dominant commercial culture." Lipsitz asserts that working-class participants in the Mardi Gras Indian tribes, in part because they are responding to "oppressive social conditions" in their daily lives, generate and maintain a storytelling tradition that has the ability to withstand commodification by the culture industry. Lipsitz also analyzes the form and function of the body of Indian songs, the elaborate costumes, and the languages utilized by participants and the dancing, as "a symbolic form of combat." He concludes that the Mardi Gras Indian narrative offers a central theme of resistance, an opportunity to "collectively author an important narrative about their own past, present, and future," and a set of shared stories that reinforce community values, cooperation, and fervent celebration.

In the final section of essays, focused on contemporary African–Native American subjectivity, Patricia Riley analyzes Alice Walker's novel *Meridian* as an African Cherokee text that "firmly links together the collective struggle for freedom undertaken historically by Native American and African American peoples," Sharon P. Holland discusses African–Native American subjectivity and literary representation in Nettie Jones's *Mischief Makers* and Leslie Marmon Silko's *Almanac of the Dead*, and Paul Pasquaretta explores African–Native American subjectivity and the blues in works by Toni Morrison and Sherman Alexie.

Riley argues that Walker brings together African American and Lakota Sioux civil rights struggles and links through dreams violence enacted against African Americans and Native Americans. She also examines Meridian, the title character, and proposes that she functions in much the same manner as a Lakota sacred clown, the *heyoka,* and that Meridian's great-grandmother, Feather Mae (perhaps drawn from Walker's own Cherokee great-grandmother), having descended into the Cherokee Serpent Mound, experiences a "spiritual rebirth" and "communion" with the Cherokee Grandmother Sun. Riley suggests that Meridian's actions in Chicokema mirror the role of many Native American shaman traditions and that the "Cherokee mythological figure of the Wild Boy is feminized and reconfigured as 'The Wild Child'" in *Meridian*. Finally, Riley maintains that Walker has "consistently made a point of expressing her own African–Native American identity and subjectivity" within her writing, in spite of the sometimes angry critical responses, and that "this re-membering is not an attempt to disidentify with blackness . . . rather, it is an attempt to own all the shades of the race and all the ancestors who brought these shades into being."

In the second essay on contemporary African–Native American fiction, Sharon P. Holland also raises issue of political collaboration between African Americans and Native Americans and discusses Toni Morrison's "strategy of literally emancipating traditional canonical literature from the bondage of critical discourse in order to discover a disguised or suppressed presence." Holland notes that such a strategy for Afro-Native literature must consider "emancipation and sovereignty," as promoted by Robert Warrior in his essay on "Intellectual Sovereignty," and that this same strategy was observed by Kevin Mulroy among the African–Native American Seminole nation: "'at first freedom meant simply an escape from bondage but ultimately it would come to embody the larger notion of self-determination.'" Holland finds that African–Native American subjectivity is developed in contemporary literatures, noting the character Rayona in Michael Dorris's *A Yellow Raft in Blue Water* as well as the role of John Horse in Alice Walker's *Temple of My Familiar*, and she then focuses on a critical analysis of Nettie Jones's *Mischief Makers* and Leslie Marmon Silko's *Almanac of the Dead*. Holland discusses silences, passing, and class as they relate to Afro-Indian identity in *Mischief Makers* and explores the development of an Afro-Native narrative that disrupts existing racial categories in *Almanac*, arguing that the knowledge of early Black Indian history leads to freedom and self-determination. Finally, Holland claims that there is a conflict between African–Native American subjectivity and the language available to represent this subjectivity, especially the "white/black dichotomy" she notes early in the essay, because this particular dichotomy leaves out Native Americans entirely, and even an expansion to "'blackness,' 'Indianness' and 'whiteness' as categories" erases the reality of Black Indian history and subjectivity.

In the final essay of the collection, Paul Pasquaretta argues that in the writings of Morrison and Alexie, the blues represents the intersection of the experiences of African Americans and Native Americans. He notes that many of Morrison's works, including *Beloved, Song of Solomon,* and *Paradise,* explore African–Native American subjects and issues. In a reading of *Song of Solomon,* Pasquaretta asserts that Milkman's "most significant discovery on his journey to Virginia is the identity of his Native American grandmother" (Sing Byrd), as well as his discovery that his grandfather was also raised by a Native American woman (Heddy Byrd, Sing's mother). As singing becomes a powerful metaphor in the novel, the African–Native American roots lead to the blues, which Pasquaretta posits as a historical collaboration between Native Americans and African Americans. This collaboration emerges as an important site of musical inquiry in Alexie's works, for "in poems such as 'Red Blues' and 'John Coltrane Blowing,' the speaker describes 'drum[s] that sound . . . like the blues,' Robert Johnson and Crazy Horse playing slide guitar, and John Coltrane blowing a 'tender tenor pain' for the Indian boys." Alexie merges elements of blues, jazz, gospel, and Native American pow-wow music and drumming in his writing, mirroring and honoring the African–Native American cultural collaborations that preceded him. Finally, Pasquaretta notes, Alexie and Morrison's explorations of African–Native American experience discover elements sometimes as "divisive as they are binding," for they claim a common history of colonization and a shared history of cultural collaboration, the latter allowing both African American and Native American writers to continue to broaden the scope of their explorations and their literary tools.

## Conclusion: "This Is Where I Live!"

It is my intention in this collection to address the conflict between language and African–Native American subjectivity, to think past the limiting black/white racial dichotomy established in the United States, to re-cognize the existence and importance of African–Native American literature, to promote a critical discussion of African–Native American literatures, and to examine the merging of numerous culturally inscribed African American and Native American literary traditions. These essays critique and explore a rich and distinctive body of African–Native American literature and suggest some of the many approaches critics might adopt in their exploration of this literary tradition, thus forming a meridian that falls between African American and Native American boundaries. Working outside of the established cultural, racial, and literary boundaries often requires the assumption of trickster qualities, provoking a challenge to the community through the derailment of established guidelines. As for African–Native American writers such as Long Lance, many eventually assume the role of the trickster to survive and maintain their identity. In an African Cherokee trickster tale, Rabbit refuses to join the community in digging a well during the drought, and the community attempts to punish her for drinking from the well, but in the end, she escapes to the thicket. For African-Native Americans, perhaps this represents a retreat to what Karen Blu describes as a "tangle"[263] of identity for the Lumbee, a safe haven that still allows the multiple branches of a complex identity to intertwine:

> Once upon a time there was such a severe drought that all streams of water and all lakes were dried up. In this emergency the beasts assembled together to devise means to procure water. It was proposed by one to dig a well. All agreed to do so except the hare. She refused because it would soil her tiny paws. The rest, however, dug their well and were fortunate enough to find water. The hare beginning to suffer and thirst, and having no right to the well, was thrown upon her wits to procure water. She determined, as the easiest way, to steal from the public well. The rest of the animals, surprised to find that the hare was so well supplied with water, asked her where she got it. She replied that she arose betimes in the morning and gathered the dewdrops. However, the wolf and the fox suspected her of theft and hit on the following plan to detect her:
>
> They made a wolf of tar and placed it near the well. On the following night the hare came as usual after her supply of water. On seeing the tar wolf she demanded who was there. Receiving no answer she repeated the demand, threatening to kick the wolf if he did not reply. She receiving no reply kicked the wolf and by this means adhered to the tar and was caught. When the fox and the wolf got hold of her they consulted what it was best to do with her. One proposed cutting her head off. This the hare protested would be useless, as it had often been tried without hurting her. Other methods were proposed for dispatching her, all of which she said would be useless. At last it was proposed to let her loose to perish in a thicket. Upon this the hare affected great uneasiness and pleaded hard for her life. Her enemies, however, refused to listen and she was accordingly let loose. As soon as she was out of reach of her enemies she gave a whoop, and bounding away she exclaimed: "This is where I live!"[264]

The thicket, a safe haven for an African-Native American, raises key points of inquiry into the African–Native American literary tradition: does such a tradition "exist" without widespread acknowledgment, or when it remains obscured by a thicket? What happens when Brer Rabbit meets Coyote? What sound does an African–Native American trickster writing alone in the forest make?

One answer to these questions might be found in the *Narrative* of Frederick Douglass, at the close of chapter two, when he discusses the monthly passage of slaves to the Great House Farm, his master's central plantation: "While on their way, they would make the dense old woods, for miles around, reverberate with their wild songs, revealing at once the highest joy and the deepest sadness. They would compose and sing as they went along, consulting neither time nor tune. The thought that came up, came out—if not in the word, in the sound;—and as frequently in the one as in the other. . . . This they would sing, as a chorus, to words which to many would seem unmeaning jargon, but which, nevertheless, were full of meaning to themselves."[265]

The woods are a site for both sorrow and joy: sorrow expressed in the testimonies against slavery, and joy in the fleeting freedom to express themselves while in the woods, in the meridian between plantations and masters. Yet these same woods marked by freedom of expression and the maintenance and development of an African American oral tradition are also marked by the lack of European American witnesses to this tradition. Although the dearth of outside witnesses enables the free expressions of slaves, it simultaneously works against their freedom because these testimonies go unacknowledged by European American witnesses who hold the power to bring the meaning of these expressions into the political arena, to acknowledge the humanity of African Americans by valuing their cultural productions. Thus Douglass exhorts the reader, his European American witness, to engage in an act of imagination to understand the slaves' songs, to give the "unmeaning jargon" a meaning:

> I have sometimes thought that the mere hearing of these songs would do more to impress some minds with the horrible character of slavery, than the reading of whole volumes of philosophy on the subject could do. . . . If anyone wishes to be impressed with the soul-killing effects of slavery, let him go to Colonel Lloyd's plantation, and, on allowance-day, place himself in the deep pine woods, and there let him, in silence, analyze the sounds that shall pass through the chambers of his soul,—and if he is not thus impressed, it will only be because "there is no flesh in his obdurate heart."[266]

It may require a similar act of imagination for some witnesses from outside of the African–Native American community to acknowledge the existence of an African–Native American literary tradition, not because it does not exist but because it requires an empathy found only in introspection and the willingness to witness a world previously existing but unfamiliar to the reader. The woods, so often a site of interaction between escaped African slaves and Native Americans, serve as a potent metaphor for the muffled expression of African–Native American literature. It requires an act of imagination to place oneself within an African–Native

American tradition; although the African American (and Native American) slaves were in the forest all along and were also highly visible on the plantation, the lack of acknowledgment from outside communities required Douglass to demand an act of imagination and empathy on the part of the readers of his narrative to "analyze the sounds" and prompt them to engage with the human being behind the slave.

The answer lies in the hands of the reader of the African–Native American text, and I turn to William Andrews's study of African American autobiography to introduce his concept of the "implied reader." Andrews argues that a "successful reading" of a text depends on the relationship between the subject narrator and the "implied model" for a reader, the mirror through which the reader "might be guided or measure themselves."[267] Andrews asserts that before the 1840s, African American autobiographers were "most concerned" with "identifying themselves . . . with the characterized fictive reader," but subsequent autobiographers, rather than hoping for an empathetic and charitable reader, demanded that the reader change his or her fundamental perspective:

> Bibb's explicit demand in this passage is to be judged by a standard of "reason," not hair-splitting morality. He does not take time to explain what this alternative to abstract Victorian morality is. Instead, he dismisses the fictive reader as unreasonable and implicitly calls for a reader who can interpret his actions according to the standards that emerge dramatically and pragmatically in the narrative itself. In this sense, Bibb structures into his autobiography an implied reader, someone who can read his story and judge him according to a set of norms, both moral and aesthetic, that text and author—not the predominant culture—require.[268]

Works of African–Native American literature require an implied reader who does not follow fictive norms but instead accomodates him- or herself to the new parameters of a work of mixed-race literary expression. Such a reader interprets the work not by following a master racial or literary discourse but by allowing a new identity to develop and be presented according to the "standards that emerge dramatically" from the African–Native American text. Such a reader is invited into Douglass's "deep pine woods," into a text that requires analysis on its own terms, through the lens of African–Native American subjectivity. By becoming the narrator's implied reader, the reader offers him- or herself a site for introspection, "involving the reader in a decision about his [or her] own identity,"[269] an opportunity for re-cognition of African–Native American literature, and an analysis that presents the best opportunity to develop an understanding of this fascinating and rich American literary tradition. Such a reader will hear the lonely songs of Frederick Douglass's slaves on their way to the Great House farm, "'drum[s] that sound . . . like the blues,' Robert Johnson and Crazy Horse playing slide guitar," Okah Tubbee on the musical tomahawk, "and John Coltrane blowing a 'tender tenor pain' for the Indian boys," having attuned one's ears to the sounds trumpeted by an African–Native American writer.

## Notes

The quotation from John Horse, the Seminole leader who refused to attack the political rivals of Coahuila's leader in Mexico, continues: "'How can I take up a gun and kill you, who are my brother, or how can I take up a gun for you and kill that other man, who is also my brother?'" (qtd. in William Loren Katz, *Black Indians: A Hidden Heritage* [New York: Atheneum, 1986], 74.) Although John Horse was attempting to negotiate a politically sensitive situation, his statement is particularly significant for an African–Native nation whose mixed-race identity substantially complicates a monolithic construction of race and political strategy. This quotation is also used in a slightly different form as a chapter title in Katz's *Black Indians*.

1. Katz, *Black Indians*, 23.

2. See also Herbert Aptheker, *American Negro Slave Revolts* (New York: International Publishers, 1969), 163.

3. See Ivan Van Sertima, *They Came Before Columbus* (New York: Random House, 1976), and *African Presence in Early America*, ed. Ivan Van Sertima (New Brunswick, N.J.: Transaction Publishers, 1992).

4. Jack D. Forbes, *Africans and Native Americans: The Language of Race and the Evolution of Red-Black Peoples*, 2d ed. (Urbana: University of Illinois Press, 1993), 9.

5. Ibid., 14.

6. Ibid., 2.

7. Ibid., 26.

8. Almon Lauber, "Indian Slavery in Colonial Times within the Present Limits of the United States," *Studies in History, Economics, and Public Law* 54.3 (1913): 48.

9. Ibid., 51–54.

10. Ibid., 62.

11. Ibid., 60.

12. Ibid., 71–72.

13. Ibid., 68. Native American slaves are also recorded in Montreal in 1670 (92). In Louisiana, colonists enslaved Native Americans for "agricultural pursuits" (83), or plantation slavery, and the farmers in the Illinois territory "increased the results of their industry by the extensive use of Indian slaves" (84). The French military used Native American female slaves for cooking and "domestic labors" (84) and male slaves for "erecting fortifications, performing other heavy labor, and as guides in military expeditions" (84). In 1708, Bienville proposed exchanging Native American slaves for African slaves from

the West Indies (78), and "[u]ntil well into the latter half of the eighteenth century Indian slaves were held by the settlers of Detroit" (74–75).

14. Ibid., 154.

15. Ibid., 155, 158.

16. Ibid., 118.

17. Ibid., 119–21. The Carolina colonies realized a substantial profit from the export and sale of slaves to other colonies on the mainland and in the Caribbean; they exported more Native slaves than any other English colony, the traders paying twenty shillings per slave to the colonial government at the time of exportation (240–41). Some of the Native American slaves exported to the plantations in the Caribbean would subsequently be sold back to plantations in the United States, many of them having become African–Native American slaves both culturally and racially.

18. Ibid., 123–24.

19. Ibid., 127.

20. Ibid., 201–7.

21. Ibid., 223.

22. Ibid., 207–9.

23. Ibid., 197.

24. Ibid. Apparently, the colonists in Virginia and New York did the same: "A letter of Governor Spotswood to Lord Dartmouth, March 11, 1711, tells of his attempt to persuade Indians to allow their children to attend the Indian college by remitting their annual tribute of skins and declares that 'they were a little shy of yielding to his proposal, and urged the breach of a former contract made long ago by this government, when instead of their children receiving the promised education, they were transported, as they say, to other countries and sold as slaves'" (qtd. in ibid., 197–98). In July 1715, Colonel Heathcote wrote home to Secretary Townsend: "'The Indians complain that their children, many of whom were bound out for a limited time to be taught and instructed by the Christians, were, contrary to the intent of their agreement, transferred to other plantations and sold for slaves, and I don't know but there may be some truth in what they allege'" (qtd. in ibid., 200).

25. Ibid., 315.

26. Ibid., 316.

27. Ibid., 317.

28. Forbes, *Africans and Native Americans*, 207–8. Forbes documents many more African–Native American slaves, including:

> 1773 Ran away with "a Negro Fellow named Fortune . . . a Wench named Aminta . . . has much the Look of an Indian, and is so, her Mother having been brought from the Spanish Main to Rhode Island, has long black hair." (207)

> 1775 Ran away from Bute County, North Carolina, "a Slave named Charles, of the Indian breed." (207)

> 1776 Ran away from Amherst County a "Negro Fellow named Ben." He used the name John Savage on a previous flight "and has an Indian Woman for his wife who some Time ago lived in Goochland." (207)

1764 "... a Mulatto or Mustee slave called 'Tony' ran away from New Bern, North Carolina ... had 'long stiff black hair, and greatly the looks and colour of an Indian ...'" (208)

1748 Ran away from Cohansey in New Jersey "a very lusty Negro Man named Sampson, aged about 58 years, and has some mixture of Indian Blood in him. ... He has taken with him a boy named Sam, who was born of an Indian woman, and looks much like an Indian only his Hair. ... They both talk Indian very well, and it is likely have dress'd themselves in an Indian dress, and gone towards Carolina." (208)

1771 Ran away "a young mulatto or mustee wench, named Mary." Well known at Ashley-River "where she formerly lived, and was enticed away by her mother, an Indian wench, named Sarah, who lives at ... Stono Plantation." (209)

29. Ibid., 226. See Forbes's chapter titled "Mustees, Half-Breeds, and Zambos" in ibid., 221–38.

30. Rhett S. Jones, "Black and Native American Relations before 1800," *Western Journal of Black Studies* 1 (Sept. 1977): 156. Jones argues that "Britons in North America were only slightly more successful in preventing a Black-Indian alliance than their cousins in the Caribbean, and were not able to prevent Blacks from fleeing to the Indians. The Senecas and Onodagas of northern New York aided many runaways, while the Minisinks of Long Island welcomed fugitives into their tribe. Even tribes as closely allied to the English as the Iroquois sometimes refused to return Blacks who had taken refuge among them. Blacks were also accepted by the Chippewa and more than earned their keep by serving as translators for the French, the English and their Indian brethren. ... In English Connecticut, rebellious Blacks and Indians destroyed a number of buildings in Hartford. ... In Louisiana in 1727, the authorities discovered a small Afro-Indian village armed and prepared to defend itself, and the very next year they located a similar settlement. Despite this evidence of Black-red cooperation the French colonists armed adult male slaves against red folk. In 1730, this policy backfired when a number of armed slaves, perceiving they had much in common with the Chickasaws, conspired to unite with the Indians. A generation later one Black runaway working with the Mohawk created so much havoc in English New York that the government was forced to increase the number of troops at its frontier outposts" (155, 156).

31. Katz, *Black Indians,* 40.

32. Ibid., 12.

33. Aptheker, *American Negro Slave Revolts,* 167.

34. Hugo Prosper Leaming, *Hidden Americans: Maroons of Virginia and the Carolinas* (New York: Garland, 1995), 223.

35. Ibid., 224.

36. Ibid., xx.

37. Richard Price, *Maroon Societies: Rebel Slave Communities in the Americas* (Garden City, N.Y.: Anchor Press, 1973), 11–12.

38. See Daniel F. Littlefield Jr.'s works on African slaves and Native Americans: *Africans and Seminoles: From Removal to Emancipation* (Westport,

Conn.: Greenwood Press, 1977), *The Cherokee Freedmen: From Emancipation to American Citizenship* (Westport, Conn.: Greenwood Press, 1978), *Africans and Creeks: From the Colonial Period to the Civil War* (Westport, Conn.: Greenwood Press, 1979), and *The Chickasaw Freedmen: A People without a Country* (Westport, Conn.: Greenwood Press, 1980). See also Theda Perdue, *Slavery and the Evolution of Cherokee Society, 1540–1866* (Knoxville: University of Tennessee Press, 1979).

39. See Barbara W. Brown and James M. Rose, *Black Roots in Southeastern Connecticut, 1650–1900* (Detroit: Gale Research Co., 1980), for a wealth of evidence on African-Native Americans in Connecticut; much the same has long been occurring throughout the rest of New England.

40. See Kenneth Wiggins Porter, *The Negro on the American Frontier* (New York: Arno Press and the New York Times, 1971), for a variety of articles on African-Native interaction in the western United States. See also Donald A. Grinde and Quintard Taylor, "Native American and Black Interaction in the American Southwest during the Colonial Period," *Hampton Institute Journal of Ethnic Studies* 9 (May 1981): 52–60; and Quintard Taylor, "Blacks in the American West: An Overview," *Western Journal of Black Studies* 1.1 (Mar. 1977): 4–10.

41. Bernice F. Guillaume, "Character Names in *Indian Trails* by Olivia Ward Bush (Banks): Clues to Afro Assimilation into Long Island's Native Americans," *Afro-Americans in New York Life and History* 10.2 (July 1986): 45–47.

42. Guillaume argues:

> Indeed, researchers wanted to believe that "true" native cultures died due to intermarriage with Afro-Americans. This attitude was rooted in a deep-seated prejudice against mixed-bloods, stemming from pseudo-scientific theories of racial origins. Mixed-bloods were considered genetically inferior hybrids who inherited the "worst" traits of the parent races. At the same time, the visible demise of Native Americans and the potential insurgency of Afro-Americans after the Civil War made most scientists see Afro-Indians as a corruption or debasement of their "noble savage."
>
> "Race purity" was a pre-requisite for researchers observing Native American societies in North America. If a group appeared Afro-Indian, it was either passed over or awarded a superficial investigation. Consider the remarks of Mark R. Harrington regarding the Shinnecock reservation:
>
> > It seems to be a negro settlement pure and simple. . . . But . . . many of the people have Indian blood. Some are black and wooly headed, having at the same time facial characteristics distinctly Indian. Others have the straight hair and light color of the Indian, but the flat nose, dull eyes and thick lips of the negro.
>
> Local historians agreed that African intermarriage hurt Native Americans. Martha B. Flint (1896) says that the Shinnecocks were "much degraded by negro admixture. They have even lost the traditions of their forefarthers." (ibid., 48–49)

43. James H. Johnston, "Documentary Evidence of the Relations of Negroes and Indians," *Journal of Negro History* 14 (Jan. 1929): 29–30.

44. Quoted in Johnson, "Documentary Evidence," 30.

45. Taylor, "Blacks in the American West," 5.

46. Katz, *Black Indians*, 119.

47. Ibid., 117–18.

48. Taylor, "Blacks in the American West," 6.

49. Porter, *Negro on the American Frontier*, 398.

50. Littlefield, *Africans and Creeks*, 145.

51. Ibid., 256.

52. Ibid., 256–57.

53. Ibid., 257–58.

54. Littlefield, *Africans and Seminoles*, 5. See also Kevin Mulroy, *Freedom on the Border: The Seminole Maroons in Florida, the Indian Territory, Coahuila, and Texas* (Lubbock: Texas Tech University Press, 1993).

55. Littlefield, *Africans and Seminoles*, 5.

56. Ibid., 12–13.

57. Ibid., 80–81.

58. Gwendolyn Midlo Hall, *Africans in Colonial Louisiana: The Development of Afro-Creole Culture in the Eighteenth Century* (Baton Rouge: Louisiana State University Press, 1992).

59. Lorenzo Greene, *The Negro in Colonial New England* (New York: Atheneum, 1968), 198.

60. Ibid., 200.

61. Ibid., 200 n.59.

62. Ibid., 124–42.

63. Rebecca Bateman, "African Frontiersmen: The Black Carib of St. Vincent Island," *Papers in Anthropology* 22 (Spring 1981): 124.

64. Catherine Lynn Macklin, "Crucible of Identity: Ritual and Symbolic Dimensions of Garifuna Ethnicity" (Ph.D. diss., University of California at Berkeley, 1986), 161–62.

65. Ibid., 159–60.

66. Don Justo and Justin Flores, *Tumba Le: A Garifuna Novel* (Los Angeles: Don Justo, 1977).

67. For an encapsulation of these scholarly arguments, see W. K. McNeil's introduction to *Native American Legends: Southeastern Legends—Tales from the Natchez, Caddo, Biloxi, Chickasaw, and Other Nations*, ed. George E. Lankford (Little Rock: August House, 1987), 13–28. Lankford's collection of southeastern folktales also contains examples of African-Native folktales. See also Alan Dundes, "African Tales among the North American Indians," *Southern Folklore Quarterly* 29 (1965): 207–19.

68. Of course, as many other Native nations are partially or entirely African-Native nations (as many "African American" communities are in reality African–Native American communities), there are surely other significant bodies of African-Native folklore.

69. William C. Sturtevant, "Seminole Myths of the Origin of Races," *Ethnohistory* 10 (1963): 83.

70. Alan Dundes, "Washington Irving's Version of the Seminole Origin of Races," *Ethnohistory* 9 (1962): 259.

71. Dundes, "African Tales," 122–23.

72. Dundes, "Washington Irving's Version," 260.

73. Sturtevant, "Seminole Myths," 84.

74. William Gerald McLoughlin, Walter H. Conser Jr., and Virginia Duffy McLoughlin, "A Note on African Sources of American Indian Racial Myths," in *The Cherokee Ghost Dance: Essays on the Southeastern Indians, 1789–1861* (Macon, Ga.: Mercer Press, 1984), 255.

75. Dundes, "African Tales," 122.

76. Ibid., 123.

77. Sturtevant, "Seminole Myths," 82. It is also possible that Lucien Spencer, the reporting Indian Bureau agent, misunderstood or intentionally misinterpreted the section of the myth that applied to Africans; perhaps there was no negative implication to their decision to remain black.

78. Ibid., 82.

79. Ibid., 84.

80. Dundes, "African Tales," 115.

81. Ibid., 117.

82. Lankford, *Native American Legends*, 242.

83. Mary Ellison, "Black Perceptions and Red Images: Indian and Black Literary Links," *Phylon* 44.1 (1983): 45.

84. Ibid.

85. Cuffe's son, Paul Cuffe Jr., also published an autobiography, *Narrative of the Life and Adventures of Paul Cuffe, a Pequot Indian: During Thirty Years Spent at Sea, and in Travelling in Foreign Lands* (Vernon, N.Y.: Horace N. Bill, 1839). Paul Cuffe Jr. (1792–?) made his first voyage with his father at the age of twelve. He spent two years in a Quaker high school before shipping out again. He sailed from port to port, escaped capture several times by the English during the War of 1812, and fought pirates off the coast of Florida. In 1839, he published a short autobiographical narrative with a long title, *Narrative of the Life of Paul Cuffe, a Descendant of an Indian family, which formerly resided in the eastern part of Connecticut and constituted a part of that fierce and warlike tribe of Indians called Pequots, of whose exploits in the Early Wars of New-England, the reader may become acquainted by perusing "Trumbull's History of the Indian Wars."* It is not a journal but a travel narrative that uses a number of rhetorical strategies. Like his father's narrative, Paul Cuffe Jr.'s is structured in the language of exchange and economic trade. Unlike his father's narrative, his is clearly attendant to an audience that will appreciate a swashbuckling pirate story, an anthropological and geographic exploration of the nations where he lands, and a war narrative. Cuffe also identifies as Pequot in the title of his narrative; perhaps he chose to do so because he identified more closely with the Pequot nation than with African Americans, or perhaps he and/or the publisher decided that the popular Indian autobiography was a form that would sell more copies. In any case, it is clear that the title capitalizes on the European American interest in the "fierce and warlike" (but now safely diminishing) Pequot nation. Cuffe alternates between his use of anthropological language that examines the "primitive" in his native setting or relates the woes of Robinson Crusoe

among the cannibals on the island of Juan Fernandez and a mixed-race-conscious discourse through which he declares his respect for a mulatto chief magistrate he encounters in Haiti.

86. See the excellent introduction to *On Our Own Ground: The Complete Works of William Apess, a Pequot,* ed. Barry O'Connell (Amherst: University of Massachusetts Press, 1992), xiii–xxvii, for a thorough treatment of Apess's background and his writing.

87. William Apess, *A Son of the Forest: The Experience of William Apes, A Native of the Forest, Written by Himself* (New York: By the author, 1829), *The Increase of the Kingdom of Christ: A Sermon* (includes *The Indians: The Ten Lost Tribes;* New York: By the author, 1831), *The Experiences of Five Christian Indians of the Pequot Tribe* (Boston: By the author, 1833), *Indian Nullification of the Unconstitutional Laws of Massachusetts Relative to the Mashpee Tribe; or, The Pretended Riot Explained* (Boston: Jonathan Howe, 1835), and *Eulogy on King Philip, as Pronounced at the Odeon, in Federal Street, Boston* (Boston: By the author, 1836).

88. Ann Plato, *Essays: Including Biographies and Miscellaneous Pieces, in Prose and Poetry* (New York: Oxford University Press, 1988).

89. James W. C. Pennington, *A Text Book of the Origin and History, &c. &c. of the Colored People* (Hartford, Conn.: L. Skinner, 1841); William Wells Brown, *The Black Man: His Antecedents, His Genius, and His Achievements* (Boston: J. Redpath, 1863); Charles Alexander Eastman, *Indian Heroes and Great Chieftains* (Boston: Little, Brown, 1918); Charles Alexander Eastman, *The Indian To-Day; The Past and Future of the First American* (Garden City, N.Y.: Doubleday, Page, 1915); Robert Benjamin Lewis, *Light and Truth; Collected from the Bible and Ancient and Modern History, Containing the Universal History of the Colored and Indian Races, from the Creation of the World to the Present Time* (Boston: By a Committee of Colored Gentlemen, B. F. Roberts, Printer, 1844), 277.

90. The latest edition is Okah Tubbee and Laah Ceil, *The Life of Okah Tubbee,* ed. Daniel F. Littlefield Jr. (Lincoln: University of Nebraska Press, 1988).

91. James P. Beckwourth, *The Life and Adventures of James P. Beckwourth as Told to Thomas D. Bonner* (Lincoln: University of Nebraska Press, 1972).

92. See Hertha D. Sweet Wong, *Sending My Heart Back across the Years: Tradition and Innovation in Native American Autobiography* (New York: Oxford University Press, 1992), esp. 25–56 and 91–104, for a discussion of the coup tale and Crow autobiography. See also "Preliterate Traditions of American Indian Autobiography" and "The Preliterate Traditions at Work" in H. David Brumble, *American Indian Autobiography* (Berkeley: University of California Press, 1988), 21–47 and 48–71.

93. James Seamon Cotter Jr., *The Band of Gideon, and Other Lyrics* (Boston: The Cornhill Company, 1918). Cotter's father, Joseph Seamon Cotter (1861–?), of Louisville, Kentucky, was the author of numerous works of poetry and drama, including *Links of Friendship* (Louisville, Ky.: Bradley and Gilbert, 1898) and *Collected Poems* (1938; rpt., Freeport, N.Y.: Books for Li-

braries Press, 1971). Cotter Sr. was also an educator, a close friend of Paul Laurence Dunbar, and a successful poet in his own right.

94. Olivia Ward Bush-Banks, *The Collected Works of Olivia Ward Bush-Banks*, ed. Bernice F. Guillaume (New York: Oxford University Press, 1991).

95. See Guillaume, "Character Names," for a discussion of Bush-Banks's play.

96. Bernice F. Guillaume, Introduction to *The Collected Works of Olivia Ward Bush-Banks*, ed. Bernice F. Guillaume (New York: Oxford University Press, 1991), 3.

97. Ibid., 7.

98. Ibid., 8, 10.

99. Ibid., 18.

100. Ibid., 7–8.

101. Donald B. Smith, "From Sylvester Long to Chief Buffalo Child Long Lance," in *Being and Becoming Indian*, ed. James Clifton (Chicago: Dorsey Press), 189. See also Donald B. Smith, *Long Lance: The True Story of an Imposter* (Toronto: Macmillan, 1982). Chief Buffalo Child Long Lance, *Long Lance* (New York: Cosmopolitan, 1929).

102. Smith, "From Sylvester Long," 189.

103. Ibid., 187.

104. Ibid., 198.

105. Ibid., 199.

106. Ibid.

107. "In spring 1922, Long Lance became restless. For months he had covered city hall. He had been given no more Indian assignments since the previous fall, so he decided to liven up the municipal meetings with a mock terrorist attack. Donning a mask, he slipped into the council chamber and placed inside the door of the mayor's office a gas inspector's bag that looked suspiciously like a bomb, with a fuse sputtering sparks. City commissioners and the mayor ran for their lives, the mayor colliding with his secretary in a jammed exit door. One commissioner dived under a table. Another leaped through layers of storm window glass and fell ten feet to the ground. Over the next several days, the rival newspaper, the *Albertan*, played this prankster story for its laugh value. But the *Herald* was not amused: Long Lance was summarily fired" (qtd. in ibid., 196).

108. Karen Blu, *The Lumbee Problem: The Making of an American Indian People* (Cambridge: Cambridge University Press, 1980), 3.

109. Ibid., 238 n.1.

110. Smith, "From Sylvester Long," 189.

111. Ibid., 192.

112. Ibid., 194.

113. Ibid., 192.

114. Other African–Native American students attended Carlisle Indian school, including an African Cherokee named Crawford Goldsby (later the infamous outlaw Cherokee Bill), who was enrolled for two years from 1886–88. See Katz, *Black Indians*, 158–59.

115. Blu, *Lumbee Problem*, 233.

116. See Daniel E. Turner, "Cherokee and Afro-American Interbreeding in *The Color Purple*," *Notes on Contemporary Literature* 21.5 (Nov. 1991): 10–11.

117. See Alice Walker's comments on K. T. H. Cheatwood in her essay "In the Closet of the Soul," in *Living by the Word* (New York: Harcourt Brace Jovanovich, 1988), 87.

118. Alice Walker, *The Color Purple* (New York: Pocket Books, 1985), and *Meridian* (New York: Harcourt Brace Jovanovich, 1976).

119. John G. Niehardt, ed., *Black Elk Speaks: Being the Life Story of a Holy Man of the Oglala Sioux* (Lincoln: University of Nebraska Press, 1979).

120. Clarence Major, *Dictionary of Afro-American Slang* (New York: International, 1970).

121. Clarence Major, *Such Was the Season* (San Francisco: Mercury House, 1987).

122. Clarence Major, *Some Observations of a Stranger at Zuni in the Latter Part of the Century* (Los Angeles: Sun and Moon Press, 1989), and *Painted Turtle: Woman with Guitar* (Los Angeles: Sun and Moon Press, 1988).

123. Steve Heyward, "Against Commodification: Zuni Culture in Clarence Major's Native American Texts," *African American Review* 28.1 (1994): 110.

124. Ibid., 109.

125. Ibid., 114.

126. Ibid.

127. Ibid., 115.

128. Major, *Painted Turtle*, 144.

129. Heyward, "Against Commodification," 115.

130. Lawrence W. Levine, *Black Culture and Black Consciousness: Afro-American Folk Thought from Slavery to Freedom* (New York: Oxford University Press, 1977), 3. See also Robert Farris Thompson, *Flash of the Spirit: African and Afro-American Art and Philosophy* (New York: Random House, 1983), for a discussion of distinct African spiritual practices retained and celebrated in the Americas.

131. A. LaVonne Brown Ruoff, *American Indian Literatures* (New York: Modern Language Association, 1990), 1.

132. Henry Louis Gates Jr., foreword to *The Oxford Companion to African American Literature*, ed. William L. Andrews, Frances Smith Foster, and Trudier Harris (New York: Oxford University Press, 1997), vii.

133. Ibid.

134. Ruoff, *American Indian Literatures*, vii; Mary Hunter Austin, "Aboriginal," in *The Cambridge History of American Literature*, ed. William Peterfield Trent et al. (New York: Macmillan Co., 1946), 610.

135. Black Hawk, *Black Hawk: An Autobiography*, ed. Donald Jackson (Urbana: University of Illinois Press, 1955), 12.

136. Carter G. Woodson, "Relations of Indians and Negroes in Massachusetts," *Journal of Negro History* 5 (Jan. 1920): 45–62.

137. Porter, *Negro on the American Frontier*.

138. Herbert Aptheker, "Maroons within the Present Limits of the United States," *Journal of Negro History* 24 (Apr. 1939): 167–84.

139. James H. Johnston, "Documentary Evidence of the Relations of Negroes and Indians," *Journal of Negro History* 14 (Jan. 1929): 21–43; Wyatt F. Jeltz, "Relations of Negroes and Choctaw and Chickasaw Indians," *Journal of Negro History* 33 (Jan. 1948): 24–37; Lawrence Foster, "Indian-Negro Relationships in the Southeast" (Ph.D. diss., University of Pennsylvania, 1931).

140. William S. Willis, "Divide and Rule: Red, White, and Black in the Southeast," *Journal of Negro History* 48.3 (July 1963): 157–76.

141. Blu, *Lumbee Problem*; Rhett S. Jones, "Identity, Self-Concept, and Shifting Political Allegiances of Blacks in the Colonial Americas: Maroons against Black Shot," *Western Journal of Black Studies* 1.1 (Mar. 1977): 61–74; Jones, "Black and Native American Relations before 1800"; Jones, "Black over Red: The Image of Native Americans in Black History," *Umoja: A Scholarly Journal of Black Studies* 1.2 (Summer 1977): 13–29.

142. Julia Griffiths, *Autographs for Freedom* (Boston: John P. Jewett, 1853); *The Negro Caravan: Writings by American Negroes*, ed. Sterling A. Brown, Arthur P. Davis, and Ulysses Lee (New York: Citadel Press, 1941); Vernon Loggins, *The Negro Author: His Development in America* (New York: Columbia University Press, 1931).

143. *Call and Response: The Riverside Anthology of the African American Literary Tradition*, ed. Patricia Liggins Hill (Boston: Houghton Mifflin, 1998); *Afro-American Women Writers, 1746–1933: An Anthology and Critical Guide*, ed. Ann Allen Shockley (Boston: G. K. Hall, 1988).

144. bell hooks, *Black Looks: Race and Representation* (Boston: South End Press, 1992).

145. Jason Berry, *The Spirit of Black Hawk: A Mystery of Africans and Indians* (Jackson: University Press of Mississippi, 1995).

146. Gary B. Nash, *Red, White, and Black: The Peoples of Early America* (Englewood Cliffs, N.J.: Prentice-Hall, 1982), 285.

147. Woodson, "Relations of Indians and Negroes," 45.

148. Alexander F. Chamberlain, "African and American: The Contact of Negro and Indian," *Science* 17 (1891): 90.

149. Lankford, *Native American Legends*, 242.

150. Audre Lorde, "The Master's Tools Will Never Dismantle the Master's House," in *Sister Outsider: Essays and Speeches* (Trumansburg, N.Y.: Crossing Press, 1984), 110–13.

151. Katz, *Black Indians*, 34.

152. In South Carolina the European colonists developed a policy of separating African Americans and Native Americans: "In 1742, a Committee on Indian Affairs warned against frequent visiting by Indians because of the hazard of their associating with slaves, 'particularly in regard to their talking, and having too great intercourse with our slaves, at the out-plantations, where they camp'" (Willis, "Divide and Rule," 102). The South Carolina legislature opposed trading and intermarriage between African Americans and Native Americans, negotiated treaties with Creek and other Native nations

that required them to return all runaway African American slaves, told the Cherokee that the smallpox epidemic in 1739 that killed nearly one thousand Cherokee was caused by African slaves, pitted Native warriors against maroon nations, and created additional strategies to prevent African-Native alliances: "In 1725, Richard Ludlam, a South Carolina minister, confessed that 'we make use of a Wile for our prest. Security to make Indians & Negro's a checque upon each other least by their vastly superior numbers we should be crushed by one or the other'" (ibid., 102) And later, "Colonel Stephen Bull wrote Colonel Henry Laurens about a scheme to create Indian-Negro aversion; but first he dismissed his secretary and wrote this part of the letter in his own hand, admonishing Laurens to keep this scheme secret from all South Carolinians except for a few high officials in the government" (ibid., 105).

European Americans sowed distrust and created divisions by using African Americans to attack Native nations and Native Americans to capture escaped African American slaves. African American slaves and "free" African Americans were used in the Yamassee War, in attacks on the Cherokee nation in 1715, in attacks on the Creek nation, in attacks on the Chickasaw nation, and in the Second Natchez War (1729) against the Choucha nation. In the attacks on the Choucha, the African American slaves had been accused of plotting a rebellion with the Choucha nation; when they denied doing so, the French "armed the Negroes and ordered them to attack this tribe as the sole means of saving their own skins" (ibid., 106). The European American colonists took every opportunity to remind Native nations that they could not trust African Americans and predicated African American survival on Native American destruction.

153. Ibid., 157–76.

154. European Americans employed Native nations to capture and return escaped African American slaves. The prices they paid to Native slave catchers were generous: one musket and three blankets (the equivalent of several months of hunting for deerskins), in one instance. European American slaveowners were sometimes less interested in retrieving their slaves than they were in having the escaped slaves scalped or killed, thus sending a clear message to the African American slave community: "Whites did not employ Indians as slave catchers only to recover valuable property and to punish offenders. They also employed them to make their slaves hate Indians. In 1776, some Maroons established themselves on Tybee Island; the Charles Town government secretly arranged for Creek slave catchers to kill these Maroons. Colonel Stephen Bull explained that this would 'establish a hatred or aversion between Indians and Negroes'" (ibid., 106). When some members of the Creek nation scalped fugitive African American slaves, John Stuart insisted that "this cannot fail of having a very good Effect, by breaking that Intercourse between Negroes and Savages which might have been attended with very troublesome consequences had it continued" (ibid., 109).

155. Quoted in Walker, *Living by the Word*, 87.

156. Jonathan Brennan, Introduction to *Mixed Race Literature*, ed. Jonathan Brennan (Stanford, Calif.: Stanford University Press, 2002), 20.

157. See Wong, *Sending My Heart Back*, 43–44, for a discussion of the acquisition of names among the Plains Indians.

158. Apess, *On Our Own Ground*, 10–11.

159. Carol Roh Spaulding, "The Go-Between People," in *American Mixed Race: The Culture of Microdiversity*, ed. Naomi Zack (Lanham, Md.: Rowman and Littlefield, 1995), 98.

160. Quoted in Sharon P. Holland's essay in this volume, p. 262.

161. John Marrant, *A Narrative of the Life of John Marrant* (London: n.p., 1787); Tubbee and Ceil, *Life of Okah Tubbee*; Michael Dorris, *A Yellow Raft in Blue Water* (New York: Warner Books, 1987); James Seamon Cotter Jr., *Complete Poems*, ed. James Robert Payne (Athens: University of Georgia Press, 1990; see "The Mulatto to His Critics" [p. 27], among others).

162. Forbes, *Africans and Native Americans*, 90.

163. Langston Hughes, *The Big Sea: An Autobiography* (New York: Thunder's Mouth Press, 1986), 13–14.

164. Ibid., 12.

165. Ibid., 17.

166. Quoted in Arnold Rampersad, Introduction to *The Big Sea*, by Langston Hughes (New York: Thunder's Mouth Press, 1986), 18.

167. Samson Occom, *A Sermon Preached at the Execution of Moses Paul* (Bennington, Vt.: William Watson, 1772); George Henry, *An Account of the Chippewa Indians* (Boston: By the Author, 1848); George Copway, *The Life, History, and Travels of Kah-ge-ga-gah-bowh (George Copway), a Young Indian Chief of the Ojebwa Nation, a Convert . . .* (Albany, N.Y.: Weed and Parsons, 1847).

168. Guillaume, Introduction, 7.

169. Beckwourth, *Life and Adventures*, 95–96, 100.

170. Ibid., 262–63.

171. Ibid., 296.

172. C. A. Weslager, *The Delaware Indians* (New Brunswick, N.J.: Rutgers University Press, 1972), 68.

173. Apess, *On Our Own Ground*, 20.

174. Frances Smith Foster, *Witnessing Slavery* (Westport, Conn.: Greenwood Press, 1971), 45.

175. Arlene R. Keizer, "Religious and Didactic Poetry," in *Oxford Companion to African American Literature*, 593.

176. Kenny Jackson Williams, "Ann Plato," in *Oxford Companion to African American Literature*, 583.

177. Debra Walker King, "Alice Walker," in *Oxford Companion to African American Literature*, 749.

178. Bernard L. Peterson Jr., "Drama," in *Oxford Companion to African American Literature*, 228.

179. Katz, *Black Indians*, 118; Reuben Holmes, *The Five Scalps* (St. Louis: Jefferson Memorial, 1938).

180. Katz, *Black Indians*, 185.

181. Ellison, "Black Perceptions and Red Images," 48; Mary Alicia Owen,

*Old Rabbit, The Voodoo, and Other Sorcerers* (London: T. Fisher Unwin, 1893), 9, 180–86.

182. Ibid., 51–52.

183. Apess, *On Our Own Ground*, 10–11.

184. Chief Buffalo Child Long Lance, *Long Lance* (Jackson: University Press of Mississippi, 1995), 222–23.

185. Ibid., 80–81.

186. Beckwourth, *Life and Adventures*, 42.

187. Ibid., 66–67.

188. Ibid., 97.

189. Ibid., 177.

190. Ibid., 299.

191. Ibid., 331.

192. Marrant, *Narrative of the Life of John Marrant*, 2–4.

193. Ibid., 17.

194. Tubbee and Ceil, *Life of Okah Tubbee*, 31.

195. Copway, *Life, History, and Travels*, 62.

196. Ellison, "Black Perceptions and Red Images," 44.

197. See Henry Louis Gates Jr., *The Signifying Monkey: A Theory of Afro-American Literary Criticism* (New York: Oxford University Press, 1988).

198. Ibid., xxiv.

199. Ibid., 18.

200. See Maya Deren, "Some Elements of Arawakan, Carib, and Other Indian Cultures in Haitian Voudoun" (appendix B), in *The Divine Horsemen: Voodoo Gods of Haiti* (New York: Dell Publishing, 1970), 271–86.

201. Sheldon H. Harris, *Paul Cuffe: Black America and the African Return* (New York: Simon and Schuster, 1972); Paul Cuffe, *Captain Paul Cuffe's Logs and Letters, 1808–1817: A Black Quaker's "Voice from within the Veil,"* ed. Rosalind Cobb Wiggins (Washington, D.C.: Howard University Press, 1996).

202. *Genius in Bondage: Literature of the Early Black Atlantic*, ed. Vincent Carretta and Philip Gould (Lexington: University Press of Kentucky, 2001); *Olaudah Equiano: Equiano's Travels—His Autobiography—The Interesting Narrative of the life of Olaudah Equiano or Gustavus . . .* (London: Heinemann, 1969).

203. Quoted in William Scranton Simmons, *Spirit of the New England Tribes: Indian History and Folklore, 1620–1984* (Hanover, N.H.: University Press of New England, 1986).

204. Henry, *Account of the Chippewa*; George Copway, *Running Sketches of Men and Places in England, France, Germany, Belgium, and Scotland* (New York: J. C. Riker, 1851).

205. See Foster, *Witnessing Slavery*.

206. William L. Andrews, *To Tell a Free Story: The First Century of Afro-American Autobiography, 1769–1865* (Urbana: University of Illinois Press, 1986), 205–13, 144–51.

207. See John W. Roberts, *From Trickster to Badman: The Black Folk Hero in Slavery and Freedom* (Philadelphia: University of Pennsylvania Press, 1990).

208. Cuffe, *Logs and Letters*, 102.

209. Ibid., 186.

210. Ibid., 283.

211. Quoted in George Arnold Salvador, *Paul Cuffe, the Black Yankee, 1759–1817* (New Bedford, Mass.: Reynolds-DeWalt, 1969), 24.

212. Cuffe, *Logs and Letters*, 34–35.

213. Apess, *On Our Own Ground*, 157.

214. Quoted in Lewis, *Light and Truth*, 277.

215. George Washington Williams, *History of the Negro Race in America from 1619 to 1880: Negroes as Slaves, as Soldiers, and as Citizens* (New York: G. P. Putnam's Sons, 1885); Booker T. Washington, *The Story of the Negro: The Rise of the Race from Slavery* (New York: Doubleday, 1909).

216. David Cusick, *Sketches of Ancient History of the Six Nations* (Lockport, N.Y.: Turner and McCollum, 1848); George Copway, *Traditional History and Characteristic Sketches of the Ojibway Nation* (London: C. Gilpin, 1850).

217. Lewis, *Light and Truth*, 124.

218. Martin Robison Delany, *The Origin of Races and Color* (Baltimore: Black Classic Press, 1991).

219. Nathan J. Cuffee and Lydia A. Jocelyn, *Lords of the Soil: A Romance of Indian Life among the Early English Settlers* (Boston: C. M. Clark, 1905).

220. Littlefield, ed., *Life of Okah Tubbee*, 131.

221. Katz, *Black Indians*, 9.

222. Apess, *On Our Own Ground*, 10.

223. Long Lance, *Long Lance*, 4.

224. Plato, *Essays*, 111–12.

225. Ibid., 118.

226. Ibid., 22.

227. Elleanor Eldridge, *Memoirs of Elleanor Eldridge* (Providence, R.I.: B. T. Albro, 1838).

228. Daniel F. Littlefield Jr., Introduction to *The Life of Okah Tubbee*, by Okah Tubbee and Laah Ceil (Lincoln: University of Nebraska Press, 1988), viii.

229. Ibid., xxv.

230. Tubbee and Ceil, *Life of Okah Tubbee*, 17.

231. Ibid., 26.

232. Ibid., 27.

233. Bush-Banks, *Collected Works*, 6.

234. Guillaume, "Character Names," 45.

235. See Hertha D. Sweet Wong, "Taking Place: African–Native American Subjectivity in *A Yellow Raft in Blue Water*," in *Mixed Race Literature*, ed. Brennan, 172–74.

236. Dorris, *A Yellow Raft in Blue Water*, 25.

237. George Herzog, "African Influences in North American Indian Music," in *Papers Read at the International Congress of Musicology*, ed. Arthur Mendel, Gustave Reese, and Gilbert Chase (New York: Music Educators National Conference, 1939), 130–43.

238. Ibid., 142.

239. See George Lipsitz's essay in this volume, p. 235.

240. Herzog, "African Influences," 135.

241. Quoted in Jason Berry, Jonathan Foose, and Tad Jones's essay in this volume, p. 210.

242. Berry, *Spirit of Black Hawk*, 98.

243. The Calinda (or Kalinda) was one of the African dances performed at Congo Square in the 1800s. See Berry, Foose, and Jones's essay in this volume, p. 203.

244. For another example of African-Native dance, see Katz, *Black Indians*, 58, on the Seminole: "For U.S. slaveholders, the armed, uppity Black Seminoles were an intolerable problem. . . . They carried guns, were allowed to travel long distances, and acted 'impudently' free. These were not slaves, complained U.S. masters, but people who kept their African names, dressed in fine Seminole clothing and turbans, *adopted Seminole stomp dances* [my emphasis], sang Seminole and African songs."

245. See Berry, Foose, and Jones's essay in this volume, p. 201.

246. Dee Brown, *Bury My Heart at Wounded Knee* (New York: Pocket Books, 1970), 409.

247. See Lipsitz's essay in this volume, p. 220. Berry, Foose, and Jones note that "although the Indians are a preponderantly male tradition, many women have masked and marched with tribes over the years. They are known as Queens and usually occupy an ancillary slot by virtue of their relationship to the Big Chief" (in this volume, p. 207).

248. Kathryn VanSpanckeren, "The Mardi Gras Indian Song Cycle: A Heroic Tradition," *Melus* 16.4 (1989–90): 41.

249. Quoted in Lipsitz's essay in this volume, p. 222.

250. See Berry, Foose, and Jones's essay in this volume, p. 206.

251. Ibid., 209.

252. Ibid.

253. VanSpanckeren, "Mardi Gras Indian Song Cycle," 41.

254. See Lipsitz's essay in this volume, p. 224.

255. See Berry, Foose, and Jones's essay in this volume, p. 202.

256. Lauber, "Indian Slavery in Colonial Times," 68.

257. Ibid.

258. See Berry, Foose, and Jones's essay in this volume, p. 205.

259. Ibid., 201–2.

260. Ibid., 209.

261. Samuel Sewall, *The Selling of Joseph: A Memorial* (Boston: Bartholomew Green and John Allen, 1700).

262. Foster, *Witnessing Slavery*, 7.

263. Blu, *Lumbee Problem*, 232.

264. "The Rabbit and the Tar Wolf [second version]," in *Harper American Literature*, ed. Donald McQuade (New York: Harper and Row, 1987), 739–40.

265. Frederick Douglass, *Narrative of the Life of Frederick Douglass* (New York: Bedford Books, 1993), 46–47.

266. Ibid., 31–32.
267. Andrews, *To Tell a Free Story,* 29.
268. Ibid., 30.
269. Ibid., 29.

# PART I

# African–Native American
# Folklore

DAVID ELTON GAY

# *1   On the Interaction of Traditions: Southeastern Rabbit Tales as African–Native American Folklore*

Recent historical writing on the Native American cultures of the Southeast has begun to illuminate the dynamic and changing nature of these cultures throughout the colonial period.[1] Rather than imagining the cultures as static or attempting to reconstruct the precontact cultures, this new work focuses on the southeastern cultures' constant adaptation to the changing political and economic circumstances following European contact and colonization.[2] Although research on Native American interaction with Europeans has dominated this new historical analysis, it is clear that Native American contact with African slaves also brought about major cultural changes within the tribes and among the African slaves. As both slaveholders and slaves, Native Americans were in close contact with African slaves from their earliest arrival in the Southeast. One of the results was the emergence of a new syncretic culture for both Native Americans and African slaves. Folk narratives, especially the Rabbit stories that are common to both communities, offer clear evidence of the intense interaction and cultural syncretism between Native American and African American cultures.

The dominant paradigm in the study of these stories has not, however, been concerned with them as the product of the emerging culture of the seventeenth- and eighteenth-century Southeast. Instead, arguments have focused on whether or not the stories are of African origin. Joel

Chandler Harris was certain that the stories he collected in his Uncle Remus books had originated in Africa and thus rejected the notion that any were of Native American origin.[3] Harris's stories and assertions about them helped shape later assumptions.[4] The fullest argument in favor of the African origin of the tales is Alan Dundes's "African Tales among the North American Indians." Through the comparative study of certain key motifs, Dundes attempts to prove the African origin of the Rabbit tales. Much of his argument rests on the assumption that these motifs are, in fact, so characteristically African that any Native American or African American tale having these motifs must be of African origin. Dundes thus takes it as proven, for instance, that "Motif H 1154.6, Task: capturing squirrel and rattlesnake" is of African origin because in Stith Thompson's motif index "one finds only one reference and that is to Harris's 'Brother Rabbit Submits to a Test,' in *Nights with Uncle Remus.*"[5] Dundes then produces some examples of the tale from Africa and concludes his proof. Each of his explanations of why a particular motif or tale type must necessarily be African or African American proceeds in the same way. He asserts that "since Rabbit is not a trickster figure outside of the southeast in American Indian folklore and there can be no question that African narrative elements were introduced into American Indian tales, one can plausibly argue that the rabbit trickster figure so popular in American Negro tradition is African, not American Indian." He concludes by insisting that "[t]he burden of proof should be on those espousing an American Indian origin theory. . . . No doubt when some enterprising student undertakes a tale type index for Africa or even just East Africa, the amount of evidence for the African influence on American Indian folklore will be overwhelming."[6]

It is true that at the time his article was written there were few type and motif indices for Africa, but this was equally true, and remains so, for Native American narratives. Even recent anthologies of Native American oral narrative rarely have type and motif indices attached.[7] And further, Stith Thompson's *Motif Index* is notorious for its lack of coverage of non-European traditions and the inconsistency of its citations.[8] One thus cannot argue that a particular motif is characteristic of African or African American tradition, as Dundes does, simply because that motif shows up in the type and motif indices for Africa or because the only source for that motif in Thompson's work is of African or African American origin.[9] Contrary to Dundes's insistence that Rabbit does not appear as a trickster outside the Southeast and therefore must have come from Africa, Rabbit is found in the stories of the Northeast, which suggests that Rabbit did in fact originate at least in part in Native American narrative.

Some of the tales Dundes cites as African exemplars also differ considerably in style and structure from those found in the Southeast, which makes it unlikely that they are the source, or the sole source, for the southeastern tales. But since Dundes does not discuss the style or structure of the tales, nor any complete tale at all, relying instead on the mistaken idea that a shared motif between African or African American and Native American stories means they are of African origin, these structural and stylistic differences pose no problem for his thesis of African origins. While avoiding these problems with his thesis allows Dundes to engage in an energetic polemic for the African origin of the Rabbit tales, it substantially weakens his argument.

The proponents of the African origin of the Rabbit stories have also based their conclusions about the nature of the southeastern Rabbit tales on a limited and incompletely recorded body of narrative from African, African American, and Native American peoples, none of which was collected before the mid-nineteenth century and most of which was collected in the twentieth century. And of these peoples, the folk narrative of the southeastern Indians is the least well collected and studied. W. G. Tuggle's nineteenth-century collection of Creek stories was the first from the Muskogean-speaking peoples of the Southeast, but it has serious limitations since it was collected through translators (Tuggle did not speak Creek) after the Removal.[10] As with all collections of southeastern Indian materials, it comes too late to allow for accurate determination of the nature of precontact story cycles or for the discovery of the origins of tales.

John Swanton's *Myths and Tales of the Southeastern Indians*, which draws from Tuggle's collection as well as from Swanton's own fieldwork, is the most extensive anthology of southeastern Native American narrative, but it has several problems as a source. Swanton's collection contains no texts in the original languages, which makes it difficult to get at their original forms. Swanton also reworks the texts he took from Tuggle's collection, so that the texts as he presents them are one step further away from the form and style of the originals.[11] And it is clear that "Swanton did not intend [*Myths and Tales of the Southeastern Indians*] to be a definitive collection."[12] He had already used many of the stories he collected in his other publications, and this collection was his "way of getting his remaining texts—largely unanalyzed—into print and thus available for study."[13] Thus, while his work remains the largest collection, even Swanton realized its limitations in representing the narrative repertoire of the southeastern Indians.

Although George Lankford supports the notion of African origins in his *Native American Legends*, he does address the problems with the thesis.[14] Lankford notes that some motifs in the Native American Rabbit tales are known throughout Native American narrative, while others are widely distributed in the Midwest and Northeast, areas contiguous to the Southeast.[15] Though some motifs in southeastern narratives are shared with African and African American tales, the widespread distribution of many in Native American cultures outside of areas influenced by black cultures argues against their use as a diagnostic of African derivation. Lankford raises another significant problem for the African origin thesis when he points out that "[h]ow the transmission [of stories] occurred is not known."[16] In fact, no proponent of African origins suggests a viable mechanism for the transmission of the stories from one culture to the other, a failure that is obvious in many of the essays in William Bascom's *African Folktales in the New World*. In the essay "Bird's Head (Leg) under Its Wing," for instance, Bascom summarizes a number of African and African American folktales that are similar along with tales from Native American tribes from Arizona and New Mexico that are, he claims, related.[17] It is possible that Bascom's suggestion is correct, but he does not explain how the transmission of an African folktale to these tribes occurred. Comparing folktales to "determine whether or not they are similar enough to be considered historically related" is only the first part of the task of demonstrating a genetic relationship.[18] A genetic relationship cannot, however, be established solely on the basis of the similarity of stories in two cultures. One must also provide a means for the transmission of the tales from one culture to the other. Without a means of transmission, tales that are similar in different cultures should be attributed to independent creation.

Similar tales in different traditions that are in contact are, however, likely to influence each other, creating new forms of the tales that do not have their origins in a single tradition. This is in fact the most likely explanation for the similarities in many of the stories discussed by Dundes, Bascom, and Lankford. Realizing that cultural contact was a major factor in shaping the tales, Lankford proposes an alternative view of the origin of the Rabbit: the Southeast, as a melting pot of traditions, had several tricksters, one of the most important of whom was the Rabbit of northern fame. The addition of tales and motifs from Africa increased the body of trickster tales, many of which were adapted by giving the trickster the identity of Rabbit—a tendency increased by the discovery that the Africans, too, knew Rabbit.

Lankford goes on to note that the attention given to African origins "led to the creation of an illusion, that there was a single important trickster in the Southeast, whereas Rabbit may earlier have been but one

among several."[19] While his explanation comes closest to accounting for
the likely dynamics of the interaction of the different traditions, it still
has a major problem—Lankford believes that the influences were one-
way, that "[m]ixed into the Southeastern trickster tales with no indication of distinctiveness is a large number of stories taken by Native Americans from Africans."[20] Because Lankford is certain that the stories come
from Africa, he suggests that it was the Native American storytellers who
changed the name of the trickster from Anansi to Rabbit in order to ac-
culturate the tales to their own trickster cycle—without noting that the
trickster is also Rabbit among African American storytellers. The fact
that the name of the Native American trickster is the common name for
the trickster among both groups of storytellers is one indication of Native American influence on the story cycle. If the influence of the African slaves was as strong as the proponents of African origins of the Rabbit tales suggest, it is unlikely that the slaves would have adopted the
Native American name for the trickster. The focus on discovering origins has caused most researchers to overlook the fact that the Native
American and African American versions of trickster stories more closely
resemble each other than their supposed African exemplars. These similarities between Native American and African American stories, which
are too close to be attributed to independent invention, are further evidence of the long-term interaction between the two southeastern traditions, an interaction that creates a new southeastern tradition shared by
both groups.

The Tar Baby story is an excellent example of the close connection
between the folk narrative of the two cultures. A Cherokee version giv-
en by James Mooney goes as follows:

> Once there was such a long spell of dry weather that there was no more
> water in the creeks and springs, and the animals held a council to see
> what to do about it. They decided to dig a well, and all agreed to help
> except the Rabbit, who was a lazy fellow, and said, "I don't need to dig
> for water. The dew on the grass is enough for me." The animals did not
> like this, but they went to work together and dug their well. They no-
> ticed that Rabbit kept sleek and lively, although it was still dry weather
> and the water was getting low in the well. They said, "That tricky Rab-
> bit steals our water at night," so they made a wolf of pine gum and tar
> and set it by the well to scare the thief. That night the Rabbit came, as
> he had been coming every night, to drink enough to last him all next day.
> He saw a queer black thing by the well and said, "Who's there?" but the
> tar wolf said nothing. He came nearer, but the tar wolf never moved, so
> he grew braver and said, "Get out of my way or I'll strike you." Still the
> wolf never moved and the Rabbit came up and struck it with his paw,

but the gum held his foot and it stuck fast. Now he was angry and said, "Let me go or I'll kick you." Still the wolf said nothing. Then the Rabbit struck again with his hind foot, so hard that it was caught in the gum and he could not move, and there he stuck until the animals came for water in the morning. When they found who the thief was they had great sport over him for a while and then got ready to kill him, but as soon as he was unfastened from the tar wolf he managed to get away.[21]

This Cherokee version of the Tar Baby story is typical of the Native American traditions in the Southeast, which show the variations characteristic of oral traditions.[22] One basic variation is the reason Rabbit gets into trouble. The Cherokee, Hitchiti, and Natchez envision Rabbit both as a water thief and a food thief. In a Natchez version of the story Rabbit gets access to the water by killing a gray squirrel and covering himself with its skin, thus pretending to be the gray squirrel.[23] This gives Rabbit access to the water, but when the skin becomes hard Rabbit must get rid of it; he then has to get water by sneaking up to the well at night. He gives himself away by offering some guests water. They quickly realize that Rabbit's explanation that it is dew he has collected is a lie when they find his tracks around the well. After being caught, Rabbit tricks the animals into throwing him into the briar patch. George Lankford gives a Biloxi version of the story in which Rabbit also escapes by tricking a Frenchman into throwing him into the briar patch.[24]

In Creek, Hitchiti, Alabama, and Koasati versions of the tale, Rabbit steals vegetables from a man's garden.[25] In a Koasati version Rabbit escapes from captivity and is pursued by the animals. He takes refuge in a hollow log where the other animals are unable to get to him.[26] They leave Crane to guard the log, but Rabbit tricks Crane and kills him. He does not escape cleanly, though, since Dog sees him and chases him—and this, the Koasati tale tells us, is why rabbits still fear dogs. Of the various versions of the tale in the Southeast, the Uncle Remus story is unusual in not having Rabbit's theft as a motivation. Instead, Brer Fox is trying yet again to catch Brer Rabbit, who then escapes when he tricks Brer Fox into throwing him into the briar patch.[27]

Rabbit does not always escape. As Harris's Uncle Remus says, when asked if fox ever caught rabbit, "He mout, en den agin he moutnent. Some say Jedge B'ar come 'long en loosed 'im—some say he didn't."[28] The Alabama are certain that Rabbit doesn't escape: "Rabbit was stealing potatoes. Then the people made a tar image in the shape of a man and set it near the potato field to scare him away. When Rabbit came near he asked it for potatoes, but it would not give him any. Then he said he would hit it with his fist, but his hand stuck to it. When he hit it with his other

fist that stuck also. He kicked it and his foot stuck. The same thing happened to the other foot. Then they wrapped him up in it. They wrapped
the tar round and round him and killed him."[29] A Hitchiti variant also
tells that after the people caught Rabbit for stealing vegetables, the "man
who had charge of the garden came . . . and beat him to death."[30]

The closeness of the Native American and African American traditions is reflected in this Tar Baby story from the Sea Islands, which could
easily be taken for a Native American version:

> Ber Wolf had a pease patch. An' every night somebody go in de pease
> patch an' eat the pease. So Ber Wolf made a tar baby an' set him up in de
> yard. So Ber Rabbit went in de patch, an' he meet de tar baby standin'
> up. So Ber Rabbit said, "Good-mornin', gal!" Tar baby ain't got no man-
> ners, say nothin'. Say, "Man I slap you." His hand fasten. Ber Rabbit say,
> "I got anoder han'." So he hit him wid dat han'. Dat one fasten. Ber Rab-
> bit said, "I got a head." Say he butt him wid de head. De head fasten. "Gal,
> don't you see I got a foot?" So he kick him wid de foot. De foot fasten. "I
> kick him wid de oder foot." Dat one fasten. Ber Rabbit said, "I got a
> mout'." De mout' fasten. Den Rabbit say, "Tu'n me loose!"
>   Next t'ing come along Wolf. Wolf say, "I ketch yer, t'ief! You eat all of
> my pease. I putshyer head down on de choppin'-block an' chop em off."—
> "Oh, don't duh dat! Dat will kill me." Say, "I want ter kill you." Say, "I'll
> t'row you in the creek, drown you."—"Ah, don't duh dat," he say. "I'll
> t'row you in de briar-patch," he say. "Yes, Ber Wolf, t'row me in de briar
> patch! Den you'll kill me." When Ber Wolf t'row him in de briar-patch,
> Rabbit say, "Ping! Ping! Dat's de place my mammy done born me!" So
> dat ol' rabbit git away."[31]

The stories from the southeastern tradition do, of course, have strong
affinities to European and African stories of the tar baby, but they consistently agree in the details of the story, as can be seen when full versions of the stories and not only individual motifs are compared.

George Lankford, for instance, gives a Bakongo version of the Tar Baby
story in his anthology as a probable exemplar for the southeastern stories.[32] The Bakongo tale differs from the southeastern versions in several major ways. The most immediately noticeable difference is structural—what are always two different Rabbit stories in the Southeast appear
in the Bakongo version as one story with two incidents. In the Bakongo
story the rabbit first tricks the antelope out of food and then steals from
his well. In the first incident in the African tale the rabbit and the antelope agree to dig a well. They are eating before they go off to work on the
well, and the antelope suggests that they finish and then begin work. The
rabbit suggests instead that they hide the food and return to it later. The
antelope agrees, and they go off to work. The rabbit then tells the ante-

lope that he hears his family calling—his wife is having children and he must return to name them. By using this trick several times, the rabbit escapes working on the well and gets to eat the hidden food. When the antelope finds that the food is gone, he accuses the rabbit of stealing it. The rabbit gets angry and dares him to take casca, a purge or emetic.

> "Let us both take it," said the antelope, "and let him whose tail first becomes wet be considered the guilty one." So they took the casca and went to bed. As the medicine began to take effect upon the rabbit he cried out to the antelope:
> "See, your tail is wet!"
> "Nay, it is not!"
> "Yes, it is!"
> "No, but yours is, dear rabbit, see there!"
> Then the rabbit feared greatly and tried to run away. But the antelope said: "Fear not rabbit; I will do you no harm. Only you must promise not to drink the water of my well, and to leave my company forever."[33]

This story is well known in the Southeast. It is "Mr. Rabbit Nibbles up the Butter" in the Uncle Remus stories, and though it is the same tale type, the southeastern story differs significantly from the African story in its resolution and meaning.[34] In the southeastern stories, Rabbit escapes any punishment for his actions through trickery rather than revealing himself through a test and suffering for it, as in the Bakongo story. In the Uncle Remus version, after Rabbit's theft is discovered he suggests that someone else has stolen the butter. To prove this, he smears butter on Brer Possum's mouth and then offers his deception to Brer Fox as proof that Brer Possum was the thief. Brer Fox does not quite believe Brer Rabbit and proposes that they build a bonfire and jump over it. Both Brer Fox and Brer Rabbit make the jump, but Brer Possum falls in—which further indicates his supposed guilt and allows Rabbit to escape. When questioned about the unfairness of the ending, Uncle Remus explains, "In dis worril, lots er fokes is gotter suffer fer udder fowkes sins. Look like hit's mighty onwrong; but hit's des dat away."[35] The change in the ending and the explanation that Uncle Remus gives for the tale are both the products of the slave culture of the Southeast. As Lawrence W. Levine notes, "The rabbit, like the slaves who wove tales about him, was forced to make do with what he had. . . . [And] he resorted to any means at his disposal—means which may have made him morally tainted but which allowed him to survive and even to conquer."[36] Thus, while the tale's new ending may have disturbed the imaginary young white boy listening to Uncle Remus, it fit well the real conditions of African and Native American slavery.

The second incident of the Bakongo story is the Tar Baby story proper. It is similar to the southeastern stories about the tar baby, but with some differences. In the Bakongo story the antelope learns from a bird that the rabbit is stealing his water. The "antelope was greatly enraged, and determined to kill the rabbit. So the antelope laid a trap for the silly little rabbit. He cut a piece of wood and shaped it into a figure of an animal about the size of the rabbit; and then he placed this figure firmly in the ground near to the well, and smeared it all over with birdlime." As expected, the rabbit comes along and is insulted when the figure refuses to respond to his greeting. In his anger the rabbit hits the figure with his paws, stomach, and head, and thus becomes inextricably stuck to it. The antelope comes along and, finding the rabbit stuck to the figure, laughs at him and then kills him.[37] There are several ways that Rabbit's theft is discovered in the southeastern stories, though none have a bird as the carrier of the news, and the figure is made from tar, not smeared with something sticky—a detail that argues for considering the versions of the story collected from African Americans and Native Americans as, at the very least, a southeastern oicotype of the tale, a version of the story unique to the region.[38] And Rabbit uses the same tricks to escape in both Native American and African American versions of the story. A Hitchiti story tells how Rabbit escapes from a man who has caught him:

> Next day the man who was master of the water discovered him. He said to him, "You are the one who has been stealing and drinking the water," but Rabbit answered, "I have not stolen any water from you. . . ." The man said, "Was it not you who stole the water from me?" and Rabbit said, "I have never stolen any water from you." "If that is so, I will let you go, but you must look out for me. If you find who has been stealing the water you must tell me," he said. Rabbit said, "All right." So the man let him go and he ran off and disappeared.[39]

The trickery involved in Rabbit's escape here is similar to that in the Uncle Remus story about Brer Rabbit eating the butter. As in the African American version, the key to Rabbit's escape is his ability to dupe someone into believing that he did not commit the theft—though in this case, Rabbit makes his escape without getting anyone else killed.

That the African American and Native American versions are more similar to each other than to any African tale strongly suggests that the tales were shaped by the interaction of traditions in the Southeast rather than the one-way African-to–Native American influences posited by the proponents of the African origins of the tales. There are several likely contexts for such interactions. James Mooney long ago noted that Native Americans and African Americans had a long association as slaves in the colonial South—a situation that would have allowed for the constant exchange of cultural materials. As Mooney writes, "it is not commonly known that in all the southern colonies Indian slaves were bought and sold and kept in servitude and worked in the fields side by side with negroes up to the Revolution." Not only did the Indians serve as slaves, but "as the coast tribes dwindled they were compelled to associate and intermarry with the negroes until they lost their identity and were classed with that race."[40] The use of English as the language of the slave culture would also have facilitated the interaction of the two cultures, since neither would have been able to depend on the linguistic resources of their native languages for storytelling or for daily life. This intimate long-term contact would have been the perfect medium for the interaction of traditions.[41] The other likely source for the mutual influence of the two cultures was through the intermarriage of Native Americans and African Americans and through the slaves held by Indians. Indian-black intermarriage, with acculturation of the black spouse into Native American culture, was common throughout the early period and continued even after the Removal in the 1830s and 1840s. Among the Creeks and Seminoles especially, where intermarriage and adoption of blacks into the tribes were common, this would have been an excellent conduit for stories to pass both ways—from blacks to Indians, and from Indians to blacks. Intermarriage between Creeks and blacks was common enough for Tuggle to record this quip: "A Creek said to a Cherokee (Wm. P. Ross), 'You Cherokees are so mixed with Whites that we cannot tell you from Whites.' The Cherokee Ross replied, 'You Creeks are so mixed with Negroes that we cannot tell you from Negroes.'"[42]

Even though we know the probable routes of transmission, it remains unlikely that the origin of the tales can ever be established. No collection of Native American, African, or African American tales exists from the periods in which we must seek that answer. As Richard M. Dorson writes, "The fact is we know very little about the slaves' repertoire of folktales since no folklorists were around before the Civil War."[43] We know as little about the Native American repertoire. The first collections of the Rabbit tales are too late to allow us to know what the earlier traditions were like, and thus we cannot know whether a precontact southeastern Native American Rabbit cycle existed or not, just as we cannot know if the African slaves brought trickster stories with them, nor what sort they were if they did. Even Dundes notes that "for a number of tales it is extremely hard to say whether it is a European or African tale type."[44] This inability to establish the origins of the tales with certainty makes searching for their origins of limited use. It is, in fact, largely a distraction from the study of the cultural interactions between Native Americans and African Americans, interactions that produced a cycle of stories unique to the southeastern United States.

## Notes

1. See, for instance, Colin G. Calloway, *New Worlds for All: Indians, Europeans, and the Remaking of Early America* (Baltimore: Johns Hopkins University Press, 1997); James H. Merrell, *The Indians' New World: Catawbas and Their Neighbors from European Contact through the Era of Removal* (New York: W. W. Norton, 1991); Joel W. Martin, *Sacred Revolt: The Muskogees' Struggle for a New World* (Boston: Beacon Press, 1991); J. Leitch Wright Jr., *Creeks and Seminoles* (Lincoln: University of Nebraska Press, 1986), esp. chap. 3, "The Black Muscogulges" (73–100), on the interaction between Indians and blacks; Daniel H. Usner Jr., *Indians, Slaves, and Settlers in a Frontier Exchange Economy: The Lower Mississippi Valley before 1783* (Chapel Hill: University of North Carolina Press, 1992); and Daniel J. Littlefield Jr., *Africans and Creeks: From the Colonial Period to the Civil War* (Westport, Conn.: Greenwood Press, 1979).

2. The work of John Swanton, for instance, the great scholar of the southeastern tribes, was largely an effort to recover the precontact cultures. His short, fictional reconstruction of precontact Creek life in Elsie Clews Parsons's *North American Indian Life: Customs and Traditions of Twenty-three Tribes* (1922; rpt., New York: Dover, 1992), 127–46, epitomizes Swanton's project. Charles Hudson's *The Southeastern Indians* (Knoxville: University of Tennessee Press, 1976), the most recent handbook on the southeastern tribes, has a similar focus.

3. See Joel Chandler Harris, Introduction to *Uncle Remus: His Songs and Sayings,* ed. Robert Hemenway (New York: Penguin Books, 1982).

4. "Perhaps the first indication that American Indians had borrowed African tales from Negro slaves and ex-slaves was the noting of a large number of parallels in Joel Chandler Harris's 'Uncle Remus' tales and the tales collected from the Cherokee and the Creek" (Alan Dundes, "African Tales among the North American Indians," *Southern Folklore Quarterly* 29 [1965]: 207). See also Alan Dundes, "African and Afro-American Tales," *Research in African Literatures* 7 (1976): 181–89; and Foreword to William Bascom, *African Folktales in the New World,* (Bloomington: Indiana University Press, 1992), vii–xx.

5. Dundes, "African Tales among the North American Indians," 212.

6. Ibid., 218–19.

7. Stith Thompson's *Tales of the North American Indians* (1929; rpt., Bloomington: Indiana University Press, 1966) is one of the few collections of Native American narrative with an extensive comparative apparatus based on tale type and motif. Collections like John Swanton, ed., *Myths and Tales of the Southeastern Indians* (1929; rpt., Norman: University of Oklahoma Press,

1995), George Lankford, ed., *Native American Legends: Southeastern Legends—Tales from the Natchez, Caddo, Biloxi, Chickasaw, and Other Nations* (Little Rock, Ark.: August House, 1987), and Brian Swann, ed., *Coming to Light: Contemporary Translations of the Native Literatures of North America* (New York: Random House, 1994), are more typical in their almost complete lack of reference to comparative materials or to tale types and motifs.

8. On the limitations of Thompson's work for non-European traditions see, for instance, Hasan El-Shamy, Introduction to *Folk Traditions of the Arab World: A Guide to Motif Classification*, vol. 1 (Bloomington: Indiana University Press, 1995), xiii–xiv and xxi–xxii.

9. Dundes, "African Tales among the North American Indians," 218.

10. Tuggle's writings are available in *Shem, Ham, and Japeth: The Papers of W. O. Tuggle,* ed. Eugene Current Garcia with Dorothy B. Hatfield (Athens: University of Georgia Press, 1973).

11. An idea of how these looked can be gotten from Geoffrey Kimball's recent retranscription and retranslation of some of Swanton's Koasati texts. His results show that Swanton's arrangements of the texts do not follow the structure and style of the originals very closely—in fact, as translated and transcribed by Kimball from the original language, the texts are far more typical of Native American narrative than Swanton's anthology would lead one to believe. See Geoffrey Kimball, "Two Koasati Traditional Narratives," in *Coming to Light,* ed. Swann, 704–13.

12. George Lankford, Introduction to *Myths and Tales of the Southeastern Indians,* ed. Swanton, xiv.

13. Ibid., xiii–xiv.

14. Lankford, *Native American Legends,* 222–42.

15. For example, the motifs "Bungling Host" (J2425) and "Sham Doctor" (K1955) (ibid., 225). In *African Folktales in the New World* (Bloomington: Indiana University Press, 1992), William Bascom also draws attention to widely scattered Native American parallels to many African and African American tales.

16. Lankford, *Native American Legends,* 229.

17. Bascom, *African Folktales in the New World,* 71–82. Bascom gives them as the Tewa, Zuni, and Zia. In a later essay he lists versions of another folktale from a number of tribes, mostly from Mexico, the Southwest—for instance, various bands of the Apache and the Hopi—and the Yokut of central California, again without explaining how African tales came to these tribes (116).

18. Ibid., 83.

19. Lankford, *Native American Legends,* 240.

20. Ibid., 229. Dundes also assumes, based on his comparisons, that the influence was one-way, from Africans to Native Americans, and so denies any possibility of Native American origin or influence on the form of the tales.

21. James Mooney, trans., *Myths of the Cherokee* (1900; rpt., New York: Dover, 1996), 271–72.

22. In *The Black Ox: A Study in the History of a Folktale,* Folklore Fellows Communications 70 (1927; rpt., New York: Arno Press, 1980), Archer Tay-

lor explains that "probably every tale in circulation among the folk . . . is at the same time a definite entity and an abstraction. It is a definite entity in the particular form in which it happens to be recorded; it is an abstraction in the sense that no two versions ever exactly agree and that consequently the tale lives only in endless mutations" (4).

23. Swanton, *Myths and Tales of the Southeastern Indians*, 258–59.

24. Lankford, *Native American Legends*, 237–38.

25. Swanton, *Myths and Tales of the Southeastern Indians*, 68, 110, 161, and 208–9.

26. Ibid., 208–9.

27. Harris, *Uncle Remus*, 55–59 and 62–64.

28. Ibid., 59.

29. Swanton, *Myths and Tales of the Southeastern Indians*, 161.

30. Ibid., 110.

31. Elsie Clews Parsons, ed., *Folklore of the Sea Islands, South Carolina* (Memoirs of the American Folklore Society No. 16) (Cambridge, Mass.: American Folklore Society, 1923), 26–27.

32. Lankford, *Native American Legends*, 235–38.

33. Ibid., 235–36.

34. Harris, *Uncle Remus*, 99–102.

35. Ibid., 102.

36. Lawrence W. Levine, *Black Culture and Black Consciousness: Afro-American Folk Thought from Slavery to Freedom* (New York: Oxford University Press, 1977), 112. See also William Courtland Johnson, "Trickster on Trial: The Morality of the Brer Rabbit Tales," in *"Ain't Gonna Lay My 'ligion Down": African American Religion in the South,* ed. Alonzo Johnson and Paul Jersild (Columbia: University of South Carolina Press, 1996), 52–71.

37. Lankford, *Native American Legends*, 237.

38. This is the kind of detail expected in a region where tar is used. As Mooney points out, "The famous 'tar-baby' story has variants . . . wherever, in fact, the piñon or pine supplies enough gum to be molded into a ball for Indian uses" (*Myths of the Cherokee*, 233–34). It is unlikely that the widespread knowledge of the tale in Native American narrative can be explained by an African origin.

39. Swanton, *Myths and Tales of the Southeastern Indians*, 110.

40. Mooney, *Myths of the Cherokee*, 233.

41. On the culture of the black slaves see, among others, John W. Blassingame, *The Slave Community: Plantation Life in the Antebellum South,* rev. ed. (New York: Oxford University Press, 1979); Charles Joyner, *Down by the Riverside: A South Carolina Slave Community* (Urbana: University of Illinois Press, 1985); and Levine, *Black Culture and Black Consciousness.*

42. Tuggle, *Shem, Ham, and Japeth,* 37.

43. Richard M. Dorson, "African and Afro-American Folklore: A Reply to Bascom and other Misguided Critics," *Journal of American Folklore* 88 (1975): 155.

44. Dundes, "African Tales among the North American Indians," 216.

SANDRA K. BARINGER

## 2 Brer Rabbit and His Cherokee Cousin: Moving Beyond the Appropriation Paradigm

On the issue of cultural appropriation in the context of ethnic and multicultural studies, Gayatri Chakravorty Spivak, bell hooks, and others defend the "strategic essentialism" of ethnic minorities as a defense against "excessive commodification" of their cultural production by whites.[1] Informing this discussion is the concept of "signifyin'," described by Henry Louis Gates Jr. in his seminal text *The Signifying Monkey.*[2] Coco Fusco exemplifies the discussion of these signifying strategies—the practice of "taking elements of an established or imposed culture and throwing them back with a different set of meanings"—in her collection of essays *English Is Broken Here.* Acknowledging that such syncretism has "enabled disempowered groups to maintain their outlawed or marginalized traditions,"[3] Fusco criticizes the celebration of multicultural interchange when a dominant culture is borrowing from an oppressed culture. She argues that cultural interchange under such a rubric amounts to "postmodern fetishizing of the exchange of cultural property" that "seems less like emancipation and more like intensified alienation."[4] In other words, she seems to say, what is a culturally positive signifying practice when practiced by marginalized or disempowered groups amounts to appropriation or fetishization when practiced by a dominant group.

The stances of these critics has tended to shift attention in the multicultural arena away from the dynamics of cross-cultural exchange and other "strategically essentialist" practices of signification and transformation to the more limited subtopic of the power dynamics of cultural appropriation. One can generally agree with these critics that rampant cultural borrowing by whites of minority cultural property—as Fusco puts it, "rampant commodification of one's cultural heroes"[5]—has historically offered little in exchange to the minority communities from which such property has been borrowed. For example, blacks and American Indians have gained little recognition or other recompense for the commodified evolution from the Brer Rabbit stories to Joel Chandler Harris's Uncle Remus stories, Disney's *Song of the South,* and even Bugs Bunny. But issues of cross-ethnic cultural exchange warrant examination beyond the issue of appropriation.[6] Cultural syncretism that has occurred historically demands analysis, for example, of how dominant histories have distorted or erased Indian, African, and Black Indian syncretic practices and their cultural products, and to what end. Once revealed, these practices and products have interesting things to say about the dynamics of cross-cultural contact and about the cultures themselves. They show how such contact can stimulate creative and historically salient retellings of old stories. They demonstrate, in this instance, the profound connections between African American and Indian concepts about the world and about the spirit world. An appreciation of the value of cultural syncretism is increasingly important because in the contemporary, postmodern arena, signifying practices are rarely just two-way but rather increasingly complex.

The Rabbit stories of the southeastern United States are interesting in regard to these questions because even the seemingly simple question of which culture dominated becomes complex. African slaves were unequivocally an oppressed culture, or collection of cultures, in the South, but the Cherokees and the other four Civilized Tribes were both oppressor and oppressed. Their own course of syncretism and assimilation with white settlers in the South reached its zenith in the late eighteenth century, to the point where the affluence of slaveowning Cherokee plantation owners in the early nineteenth century precipitated the forced Removal of the Cherokees in 1838. At the same time, many Indians became slaves during the seventeenth and eighteenth centuries and blended into the African American population. Though subsequent generations may have been African in appearance to white slaveowners, cultural retentions from parents and other caregivers, disrupted as slave communities may have been by white slaveowning practices, did not disappear. There were yet other Indians who managed to avoid both slavery and forced Removal and whose descendants remain in the Southeast, some of them intermingled with descendants of escaped slaves. In the 1920s it was estimated that one-third of African Americans had some Indian ancestry. More recently it has been asserted that "today just about every African American family tree has an Indian branch."[7] Oral tradition maintained by African American elders in the South prior to the northward migration "kept alive the memories of bonds and ties with Native American cultures."[8]

Given all this contact, interaction, and intermarriage, it makes sense that the rabbit, among several African trickster figures, would have become the dominant trickster figure among the slaves. There would have been both egalitarian cross-cultural exchange among storytelling African and Indian slaves, and also signifying practices—"taking elements of an established or imposed culture and throwing them back with a different set of meanings"—by slaves upon dominant Cherokee and/or white folklore. The significance of dancing and drumming to both cultures as a means of communicating with the spirit world underlies the fact that dancing has continued to be associated with the rabbit trickster in both Cherokee and African American stories. Though the Cherokee Rabbit stories do not involve agriculture so much as the Brer Rabbit stories do, the position of the rabbit trickster as a bothersome creature in Cherokee folklore is consistent with a gardening culture. Brer Rabbit stories, however, carry garden thievery to plantation proportions. The eating of greens may well have been a matter of survival to underfed slaves. It would have been easy, if not inevitable, to identify with the nervous, fast-nibbling, and fleet-footed animal who pilfered the master's fields under cover of darkness. And from there, the transition to swashbuckling swindler of wolves is but a short step.

Even before Joel Chandler Harris first published his Uncle Remus stories in 1883, ethnologists had noted the similarities between Brer Rabbit stories and Rabbit stories among the Creek and Cherokee—in particular, two almost identical tales: the well-known Tar Baby tale,[9] and Rabbit's race with the turtle or terrapin, wherein Turtle prevails not because Rabbit is overconfident and easily distracted as in Aesop's fable but because Turtle invokes the aid of all his relatives to pop up and impersonate him at every turning point in the race. Late nineteenth-century scholars asserted that the African slaves had gotten Brer Rabbit stories from Native American sources, or that they had gotten them from European sources.[10] The issue was most comprehensively addressed in Aurelio M. Espinosa's 1930 article on the tar baby in the *Journal of American Folk-Lore* in which he accounts for 158 versions of the tale worldwide, of which twenty-nine are Native American.[11] He concludes that the story is of Hindu origin, spreading to Europe, and reaching Africa and the

Americas through Hispanic and Portuguese mariners. Espinosa's hypothesis is plausible but overlooks the possibility of prior independent contact and migrations.[12]

The 1972 edition of the *Funk and Wagnalls Standard Dictionary of Folklore, Mythology, and Legend* comments that "both character and category" of Rabbit folklore "has tended to be exaggerated" due to the popularity of the Uncle Remus version,[13] a somewhat odd assertion that is not only dismissive of Cherokee and Creek folklore but can only be interpreted as an inability to recognize African American folklore as significant in its own right. This standard reference tool also offhandedly asserts that the Tar Baby story was borrowed by Native Americans from European sources. Though its ensuing remark that such tales "have been completely recast in setting, characters, cultural background, style, and thematic emphasis to suit the native pattern"[14] gives a rather global overview of every way in which a minimal plot can be adapted to serve the social, political, and aesthetic needs of a particular culture, this standard reference ignores the issue of African–Native American contact and interchange, as have most scholars.

A 1965 article by Alan Dundes defending African origin implies that all Rabbit tales in Native American folklore come from Africa. Dundes provides a good bibliographic history of the dispute over origins, though he curiously omits Espinosa's work, mentioning it only by way of contesting a remark from Franz Boas in which Boas aligns himself with Espinosa.[15] But Dundes's general conclusion is overbroad:

> In West Africa, the most common trickster figure is the tortoise. But it is a known fact that Negro slaves came from East Africa as well and in East Africa it is the hare which is the principal trickster figure. Therefore since the rabbit is not a trickster figure outside the southeast in American Indian folklore and since there can be no question that African narrative elements were introduced into American Indian tales, one can plausibly argue that the rabbit trickster figure so popular in American Negro tradition is African, not American Indian. In any case, the burden of proof should be on those espousing an American Indian origin theory.[16]

One problem with Dundes's argument is that in setting out to prove that Native Americans have borrowed tales from Africans, he focuses primarily on a strategy of disproving European origins for African tales. Another problem is that he sometimes simultaneously relies on the Arne-Thompson tale type index for much of his evidence and dismisses the implications that don't suit him.[17] Furthermore, it is often far from clear to which index he is referring.

Finally, Dundes's argument is based on a misstatement of fact: Rabbit stories were *not* limited to the southeast. Paul Radin has established that Hare stories were widespread among tribes of the north-central area of the continent. Distinguishing between rabbits and hares may be important for rabbit breeders, but it seems an insignificant distinction among shapeshifting tricksters, and Dundes himself conflates the two in discussing African origins. When Dundes argues that rabbit trickster tales occur only among southeastern Native American tribes, he fails to take into account Radin's 1956 book on the Winnebago, which in addition to relating a full cycle of Hare stories refers to Hare stories among the Menominee, Ponca, Iowa, and Ojibwa, all tribes of the north-central area of the continent. It is true that Radin is preoccupied with making a distinction between a trickster and a culture hero and thus argues that some of Hare's trickster characteristics, at least among the Winnebago and Iowa, "have been purged in order to make him conform more perfectly to the picture of a true culture hero."[18] But Radin's distinction between trickster and culture hero is somewhat insignificant in an argument of origins. One could likewise argue that Brer Rabbit is more of a culture hero than a trickster. Clearly, indigenous rabbit folklore in North America predated the Middle Passage from Africa.

It is important to start with this observation that the American Indian elements in the Brer Rabbit stories have been largely overlooked or dismissed, though the origin question seems less interesting overall than the process of intermingling elements, divergent paths, and surviving themes. The African American Brer Rabbit is a uniquely American creation, having been influenced not by European-based Rabbit stories, as some have claimed (at least, not much), but by the transmission of stories from a variety of African cultures, by contact with Native American communities, and by the subsequent evolution of the tales to reflect unique aspects of the slave experience in the American South. Gross oversimplifications such as Dundes's assertion that the rabbit trickster is African and not American Indian trivialize the complexities of cultural exchange. That sort of argument of origins is a form of essentialism, but not the sort of "strategic essentialism" that furthers subaltern interests. Rather, it effaces opportunities for the study of cultural exchange, which is more complex than one oppressor versus one oppressed. Players in cultural trade may have different sorts of assets and liabilities, as the Cherokees did during slavery, and the study of literary motifs as artifacts of that cultural trade may serve to enhance our understanding of cultural survival. Like Turtle's cousins popping up at every turn in Rabbit's race, common motifs such as dance and music and particular trajectories of resistance as in the case of the slave stories demonstrate the operation of particular strategies of cultural continuity and the different needs of tribal and slave cultures.

One interesting cross-cultural motif illustrated in the Rabbit tales appears in a group of tales that can be described as the "raining fire" stories. In one African American folktale about Brer Rabbit and Alligator, Alligator asks Brer Rabbit what trouble is. Brer Rabbit replies, "I'll show you trouble," and sets the marsh grass on fire, burning Alligator's hide and thus giving it the rough and scaly appearance it has today. This tale seems to be a variation on an African version from the Ibo of Nigeria in which the "dupe is persuaded to get into grass in order to learn new dance." But there is no alligator and no rabbit named in the Ibo reference, nor a reference to "trouble."[19]

More than to the Ibo, the tale of Brer Rabbit and Alligator bears similarities to Creek and Cherokee stories. In the Cherokee story of how Otter lost his coat, Rabbit takes Otter camping to a sacred place, the "Fire Falling from the Sky Spot." He persuades Otter to take his coat off for the night so it won't get damaged by the falling fire and then, after Otter goes to sleep, sends him into a panic by throwing hot embers from the fire up into the air with a shovel. Otter, like Alligator, escapes into the water.[20] In the Creek version, it is Panther (Maneater) rather than Alligator who gets rained on. This raining-fire technique also appears in a tale of Simon Brown, the ex-slave storyteller whose turn-of-the-century stories are recounted in William J. Faulkner's *The Days When the Animals Talked: Black-American Folktales and How They Came to Be.* In one of Simon Brown's Brer Rabbit stories, "yellow balls of fire" (Brer Rabbit's friends the hornets) rain down on Brer Fox and Brer Wolf.[21] Brown also tells of how he himself, as a boy, drove the patrollers away from a slave prayer meeting by throwing open the door and tossing a shovelful of hot embers in their faces.[22]

In all these stories, an underdog turns on a predator by wielding a powerful cosmic force, fire. In the Creek tale, Rabbit follows up this feat by causing an ocean to spring up between himself and the angry panther. In this abrupt shift to global proportions from what had up to that point seemed a quaint, though somewhat brutal, fable of one-upmanship, one gets a glimpse of the supernatural powers and themes that underlie trickster stories. The original meaning of the raining-fire motif in the Cherokee and Creek stories is old and most assuredly has inaccessible sacred connotations. The giant horned snake Uk'ten is the original cosmic monster of Cherokee monster slayer stories; similar horned serpents appear in indigenous folklore all over North America from Canada to

Mexico. The Cherokee folklorists Jack and Anna Kilpatrick compare Uk'ten to the European fire-breathing dragon, speculating as to a common Mesozoic origin. When Uk'ten was finally slain, "he caused it to rain hot fire. The fire rained until he was completely dead."[23] But fire was also used by the Cherokee warrior who fought Uk'ten. The ritual slaying of Uk'ten involved running from one to the next of seven consecutive "protective, purifying fires."[24]

So when Simon Brown rains fire on the patrollers from the church door, he is invoking sacred power, just as the black preacher inside may be raining metaphorical fire on his parishioners. This mode of articulation is a natural outgrowth of a slave culture in which some combination of variations on these stories were heard from earliest childhood. The storyteller might or might not know the Uk'ten stories, but in a way of knowing the world in which animals are understood to connote spiritual power, the signification of raining fire is likewise understood if not articulated. The fire constitutes not only deadly force but supernatural force—sometimes the only force available to a totally subjugated people.

The most powerful thing a trickster can do is to kill a monster or a witch, and in fact, that is what happens in the story in which Brer Rabbit kills Old Mammy Witch Wise, "the last witch what ever live." It is conventional wisdom in African American folklore that witches often take off their skins at night before they go flying around in other forms.[25] At the behest of the other oppressed animals, Brer Rabbit comes up with a plan: he sneaks up to the witch's house one night, finds her skin on the porch, and rubs the inside all over with hot pepper. When she comes back and tries to put it on, the pain causes her to "fall over in a fit," and the other animals burn her.[26] But the motifs are the same as in the Cherokee story about Rabbit and Otter: burning and removable skin.

Stories get told and retold, almost never twice the same, and it is the interactive and evolving part of storytelling that is effaced from these stories in the anthropologically oriented ventures in recording them over the past hundred years. This interactive dynamic is the reason why it would be impossible to show that all Brer Rabbit stories come from Africa, or all Brer Rabbit stories come from the Cherokees. Any such argument of origins misunderstands the way oral storytelling works. A further analysis of the interaction will be facilitated by a brief account of historical contact.

Much of the ethnographic documentation of slave folklore has come from the Gullah people of the Carolina and Georgia coastal areas, many of whom were relative latecomers from Africa in the nineteenth century and thus the focus of studies seeking to trace specific African origins and retentions. As a result of this focus, it has been easy to lose sight of the long history of Africans in the Western Hemisphere. There is considerable basis for speculation, though no hard evidence, of transatlantic contact between Africa and the Americas in pre-Columbian times: the nature of Atlantic currents; the presence of bananas, the yellow type of which was indigenous to South America, in West Africa; controversies over the diffusion history of cotton and yams; similarities of Olmec sculpture to African styles.[27] At any rate, systematic introduction of African slaves into Virginia and the Carolinas was well under way in the early seventeenth century. Thus the span of widespread African slavery in this area can be said to encompass two and a half centuries, longer than the history of the United States and ample time for extensive intermingling of new influences into an African-based culture.

The major tribes in Georgia and the Carolinas were the Cherokee and the Creek. Some of the smaller coastal tribes such as the Catawba along the Carolina coast were diminished almost to the point of extinction (at least in comparison to the Five Civilized Tribes: Cherokee, Creek, Choctaw, Chickasaw, and Seminole) by way of a combination of epidemics, enslavement, and assimilation; it could be argued that such "disappearing" tribes were assimilated into African slave culture as much as into white or Cherokee communities.[28] As the Atlantic coastland was converted into a plantation economy, some Cherokees and Creeks acquired African slaves. Slavery existed among these tribes prior to contact with whites but was of an essentially different character. Slaves were captives, usually women and children, taken in battle; they were not generally viewed as a commodity for economic trade and profit. But by the end of the seventeenth century the Cherokee became dependent on European trade goods to the extent that they engaged in warfare with the coastal tribes—the Catawba, the Guales, and others—to obtain slaves for trade.[29] At the same time, there was an active trade in Indian slaves, including Cherokee, throughout the eighteenth century. James Mooney explains, "as the coast tribes dwindled they were compelled to associate and intermarry with the negroes until they finally lost their identity and were classed with that race, so that a considerable proportion of the blood of the southern negroes is unquestionably Indian."[30] Mooney's characterization is an outsider's view, that is, a definition of identity based on physical appearance (to a white eye) rather than sensitivity to evidence of cultural syncretism: social structures within a slave community and with relation to the dominant culture, spiritual beliefs and attitudes, and the blended body of orally transmitted folklore that expresses and influences ways of knowing and relating to the world.

European intermarriage with Creek and Cherokee women contributed to a more Europeanized model of agriculture and slave ownership among the Cherokees who escaped slavery. They continued to have a significant presence in the region until Andrew Jackson's defeat of the Cherokees and of the U.S. Supreme Court culminated in the 1838 Trail of Tears, the forced march of the Cherokees to the Indian Territory (what was to become Oklahoma). Thus it is fair to say that considerable contact occurred among Cherokees and Africans for over two hundred years prior to the forced Removal of the remaining Five Civilized Tribes to Oklahoma. One can even speculate that some of James Mooney's information is traceable to one of these African slaves: Mooney discusses a Cherokee prophet, Yona-gusksa, "the most prominent chief in the history of the eastern Cherokee," who died in 1839, noting that he was survived by "an old negro slave named Cudjo, who was devotedly attached to him."[31]

There are many cultural affinities between Africans and Native Americans that neither group shared with European settlers. According to Theda Perdue, "both emphasized living harmoniously with nature and maintaining ritual purity; both attached great importance to kinship in their social organization; and both were accustomed to an economy based on subsistence agriculture."[32] Prior to Christian influence, both had similar concepts of an afterlife in which the soul of the dead person made a journey to another world, though details of these concepts differed. A soul could become lost and condemned to perpetual wandering for various reasons: despicable behavior, as in the African American tale of the King Buzzard recorded by Edward C. L. Adams in *Tales of the Congaree*,[33] through a curse, or by some omission on the part of the relatives in dealing with the body. Dancing and drumming were central to the spirituality of both cultures as means of communicating with spirits. Spirits were (and are) distinguishable from the souls of the dead; people communicate with spirits through dancing and drumming.

Spirits are often, but not always, associated with particular animals. Camara Laye, in his autobiography *The Dark Child: The Autobiography of an African Boy*, commented on the affinity of his mother with her "totem," the crocodile, which enabled her to draw water from the Niger without being attacked by crocodiles.[34] Frequent mention is made in *Drums and Shadows*, a compilation of interviews with former slaves and their Gullah descendants, of inherited food taboos related to particular animals. Such affinities with particular animal spirits among Native Americans are usually inherited matrilineally as clan associations.

Though the rabbit is not a particularly important animal in terms of Cherokee dance and ritual,[35] it is significant in terms of the number of stories that are told about it. It is the primary trickster figure in Cherokee and Creek folklore; it could fairly be said that the rabbit is the main trickster figure among southeastern tribes in general, but the largest story collections available were obtained from the Cherokee and Creek. James Mooney recorded twelve Rabbit tales, including versions of the Tar Baby story and the race between the rabbit and the terrapin. My overview of Cherokee Rabbit stories is based primarily on Mooney's ethnological treatise published in 1898 and on Gayle Ross's 1994 book *How Rabbit Tricked Otter and Other Cherokee Trickster Stories* (compiled from Mooney, Jack and Anna Kilpatrick, Jack Gregory, Rennard Strickland, and other Cherokee storytellers). In the Cherokee tales, Rabbit is a talented singer and dancer who occupies the position of the messenger for the council who goes around to notify everyone of meetings and dances. Since the published Cherokee stories are far fewer than the published Brer Rabbit stories, it is possible to summarize them herein: the following is a fairly comprehensive summary of the stories contained in these two sources.

On two of these missions, Rabbit steals Otter's coat and conspires to denude Possum's tail, both in order to feed his own vanity before the other animals at the gatherings. On another occasion—in a sequence of events that could be read as a satirical political commentary—Rabbit abuses his position by involving Possum in a scheme to deliver a phony message from the council that "everyone must take a mate at once, and then we'll be sure to get our wives." Possum can't keep up and arrives late at the first town, where Rabbit has already gotten himself a wife. So they go on to a second town, purportedly to get a wife for Possum, but Rabbit dupes him by announcing that "as there had been peace so long that everybody was getting lazy the council had ordered that there must be war at once and they must begin right in the townhouse." Consequently Possum walks into the middle of a fracas and survives only by playing dead; Rabbit escapes.[36] This is the most overtly "political" of the Cherokee stories, and it will be discussed further in due course.

Rabbit helps Wildcat capture a turkey with his talents as a leader in song and dance.[37] This story echoes that of the Cherokee culture hero Stone Coat who provided hunting songs to lure turkeys from their hiding places; turkey hunters wear simulated wildcat ears when following the turkey hunting ritual described among the eastern Cherokee at Big Cove.[38] Rabbit also escapes from the wolves through his singing and dancing talent; he gets the wolves so involved in stamping their feet that he eventually makes his getaway.[39] Parody and mimicry are key to Cherokee mask dancing;[40] such stories in which Rabbit tricks an opponent by mimicking his adversary—or, better yet, putting words in the adversary's mouth—inform contemporary black signifying practice:

> "Why do you say that?" said the (suspicious) old Turkey.
> "O, that's all right," said the Rabbit, "that's just the way he [Wildcat] does, and we sing about it."[41]

The dialogue brings to mind the rapper Ice-T's defense of his song "Cop Killer," a first-person narration from the killer's point of view.

Rabbit is made to appear foolish when he has dinner at Bear's house; Bear splits open his side to get some grease to put in the stew, and when Rabbit tries to do the same, he practically kills himself.[42] Deer also prevails over Rabbit: Rabbit loses the race with Deer for the antler prize by getting caught cheating, but he gets back at Deer by convincing him to let him file his teeth down to blunt nubs. But then Deer tricks Rabbit into a jumping contest that ends with Deer conjuring the stream Rabbit has jumped across into an ocean with Rabbit stranded on the other side. In Mooney's version, "the Rabbit was never able to get back again and is still on the other side. The rabbit that we know is only a little thing that came afterwards."[43]

The one truly heroic thing that Rabbit appears to have done is kill Flint, a giant who lived in the mountains, whom the animals hated "because he had helped to kill so many of them."[44] He invites Flint to dinner, waits for him to fall asleep, and drives a stake into his middle, exploding him into the pieces of flint that we now find in many places.[45]

Thus among Mooney's twelve stories, Rabbit is the butt of the joke in six, counting the Tar Baby and Terrapin Race stories with which we are already familiar (the other four are being discovered in Otter's coat, injuring himself at Bear's house, losing the race to Deer, and being tricked into banishment by Deer). Among the six stories in which Rabbit prevails in some fashion, he tricks Possum twice, ruins Deer's teeth, escapes from the wolves, helps Wildcat catch a turkey, and kills Flint. Though two of the stories involve Rabbit's skills in song and dance, only the last, in which Rabbit kills Flint, involves action of epic and clearly supernatural scope.

Though it is difficult to argue with Mooney's judgment that Rabbit is "first and most prominent in the animal myths,"[46] the Rabbit stories must be kept in perspective. There is a large body of stories about other animals that is beyond the scope of this discussion, as well as creation stories, historical legends, and stories about supernatural people. For instance, Deer and Bear prevail over Rabbit in the Cherokee stories because they are more significant figures in Cherokee cosmology. Deer was the primary target for hunting, and the deer spirit, described by Mooney as "powerful chief of the deer tribe . . . 'Little Deer,'" protects the deer from all but knowledgeable hunters and wreaks revenge on those hunters who kill without offering the appropriate prayer. Bears occupy an even higher position, understood to be transformed Cherokee who, as essentially human, can talk if they want to.[47]

Rabbit's role in Cherokee literature could be described as a cuddly buffoon.[48] This characterization marks the major parting of the ways between the Cherokee Rabbit and Brer Rabbit: the former becomes a nostalgic ne'er-do-well used to convey moral principles to children, whereas Brer Rabbit evolves into a swashbuckling antihero. This distinction is most clearly seen in the Cherokee storyteller Gayle Ross's collection, a children's book with illustrations (by a Cherokee artist) of Rabbit as a cute, wide-eyed creature. The collection includes four additional stories not related by Mooney. In one, Rabbit tries to throw a noose around a duck, gets carried up into the air, falls into a hollow tree stump, and gets some children to let him out by singing to them. In another, "Rabbit Steals from Fox," Rabbit gets Fox's fish by playing dead in the road in three different places. Versions of this story appear in both Iroquois and African American folklore.[49] "Rabbit Sends Wolf to the Sunset" ends with the same joke as William J. Faulkner's "How the Cow Went under the Ground"; it is also the only one of the Cherokee Rabbit tales to involve an animal not indigenous to North America (the cow). The fourth Ross story not in Mooney's collection, "Rabbit Dances with the People," tells of how Rabbit steals the dance mask of a boy who is very popular with the girls.

Before attempting any more generalizations, it may be useful to compare the Rabbit stories documented among the Creeks around the turn of the century, that is, roughly contemporaneous with Mooney's collection from the Cherokees. The Creeks, though longstanding enemies of the Cherokee, occupied the territory contiguous to the Cherokee on the south, in Georgia and Alabama prior to Removal. Frank G. Speck compiled six Rabbit stories, among them the Turtle Race and the Tar Baby.[50] A third story is actually an elaborate sequel to the Tar Baby story, in which Rabbit has to escape first from a bag and then a hollow tree. "Rabbit Outwits Tie-Snake," in which Rabbit tricks two snakes into pulling on opposite ends of a grapevine, each thinking Rabbit is pulling the other end,[51] is actually a contest over water rights, like most versions of the Tar Baby story. Only one story, where Opossum gets Rabbit killed by telling him how to get some persimmons by butting his head against a persimmon tree, seems unrelated to other stories elsewhere.

The sixth story, in which Rabbit rains fire on Panther and then causes an ocean to spring up between them, conflates the Cherokee Rabbit versus Otter story (raining fire) and Deer versus Rabbit (making the ocean). In the Creek version Rabbit, not Deer, creates the ocean, and Panther, not Rabbit, ends up on the other side. It should be noted that "Panther" in these stories, often translated as "Maneater" or "Wildcat," refers to the southeastern American mountain lion—not an African animal.[52] Nevertheless, the motif of the wide ocean compels an acknowledgment of awareness of land on the other side. The theme of insurmountable separation was a resonant one for African slaves who experienced the Middle Passage.

The appearance of tobacco spitting in the African American Rabbit stories would appear to be an instance of Native American influence. Rabbit spits at the wolves in the Cherokee story—a way, as Ross points out, "to put a powerful curse on them."[53] In one of the Creek stories, Rabbit spits tobacco juice in Heron's eye when Heron sticks his head in the tree.[54] One might recall that this is what happens to Brer Wolf when he's at the door of Brer Rabbit's house, having killed his wife and children; Brer Rabbit spits tobacco at him to make his final escape.[55] Tobacco is an indigenous American plant, grown by the southeastern tribes and used for religious and ceremonial purposes.

The best known collection of African American Brer Rabbit stories, the Uncle Remus stories of Joel Chandler Harris, has been criticized and vilified for Harris's creation of the character of Uncle Remus, for Harris's exaggerated and inaccurate rendering of dialect, and, according to Bernard Wolfe, Harris's whitewashing of the "malevolent" character of Brer Rabbit himself.[56] A better comprehensive source is Richard M. Dorson's 1956 collection, *American Negro Folktales*, which includes seventeen Rabbit tales. But more useful in considering Indian influence is Edward C. L. Adams's folklore collection from South Carolina, *Tales of the Congaree*. First published in 1928, it reflects a picture of Brer Rabbit that has particular affinity with the Cherokee concept of Rabbit as messenger, singer, and dancer. An excellent recent collection is William J. Faulkner's posthumously published *The Days When the Animals Talked*, a group of stories told to Faulkner as a boy starting in 1900 by the former Virginia slave Simon Brown. The first part of the book is stories of slave life, and the second part consists of twenty-two Brer Rabbit stories. The stories, told to Faulkner in Gullah dialect,[57] are retold by Faulkner in standard English.

Lawrence W. Levine's discussion of Brer Rabbit as trickster in slave folklore ascribes to him a tripartite didactic function: role model for the slave, warning about the duplicity of others, and explication of a fatalist vision of the cosmos.[58] According to Levine, the Hare or Rabbit was the primary trickster figure in East Africa and Angola; he says the trickster

of the Yoruba, Ibo, and Edo was the Tortoise, and the Anansi spider trickster was prevalent in "much of West Africa including Ghana, Liberia, and
Sierra Leone."[59] Though Melville J. Herskovits's comment that "many
elements of the Uncle Remus stories are encountered in the sacred
myths" of Africa[60] has apparently gone unchallenged, Levine and Wolfe
have focused their readings of Brer Rabbit as satire on human behavior
and thus have paid scant attention to supernatural aspects of the stories.

Many tales obliquely refer to Brer Rabbit's avocation as a doctor. This
aspect of his character is not present in Faulkner's collection and appears
only once in Dorson's, where it is incorporated into the Tar Baby story.[61]
But it appears frequently in miscellaneous tales printed in the late nineteenth century. One such tale is Christenson's version of about who stole
the butter, wherein Brer Rabbit keeps going off ostensibly to deliver ba-
bies.[62] In another tale, also involving a joint farming venture with Brer
Wolf, Brer Rabbit "practices medicine" by disappearing while Wolf works,
though his profession is a scam.[63] Though Brer Rabbit may not actually
heal anybody in those tales, he appears to be a bona fide doctor in the story
where Brer Fox doesn't fool Brer Rabbit.[64] Furthermore, he actually kills
Mammy Witch Wise in the aforementioned tale—the ultimate feat of a
root doctor.[65]

The depiction of the supernatural in two of these miscellaneous tales
is more understandable when considered in this context. In one, all the
animals get together to store food for the winter in a house; Rabbit moves
in and scares them all away by making a noise so "outlandish . . . de beast-
ies all conclude . . . dat de Sperit, him bin tek persession er de house."[66]
In another tale, "Why Mr. Dog Runs Brer Rabbit," Mr. Dog's children,
after Mr. Dog has frozen his tail, bark "glory, glory" and "hallelujah,
hallelujah" while chasing Brer Rabbit.[67] Viewed in isolation, the supernatural motif in these two tales could be dismissed as insignificant or
satirical. But when juxtaposed with some of the Adams tales, they raise
interesting questions about transmission of African concepts of communication with spirits.

In the Red Hill Churchyard tale, Brer Rabbit is playing his fiddle in
a graveyard, the moon shining bright on the snow. All the animals, at his
sign, form a circle around the grave, and Bur Mockin'Bird starts to sing
along with the fiddle: "Dat mockin'bird an' dat rabbit—Lord, dey had
chunes floatin' all 'round on de night air. Dey could stand a chune on end,
grab it up an' throw it away an' ketch it an' bring it back an' hold it; an'
make dem chunes sound like dey was strugglin' to git away one minute,
an' de next dey sound like sump'n gittin' up close an' whisperin.'"[68] When
the music stops, Simon rises from the grave and holds a long conversa-

tion with the animals (especially the owls—"de ole folks always is say dey is dead folks"[69]). When they are finished talking, Bur Rabbit starts playing again; he steps back on the grave, and Simon is gone. Sterling Stuckey has commented at length on this story and its relation to the significance of the one-string violin in the Mali Empire and today among the Songhai of Upper Volta in the summoning of ancestral spirits. Stuckey also estimates that one out of ten slaves could play the fiddle, based on a study of the Hopeton plantation in Georgia.[70]

Adams tells a similar story, "The Dance of the Little Animals," in which Bur Rabbit ("He ain' no Christian") is playing his fiddle on Christmas in the moonlight and leads Bur Fox on a cross-country chase: "he jes tech [the fiddle] enough to wake dem hound up. . . . When Bur Fox pass 'long runnin' Bur Rabbit, den dem hound started to singin' an' cryin'. Dey sound like a choir." Bur Rabbit sits on a stump playing his fiddle and laughing as "dem hound had Bur Fox stretched like a string runnin' a race wid death."[71] This story echoes both the "glory hallelujah" baying of the dogs and two Faulkner stories in which Brer Rabbit sets the hounds on Brer Fox.[72]

Bur Rabbit's musical powers are central to all four of the Rabbit stories published by Adams. In "Bur Jonah's Goat," Bur Rabbit uses his fiddle to get Bur Wolf to sing a false confession that he stole the goat that Bur Rabbit stole.[73] As in the Cherokee tale of Rabbit and the turkeys and numerous other Brer Rabbit tales, the temptation to sing along is irresistible. What is clear in the Adams version is that this power is tied to the fiddle.

The fourth and final Rabbit story in Adams tells how Bur Rabbit gets back at Bur Spider for cutting his web loose and dropping Bur Rabbit in the river. When they get to the dance they are going to, Bur Rabbit sings a song all about what Bur Spider did: "he make all de gals 'shame' (for makin' great miration over Bur Spider) an' dey turn dey back on Bur Spider an' wouldn't have nothin' to do wid him."[74] This story is significant in two ways. First, the spider was one of the primary tricksters of West Africa: Anansi, rendered as "An Nancy" in some American transcriptions.[75] Clearly, in African American folklore,[76] the rabbit has prevailed over the spider as the primary trickster, even though far more slaves came from western Africa than from eastern Africa where the rabbit trickster is more prevalent. Second, the rabbit prevails over the spider in this story because he possesses the power of song and dance. The contest between Rabbit and Spider here invites comparison to the Creek contest between Rabbit and Panther and the Cherokee contest between Rabbit and Deer— all seemingly allegories of power struggles among the supernatural.

The story of the rabbit and the spider, less than one page long, is a historical narrative of the transmission of spiritual power. Several trickster figures crossed over from Africa in the Middle Passage, but through the fragmentation and reassemblage of multiple voices that one would expect in intercultural oral transmissions, it is the rabbit who prevailed among the significant African animal spirits in the southeastern United States—he holds the power of music and dance that is the key to communicating with the spirit world both among Africans and among Native Americans.[77] And it is the Adams stories in which the consistent similarity with the Cherokee Rabbit appears: the rabbit trickster as musician and dancer.

Herskovits says that the African American animal tales "indicate that the body of African mythology and folktales has been carried over in even less disturbed fashion than has hitherto been considered the case. The changes that have occurred understandably reflect the flora, fauna, and other elements in the everyday experience of the Negroes in their new habitat. The stories also are changed, in that the supernatural figures among the characters are no longer vested with the power and forms of gods, as they are in African mythologies."[78]

Though the power of African supernatural figures may have been impaired or changed form, as shapeshifting tricksters are wont to do, the Adams Rabbit stories would seem to contest Herskovits's latter assertion and its restatement in Levine's assertion that "divine tricksters such as the Dahomean Legba or the Yoruban Eshu and Orunmila did not survive the transplantation of Africans to the United States and the slave's adaptation to Christian religious forms."[79] On the contrary, these tricksters *evolved* to construct the Brer Rabbit described by Bernard Wolfe and Richard Levine as an antihero of resistance to the slaves' masters, personified as the dupes Wolf, Fox, Alligator, and Bear. This Brer Rabbit is not as "weak" and "relatively powerless" as Levine sees the African and African American animal tricksters.[80] But insofar as the stories reflect new "flora, fauna, and other elements," this can be seen as true in the Brer Rabbit stories in general. Most of them involve tricks on Brer Fox, Brer Bear, or Brer Wolf—clearly more American than African predators. Brer Possum also figures in a number of the stories. Many of them involve farming such as the slaves were engaged in. Faulkner's (and the Cherokee) story of how the cow went underground is only one example. Of Faulkner's twenty-two stories, four involve cultivation: two of peanuts (pinders), one of corn, and one of things rabbits like, such as collards, turnips, and carrots. There are many versions, in Dorson and elsewhere, of Brer Rabbit getting some other animal to do all the farm work for him.[81]

Though the Cherokees cultivated crops, their Rabbit stories, except for the cow that went underground, do not include any of these tales of farming one-upmanship that are so prevalent in the African American stories. The story in which Brer Rabbit uses another animal as his riding horse is also more African American both in the sense that it doesn't appear in Cherokee or Creek folklore and in the sense that it is a story of dominance and submission.[82] Whatever the sources may have been in African folklore, or even in Mr. McGregor's garden, these stories are concerned with the politics of oppression on the plantation and during Reconstruction. Brer Rabbit seems to become more human in the stories in which he is dealing with oppression through guile, subterfuge, and revenge. One could argue that a divine trickster plays tricks more often for entertainment than for survival. Brer Rabbit in this role reflects the Ojibwa critic and novelist Gerald Vizenor's conception, more than the Cherokee rabbit does, of the divine trickster as the destabilizer of political tyranny.[83]

By the time Simon Brown was telling Brer Rabbit stories to William J. Faulkner, the politics of Reconstruction were there to be told as well. "Brer Rabbit's Protest Meeting"[84] is an allegory about voting rights in the Reconstruction era: Brer Rabbit calls a meeting to discuss the oppression of the short-tailed animals, but Brer Lion takes over and kicks the short-tailed animals out of the meeting house. Brer Rabbit calls on the Lord for deliverance: "one day, by and by, He will answer our prayer, and that's for sure." Simon Brown's Brer Rabbit was an evolution of Wolfe's "malevolent rabbit" into what Radin would term a culture hero. Faulkner says, "Brer Rabbit was virtuous, on the side of God."[85] Simon Brown's Brer Rabbit not only ties the tiger to a tree and distributes food and water to all the animals, he rescues all the captives from the dragon's lair, slays the dragon *and* the lion, goes back for the dragon's treasure, and assigns Judge Hooting Owl to divide the treasure "among all the little creatures who deserved it."[86]

Gates has demonstrated the transformation—into the African American signifying monkey—of the divine humanoid West African trickster Esu, "sole messenger of the gods, . . . he who interprets the will of the gods to man; he who carries the desires of man to the gods . . . guardian of the crossroads, master of style and of stylus, the phallic god of generation and fecundity, master of that elusive, mystical barrier that separates the divine world from the profane."[87] It seems clear from the Adams stories and supporting evidence from other stories cited above that similar divine powers were transmuted into Brer Rabbit. This process was most likely influenced by contact in the southeastern United States with the Native American Rabbit, messenger and singing, dancing entertainer to the people.

Certainly it would have been easier, in terms of religious and political oppression, for slaves to attribute the power of calling the dead from their graves to a fiddle-playing rabbit than a fiddle-playing Yoruba trickster with a large phallus. And in turn, the rabbit's similarity to the black preacher was perhaps best masked. Just as, in Faulkner's story, young Simon Brown steps from behind the rabbit persona to rain fire on the patrollers, the black preacher in African American folklore sometimes acted like Brer Rabbit. One verse in an old African American folksong, dating back to at least 1836, goes: "Some folks say that a preacher won't steal / I caught two in my cornfield / Preachin' and prayin' all the time / And pullin' my melons off the vine."[88] Like Brer Rabbit, black preachers might do what they have to do to survive.

Mooney's speculation that many of the Cherokee animal stories are "worn down fragments of ancient sacred traditions"[89] could be applied as well to the African stories. But whereas the African stories probably have involved more breaking down, reassembling, and assimilation of new cultural material, some of the Cherokee stories may well be more like "worn down fragments" due to the lesser degree of dislocation and rupture of oral tradition. Certainly the Cherokees have suffered severe depredations from the white invaders, but even in the forced Removal to Oklahoma they have been able to maintain a cultural unity that African tribal units have not. Thus the ancient attributions of specific roles and characteristics to specific animal identities has probably been maintained in Cherokee lore. As Ross says: "Each animal had its place. Buzzard was known as a great doctor, while Turtle knew the secrets of conjuring. Frog was the marshall at the council house. Rabbit's job was to be the messenger. He was to spread important news. He was also a good singer and often led in the dance. But Rabbit was the leader of them all in mischief, and his bold ways were always getting him into trouble."[90] Just as Raven is the primary trickster in the Pacific Northwest and Coyote in the Southwest, these roles seem fairly stable among eastern tribes. If the Cherokee rabbit seems more childlike than the African American Brer Rabbit, this aspect is consistent with the relative status of the Cherokee rabbit in comparison to the African American trickster rabbit bearing all that trans-Atlantic baggage on his shoulders. The mixing that has occurred in the African Diaspora has lent a certain dynamism to the African American trickster stories that is not, overall, inconsistent with the destablizing and yet timeless role of the rabbit trickster in the Cherokee stories.

Interesting as these interpretations are, it is risky to make too many generalizations on the basis of the work of a few storytellers and transcribers. Mooney's talent was as an ethnographer, not a storyteller. As in Richard Dorson's work, a lot seems to have gotten lost in the sometimes cryptic retelling. Stories vary, and though the African American rabbit may seem to be more dynamic than the Cherokee rabbit, neither can it be said that the Cherokee stories are frozen in time, or in an "ethnographic present." One of the tales in particular, "The Rabbit and the Possum After a Wife,"[91] depicts a hare-brained scheme that is profoundly expressive of Native American distrust of authority. When Rabbit abuses his position as messenger, a position of great fiduciary responsibility, to seduce a woman and create general mayhem if not war, the storyteller implicitly makes fun of the people for listening to such a fool—he comes to town and says everyone should get married and they do it; he says it's time to start fighting and everybody starts fighting. Obviously not a children's story, this one is not included in Ross's book. There is no way to estimate its age, but it was being told at the turn of the century when repercussions were still being felt from the violent internal political conflict engendered by the events leading up to Removal in 1839.

At the turn of the century, the Cherokees may have been disaffected with messengers, but southern African Americans, according to W. E. B. Du Bois, still had faith in their preachers, despite their human shortcomings: "It was a terrific social revolution, and yet some traces were retained of the former group life, and the chief remaining institution was the Priest or Medicine-Man."[92] The preachers were central to the only sort of community organization available to former slaves; they did not have the same degree of retained infrastructure of tribal council meetings and traditional dances that, despite efforts at suppression, have continued to be central to many Native American tribal cultures (which is not to deny that black churches, especially in the South, have provided a similar, though tribally syncretic, infrastructure). We see the community dances and council meetings in many of the Cherokee Rabbit stories. Community meetings are rare in Brer Rabbit stories, aside from those of Simon Brown. But Brown's stories, told to Faulkner during the same era in which Mooney was transcribing the tale of Rabbit and Possum after a wife, express a faith in leadership and justice that is the butt of the joke in the Cherokee story.

Certainly Faulkner's Brer Rabbit, reflecting Faulkner's background as a pastor and theologian, is a more righteous character than the "malevolent rabbit" of Bernard Wolfe's analysis. In stories other than Faulkner's, Brer Rabbit's actions are often nothing less than despicable. He serves as a cultural antihero, first for slaves, then for southern blacks of the Jim Crow era, and finally for the urban black migration, much as the myths constructed around the James/Younger gang and other outlaws who "lit out for the Territory" created antiheroes of the rural westward migration. Though Cherokees were forcibly removed from their home-land, the Cherokee nation remains the largest tribe in the United States, still maintaining two geographical cultural centers—in the Carolinas and in Oklahoma—and the need for the ongoing articulation of resistance against a dominant culture represented by a cultural antihero has been less compelling. The Cherokee rabbit is in a sense outside of time, a crea-ture of the past gone across time's ocean: both a nostalgic reminder of tradition and a warning against vanity, double-dealing, and gratuitous rabble-rousing.

Animal tales in all cultures are probably often at some level satiri-cal commentary about human events and the human condition. Like all literature, some animal stories are timeless, and some reflect particular historical conditions and events. Often, they do both. The same figure can appear at times to be a human in animal fur and a waistcoat and at other times a giant who creates an ocean at the wave of a paw. The su-pernatural elements in the Rabbit stories constitute a common thread that runs through the Cherokee singer, dancer, and messenger, the Afri-can fiddler raising the dead, the wily and thieving agricultural Brer Rab-bit, and the defender of truth and justice for all the short-tailed animals. The rabbit may be malevolent and vengeful at times, but in the church-yard or in the dance circle, he can call up the power of the ancestors.

## Notes

1. Coco Fusco, *English Is Broken Here: Notes on Cultural Fusion in the Americas* (New York: New Press, 1995), 27, 71. See also bell hooks, "Eating the Other," in *Black Looks: Race and Representation* (Boston: South End Press, 1992), 21–40, esp. 30–33.

2. Henry Louis Gates Jr., *The Signifying Monkey: A Theory of African-American Literary Criticism* (New York: Oxford University Press, 1988).

3. Fusco, *English Is Broken Here*, 34.

4. Ibid., 22.

5. Ibid., 30.

6. Contemporary folklorists, of course, acknowledge the pervasiveness of borrowings of cultural motifs, but my focus is on the ramifications of such borrowings for multicultural studies, not for the study of folklore per se.

7. William Loren Katz, *Black Indians* (New York: Atheneum, 1986), cited in bell hooks, "Revolutionary Renegades: Native Americans, African Amer-icans, and Black Indians," in *Black Looks*, 194. For a more conservative esti-mate see F. James Davis, *Who Is Black? One Nation's Definition* (University Park: Pennsylvania State University Press, 1991). Davis estimates that as of

the 1980 census one quarter of African Americans had some Indian ancestry (21).

8. hooks, *Black Looks*, 189–90.

9. There are many versions of the Tar Baby story, but the only significant difference between Indian and African American versions would seem to be the characterization of the tar baby as a seductive female in some of the latter. Cherokee versions describe a "tar wolf" (see James Mooney, trans., *Myths of the Cherokee* [Washington, D.C.: Government Printing Office, 1900]). The seductress version is consistent with the overall development of Rabbit from a being who was not consistently gendered in early Cherokee stories (see Mooney's second version of "The Rabbit and the Tar Wolf," ibid., 272–73, for a female rabbit) to something of a ladies' man, at least in his own mind.

10. One example is A. Gerber, "Uncle Remus Traced to the Old World," *Journal of American Folk-Lore* 6 (1893): 244–57.

11. Aurelio M. Espinosa, "Notes on the Origin and History of the Tar-Baby Story," *Journal of American Folk-Lore* 43 (1930): 129–224.

12. And to give all voices equal attention, one should note that the Cherokee scholars Jack F. Kilpatrick and Anna G. Kilpatrick assert that the Tar Baby story was "borrowed from the Indians by Negro slaves" (*Friends of Thunder: Folktales of the Oklahoma Cherokees* [1964; rpt., Norman: University of Oklahoma Press, 1995], 35).

13. Maria Leach, ed., *Funk and Wagnalls Standard Dictionary of Folklore, Mythology, and Legend* (New York: Funk and Wagnalls, 1972), 918.

14. Ibid., 799.

15. Alan Dundes, "African Tales among the North American Indians," *Journal of American Folklore* 29.3 (1965): 207–19, quote on 210.

16. Ibid., 218–19.

17. See, for example, the paragraph on duping two animals into a tug-of-war where Dundes seems to be referring to Aarne saying the motif index clearly proves African origin but then says the tale type index is misleading in implying European origin (ibid., 213–14).

18. Paul Radin, *The Trickster: A Study in American Indian Mythology* (New York: Philosophical Library, 1956), 131.

19. Richard M. Dorson, *American Negro Folktales* (1956; rpt., Greenwich, Conn.: Fawcett, 1967), 79, for reference to the motif index; the Alligator story is in Abigail Christenson, *Afro-American Folk Lore* (Boston: J. G. Cupples, 1892; rpt., New York: Negro Universities Press, 1969), 54–57, where the feud with Alligator starts at a dance. Dorson's story is rabbit and bear.

20. Gayle Ross, *How Rabbit Tricked Otter and Other Cherokee Trickster Stories* (New York: Harper Collins, 1994), 13–17.

21. William J. Faulkner, *The Days When the Animals Talked: Black-American Folktales and How They Came to Be* (Trenton, N.J.: Africa World Press, 1993), 167.

22. Ibid., 32.

23. Kilpatrick and Kilpatrick, *Friends of Thunder*, 42–43.

24. Ibid., 46.

25. Georgia Writers' Project/Work Project Administration, *Drums and Shadows: Survival Studies among the Georgia Coastal Negroes* (1940; rpt., Athens: University of Georgia Press, 1986), 157. See also William J. Faulkner's story "The Ways of a Witch," in *The Days When the Animals Talked*, 46–51.

26. Emma M. Backus, "Why the People Tote Brer Rabbit Foot in Their Pocket," in "Tales of the Rabbit from Georgia Negroes," *Journal of American Folk-Lore* 12.45 (Apr.–June 1899): 108–15.

27. Jack D. Forbes, *Africans and Native Americans: The Language of Race and the Evolution of Red-Black Peoples*, 2d ed. (Urbana: University of Illinois Press, 1993), chap. 1, esp. 17–18 on bananas.

28. According to Mooney, who got his information from an estimate by the North Carolina governor at the time, in 1755 Cherokee "warriors" numbered 2,590, and the number of Catawba men had "dwindled" to 240 (*Myths of the Cherokee*, 39). Because of their adherence to their sacred traditions and stories, the Cherokee were described by Adair in 1775 as "a nest of apostate hornets."
In 1840 about a hundred Catawba, "nearly all that were left," moved in with the eastern Cherokee (the ones who had escaped Removal), but conflicts developed, and most of them "began to drift back to their own homes, until, in 1852, there were only about a dozen remaining among the Cherokee" (ibid., 165).

29. Theda Perdue, *Slavery and the Evolution of Cherokee Society, 1540–1866* (Knoxville: University of Tennessee Press, 1979), 19–25.

30. Mooney, *Myths of the Cherokee*, 233.

31. Ibid., 163.

32. Perdue, *Slavery and the Evolution of Cherokee Society*, 42.

33. Edward C. L. Adams, *Tales of the Congaree*, ed. Robert G. O'Meally (Chapel Hill: University of North Carolina Press, 1987), 120–21.

34. Camara Laye, *The Dark Child: The Autobiography of an African Boy* (New York: Farrar, Straus and Giroux, 1954), 74.

35. See Frank G. Speck and Leonard Broom, in collaboration with Will West Long, *Cherokee Dance and Drama* (1951; rpt., Norman: University of Oklahoma Press, 1983).

36. Mooney, *Myths of the Cherokee*, 273. Unless otherwise noted, all accounts of Cherokee Rabbit tales are from Mooney.

37. Mooney, "How the Wildcat Caught the Gobbler," in ibid., 269–70. A version of this story appears in Ponca folklore (see Radin, *Trickster*, 129).

38. Speck and Broom, *Cherokee Dance and Drama*, 92.

39. Mooney, "The Rabbit Escapes from the Wolves," in *Myths of the Cherokee*, 274.

40. Speck and Broom, "Booger or Mask Dance," in *Cherokee Dance and Drama*, 25–39.

41. Mooney, *Myths of the Cherokee*, 270.

42. According to Mooney, this story "is found with nearly every tribe from Nova Scotia to the Pacific" (ibid., 234).

43. Ibid., 277.

44. Ibid., 274.

45. Jack and Anna Kilpatrick agree with James Mooney that the story of Rabbit killing Flint is "a detail leached out of an eroded national cosmology" exemplifying the "fundamentally Iroquoian material of the Cherokee ethos"—a story in which "one senses a dramatic psychological shift from the sun-lit thought-world of the Southeast to that of the gray and granitic North" (*Friends of Thunder*, 61–62). See James Mooney, "Cherokee and Iroquois Parallels," *Journal of American Folk-Lore* 2.4 (1889): 67.

46. Mooney, "Cherokee and Iroquois Parallels," 262.

47. Ibid., 63–64.

48. The Kilpatricks discuss Rabbit's relationship to the more human trickster figure Tseg'sin' and Tseg'sin's relationship, in turn, to the Negro Jack (*Friends of Thunder*, 62, 99).

49. Dorson, *American Negro Folktales*, 91–94; Joseph Bruchac, *Iroquois Stories: Heroes and Heroines, Monsters and Magic* (Freedom, Calif.: Crossing Press, 1985), 74–78. The Cherokee are linguistically and historically related to the Iroquois. The Iroquois story about Rabbit and Fox is much more elaborate than Ross's version; Rabbit exhibits extraordinary shapeshifting and conjuring skills and ultimately dupes Fox into eating a tree.

50. Frank G. Speck, "The Creek Indians of Taskigi Town," in *A Creek Sourcebook*, ed. William Sturtevant (New York: Garland, 1987), 149–57.

51. This is a story that Dundes claims is African; see n.16 above.

52. Kilpatrick and Kilpatrick, *Friends of Thunder*, 30–33. The Kilpatricks also note that Maneater often has human qualities in Cherokee stories. Maneater replaces the wolf as the dupe in the version here cited of how the cow went underground.

53. Ross, *How Rabbit Tricked Otter*, 28.

54. Speck, "Creek Indians," 153.

55. Christenson, *Afro-American Folk Lore*, 34.

56. Bernard Wolfe, "Uncle Remus and the Malevolent Rabbit: 'Takes a Limber-Toe Gemmun fer ter Jump Jim Crow,'" *Commentary* 8 (1949): 31–41.

57. Faulkner, *The Days When the Animals Talked*, 7.

58. Or as Lawrence W. Levine says, Brer Rabbit functions "as black slave, as white master, as irrational force" (*Black Culture and Black Consciousness: African American Folk Thought from Slavery to Freedom* [New York: Oxford University Press, 1977], 120–21).

59. Ibid., 103.

60. Melville J. Herskovits, *The Myth of the Negro Past* (1941; rpt., Boston: Beacon Press, 1958), 75.

61. Dorson, *American Negro Folktales*, 75.

62. Christenson, *Afro-American Folk Lore*, 73–80.

63. Emma M. Backus, "Tales of the Rabbit from Georgia Negroes," *Journal of American Folk-Lore* 12.45 (Apr.–June 1899): 108.

64. Emma M. Backus, "Folk-Tales from Georgia," *Journal of American Folk-Lore* 13.48 (Jan.–Mar. 1900): 24.

65. Backus, "Tales of the Rabbit from Georgia Negroes," 109.

66. Charles C. Jones Jr., *Negro Myths from the Georgia Coast* (1888; rpt., Detroit: Singing Tree Press/Book Tower, 1969), 52.

67. Backus, "Tales of the Rabbit from Georgia Negroes," 112.

68. Adams, *Tales of the Congaree*, 235.

69. Ibid., 236.

70. Sterling Stuckey, *Slave Culture: Nationalist Theory and the Foundations of Black America* (New York: Oxford University Press, 1987), 17–22.

71. Adams, *Tales of the Congaree*, 240–41.

72. Faulkner, "Brer Rabbit Keeps His Word," in *The Days When the Animals Talked*, 95; "Brer Fox Meets Mister Trouble," in *The Days When the Animals Talked*, 137.

73. Adams, *Tales of the Congaree*, 237–38.

74. Ibid., 242.

75. Georgia Writers' Project, *Drums and Shadows*, 108, 169.

76. Though I use the term "African American folklore" here, it should be understood that this body of folklore is syncretic in nature. Indeed, the thesis of this essay is that it is pervaded by Indian influences. Nevertheless, it is important to distinguish a general African American cultural entity in the United States from more specifically black Indian cultural entities such as the Lumbees, and for that reason I have generally avoided use of "Black Indian" or similar terms in this discussion.

77. The spider is, of course, not unknown in American Indian literature; Spider Woman is a major figure in the American southwest. But Spider Woman is totally unlike the lecherous Anansi. This author is aware of one Cherokee Spider story and two Muskogee (Creek) Spider stories, all appearing in the children's anthology *Spider Spins a Story: Fourteen Legends from Native America*, ed. Jill Max (pseud. for Kelly Bennett and Ronnie Davidson) (Flagstaff, Ariz.: Rising Moon, 1997). The spider is female in all three stories. Water Spider is bringer of fire to the people in the Cherokee story, and of these three southeastern-origin stories, it is the one, due to the water-crossing motif, that is most provocative of speculation about African influence.

78. Herskovits, *Myth of the Negro Past*, 275.

79. Levine, *Black Culture and Black Consciousness*, 103.

80. Ibid.

81. Though corn and peanuts have been important food sources in Africa since the seventeenth century or earlier, they are indigenous to America, having reached Africa most likely by way of Brazil. See Forbes, *Africans and Native Americans*, 60.

82. The riding horse story appears in folklore of the Maroons, escaped African–Native American slaves in the Caribbean (see Robert Perez, "Brer Rabbit and Ba Nansi: Were They Shipmates?" paper presented at the University of California at Riverside, Winter Conference in History, January 10, 1996). This story seems to echo the closing words of Maya Deren in *Divine Horsemen: The Living Gods of Haiti* (New York: McPherson and Company, 1953), 262, describing an episode of Voudoun possession: "the journey around is long

and hard, alike for the strong horse, alike for the great rider." Elsewhere Deren asserts that "the African culture in Haiti was waved by the Indian culture which, in the Petro cult, provided the Negroes with divinities sufficiently aggressive (as was not true of the divinities of the generally stabilized African kingdoms) to be the moral force behind the revolution. In a sense, the Indians took their revenge on the white man through the Negro" (11).

Perhaps the most singular contemporary retelling of the riding horse story is contained in Toni Morrison's *Tar Baby* (New York: Plume Penguin, 1982), wherein the protagonist, Son, a black man from Florida who is also Brer Rabbit, escapes into the swamps of the Caribbean Isle de Chevaliers to run with the blind ghosts who "gallop; they race those horses like angels all over the hills where the rain forest is" (306).

83. Vizenor is a prolific critic and editor, but he has perhaps most fully explored his concept of the trickster in two of his novels, *Griever: An American Monkey King in China* (Normal: Illinois State University Fiction Collective Series, 1987) and *The Trickster of Liberty: Tribal Heirs to a Wild Baronage* (Minneapolis: University of Minnesota Press, 1988).

84. Faulkner, *The Days When the Animals Talked*, 115–21.

85. Ibid., 6.

86. Ibid., 84. The role of the owl in this tale is evidence, perhaps even more so than the dragon, of European American influence: the owl in both African and Native American cosmogony is a bad omen and messenger of death.

87. Gates, *Signifying Monkey*, 6.

88. Alan Lomax, "Part 4: The Negro South," in his *Folk Songs of North America* (New York: Doubleday, 1960), 445–595, quote on 509.

89. Mooney, "Cherokee and Iroquois Parallels," 34.

90. Ross, *How Rabbit Tricked Otter*, 6–7.

91. Mooney, "Cherokee and Iroquois Parallels," 278.

92. W. E. B. Du Bois, "Of the Faith of the Fathers," in *The Souls of Black Folk* (New York: Penguin/Signet, 1969), 210–25, quote on 216.

# PART 2

# African–Native American Captivity and Slave Narratives

JOHN SEKORA

## 3  Briton Hammon, the Indian Captivity Narrative, and the African American Slave Narrative

American slaves thought themselves the most forsaken of God's children, Frederick Douglass often remarked, until they met American Indians. To Douglass, African American writing took up two issues—freedom and identity—and sought to decolonize both. To us, the slave and the Native are ironically important—liminal figures who resist the master narratives of Early America, those scripts that inscribe them in silence. They occupy the margins that define a center, margins through which literary genres and physical safety are keenly debated. For the same acts of self-writing, self-disclosing, and self-authorizing by which they lay claim to their own lives are those by which they endanger those lives. Self-revelation becomes self-endangerment. As ironic as anything is the intertwining of Native American and African American experience that would give us the slave narrative—the form Douglass brought to its epitome.

Since the Enlightenment every age has viewed itself as somehow unique, special, or distinctive. Voices of every generation have declared that they stand at some pivotal point in the movement of human history. And as surely, later generations have declared that their ancestors were wrong. Are we not bound together to testify—if not shout—that something extraordinary, something distinctive is at work in our own time, if only in the modest, academic enterprise of biography and autobiography?

We can demonstrate with ease (at least to our contemporaries) that we are present at the creation of a new understanding of life-writing. Speaking of autobiographical studies generally, James Olney has remarked the sudden, unpredicted, and unprecedented appearance of a vast number of papers and monographs on the form. Speaking of life stories by and about women, Carolyn Heilbrun has noted "an explosion" of new books and new theories since 1970. Speaking of African American writing, Arnold Rampersad marks the passing of a heroic age of autobiography into a different but present age of biography. Speaking of that distinctively American form of life-writing, the slave narrative, Darwin Turner and I have called attention to the plethora of critical studies published since 1969—far more, that is, in the last twenty-five years than in the previous 150.[1]

Perhaps we are all encircled by generational chauvinism. Equally likely, however, we are onto something. One measure of the power of autobiographical study is the intensity of resistance it has spurred among our colleagues. While some traditional critics dismiss autobiography as a minor form, hardly deserving of the honorific of *genre,* some contemporary theorists dismiss all genre criticism as thoroughly discredited. Others say the very notion of autobiography contradicts the concept of a transmissible form or tradition. Similar arguments abound about African American writing. Rampersad reports challenges to his use of European theories to explain African American lives. Although some historians see only factual value in the slave narratives, some literary critics would segregate them as an ur-literary form. In one of the baldest dismissals of the narratives, several critics have denied them any distinctive place because, they say, all American writing deals with bondage. What all this suggests is that life-writing is disturbing—and to an unusual degree. Disturbance breeds resistance, and resistance provides more glib answers than articulated (and difficult) questions.

Few forms of life-writing have been more disturbing than the slave narrative. And few have met more resistance. Indeed, one can say that after the Civil War slave narratives were subjected to cultural repression, a repression that has only recently and partially abated. Notwithstanding twenty-five years of scholarly activity, something important remains—a profound categorical uncertainty. The issue is particularly pressing because virtually every student of African American writing now seeks to use the narratives as a starting point for one type of study or another. Rampersad argues eloquently that "no single genre holds sway over a culture as powerfully as does autobiography over Afro-American literary expression" and traces the autobiographical hold back to the power of the narratives.[2] Describing the impulse for her own writing, Alice Walker states simply, "Our literary tradition is based on the slave narratives."[3] It is no detraction from the herculean studies of recent years to note that almost all begin with what is essentially a conclusion. What is now needed is to discover and to explain how the genre of the slave narrative emerged from an earlier historical context in which the literary category of "slave narrative"—name and practice alike—did not exist. Yet the question of autobiography is compassed by others. Does the category slave narrative signify one thing or several? Is it a unified genre? If so, around what principle or practice? From what earlier African American and/or Anglo-American forms did it emerge? And, if not autobiography, what else can it be?

Fully to answer such questions would require a powerful union of theory and history. The ideal account of the slave narrative would, I presume, mediate between the formal analysis of individual texts and a doubled, decade-by-decade history of narrative forms and of the evolution of social life in America, particularly the institution of slavery. Far more modestly, I propose here to look at one moment in that history in order to suggest that the type of question one asks largely determines the quality of answer, and that all such questions are more problematic than was once believed. For in American writing the slave narrative is unique; it resembles other forms, but other forms do not resemble it. Slavery was indeed the great divider of human beings, one from another. And we must know what we do not know about the slave voice in the slave narrative.

---

How black writing began in America has been a topic of growing interest for several decades. In a major example, we know that the work held to be the earliest slave narrative, by Briton Hammon, was published in Boston in 1760 by Green and Russell. Years of speculation notwithstanding, we know virtually nothing else about Hammon, his printers, the circumstances of publication, or the social climate his narrative entered. Even the mere fact of publication is a thorny issue. For, according to most historians of early America, the mid-eighteenth century was a harsh time for *all* people of color—slave, free black, or Native American.

From the early 1740s distrust between white settlers and Natives in most colonies had deteriorated beyond a tense contest for land. Even before the outbreak of open warfare in the middle of the next decade, white political figures frequently denied that there could be anything like a friendly or peaceable tribe. With the coming of actual war, such attitudes hardened into the genocidal. Toward free blacks the policy was less extermination than malevolent neglect. The tiny groups of free blacks in, say, Charleston or Boston were threatened by greater fertility of slaves in the South and by a large influx of Africans into the North. Where skilled labor had previously been found in creole and free black communities, now it was being cultivated exclusively among bound slaves. In the large towns of the North, increased numbers of slaves meant that all labor was cheaper to secure, and a new young slave was much more profitable than an old one. In such circumstances, "freedom" often went to the old who had outlived their strength; "freedom" meant having to earn one's living after one was too infirm to work. Often driven from their previous settlements, "free" blacks were confined to woods or hovels on the outskirts, left to die out of sight.[4]

Attitudes toward slaves were likewise undergoing swift change. Results were checkered, since each region adjusted differently to a rapid growth in the slave population. In the Carolina and Georgia low country the increase was so great, whites said, that they were in danger of being inundated. In *Black Majority* (1974), Peter Wood has described the white response as a brutal, inflexible system grounded in fear, separation, and surveillance. In the region of the Chesapeake, planters expressed a similar but more moderate anxiety over the fact that for them slavery was going well. They were wary because their slaves were living well enough and long enough to reproduce themselves. A higher birthrate created, for the first time in colonial history, a balance of males and females and further chances for families and reproduction. Economic growth was most pronounced above the Chesapeake in the northern colonies; with that growth came the call for more bond laborers. Until the 1740s, the North had been least interested in the direct import of slaves and most interested in assimilating those already arrived. During the next twenty years, however, many more large shipments of slaves arrived than ever before, reaching a peak in the late 1750s, when a wartime blockade stopped the supply of white indentured servants from Ireland and Germany. The new numbers halted or delayed whatever assimilation had been going on and gave rise in its stead to novel legal codes and increased vigilance. In his "Observations Concerning the Increase of Mankind" in 1751, Benjamin Franklin probably spoke for all regions in his concern for the future, for slavery had already "blacken'd half America."[5] Elsewhere he had written of a curious interplay of settlers' attitudes toward Indians and toward slaves. Although Franklin the printer and bookseller did not pursue the point, other booksellers eventually did. But that is to get ahead of the story. For 1760, the question is clear and stark: Why were hostile or indifferent white printers willing to invest in an African American subject?

Perhaps not all were indifferent. An informal, speculative consensus holds that the work was done by some radical printer, an early Tom Paine, with an incipient sense of egalitarianism. This notion is inspired by the nineteenth-century crest of the abolitionist movement, led as it was by such printing families as the Phillips, the Lundys, and the Garrisons. The elder John Phillips was first apprentice, then partner, to a printer in Charleston. His son John was the first mayor of Boston. His son Wendell was the noted abolitionist and an associate of Douglass and Garrison. Lundy was the printer and publisher of *The Genius of Universal Emancipation*. Garrison, who had been an apprentice to Lundy, said that abolition depended upon printers, who would "scatter tracts, like raindrops, over the land, on the subject of slavery."[6] William Wells Brown said the happiest months of his early life were spent as apprentice to Elijah Lovejoy at the *St. Louis Times*.[7] Much earlier, Samuel Sewall, one of Boston's earliest printers, became a judge of the superior court (and later, chief justice) and while on the bench published *The Selling of Joseph: A Memorial* (1700), a record of a slave sale and probably the earliest antislavery document in America. (The pamphlet was printed by Bartholomew Green, grandfather of John Green, who in his turn printed Briton Hammon.) Printing as an occupation likely produced on both sides of the Atlantic more activists for abolition than any other calling.

The eighteenth-century situation, nonetheless, was largely different. Green and Russell were not radical printers. Boston did not in fact possess a radical or underground or opposition press in 1760—nothing like those in place at the time in London or Paris. The story of Briton Hammon was published because of a peculiar set of circumstances obtaining at the beginning of the decade. These can be simplified into four: (1) the impact of the Seven Years War, particularly upon the economy of Boston; (2) the singular appeal for the moment of the captivity form in which Hammon appears; (3) the social status of Hammon's printers; and (4) Hammon himself, considered in terms of his age, his owner, his education, and his position in a system of domestic slavery. Because the subject is large, what follows will be but part of a part—the role of the captivity narrative and its influence upon later black writing.

In retrospect it may seem paradoxical that the first narrative by an American slave should be a tale of *Indian* captivity—but only in retrospect. From the eighteenth-century perspective it seems inevitable. For if the story of a black man or woman was to be told at all, it would necessarily be shaped into a popular form. No form was more popular than the captivity narrative, and no figure loomed larger in the colonial imagination than the Native American. Of the four narratives published between 1680 and 1720 that could legitimately be called "best-sellers," three were captivities (the other was *Pilgrim's Progress*). Northeastern readers between 1740 and 1760, when they sought literary and historical fare, turned not to essays or poetry but to descriptions of actual life in the new land: travel books, captivity narratives, and Indian treaties. A typical mid-century American bookshelf, according to Lawrence Wroth, was loaded down with accounts of Indian negotiations and the popular captivities.[8] Compared with dry-as-dust histories, these were expansive works, works to stretch the imagination yet of undoubted practical value. Pushing the imagination ever westward, they described the large and potent nation represented by the colonies and sought to bring accord and coherence to the whole. They were of use, too, in the ideological construction of the American myth, for booksellers used them to convey alternating attitudes toward Native Americans. Accounts of Native treaties showed them in noble mien; the captivities displayed their putative savagery. The cruelty described in the one justified violating the treaties described in the other. This ambiguity on the part of the educated would play as important a role in sustaining slavery as in reducing the Native American population.

Historians have traced this division to the last decades of the seventeenth century, making it coterminous with the captivity narrative itself. From its beginnings the captivity narrative had provided a theologically powerful as well as physically useful version of Manifest Destiny. The short title of one of Cotton Mather's tracts suggests the formula at its most succinct: *Humiliations Follow'd with Deliverances* (1697). English settlers might be thwarted or humbled, yet such reverses would be merely temporary, for Providence would surely deliver them to glory. The subtitle suggests the mythology of the genre and its influence on later narratives: *A Brief Discourse on the Matter and Method of That Humiliation Which Could be an Hopeful Symptom of Our Deliverance from Calamity. Accompanied and Accommodated with a Narrative of a Notable Deliverance Lately Received by Some English Captives, from the Hands of Cruel Indians. And Some Improvements of That Narrative. Whereto Is Added a Narrative of Hannah Swain, Containing a Great Many Wonderful Passages, Relating to Her Captivity and Deliverance.* Another tract printed in Boston by Bartholomew Green, the grandfather of the printer of Briton Hammon's autobiography—the Green family printed most of the writings of the Mather family—this possesses several characteristics that endured. The captivity would meditate upon events as much as relate them. Typographically, the largest word by far on Mather's title page is *Humiliations,* and his emphasis is on *collective* humiliation and deliverance. The individual lives he recounts are analogical, the ground upon which the Lord works for all of New England. The natives who must be subdued in the process are doubly foul—heathen as well as brutal. Mather, like later booksellers and clergymen, feels free to introduce and otherwise "improve" the stories that come to his hand. The talismanic legend so important later, "written by her own hand"—as in Mary Rowlandson's tale of 1682—would distinguish such efforts from those "improved" by booksellers. Mather taught several generations of readers to see God's handiwork in the narrative's blend of sensation and piety, of blood and holy water—precisely the combination that gave it its extraordinary popularity. Present from the beginning too is an enveloping hostility toward virtually all aspects of Native life. This could be separate from or joined to repulsion against slaves. Jonathan Dickinson's *God's Protecting Providence* (1699) presents a pointed comparison of what he considers the disgusting habits of Indians and blacks. Finally, Mather's formula of trial by captivity leading to physical and spiritual salvation would be transferred from the captivities directly to the slave narratives of the abolitionist period. Between Cotton Mather and William Lloyd Garrison readers might be taught that a man or woman need no more be degraded by slavery than by captivity.

Because of constant tension between settlers and tribes in the North and West, the captivities always possessed a timeliness. But that relevance was aggravated with each new quarrel. A new narrative or (more often) a new edition of a previous one appeared most years during the eighteenth century. The most serious quarrel of all, the Seven Years War, led in the 1750s and early 1760s to a new round of narratives and editions. In the early 1750s the narratives were appearing at the rate of about one every six months. When the war intensified at mid-decade and invective against both Indians and the French rose sharply, they appeared nearly twice as often, or every three or four months. Put another way, with the coming of a major conflict that brought several early British defeats, the Indian and the tales in which he figured so prominently were more central than they had been at any time since the early settlement. In the practical terms of the bookseller, war fever served to heat the presses. As more persons and families claimed contact with the Indians, an apparatus was needed for verification, composition, and publication—as abolitionists would discover eighty years later. As their tales grew more and more horrific, so grew the use of legitimizing prefaces and afterwords that testified to the piety and reliability of the narrator—as, for example, in Reverend Gilbert Tennent's preface to Robert Eastburn's *Faithful Narrative* (1758)—devices the abolitionists also retrieved.

By 1760 when Hammon's narrative was published, Green and Russell were probably the foremost of the approximately two dozen printers in Boston, the publishing center of the colonies. But they were not the leading printers of captivities; this distinction was held by the partnership of Fowle and Draper. Bound to Green and Russell by family business, Fowle and Draper specialized in the short pamphlet relating either Indian captivity or military expedition or, ideally, as in the case of Peter Williamson, both at once. During the North American phase of the war they brought out as many of each as they could obtain, including early in 1760 the captivity tale of a young white man named Thomas Brown. Brown has largely disappeared from the annals of America, yet he represented a group of utmost importance at the moment, the young soldiers who, having defeated the enemy, returned to a devastated economy in Massachusetts that could not provide for them. To his printers his story must have seemed perfect for the disconsolate mood of early 1760, condemning as it did the French army and several Indian tribes with equal virulence. Not only did it describe the horrors of Indian captivity, but like Peter Williamson's narrative it also related the details of numerous battles, first from the British, then, after Brown's capture, from the French point of view. It must have pleased its audience as much as its printers, for three editions were called for by summer. It must also have been widely read, since examples of the first two editions have virtually disappeared. While full of the blood and piety that mark the most successful examples of the genre, Brown's tale stretched the captivity narrative in several directions. Born in 1740, Brown is but sixteen or seventeen when he is taken into the army, injured, left for dead, and finally captured—he is only twenty when he escapes. A full title page speaks of the *plain* narrative, first of uncommon sufferings, then of remarkable deliverance; his great loss, that he has been absent from his father's house for three years and eight months. The maxim of miraculous deliverance, purchased by terrible pain, of course, is repeated. Yet here it has been expanded to accommodate the sensational experiences of a very young man who describes scalpings, decapitations, eviscerations, and burnings to death; who kills his own prisoners rather than allow them to escape; and who does not so much escape himself as negotiate coolly with his captors for his release. In the long history of the captivity genre, this is indeed remarkable material.

It is therefore all the more arresting to discover a finely wrought preface explaining that Brown is too young to interpret properly the significance of his own life: "As I am but a Youth, I shall not make those Remarks on the Difficulties I have met with, or the kind Appearances of a good God for my Preservation, as one of riper Years might do; but shall leave that to the Reader as he goes along, and shall only beg his Prayers, that Mercies and Afflictions may be sanctified to me, and relate Matters of Fact as they occur to my Mind."⁹ The closing portion of the narrative is likewise of religious piety and humility, justifying the preceding pages by glorying in divine providence: "After repeated Application to General Amherst, I was dismissed, and returned in Peace to my Father's House the Beginning of *Jan.* 1760, after having been absent 3 Years and almost 8 Months. 'O! that Men would praise the LORD for his Goodness, and for his wonderful Works to the Children of Men!'—'Bless the LORD, O my soul!—.'"¹⁰

At the nadir of his years among the unnamed Indians, when his pains are greatest and hopes faintest, Brown allows himself one brief expression of despair: "I fared no better than a Slave."¹¹ It is at this point that the relation between Brown and Hammon can be glimpsed and the distinctive flavor of Briton Hammon's story for a northeastern audience can be appreciated, for he is a bondsman doubly bound—a person of color and an outsider in eighteenth-century New England, captured and violated by a people whose skin is as dark as his. (One can imagine the expected, self-comforting response: "What those people won't do to one another!") While possessing all the attractions of earlier captivity narratives like Brown's, this first slave story has an additional, invaluable polemical ingredient for a colony besieged externally by a real enemy and internally by its own racial myths. It is as if he said, "Ah, if those terrible Indians would be so cruel to one whose skin color is so close to their own, imagine, oh fair maidens, what they would do to *you!*"

Precisely when in 1760 Hammon's *Narrative* was published is not known, but it was certainly after Brown's.¹² It probably appeared after the third edition of Brown's narrative had been placed on sale, most likely later summer or early fall. It was advertised in all of the July 1760 issues (7, 14, 21, and 28) of *The Boston Evening-Post*, a weekly newspaper. The connections between the firm of Fowle and Draper and that of Green and Russell were as much personal as commercial. John Green (1731–87) was the last member of America's earliest printing dynasty, the oldest family of printers and booksellers in New England. The great-grandson of Samuel Green, who had taken over Stephen Day's Cambridge Press in 1649, he was the son of Bartholomew Green Jr. He was also closely tied to the Draper family; his father was brother-in-law of John Draper. After apprenticeship with John Draper, he married Draper's daughter, Rebecca (an event that turned his aunt into his mother-in-law). Once established for himself, John Green formed a service relationship with another Draper, Samuel, who was a nephew of John Draper. This connection between the two main printing families in the printing center of the colonies allowed for the convergence of loyalist political sympathies and the sharing of indispensable government contracts. Green's partner, Joseph Russell (1734–95), had a further connection with the Fowles, for he had been apprenticed to Daniel Fowle, brother of Zechariah. For the business association to work, moreover, the two firms shared capital, type, paper, and completed volumes. And to make exchanges easier, they were located close to one another. Fowle and Draper kept a large shop on Marlborough Street; Green and Russell were a short distance away on Queen Street. Such proximity was often required. For instance, Green and Russell were the nominal printers of Nathaniel Ames's popular *Astronomical Diary and Almanack*. In practice, Green and Russell printed one half-sheet, Fowle and Draper another. The full edition was gathered, sold at both shops, and its profits shared. Besides such routine arrangements, the two firms shared rush jobs for the government; whenever the governor or council wished speedy completion of a large printing order, Green and Russell often divided the tasks with Fowle and Draper. The strong bond between the two firms represented a sign of the needful sharing of profits and privileges in printing at a time when there was relatively little to go around—and most of that was controlled, one way or another, by the colonial government. Most firms sought such cooperation; Fowle and Draper's work with Green and Russell was simply one of the most successful efforts, especially at keeping profits and influence within the family.

To the trained eye, a connection of some sort between the two firms beyond the conventions of the day could be deduced from the title pages of Brown's and Hammon's narratives. Using essentially the same layout and typographical style, they give greatest emphasis to the word *Narrative* and to the name of their respective subjects. Both undergo uncommon sufferings, while Brown's deliverance is "remarkable" and Hammon's is "surprising." Brown is recorded as the one "*Who returned to his Father's House the Beginning of Jan. 1760, after having been absent three Years and about eight Months.*" Although Hammon's delayed return is not given the accent of italics, it does receive certain prominence, for it was he "who returned to *Boston*, after having been absent almost thirteen years." Hammon, like Brown, could represent the many young men pulled from their homes who were returning in 1760. Under the heading of "CONTAINING," each title page provides a precis of events, with stress upon the sensational, especially torture and murder. At work here is apparently a common house style, since far more resemblance exists between Fowle and Draper and Green and Russell than between either and any other Boston printers.

Thus it may be to an element of formula that we owe our recognition of Briton Hammon as a black man. Both firms preferred to use some legend beneath the name of the subject of a narrative. With Brown we get "of Charlestown, in New England." For Hammon, in smaller type, it is the crucial liner "A Negro Man,—Servant to. . . ." Had the first half of that line been omitted, we never could have been certain of Hammon's blackness, for the text itself contains no reference. (The title page calls Hammon "Servant to General Winslow," and he may have been simply that. The earliest putative slave narrative may have been written by a man who was not a slave at all, and that would be one of the least surprising facts about it.) That line may be considered essential to the next, since General Winslow (who has no role in the tale other than, passively, as Hammon's master) is given nearly as much prominence of name as Briton Hammon himself. In the retrospect of two centuries, what is most arresting about this reference to blackness is how *little*—in significance as well as size—is made of it. Although centrally located for the eye on the page, it is almost buried there—needed as identifying legend but less important than the *three* notices on the page of Hammon's subservience to Winslow. (The penchant for identifying legends is carried over to the text, where his slain comrades are identified as "*Elkanah Collymore* and *James Webb*, Strangers, and *Moses Newmock*, Mollatto."][13] Winslow is named and then in the synopsis becomes "his Master" and "his *good old Master.*" He is thus a formidable absence in the story, which has no obligation to feature slavery when it can emphasize stewardship. It possesses in this light a message of social value beyond the standard propaganda of captivity narratives. As Brown's tale is encased in an envelope of filial piety, so Hammon's is wrapped in a coat of social and occupational piety, addressed in its sanctity to all servants black and white, young and old, throughout the colonies. It is a social appeal all the greater in a city where and a time when many young men were being carried off and killed by warfare, leaving the remaining servants with more work, more influence, more responsibility, and more numerical prominence.

Subordination is indeed the central issue of Hammon's brief preface. In language echoing Brown and the most carefully crafted sentence in the tale, Hammon asserts the singularity of his situation: "*As my Capacities and Condition of Life are very low, it cannot be expected that I should make those Remarks on the Sufferings I have met with, or the kind Providence of a good GOD for my Preservation, as one in a higher*

*Station: but shall leave that to the Reader as he goes along, and so I shall only relate Matters of Fact as they occur to my mind.*"[14] Hammon concludes with the same biblical quotation as Brown, and, like Brown, he clearly has something to teach his contemporaries about the "Matters of Fact" pertaining to those whose conditions are low. What his tale can suggest to us is that to have a genuinely unusual publishing event in the mid-eighteenth century, such as a captivity narrative with a black subject, several remarkable circumstances would have to flow together.

With the *Narrative of Briton Hammon* such a coincidence did indeed occur: (1) In 1760, Boston was suffering a postwar economic and political depression.[15] (2) The governor, the council, and the ruling class generally were eager temporarily to accommodate new or unusual groups, particularly returning soldiers and their families. (3) The perennially popular captivity narrative now had an acute political significance, as it roused the populace and flayed the enemy. (4) Thomas Brown's narrative was uncommonly successful, partly because he was an uncommon subject for a captivity, partly because he was such an apt one in 1760. A relatively marginal figure in the life of the colony before the war, Brown was of much greater importance now as a soldier, an enemy of the French and Indians, and a young man seeking stability and familiarity after the fighting. (5) Brown's printers, Fowle and Draper, were solid establishment figures, who (6) had strong business ties with Green and Russell. (7) Green and Russell, in their turn, were even closer to the needs and purposes of colonial government. (8) The subject of their captivity tale, Briton Hammon, is another marginal figure whose social consequence had increased because of the war.[16] He was of the right age and the right social history, voiced the right social pieties, and represented that group of slaves who, because of the death and impoverishment of white men, were now a more prominent feature of the Boston economy. To give a quick illustration: In 1750 a fairly prosperous chandler's shop was operated by a middle-aged white couple, their son, and a single black slave. By 1760 the son had been killed in the war; the father had sickened at the news and, after two years of lingering illness, died. Both mother and slave overtaxed themselves, but he recovered and took full control of the business. (9) Finally, both Brown and Hammon tell their audience, chastened and anxious as they themselves are, that with God's grace and their cooperation life can once more return to normal—an appealing message anytime, particularly so in Boston in 1760.

In order to carry the story of the captivities into the nineteenth century, it would be possible to list at least fifty characteristics that link Hammon with Douglass or Hammon with *Clotelle* and *Our Nig*.[17] What stands out among such a welter of influences, however, are two enduring traits. As obvious as it is significant, the captivity narrative taught its readers that only barbarians would hold other human beings captive. In the hands of such writers as William Wells Brown and Harriet Jacobs that would prove a potent message indeed. In the eighteenth century, slave writing was simply conscripted into the vagaries of American bookselling. In the nineteenth century, however, some slave writers could themselves determine such movements. Briton Hammon's presence as a subject for a captivity expanded the scope of the captivity tale for a time, but at the same time it created the terms of possibility for the slave narrative. As a slave writing, a captivity undermines that form but strengthens alternative life stories for other slaves; so the meaning of one narrative is sometimes another one. The earlier tale of Native captivity is easily turned to the later story of southern bondage. One escape teaches another.

One kind of mythmaking likewise teaches another. For two centuries influential white Americans used stories of Indian captivity to invent a cultural history for a people who otherwise lacked one. They took an "American" event, white settlers held by native peoples, and declared it ordained, unique, and indigenous. Then it became a symbolic structure through which all reality would be passed: What happened to the captives could occur to the nation as a whole, and in the revolution of the decade after Brown and Hammon it soon would. (As the captivity narrative provided the pattern for understanding the Revolutionary War, the slave narrative did so for the Civil War. In the earlier century the American colonies were held in thrall by a distant uncaring foe; in the nineteenth century, one region held back the moral and economic progress of the nation as a whole. In each instance an entire nation is in bondage.) Learning that lesson, formerly enslaved writers turned the narrative into the only moral history of American slavery that we have. Outside its pages, slavery was a wordless, nameless, timeless time. It was time without history and time without immanence, the only duration slaveholders would permit. The slave narrative changed that forever. Many writers were quite aware that they were reshaping for their own lives the Christian story of the crucifixion within the national crisis of human slavery, and they were not daunted. They found a symbolic structure to give a measure of fixity to a life of painful flux. In this sense, to recall one's history is to renew it.

## Editor's Note

John Sekora's essay ends somewhat prematurely, an unfortunate reflection of his sudden death while on a trip to New York. We had completed our discussions of his essay just before he left on his trip, and John had developed several ideas to further link African American and Native American literary representations, but after his death his notes could not be discovered by his family. I would like to briefly discuss a few of his ideas for the final revision while leaving his original essay intact.

Among the issues Sekora planned to discuss further were eighteenth-century Native American autobiographies and their relationship to eighteenth-century African American autobiographies. Just as Native Americans and African Americans served as liminal figures in Early America, actively resisting the master narratives in which they were misrepresented by European Americans, they both undertook to resist through acts of writing. Such African American autobiographical acts as Briton Hammon's narrative hold fascinating parallels with early Native American autobiographies, similarities that merge in early African–Native American autobiographies such as those by John Marrant or William Apess. *The Letters of Eleazar Wheelock's Indians*, written between 1763 and 1766, contain life-writing by Native Americans at Wheelock's Indian missionary school at Dartmouth.[18] Like the eighteenth-century African American autobiographies, they contain descriptions of missionary work by Native Americans who served, as did many African American autobiographers, as missionaries to Native American nations. Eighteenth-century African American and Native American autobiographies draw from Christian conversion narratives as well as travel narratives. A. LaVonne Brown Ruoff argues that African American slave narratives and Native American autobiographies were influenced by spiritual confessional writing and that "some Indian authors, or their editors or publishers, also incorporated aspects of slave narratives, which themselves were influenced by religious narratives."[19]

Another clear parallel lies in the Native American writers' demands for freedom, for example, the letters of David Fowler, which are confessional, like much eighteenth-century African American writing, but also express anger at his treatment by Eleazar Wheelock[20] or, in African–Native American autobiography, works by Paul Cuffe and William Apess, which contain demands for Native American and African American freedom. In fact, the early African–Native American autobiographies are rich sites from which to explore the later merging between African American and Native American literary traditions, particularly if one is interested in exploring the influences of early captivity narratives on slave narratives. Captivity narratives (or signifying responses) were written not only by European Americans who had undergone Native American captivity but by African Americans in slavery and Native Americans, enslaved or otherwise deprived of freedom and civil rights. As Ruoff argues, Native American autobiographers were often responding to the market in popular captivity narratives through their own writing and "had the moral obligation to portray the harsh injustices they and their fellows suffered at the hands of Christian whites,"[21] much like European Americans such as Mary Rowlandson portrayed the harsh injustices suffered at the hands of non-Christian Native American captors. In the appendix to *A Son of the Forest*, William Apess provides a response to one of the primary claims promulgated in Indian captivity narratives, the "inhumanity of the Indians towards their prisoners" as well as to the tension of impending sexual violation that permeates the captivity narratives by European American female narrators. He counters with charges leveled against Christian armies laying waste to entire cities and perpetrating "enormities" (rapes) "at which manhood blushes."[22] Apess also includes the accounts of Colonel James Smith's captivity from his *Journal of Events* (1755–59), which, rather than vilifying Native Americans, serve to establish the parallels of their religious practices to Christianity.[23] Finally, the literary critic William L. Andrews notes a revision of the Indian captivity narrative in Henry Bibb's nineteenth-century slave narrative: "If a white man had been captured by the Cherokee Indians and carried away from his family for life into slavery, would it be a crime for the poor fugitive, whose life, liberty, and future happiness were all at stake, to mount any man's horse by the way side, and ride him without asking any questions, to effect his escape?"[24] Andrews argues that "anyone familiar with the mythology of Indian captivity narratives, which in Bibb's time were undergoing an unparalleled revival of interest in America, could empathize with such a mode of self-liberation,"[25] thus providing a clear documentation of John Sekora's assertion that the Indian captivity narrative and the eighteenth-century African American autobiography would merge to produce the nineteenth-century slave narrative.

## Notes

1. James Olney, ed., *Studies in Autobiography* (New York: Oxford University Press, 1988); Carolyn G. Heilbrun, *Reinventing Womanhood* (New York: Norton, 1979); Deborah E. McDowell and Arnold Rampersad, eds., *Slavery and the Literary Imagination* (Baltimore: Johns Hopkins University Press, 1989); and John Sekora and Darwin T. Turner, eds., *The Art of Slave Narrative: Original Essays in Criticism and Theory* (Macomb, Ill.: Western Illinois University Press, 1982).

2. Editor's note: According to Sekora's notes, this quotation comes from *Slavery and the Literary Imagination*, ed. Deborah E. McDowell and Arnold

Rampersad (Baltimore: Johns Hopkins University Press, 1989), but I was unable to locate it, as was Arnold Rampersad, who nevertheless identified it as his argument in an e-mail message to me.

3. Alice Walker, *In Search of Our Mothers' Gardens* (New York: Harcourt Brace Jovanovich, 1984), 5.

4. This and the following paragraph draw upon Gary B. Nash, *Red, White, and Black: The Peoples of Early America* (Englewood Cliffs, N.J.: Prentice-Hall, 1982), 173–78; Winthrop D. Jordan, *White over Black: American Attitudes toward the Negro, 1550–1812* (Chapel Hill: University of North Carolina Press, 1968), 276–78; Peter Wood, *Black Majority: Negros in Colonial South Carolina from 1670 through the Stono Rebellion* (New York: Knopf, 1974), 130–35; and William D. Piersen, *Black Yankees: The Development of an Afro-American Subculture in Eighteenth-Century New England* (Amherst: University of Massachusetts Press, 1988).

5. Benjamin Franklin, "Observations Concerning the Increase of Mankind, Peopling of Countries, &c.," in *Benjamin Franklin: Writings* (New York: Library of America, 1987), 373.

6. William Lloyd Garrison, *The Liberator*, Mar. 26, 1831.

7. William Wells Brown, *Narrative of William W. Brown, a Fugitive Slave, Written by Himself* (Reading, Mass.: Addison-Wesley, 1969), 8.

8. Lawrence C. Wroth, *An American Bookshelf, 1755* (Philadelphia: University of Pennsylvania Press, 1934), 101–8.

9. Thomas Brown, *A Plain Narrative of the Uncommon Sufferings and Remarkable Deliverance of Thomas Brown* (Boston: Fowle and Draper, 1760), 3. The title page calls this the third edition of Brown's narrative.

10. Ibid., 24.

11. Ibid., 19.

12. Briton Hammon, *A Narrative of the Uncommon Suffering and Surprising Deliverance of Briton Hammon* (Boston: Green and Russell, 1760).

13. Ibid., 6.

14. Ibid., 3. See John Sekora, "Is the Slave Narrative a Species of Autobiography?" in *Studies in Autobiography*, ed. James Olney (New York: Oxford University Press, 1988), 99–111, for more on Hammon.

15. See Gary B. Nash, *The Urban Crucible: Social Change, Political Consciousness, and the Origins of the American Revolution* (Cambridge, Mass.: Harvard University Press, 1979), 147–76.

16. See Pierson, *Black Yankees*, chaps. 8 and 9.

17. William Wells Brown, *Clotelle: A Tale of the Southern States* (Boston: J. Redpath, 1864); Harriet E. Wilson, *Our Nig; or, Sketches from the Life of a Free Black in a Two-Story White House, North. Showing That Slavery's Shadows Fall Even There. By "Our Nig."* (Boston: G. C. Rand and Avery, 1859).

18. *The Letters of Eleazor Wheelock's Indians*, ed. James Dow McCallum (Hanover, N.H.: Dartmouth College Publications, 1932).

19. A. LaVonne Brown Ruoff, "Three Nineteenth-Century American Indian Autobiographers," in *Redefining American Literary History*, ed. A. LaVonne Brown Ruoff and Jerry W. Ward (New York: Modern Language Association, 1990), 252.

20. H. David Brumble, *An Annotated Bibliography of American Indian and Eskimo Autobiographies* (Lincoln: University of Nebraska Press, 1981), 16, 38, 61.

21. Ruoff, "Three Nineteenth-Century American Indian Autobiographers," 252.

22. William Apess, *On Our Own Ground: The Complete Writings of William Apess, a Pequot,* ed. Barry O'Connell (Amherst: University of Massachusetts Press, 1992), 64.

23. Ibid., 81.

24. William L. Andrews, *To Tell a Free Story: The First Century of Afro-American Autobiography, 1760–1865* (Urbana: University of Illinois Press, 1986), 152.

25. Ibid.

## 4   Recapturing John Marrant

In recognizing that John Marrant's captivity narrative "inaugurates the black tradition of English literature," Henry Louis Gates Jr. undoes a century and a half of the narrative's neglect.[1] Although Marrant's narrative was among the first books written by an African American and was, from its first edition in 1785, one of the most popular of the Indian captivity narratives, it had remained largely unread since its last edition in 1835 until Gates rescued it from obscurity.[2] Even its author, whom Dorothy B. Porter identifies as "undoubtedly one of the first, if not the first, Negro ministers of the gospel in North America," is ignored by those dusty and ponderous histories of early Methodism where some literary commentators suggest he belongs.[3] When the narrative has been reproduced, moreover, it is often mistaken as a slave narrative, its editors ignoring the fact that Marrant was born a free man of some apparent means. Some reformers of the American canon, who have gone to great lengths to include figures like Olaudah Equiano and Phillis Wheatley, have ignored Marrant, favoring writers more self-consciously black or African. Because Marrant identifies himself as "black" only twice in his narrative, his work apparently lacked interest for nineteenth-century abolitionists and certainly for Protestant nativists. Up to now, he has continued to be ignored or dismissed. A new reading of Marrant's narrative, however, shows it to be a clear example of an emerging polyethnic American identity, an identity that Werner Sollors would call a "consenting" coincidence of European, African, and Native American cultures and that Mechal Sobel would recognize as an instance of a "world they made together."[4] As a witness to a sense of the American self that has been lost,

Marrant's narrative is an important document in the development of American culture as a whole.

Marrant's narrative defies the patterns frequently invoked to account for the evolution of the seventeenth-century captivity narrative into nineteenth-century fiction. Roy Harvey Pearce and Richard VanDerBeets agree that the early narratives—Mary Rowlandson's is the chief example—began as typological tracts designed to justify the ways of God to man by attesting to the redemptive power of suffering.[5] By the late eighteenth century, however, most of these tracts, originally devotional, had evolved into mere bigoted indictments against the nonwhite, non-Protestant minority, particularly the Indians, the French, and the Roman Catholics. These later narratives favored sentiment and sensationalism over fact. A contrast between the opening of Mary Rowlandson's seventeenth-century narrative and Mary Kinnan's of 1791 makes this clear. Rowlandson writes, "On the tenth of February 1675 came the Indians with great numbers upon Lancaster: Their first coming was about Sun-rising; hearing the noise of some Guns, we looked out; several Houses were burning." Mary Kinnan begins, "Whilst the tear of sensibility so often flows at the unreal tale of woe, which glows under the pen of the poet and novelist, shall our hearts refuse to be melted with sorrow at the unaffected and unvarnished tale of a female, who has surmounted difficulties and dangers, which on review appear romantic, even to herself."[6]

Although published a hundred years after the Rowlandson narrative, Marrant's narrative more closely adheres to her spirit and design than it does to those of Kinnan, his contemporary. While Marrant may have lapsed more frequently from the facts than Rowlandson, he nonetheless keeps to a similar discourse, a discourse resembling the medieval hermeneutic tradition of initiation. Like her medieval male counterparts, Rowlandson's journey takes her from the landscape of the familiar and formed into the alien and chaotic, from which she returns enlightened and reborn. Rowlandson's "proof texts" connect her journey to Daniel in the lion's den, to Jonah in the whale, to Moses and the Hebrews in the desert. Her point is always clear: her captivity is part of a cosmic design. What Auerbach says of Dante is, at least in this regard, true of Rowlandson: she does not regard history as a mere pattern of "earthly events, but in constant connection with God's plan; so that every earthly phenomenon is at all times . . . directly connected with God's plan; so that a multiplicity of vertical links establishes an immediate relation between every earthly phenomenon and the plan of salvation conceived by Providence."[7] Rowlandson's private experience has political and ultimately cosmic significance. Her testing in the wilderness is a test of the whole New England experiment; her captivity in the wilderness is a single instance of God's test for all humanity. It reproduces and relives the testing of Christ in the desert, his descent into hell, and his resurrection and apocalyptic victory.

Mary Kinnan's self-proclaimed "romantic" adventure claims no significance beyond the psychological. Her contemporary John Marrant's adventure, however, remains grounded in a typological conception of history and in that regard demonstrates Mechal Sobel's observation that among the less powerful classes in the eighteenth-century South, especially Virginia, "a wide range of values, including many that were closer to the medieval Catholic world view . . . continued to develop."[8] Unlike Kinnan, Marrant does not understand himself as the victim of frivolous circumstance but rather as an active participant in the evolution of a providential design. While Marrant has for the most part freed himself from Rowlandson's dependence on "proof texts" to clarify his typology, he recalls the events of his captivity in such a way as to make their relationship to salvation history perfectly obvious. For example, he recalls George Whitfield's first summons to his salvation at a Charleston prayer meeting in typological language—"Prepare to meet thy God, O Israel"— and throughout the narrative he remembers his experience as the antitype of scriptural events. Like Rowlandson's, his deliverance from the Indians is the "delivering of the three children in the fiery furnace, and of Daniel in the lion's den." His subsequent deliverance from a school of maneating sharks is the antitype of Jonah's, whose prayer is "the Lord did not shut me out." Furthermore, Reverend William Aldridge, Marrant's "authenticator," identifies him with David, who "without sling or stone, engages, and with the arrow of prayer, pointed with faith, wounded Goliath, and conquers the king."[9]

While Rowlandson's typology derives primarily from the Old Testament, Marrant's source, as one might expect in a post-Awakening narrative, is almost entirely the New Testament. While Rowlandson only implies that she is a seventeenth-century antitype of Christ, Marrant reconstructs his experience to leave no doubt that his model is the Messiah Himself. In this regard, he resembles Jonathan Edwards, who, unlike his contemporaries who regarded themselves only as successors to John the Baptist, insisted that the Christian minister was a type of Christ.[10] In the course of his narrative, however, Marrant has to discover his messianic identity by passing through a series of identifications with other preliminary New Testament types. In true hermeneutic style, the first of these is Lazarus. Laid ill after his initial encounter with Whitfield, Marrant languishes the requisite three days in the care of his sister, who cries out, "The lad will surely die." Whitfield arrives unannounced as the minister/Christ to effect the rebirth. Some weeks later, after Marrant has accepted his conversion, he comes to understand himself as the antitype of John the Baptist. He climbs "the fence . . . which divided the inhabited and cultivated parts of the country from the wilderness" and wanders for several weeks, surviving attacks by wolves, wild pigs, and bears, living in a tree, eating grass, and drinking muddy water.[11] After his capture by the Cherokee, he announces the gospel to a Herod-like king and his Salome-like daughter, but unlike his scriptural type, he keeps his head and brings about the conversion of the Herod and his daughter to whom he preaches.

The ultimate identification with Christ begins with Marrant's description of a later threat of his execution: "at the appointed hour" he is stripped, "taken out and led to the destined spot, amidst a vast number of people." He is shown the "sharp pegs" that are to be struck into him and cries out, "If it be thy will that it should be so, thy will be done."[12] This prayer might be dismissed as the prayer of any pious Christian were it not followed some pages later by a lengthy description of Marrant's return from capture, composed entirely of incidents contrived to echo John the Evangelist's account of Christ's life after the resurrection. In his absence Marrant's family had searched for him for "three days," and finding what they supposed was "his carcass torn," they buried it. Dressed in new clothes borrowed from the Indian king, he returns to the familiar world only to be turned away by neighbors, an uncle, his brother, and finally his own mother, all of whom are gathered to mourn in their own version of an upper room. Only his youngest sister recognizes him, but, predictably, when she announces that he has returned, they all Thomas-like refuse to believe. Ultimately they are convinced, clasp him about the neck, and rejoice, Marrant adding, "Thus the dead was brought to life again."[13]

Marrant's almost exclusive dependence on a typology of rebirth and resurrection separates his text further from Rowlandson's less evangelical imagery and reflects the strong influence of Whitfield and the other preachers at whose hands he experienced his conversion. Moreover, while Rowlandson's captivity brings about only a series of perceptive changes, Marrant undergoes a complete change of identity, the fullness of his rebirth signified by his assuming the wardrobe of an Indian king. Marrant's emphasis on metamorphosis places him clearly in the camp of Whitfield, whose primary contribution to the ideology of American evangelism is this rhetoric of "New Birth." In fact, Whitfield's insistent defense of his particular doctrine of regeneration provoked constant disapproval. The 1738 publication of his most famous sermon, "The Nature and Necessity of Our New Birth," heralded his arrival in America and outlined the specific doctrine of regeneration for which he was best known and most frequently condemned. Summoned before a church board in Charleston, for example, Whitfield heard Alexander Garden, the Anglican rector of Saint Philip's, condemn him for defending "'the belief and expectation of a certain happy moment, when, by the sole and specific work of the Holy Spirit . . . you shall at once (as 'twere by magic charm) be metamorphosed.'"[14] No doubt Marrant's later training at the hands of the Countess of Huntingdon, for whom Whitfield served as private chaplain, and his subsequent ordination into the Methodist "connection" of which she was the almost exclusive support gave him the vehicle, rhetoric, and imagery by which to recount his own experience.

This particular "connection" and the accompanying alienation that Marrant recounts in his narrative exempt him from the charge that Houston Baker lays against other African American writers of the same period. While Wheatley, another protégé of the esteemed countess, may indeed have "moved in harmony with the larger culture of white America," and Equiano may have embraced certain dimensions of Christianity as a "comfort against life's uncertainties," as Baker suggests, Marrant's presentation of his rebirth as an early disciple of Whitfield puts him at the center of the great "transethnic" theological debate between "piety" and "reason" that violently divided America after the Awakening.[15] H. Richard Niebuhr describes it as between those who "saw the reality of the order of being other than that walled and hemmed-in existence in which a stale institutional religion and bourgeois rationalism were content to dwell" and those who did not.[16] Alan Heimert sees the conflict as *the* great debate of the eighteenth century. Already free and already in possession of the assurances of bourgeois culture, in accepting Whitfield's call to rebirth Marrant rejects what Baker sees as the universal object of the African American's search, that is, "some terms of order."[17] Like other African and white Americans after the Awakening, Marrant rejects the terms already available to him in the bourgeois world in pursuit of an uncertainty. His abandonment of bourgeois rationalism in favor of evangelical piety turns his family against him and sends him in flight from the formed city to the chaos of the countryside. After his conversion, he is, like Jesus, a prophet dishonored in his own country. His sister charges him in the language of the prevailing theological debate: he is "crazy and mad," she says, and so reports "it among the neighbors, which opened the mouths of all around against [her]." His other relatives call him "every name but that which is good." Finally, like the Jesus in Matthew 12:48 who asks, "Who is my mother? and who are my brethren?" Marrant reports, "My mother turned against me also, and the neighbors joined her, and there was no friend left to assist me, or that I could speak to."[18]

Of course, Marrant is not exempt from the charge of acculturation, but the culture with which he feels most "comfort against life's uncertainties" is neither exclusively European nor African; it is also Native American. A Cherokee brave rescues him; a Cherokee chief and his daughter are his first disciples; and unaware of the debate between rationalist and pietist, the Native Americans find his beliefs neither "crazy" nor "mad" but consistent with their own sense of a divine immanence. Significantly, Marrant's life among the Indians most clearly associates his narrative with those other contemporary captivities in which, as Slotkin points out, the figure of the European captive blends into a composite that includes hunter, trader, and Indian scout. Out of these European accounts of the late eighteenth century, the prototype of American culture heroes like Daniel Boone and Natty Bumppo begins to emerge. Indeed, Marrant's description of himself as an African returning to a European civilization dressed as a Cherokee king is close to the images we have of Leatherstocking and Boone: "My dress was purely in the Indian style; the skins of wild beasts composed my garments, my head was set out in the savage manner, with a long pendant down my back, a sash around my middle, without breeches, and a tomahawk by my side."[19]

Within the context of Whitfield's imagery of metamorphosis, such dress suggests Marrant's rebirth as a Christian; but it also suggests the appearance of a new, more complex conception of what an American might be. The costume encourages us to read him as Marius Bewley and others have read Boone and Leatherstocking, as an early embodiment of the fundamental synthesis inside the whole of American experience. Marrant's skin color requires that another component be added to Bewley's synthesis. Like his European counterparts, Marrant is caught between freedom and law, between nature and civilization, between the religion of piety and rationalist theology—Balzac's "magnificent moral hermaphrodite, [re]born between the savage and civilized states of man."[20] Marrant returns to a bourgeois culture, but black and white, as, to borrow an image that the Native American and African cultures share, a mediating "trickster" whose profound ambiguity, whose transethnic "otherness," neither the prevailing rationalism nor Mary Kinnan's sentimentality could absorb. In this regard, it may be significant that after Marrant's seminary training in Wales, the countess of Huntingdon sent him as a missionary to the Indians of Nova Scotia.

Marrant's distinction from his European counterparts is also clear from his use of language. Gates has already made Marrant's manipulation of the trope of the "talking book" the centerpiece of his argument that Marrant stands at the head of a uniquely African American tradition in letters. I would add two other considerations to that discussion. Needless to say, unlike his European counterparts Marrant did not become a popular American culture hero for any racial group: white, black, or red. While Boone's exceptional and somewhat self-aggrandizing knowledge of the wilderness assured him a place in a culture that admired Poor Richard, Marrant fell into obscurity. Never abandoning his religious stance for the cool and detached humanism of Boone or Leatherstocking, Marrant gains his freedom by what John Edgar Wideman calls "the magic of the word."[21] Unlike the similarly religious Mary Rowlandson, whose escape is entirely "Providential" and who defends herself from her captors with a shield of printed texts—so annoyed do the Indians become with her incessant Bible reading that one enterprising woman "snatched it hastily out of [her] hand, and threw it out of doors"[22]—Marrant, a trained and successful musician, adapts easily to the oral culture of the Indians and masters their spoken language. If Rowlandson appreciates written texts as a tool with which to defend the authority of a received tradition, Marrant, like Douglass and later generations of enslaved Africans after him, appreciates the capacity of language to carry him toward something new. As Baker suggests, just as Douglass's future is determined by the moment he comes to understand the "power of the word" and as every slave learned that the manipulation of the master's speech was the key to his own survival, Marrant, not a slave, also understands the relationship between freedom and language that characterizes so much African American discourse.[23] Marrant uses his skill at spoken language to win freedom from his Indian masters: "I prayed in English a considerable time, and about the middle of my prayer, the Lord impressed a strong desire upon my mind to turn into their language and pray in their tongue. I did so, and with remarkable liberty, which wonderfully affected the people. . . . I believe the executioner was savingly converted to God. . . . the first words he expressed, when he had utterance, were, 'No man shall hurt thee till thou hast been to the king.'"[24]

Moreover, Marrant shares in a significantly African American consciousness not only in his equation of freedom and language but also in his stylistic use of a particular kind of structural repetition. James A. Snead argues that the use of certain kinds of repetition helps distinguish African from European discourse. He notes particularly how the "cut" used in American jazz, that is, "an abrupt seemingly unmotivated break [an accidental da capo] with a series already in progress and a willed return to a prior series," has a counterpart in African American fiction.[25] In music and in fiction, this "cut" sets up a series of expectations for the listener/reader only to destroy them at irregular intervals. European literature, Snead argues, suppresses repetition in order to maintain the illusion of linear progression and of clearly discernible goals. This distinction is useful when we compare Marrant's "African captivity" with Rowlandson's "European captivity." Rowlandson's account is structured around twenty logically plotted chapters she calls "removes." Each "remove" takes her farther from the familiar until at around the tenth remove, she begins a trek home. Once returned, she assesses the results of her trial: her election seems sure and, like Job, her economic future is stable. She acknowledges the superficiality of her former ways, and instead of the wilderness diet of raw horse liver and grass, she rejoices, "Now we are fed with the finest of Wheat. . . . Instead of the Husk, we have the fatted calf."[26] Marrant's narrative, however, though it shares Rowlandson's European typology, never comes to rest in financial security or gastronomic reward. In fact, there is no clear linear progression in Marrant's narrative at all. His journey is not a single continuum but a pilgrimage interrupted by a series of fortuitous accidents or unexpected "cuts" that, on the one hand, literally and consistently return him "home" but, on the other hand, leave the actual outcome of his adventure open-ended and unassessed. For example, having once achieved remarkable success as a teen-aged musician in Charleston, Marrant unaccountably returns home. Admitting that he is as "unstable as water," he returns to Charleston and physically stumbles into Whitfield's revival, only to be "carried home by two men." Later, captured by Indians, he says first that "he would rather die than go home," but not long after, he has an "invincible desire of returning home."[27] Impressed by a British frigate during the Revolution, he finds himself brought home at the siege of Charleston. On board once again, he is washed overboard only to be returned home by a providential wave. The final image of the narrative has Marrant preparing to return home from England to work once more among the Indians of North America. No doubt, as pietistic propaganda, these remarkable seizures emphasize the distance between the orthodox Puritan preparationist models and those of the revivalists, but they also help define Marrant's captivity not only as a European but also, quite specifically, as an African American narrative. In Marrant's transethnic narrative, as in jazz, there is no illusion of progress or control. Instead Marrant's "cuts" make room for accident and rupture in a vision that does not equate the unpredictable with a test of faith, as does Rowlandson, but rather embraces it as yet another discovery of a "divine excellency" wholly different from anything that is reducible to received categories.

Perhaps Marrant's resistance to any single set of categories has been at the root of his neglect, and Gates's study on the reception of these early

African American texts will certainly add light to the question. Not only did Marrant defy the narrow categories of his contemporaries, he too often eludes our own. If, as Sollors argues, our well-intended ethnic categories remain as reified as our ancestors' theological categories, we will resist coming to terms with the kind of transethnic culture that Marrant epitomizes. While Marrant's appreciation for the pervasive immanence of divinity made him too "red" for many of his contemporaries, including his own family, his skin made him too "black" for others, and for yet others—perhaps his Cherokee captors, perhaps some modern readers—I am sure he is too "white." Indeed, his text is neither African, European, nor Native American but rather a kind of *coincidentia oppositorum*, a gathering of transethnic contacts that manages to retain the powerful stamp of all three. In that lies its chief significance. As an icon of possibilities, it revels in the kind of shared cultural activity that seems once to have been at the center of American experience but somehow got lost along the way.

## Notes

1. Henry Louis Gates Jr., *The Signifying Monkey: A Theory of Afro-American Literary Criticism* (New York: Oxford University Press, 1988), 145.

2. Peter Williamson's *Adventures and Suffering* (1757) and Mary Jemison's *Captivity* (1824) were two other tales that surpassed Marrant's account in number of editions. A complete list of Marrant's editions is in Dorothy B. Porter, "Early American Negro Writings: A Bibliographic Study," *Papers of the Bibliographic Society of America* 39 (1945): 192–268.

3. Dorothy B. Porter, *Early Negro Writing, 1760–1837* (Boston: Beacon Press, 1971), 404.

4. See Werner Sollors, *Beyond Ethnicity: Consent and Descent in American Culture* (New York: Oxford University Press, 1986); and Mechal Sobel, *The World They Made Together* (Princeton, N.J.: Princeton University Press, 1987).

5. Roy Harvey Pearce, "The Significance of the Captivity Narratives," *American Literature* 19 (1949): 120; Richard VanDerBeets, ed., *Held Captive by Indians: Selected Narratives, 1642–1836* (Knoxville: University of Tennessee Press, 1973), xi–xxxi.

6. Mary Rowlandson, *The Soveraignty and Goodness of God*, in *Held Captive by Indians*, ed. VanDerBeets, 42; and Mary Kinnan, *A True Narrative of the Sufferings of Mary Kinnan*, in *Held Captive by Indians*, ed. VanDerBeets, 320.

7. Erich Auerbach, *Mimesis*, trans. Willard Trask (Princeton, N.J.: Princeton University Press, 1953), 194.

8. Sobel, *World They Made Together*, 7.

9. John Marrant, *A Narrative of the Life of John Marrant* (London: N.p., 1787), 3, 12, 21. Like Marrant, William Aldridge (1738–97) was a member of the Methodist "connection" of Selina Shirley Hastings, the countess of Huntingdon (1707–91). Although he broke with her about 1777, Aldridge presided over her funeral service. His introduction to Marrant's narrative insists, "No more alterations . . . have been made than were thought necessary."

10. Alan Heimert, *Religion and the American Mind* (Cambridge, Mass.: Harvard University Press, 1966), 7.

11. Marrant, *Narrative of the Life of John Marrant*, 4, 7.

12. Ibid., 12.

13. Ibid., 20.

14. Quoted in Heimert, *Religion and the American Mind*, 37.

15. Houston Baker, *The Journey Back* (Chicago: University of Chicago Press, 1980), 12, 20.

16. H. Richard Niebuhr, *The Kingdom of God in America* (1937; rpt., New York: Harper, 1959), 110–11.

17. Baker, *Journey Back*, 1.

18. Marrant, *Narrative of the Life of John Marrant*, 5, 6.

19. Ibid., 17.

20. In Cleanth Brooks, R. W. B. Lewis, and Robert Penn Warren, *American Literature: The Makers and the Making* (New York: St. Martin's Press, 1974), 286. This college text, familiar to more mature students of American literature, offers a summary of the traditional approaches to racial questions in colonial American culture, including that of Bewley in his *The Eccentric Design* and Balzac.

21. John Edgar Wideman, "The Black Writer and the Magic of the Word," *New York Times Book Review*, Jan. 24, 1988, 1.

22. Rowlandson, *Soveraignty and Goodness of God*, 62.

23. Baker, *Journey Back*, 34.

24. Marrant, *Narrative of the Life of John Marrant*, 12–13.

25. James A. Snead, "Repetition as a Figure of Black Culture," in his *Black Literature and Literary Theory* (New York: Methuen, 1984), 67.

26. Rowlandson, *Soveraignty and Goodness of God*, 89.

27. Marrant, *Narrative of the Life of John Marrant*, 2, 4, 9, 17.

JONATHAN BRENNAN

## 5 Speaking Cross Boundaries: A Nineteenth-Century African– Native American Autobiography

Although African American and Native American literary traditions have evolved distinctly, they have also merged in texts by African–Native American authors, interconnecting the two traditions to form a hybrid text. A fascinating example of this was published in 1848, when an early African–Native American collaborative autobiography was spoken by Okah Tubbee, an African Choctaw escaped slave, to Laah Ceil, a Mohawk Delaware woman, the wife of Tubbee and editor of their autobiography.[1] Their autobiography, republished with an introduction by Daniel F. Littlefield Jr. in 1988, shares elements of eighteenth- and nineteenth-century African American and Native American literary traditions, drawing from forms that include the Christian conversion narrative, confessional writing, captivity narratives, Indian autobiographies, and slave narratives.

Although the Native American literary critic Arnold Krupat claims that after Black Hawk's autobiography in 1833, "the remaining years of the nineteenth century present no other fully developed instance of Indian autobiography,"[2] A. LaVonne Brown Ruoff states that "the only Indian woman writer of personal and tribal history during most of the nineteenth century" was Sarah Winnemuca Hopkins,[3] and Gretchen Bataille and Kathleen Mullen Sands argue that "Maria Chona's autobiography is . . . in fact, the only complete personal narrative of a nineteenth-century

Indian woman that is not romanticized, or a story of a conversion to Christianity, or a case history to illustrate ethnographic data, or a plea against unjust treatment of a tribal peoples,"[4] Tubbee and Ceil's autobiography is most certainly a "fully developed instance of Indian autobiography" as well as a narrative by a "nineteenth-century Indian woman writer of personal and tribal history" (can the two be separated?) and a "personal narrative of a nineteenth-century Indian woman" that is romanticized, a conversion story, and a plea against unjust treatment of "a tribal peoples," as well as being a "complete" personal narrative. A substantial number of Indian women's autobiographies deal with many of these issues (perhaps even exclusively) and may still be thought to be "complete personal narratives."

There appear to be two primary reasons why Tubbee and Ceil's narrative is often ignored. First, as argued by H. David Brumble, "Littlefield has also determined that Tubbee was not really, as he claimed, a Choctaw."[5] Yet this is not, in fact, what Littlefield has determined. Rather, he has determined that Tubbee was not the son of the Choctaw leader Moshulatubbee. Yet Tubbee was most certainly of mixed blood (his mother, Frances, was African American), and there is no evidence to suggest that his father was European American rather than Native American. At the time of Tubbee's birth there were substantial numbers of Choctaw living, trading, and socializing in Natchez, Mississippi.[6] Even if Tubbee's father was not Choctaw, he certainly could have been Native American.

Regardless, Tubbee's identity does not hinge on his "racial" make-up but rather on his cultural affinity. Since he probably did not know who his father was, he was left with the task of creating his identity. Since he identified as a Choctaw, believed his father to be a Choctaw, was accepted by at least some Choctaws as Choctaw, by other members of Native nations as Choctaw, and by some African Americans as well as many European Americans as Choctaw, Tubbee was for all intents and purposes part Choctaw. Although he was not the same sort of Choctaw as most, the process of identity for many Native Americans (as well as European and other Americans) became irreversibly complex after the colonization by the European settlers. The situation of on- and off-reservation members, mixed-bloods, and federally recognized and nonrecognized Native nations makes it nearly impossible to determine Choctaw lineage with any finality and creates situations in which many Choctaws are not "the same sort as most."

Brumble also asserts that Tubbee was "Indian or black."[7] This dichotomy demands that Tubbee choose either one or the other identity, yet he was not Indian *or* black; he was Indian *and* black. Like many others,

Tubbee lived in several cultures, at the very least Choctaw and African American (as well as European American and perhaps Delaware, Mohawk, and Stockbridge as well).

Since the primary prerequisite of a Native American text is at least a significant contribution by a Native American (considering the historically intrusive role of many of the "editors" of these texts), and since Tubbee's claims of Choctaw identity have been dismissed, Tubbee and Ceil's narration has been largely ignored as Native American autobiography. Yet even if we insist that Tubbee was not really a Choctaw, ignoring the significant portion of his life during which he identified as one, why has Ceil's role been discarded? Brumble acknowledges that a few pages of Ceil's autobiography are nestled within the larger autobiographical text (even giving her a brief entry in his *Annotated Bibliography of American Indian and Eskimo Autobiographies*), and he hints at her "influence" on the 1852 edition.[8] But why is she not viewed as a significant nineteenth-century Indian autobiographer?

I suspect that the reason is that although Ceil does include an autobiographical narrative within the text, the majority of the text is seen as "belonging" to Tubbee, with Ceil playing the role of the faithful scribe. Granted, a substantial portion of the text centers on Tubbee's life, and the title might indicate that his life is the sole focus of the narrative, but this limits the ways in which we can view this text. Certainly part of the narrative is a portion of Tubbee's life story; another part of the narrative is a portion of Ceil's life story. But this can also be seen as a collaborative autobiography, the creation of an identity that serves more than one individual. Ceil exercised significant control over the narrative, developing her unique style that shapes both of their voices, creating and arranging significant portions of Tubbee's life through a vision and understanding that was a collaboration between them.

Although many critics gloss collaborative issues when examining texts, particularly Native American and women's texts, it is essential to thoroughly examine the use of collaboration to understand Tubbee and Ceil's narrative. While Benjamin Franklin may have had the privilege of contributing his memoirs to his community, a literary feather in his statesman's cap, Ceil and Tubbee (and many others) had no such privilege. Many Native Americans and African Americans were literally writing for their lives. Although a substantial portion of Ceil and Tubbee's text works to establish Tubbee's identity, the establishment of such an identity was as pertinent for the life of Ceil as it was for the life of Tubbee. Tubbee's identity was not significant to only one individual; it was an essential component of the existence of an entire family.[9]

Ceil and Tubbee had four children. Although historically the children would most often "follow the condition of the mother" (i.e. if the mother was a slave then the children would be slaves as well), the terms of Tubbee's master James McCary's will stated that Warner McCary (Okah Tubbee) *and his progeny* were "to be held as slaves during all and each of their lives."[10] Thus it appears that the children of Tubbee and Ceil were in danger of being snatched into slavery. Ceil's parents were apparently concerned that either Ceil, her children, or her husband would be enslaved or otherwise come to harm because of Tubbee's legal status, and thus they denied her permission to travel to the South with him: "I knew my parents did not fully understand his plan, although it seemed so beautiful to me. 'Well,' said I, 'ask my parents, if they can, I will consent.' They did consent, providing he would not take me South, and we were married. I remained with my parents. After a short time he returned to the South."[11] Since the lives of Ceil and her children are so intimately tied to the establishment of Tubbee's identity, the process of creating such an identity becomes an urgent collaboration in which Tubbee, Ceil, and their son Mosholeh (or Bruce) all participate through the creation of a textual narrative as well as the performance of a dramatic narrative on the stage that preceded, accompanied, and expanded the written autobiography.[12] Through their communo-biography[13] they create, define, and control their identities and their lives.

A number of European American textual models provided a framework for early Native American texts. The captivity narrative was extremely popular and widely circulated; perhaps the best known was Mary Rowlandson's *The Soveraignty and Goodness of God* (1682).[14] Because the majority of captivities during the colonial period were Native Americans and African Americans captured by European Americans, it would certainly have been an appropriate literary form for African–Native American narratives. Many of these narratives fall within the category of spiritual narrative or spiritual autobiography (Saint Augustine's *Confessions* is one of the earliest Western models), which includes confessional autobiography, missionary narratives, and conversion narratives. Other forms that might have influenced Native American texts were the execution sermon, popularized by Cotton Mather,[15] and the war narrative.[16] The use of spiritual narratives as a model for a personal narrative was particularly appropriate for Native American and African American autobiographers for several reasons. Many of these writers were afforded the opportunity to write because they had greater access than others to European American culture. Many Native Americans in particular were taken from their families or nations and schooled in European American

Christian ideals. Thus, for those who accepted such a model, the Christian religious narrative was an appropriate form for their autobiography. The Christian religious narrative was not only the nearest available model but the model that afforded a marginalized writer the most credibility: "they linked Indian autobiographers to Protestant literary traditions and identified the authors as civilized Christians whose experiences were as legitimate subjects of written analysis as were those of other Christians," according to Ruoff.[17] The adaptation of a European American literary model allowed Native American and African American autobiographers the best opportunity to influence their European American audience as well as a model in which digressions critiquing European American society were more likely to be accepted.

The earliest Native American nontraditional autobiographical written texts known to me (traditional written texts being pictographic personal narratives painted on animal hides, tipis, and shields as well as narrative wampum belts, quill work,[18] tattoos, sand pictographs,[19] the pictographic symbols used by the Ojibwa to record the Mide rituals, and the *Popul Vuh* recorded in hundreds of volumes by the Quiche Maya),[20] are the letters written by Native Americans that were later published in *The Letters of Eleazar Wheelock's Indians* (1763–66).[21] Included in this collection are letters written by Samuel Ashpo (Mohegan), Hezekiah Calvin (Delaware), David Fowler (Montauk), and Joseph Johnson (Mohegan), all of whom were educated by Wheelock at Dartmouth to become Christian missionaries to their own people. Ashpo's letter describes his missionary work; Calvin writes confessional letters asking forgiveness for his sins, detailing his missionary agenda, and frequently wishing he could return home; Fowler's letters are confessional but also express anger at his treatment by Wheelock; Johnson's letters are confessional, self-examining, and they incorporate his conversion narrative as well.[22] Brumble indicates that there were Native women in Wheelock's missionary school as well, but he includes no examples of their letters from McCallum's book; perhaps he has determined that there are no "autobiographical elements"[23] in the women's writing (although the letters of Sarah Simon seem to refute this), since he does not include their letters in his *Annotated Bibliography of American Indian and Eskimo Autobiographies*.

The next example of a nontraditional (although it seems to have become a tradition by this time) Native American autobiographical biculturally composed text[24] is a series of letters and a journal currently found in *Captain Paul Cuffe's Logs and Letters, 1808–1817*.[25] Cuffe is an interesting forerunner to Okah Tubbee. His father was African American, and his mother was Wampanoag; Cuffe was pivotal in the back-to-

Africa movement. His son, Paul Cuffe Jr., would publish the *Narrative of the Life and Adventures of Paul Cuffe, Pequot Indian, During Thirty Years Spent at Sea, and in Travelling in Foreign Lands* (1839).[26] Paul Cuffe Jr. may have identified with his grandmother (Wampanoag) or he may have capitalized on the ever-present European American interest in Native American lives.

Written in 1821 and first published in 1824, *Memoir of Catherine Brown, a Christian Indian of the Cherokee Nation* is both a biography of Catherine Brown (a Cherokee European American) written by Rufus Anderson as well as a short edited selection from her journal and twelve or thirteen pages of her letters.[27] It was popular and went through several reprints. Arnold Krupat asserts that Brown defines herself in her text "exclusively in relation to salvationist discourse."[28] A discourse "dominant in the Pilgrim century, revived in the mid-eighteenth century during the Great Awakening, and residually operative even in our own time," it is a "dialect of aggressive Protestantism . . . the discursive equivalent of a glass trained on Heaven through which all this world must be seen,"[29] although I suspect that Brown, living within the juncture of several cultures, did not define herself "exclusively" through any one particular mode, although the salvationist discourse often dominates the text.

Might these texts published prior to *A Sketch of the Life of Okah Tubbee* have had any influence on Ceil or Tubbee's narrative? Tubbee was illiterate, so he would not have read any of them, but he surely would have encountered them in their oral forms, circulating among the African American community. Captivity narratives were read aloud "by clergymen to inspire rigorous faith in the face of extreme trial."[30] Although it may have been more common among European American audiences, African American church audiences would likely have heard the same, to inspire "rigorous faith" (or strict obedience) as well as to prevent African–Native American alliances by scaring the African Americans with lurid descriptions of Native American captivities.

Confessional, conversion, and missionary narratives must have pervaded the oral African American community, just as they did the Native American community, through the constant interaction between the church (missionaries) and these communities. After many years of such interaction, the African American and Native American communities were filled with converts to Christianity; the confessional and conversion narratives must have circulated widely. In addition, by the time Tubbee spoke his narrative in 1848, he had visited several Native American nations and would have been familiar with the discourse of Christian Indians, among them his own wife, Laah Ceil.

For her part, Ceil had been educated in Christian schools. She was intimately familiar with conversion, confessional, and missionary discourse. Her autobiographical narrative toward the end of *A Sketch of the Life of Okah Tubbee* is itself a conversion and missionary narrative. It is possible that she had read some of these earlier Native American texts or had heard oral accounts of the narrators' lives, especially since the administrators of the Christian Indian schools presented the students with worthy examples of other Christian Indians. Hezekiah Calvin was from her own nation (Delaware), and perhaps she had heard of him. She was likely to have heard of Samson Occom (Mohegan), who was the first Native American to publish a written text.[31] A missionary, Occom published *A Sermon Preached at the Execution of Moses Paul, an Indian*, in 1772, a text that reflected "the tradition[s] of the execution sermon then so popular in America."[32] Ceil might also have read "A Narrative of an Embassy to the Western Indians," written in 1792 (and published in 1827) by Hendrick Aupaumut, the chief of the Stockbridge, Massachusetts, division of the Mahicans,[33] which was most likely her father's nation.[34]

Regardless of what Tubbee or Ceil may have read or heard about, these prior texts are probably more useful in understanding what forms Native American writers had already used and in what ways they had used them, as general rather than specific models that Ceil and Tubbee might have used to create their own narrative, or as useful texts for comparative analysis. Although it is not clear how it transpired, Reverend Lewis Leonidas Allen, a friend of Tubbee's, edited Ceil and Tubbee's first autobiography and planned on publishing it in installments.[35] Once the decision had been made to publish an autobiography, Ceil took down Tubbee's spoken autobiography and mailed it to Allen in letters.[36]

Although Allen may have planned on published installments, Ceil and Tubbee had very different plans. One year later, a revised and expanded version was published under Ceil's name; she added significantly to the first autobiography, including sections on Tubbee's childhood, his growing musical talents, his Choctaw identity, and the powerful dreams they both experienced.[37]

The subsequent 1852 autobiography of Tubbee and Ceil shares a significant number of similarities with the Native–European American biculturally composed written autobiographies that preceded it, including themes, styles, structures, and prefatory and appendatory documentation. Such documentation accompanies early Native American and African American written narratives and texts by women (as well as others) who have been marginalized; it purports to grant them permission to speak, and it ascertains their "authentic" identities. The inclusion of such documentation allows the narrators to "convince their readers that they were members of the human race whose experiences were legitimate subjects of autobiography and whose accounts of these experiences were accurate."[38]

In the first autobiography, the "thrilling sketch" of Tubbee's life is "by Rev. L. L. Allen, Author of Pencillings upon the Rio Grande."[39] Allen exercised considerable control over the manuscript, going so far as to represent himself as the author of a biography or sketch of Tubbee's life rather than as its editor. His authority stems from his title, Reverend, as well as from his previously published work, "Pencillings upon the Rio Grande." Allen also includes a prefatory "Essay upon the Indian Character,"[40] which closely follows the prevailing tone of the "noble savage" discourse of the period: "In contemplating the Indian character, there is an interest thrown around it, which cannot fail to impress the mind of every inquiring person, although the Indian race is fading away; their palmy days being gone. . . . Nation after nation, and tribe after tribe, are passing away."[41]

Along with prefatory material, tribal histories were included in nearly every nineteenth-century Native–European American biculturally composed written autobiography. Since Native American written autobiographies have historically been shelved (in many readers' minds and in libraries) as anthropological studies rather than literary autobiographies, editors of such manuscripts included a tribal history as an essential component of an ethnographic study. For Native American authors, such a history served several purposes. First, it was an authentication of their identity, placing them genealogically in the midst of a specific Native American nation. Second, such a history allowed them to demonstrate the abuses suffered by their nation at the hands of European Americans, to provide the textual document that Europeans seemed to require to believe that acts of injustice took place. Third, since many Native Americans express themselves in terms of a relational or communal identity, an autobiography is not complete without the inclusion of the community from which their identity is derived.

Reverend Allen included a section titled "Biography" in *A Thrilling Sketch of the Life of the Distinguished Chief Okah Tubbee*, a tribal history of the Choctaws, yet the authorship is unclear. As a tribal history it is sketchy, focusing mainly on negotiations of a treaty between the Choctaws and Creeks and the Comanches and Wichitas in 1835. Littlefield believes that "it has the tone and format of a set piece which Okah Tubbee may have recited on stage."[42] If so, this section would appear to be Tubbee's attempt to reclaim his Choctaw identity, to speak himself into Choctaw history.

Tubbee and Ceil also include a history (in their "Biography" section), and it deals, like many Native American histories, with a treaty process. Mosholeh Tubbee figures prominently in these textual negotiations, as he did in the negotiations themselves, but the history also reveals the story of a missing child:

> I thought this might throw some light upon the gloom that darkens the hopes, even the dying request of the loved, the brave, the lamented, Big Chief, or Chubbee, of the Oyataw Nation, respecting the youngest son of his, who was with the pale face. Furthermore, many evil designing men, have reported that this child was dead, others that Chief Chubbee had no such child, and now had no heir living. . . . Grateful respects to the pale face friends for their care and attention from the grandfather, whose heart is warm of being pleased with his prize, as he bears a strong personal resemblance to his father, except the father was taller and heavier built also.[43]

Thus Ceil and Tubbee write Tubbee back into the history of the Choctaws, verifying his claim with an indisputable written document that accompanies the oral text they perform on the stage. Their Choctaw history is surrounded on both sides by the indisputable texts of European American authorities: prefacing their history is Allen's "Essay upon the Indian Character," offering not only a romantic conception of Indians but also an analysis of Tubbee's "beautifully significant" Indian name: "Okah Tubbee, which means Big Chief, not only referring to a great and enlarged mind but to a powerful tribe, a Chief of the Choctaw nation."[44] Allen casts Tubbee not only as Choctaw but as representative of as well as a leader in the Choctaw nation.

Following Tubbee and Ceil's "Biography" is "a view of the present condition of the Choctaw Indians written in 1846, by a highly respected and devoted Missionary, and Teacher at Fort Coffee Academy, Iowa Territory, Rev. W. G. Montgomery."[45] In this essay, Montgomery reveals the climate, the latitudinal and longitudinal location, and the mineral content of the Choctaw nation's lands. He also assures the reader that the Choctaw are capable of attaining European "civilization":

> Christianity has done much for these people, and is still doing more, they may be said to be redeemed from heathenism, and placed upon the high and elevated ground of civilization, the arts and sciences being cultivated by them to some considerable extent. They have a well drawn up, and printed constitution . . . and the temperance cause has many advocates . . . the New Testament is translated into their language . . . the weapons of war are beaten into ploughshares, and no longer is the war whoop heard, but songs of Zion may be heard from their cabins and houses.[46]

Thus Ceil and Tubbee, surrounded by the authority of the Christian church, the acknowledgment of "civilization," and even a printed constitution, may begin, as Reverend Allen acknowledges, their "true narrative drawn up from his own lips in a simple touching and beautiful style, which may be relied upon as true."[47] In this instance, although a history of Ceil's nation is not included (most likely because she was not seen by Allen, or perhaps even by Tubbee, as the true subject of this narrative), Allen acknowledges at least some of Ceil's contribution to the autobiography (as the one who does the "drawing" and as the contributor of a "simple touching and beautiful style," although he underestimates her abilities).

Like nineteenth-century African American slave narratives, *A Thrilling Sketch* is accompanied by an array of authenticating documentation. Nineteenth-century slave narratives include prefatory materials, "letters of reference, affidavits, news clippings, copies of legal documents,"[48] and a variety of appendatory documents, as well as documents inserted within the narrative itself. *A Thrilling Sketch* contains prefatory letters from Allen and Montgomery as well as an oral verification of Tubbee's identity attributed to Pochongehala.[49] Tubbee and Ceil include the names of "respectable" folk within the narrative portion of the text whenever they have an opportunity, particularly those affiliated with the church, the military, or the government. The inclusion of these names functions as an internal authentication device, a verifiable list of those who would vouch for the truth of the events in the narrative. They also include the names of every city and town visited, including dates and the names of those with whom Tubbee stayed. Furthermore, they thank the innkeepers with whom he has stayed, the Ponchartrain, Nashville, and Carrolton Railroads, and the "captain and crews of various steamers"[50] for their kindness. Such an act not only might have ingratiated Tubbee to those European Americans who had treated him decently and ensured his ability to continue to travel freely, it would also assure his readers of his Choctaw identity, since an escaped slave or even a free African American would likely have had great difficulty securing either sleeping or railroad accommodations.

In addition to names, Tubbee and Ceil also include a copy of Tubbee's appointment to Fife Major, a particularly important document because it associates him with the military:[51]

> I soon attached myself to Charles F. Hosea's Company of the Louisiana Guards, which afterward changed their names to Washington Guards. I discharged my duties honorably, and gained the confidence and esteem of many warm hearted persons. I was elected Fife Major for the Washington Battalion, and as evidence of it I insert a true copy of the order:

Special Order.
Head Quarters Regt. Louisiana Volunteers,
New Orleans, 1st May, 1844.

W. McCarey is hereby appointed Fife Major of the Field Music of the Regt. Louisiana Volunteers with full power to regulate said field music agreeably to law and the usual custom in such matters.
By order of Col. James H. Dakin.[52]

The end of Tubbee and Ceil's autobiography is marked by a substantial number of letters of reference. The letters serve to establish Tubbee's connection to Native Americans ("Mr. Okah Tubbee is hereby granted permission to visit all the Indian tribes under my control. . . . R. B. Mitchell, Ind. Sub-Ag't."), his abilities as a musician ("But I do not hesitate to add my testimony . . . of the general admiration of your talents, as a musician, unequalled perhaps by any flutist in the world"; "he is not a musician, he is music personified"), his Choctaw identity ("I have no reason to doubt your whole account of your parentage . . ."), his and Ceil's authorial success ("The history of your life, written by your wife is truly amusing. You are at liberty to have this published in any respectable newspaper"), his irreproachable behavior ("it affords me much pleasure to bear witness to his uniformly gentlemanly deportment while amongst us . . ."), and Ceil's identity and gentlewomanly deportment ("He also has with him Mrs. Tubbee, a most interesting intelligent person, and a fine specimen of the Indian tribe").[53]

The letters emanate from a number of respectable sources, including Indian agents, the commissioner of Indian affairs, reverends, members of the Fraternal Order of Masons, customs agents, average citizens, and doctors. The last category is particularly important because among Tubbee's various vocations, the practice of healing soon took precedence:

> This is to certify that Dr. Okah Tubbee boarded with me four weeks and six days, and during the time he practiced on several cases, and accomplished great cures; and so great was [sic] his cures that it was astonishing to the whole city. The house was thronged from 6 A.M. to 9 P.M.[54]

> Dr. Okah Tubbee, Toronto.
> Sir:—It is with pleasure that I certify to the good effect of your medicine on myself. I have been troubled with a pain in my side, more or less, for the last nine years, and have tried several doctors, but to no effect; but after using your medicine about four days, last February, I was relieved of the pain, and have felt none of it since.[55]

Tubbee's licenses to practice medicine in Missouri during 1850 and 1851 are also included among the authenticating documents, as are certifications that he possesses previous certifications, and two more documents that vouch for his Choctaw identity. The first appears at the end of the first section of letters of reference and describes the circumstances surrounding the death of Mosholeh Tubbee. The second is a letter of reference from members of several Native nations, including the Cayuga nation: "The Cayuga Tribe of Indians, and several parties of the other tribes residing on Grand River, were delighted with their brother Okah Tubbee a chief from the Choctaw Tribe of Indians. They were amused and instructed by his address; and the Chiefs present at his Entertainment went forward to him and gave him their hands in token of acknowledgment, before his musical performance commenced. They recommend him to their pale face friends."[56]

Another important feature of this African–Native American text is the appearance of dreams. In the body of the text, drawing from African American and Native American oral traditions and European American conversion narratives, Ceil and Tubbee relate several dreams, the first being an explanation of his invention of two musical instruments, the sauce-panana and the musical tomahawk:

> I dreamed I was an ancient Shepherd. One summer day, while my flock was resting in the shade, I sauntered out over the country. I came to a spot, where a pretty brook had once crept along, watering many flocks. But the brook was nearly gone, and the ground around was a miry swamp. There lay many sheep with broken and disjointed limbs, panting for life. They were not my sheep, and I was about to pass on. "What!" said I, "shall a shepherd pass a suffering flock, and offer no relief?" I returned, took them from the mire, and laid them on a carpet of red clover, under a shady tree. I was very thirsty, and as there was a little water in places, I began to contrive how to get a drink. I found that I had a saucepan in my pocket. . . . I thought I heard a voice, saying: "Take the sauce pan out of your pocket, and blow through the handle thereof, and there will come forth sweet strains of music, which shall cheer your flocks hereafter."[57]

The appearance of dreams and visions within African–Native American autobiography, often leading to the acquisition of special powers, is a reflection of their importance within Native American and African American cultures and as a primary component of European American Christian conversion narratives.[58] The African–Native American writer William Apess includes in his autobiography a "vivid dream [that] revealed to him the horrors of hell."[59] The Ojibwa autobiographer George Copway narrates a number of powerful visions that marked his life.[60] Tubbee's dream functions in a variety of ways. First, it was an introduction to the portion of their stage performance in which Tubbee would play his self-invented sauce-panana. The dream would also have been familiar to European American audiences as a version of the Good Samaritan parable, and thus it served to confirm Ceil and Tubbee's Christianity and thus their equality with a "civilized" Christian audience. Tubbee appears to be a Christ-like figure in the dream, a shepherd leading his Native American flocks to Christianity. The dream also draws from elements of the Christian conversion narrative and missionary narrative, introducing to European American audiences Tubbee's encounter with a mysterious voice (recalling Moses and the burning bush as well as the appearance of the angels to the shepherds before Christ's birth) and Tubbee and Ceil's mission to bring Christianity and music to Native American nations. When playing in front of a Native American audience (as they often did), the power of a dream and the importance of its enactment would be readily apparent. The dream also appears to confirm Tubbee's identity when he provides his interpretation that the suffering flock is the Native American nations and he the shepherd of restoration. Finally, it offers an opportunity to make a strong political statement about the treatment of Native American nations to a European American audience without the retribution that would accompany such a statement framed in more literal terms.

The dream/vision was also an important part of nineteenth-century African American culture and an appropriate mode of narration for a contact with God, according to Lawrence W. Levine, who describes an African American woman experiencing a vision at a church service in 1851, witnessed by Frederika Bremer:

> "she talked to herself in a low voice, and such a beautiful, blissful expression was portrayed in her countenance that I would willingly experience that which she then experienced, saw or perceived. It was no ordinary, no earthly scene. Her countenance was, as it were, transfigured."
>
> In these states of transfiguration slave converts commonly saw and conversed with God or Christ: "I looked to the east and there was . . . God. He looked neither to the right nor to the left. I was afraid and fell on my face. . . . I heard a voice from God saying, 'My little one, be not afraid for lo! I am with you always.'" "I looked away to the east and saw Jesus. . . . I saw God sitting in a big arm-chair." "I first came to know of God when I was a little child. He started talking to me when I was no more than nine years old." "I seen Christ with His hair parted in the center." "I saw Him when he freed my soul from hell." "I saw in a vision a snow-white train once and it moved like lightning. Jesus was on board and he told me that he was the conductor"[61]

Levine also observes that African American (and perhaps some Native American) slaves believed in "apparitions" and that "a Virginia correspondent of the *New York Times* wrote that in their Christian worship 'negroes are excessively superstitious. They have all sorts of "experiences," and enjoy the most wonderful revelations. Visions of the supernatural are of nightly occurrence.'"[62]

Along with the shepherd and flock dream, Tubbee relates two more dreams, one about the making of the sauce-panana and another in which Ceil appears to him before they have met. Again, Tubbee believes this dream must be performed, and he enacts its circumstances, traveling up the Ohio River in search of Ceil. The importance of such a description is not the truth or falsity of his dream but the terms in which he chooses to describe it. Such terms of vision and enactment appear in many Native American autobiographies (Black Elk's, for instance). Tubbee may have been influenced by Laah Ceil, whose control of the manuscript resulted in the appearance of these dreams in the 1852 autobiography when they had not appeared in the first version. In the portion of the autobiography that is particularly her own, Ceil includes a dream to describe her first awareness of God at two years of age; such a form draws from her traditional Delaware culture[63] as well as from the standard form of the Christian conversion narrative with which she is familiar. Just as it would have been the appropriate form for relating a conversion narrative within European American Christian society, it would have been the appropriate form in Delaware culture to discuss a supernatural contact.

Just as African American, Native American, and African–Native American autobiographers drew from multiple traditions in developing their narratives, mediating between cultural traditions, they also often served as mediators between cultural groups themselves. Although Gretchen Bataille and Kathleen Sands note that "early black writers and, until recently, American Indian narrators, were essentially unaware of the rhetorical conventions and literary models of white society,"[64] African American autobiographers such as Harriet Jacobs in her adaptation of the sentimental novel in *Incidents in the Life of a Slave Girl*[65] and Native American autobiographers were often aware of and purposely used European American textual models. They would also adopt a peaceful (non-aggressive) textual stance in order to have their stories accepted by the European American audience they hoped to sway, often tempering the political stridency of their texts to accomplish their goals. Native American autobiographers often positioned themselves in the role of mediator between the Native American nations and the United States, explaining their ability to live biculturally and their hopes for a peaceful future.

In the preface to Ceil and Tubbee's autobiography (called "Biography" in the first edition and "Indian Covenant" in subsequent editions), there is a discussion of a "universal peace" among Indian nations. The "Pipe of Peace" that is summoned is "one half white and one half red"[66] and appears to signify a peace between European Americans and Native Americans. The end of the prefatory material initiates an atmosphere of trust between the Native American narrators and the European American audience, invoking cozy and touching images of a peaceful coexistence between Native Americans and European Americans, a "warm heart," and an elderly grandfather deprived of his son. In the midst of their invocation of these comforting images, Ceil and Tubbee take the opportunity to further establish his Choctaw identity, repeating arguments that appear earlier in the autobiography: "Grateful respects to the pale face friends for their care and attention to the grandfather, whose heart is warm, being pleased with his prize, as he bears a strong personal resemblance to his father, only the father was taller and heavier built. Now may the pale face and the red man dwell peacefully together, is the desire and prayer of the grandfather."[67]

Within the autobiography itself, Tubbee and Ceil continue to represent themselves as mediators between the European Americans and the Native Americans. They discuss their visits to Native nations and their promotions of peace. In one section Tubbee reveals his plan to bring peace to the Seminoles: "a secret desire to visit that tribe soon had grown into a resolute determination, to use my endeavors to show them the hopelessness of their efforts—to impress upon their minds that at the most they would have only blood and revenge, for the blood of their kindred; and in the end, shame and disgrace, and the loss of their lands besides."[68] Tubbee also includes the reaction of Chief Powell, "who feared that I would seek to do away the Indian's hatred for the whites, and establish friendship between them."[69] Again and again, Ceil and Tubbee portray themselves as the mediators between two (or three, especially in the case of the Seminole nation) worlds, seeking "to harmonize broken and hostile tribes."[70] As problematic as the "harmonization" of Native American nations, which Ceil and Tubbee hoped to promote through music and Christianity, may seem, considering the problems Christianity had created for Native American nations, Ceil would lecture on both Christianity and Native American land rights, apparently believing, as did the African–Native American William Apess, that Christianity was an opportunity for Native American equality with European Americans. As they hoped to promote Native American rights and European American understanding of and respect for Native American cultures, they would simultaneously pacify a European American audience with promises of lasting peace, the harmonization of "hostile tribes."

Although there is a fundamental difference between the slave narratives of the nineteenth century and the autobiography of Tubbee and
Ceil, Tubbee's personal narrative is marked by numerous conventions
of nineteenth-century African American autobiography. The fundamental difference between Tubbee's autobiography and those of his contemporaries is that Tubbee, particularly in later editions (following the passage of the 1850 Fugitive Slave Act), had to deny his African American
identity in favor of his Choctaw identity. Therefore, although he had an
opportunity to speak out as an abolitionist within his text and his stage
performances, he was forced to suppress this desire along with his African identity. He did, however, retain examples of the evils of slavery in
the narration of his early life experiences, and, although he did not ally
himself with the formal abolitionist movement, he was clearly critical
of the institution of slavery.

The beginning of Tubbee's personal narrative is more attuned to the
model of the eighteenth-century rather than the nineteenth-century African American slave narrative, although it contains elements from both.
Most eighteenth-century slave narratives begin with an account of the
narrator's life before slavery, which will subsequently be contrasted with
a life in bondage. Following this is an account of the kidnapping and subsequent enslavement of the narrator.[71] This model disappeared after the
slave trade slowed and the majority of narrators were born in the United
States, not kidnapped from Africa. Since Tubbee represents himself as a
Choctaw, still living on his native soil as an infant, he narrates his memory of his early life of happiness living with his father until he is taken
from his nation to Natchez, Mississippi.

The nineteenth-century slave narrative generally begins with a description of idyllic childhood followed by a psychological rather than a
physical kidnapping, the development of the child's awareness that she
or he is a slave, in short "the loss of innocence."[72] In Harriet Jacobs's slave
narrative (1861), the protagonist, Linda Brent, declares that she "was born
a slave, but . . . never knew it till six years of happy childhood had passed
away. . . . I learned, by the talk around me, that I was a slave."[73] In the
slave narrative of Lunsford Lane (1842), he explains that he "knew no
difference between [himself] and the white children; nor did they seem
to know any in turn"; as he grew older, "they began to order me about,
and were told to do so by my master and mistress. I found, too, that they
learned to read, while I was not permitted to have a book in my hand."[74]
In Frederick Douglass's slave narrative (1850), his awareness of the hor-
rid truth of slavery comes as a child while he watches an Aunt being
whipped: "I was quite a child, but I well remember it. I never shall for-

get it whilst I remember any thing. It was the first of a long series of such outrages, of which I was doomed to be a witness and a participant. It struck me with awful force. It was the blood-stained gate, the entrance to the hell of slavery, through which I was about to pass. It was a most terrible spectacle. I wish I could commit to paper the feelings with which I beheld it."[75]

Tubbee notes that he became aware that his master was not his father, "neither in appearance nor action."[76] In other words, along with his recognition that he has been taken from his family comes his realization that the interaction between the master and himself is dictated by the terms of a master/slave relationship. He supports his assertion with the growing evidence of his bondage, the differing treatment he receives at the hands of his mother:[77]

> the slave woman . . . had two children older than myself, a boy and a girl; she was very fond of them, but was never even kind to me, yet they obliged me to call her mother. I was always made to serve the two children, but many times had to be whipped into obedience. . . . Her children were well dressed and neat; I was not only in rags, but many times my proud heart seemed crushed within me, and my cheek crimsoned with shame because of their filthy condition and I often left them off in consequence, but soon learned to take them off and wash them myself, such was my abhorrence to filth.[78]

Just as they emphasized the moment of the narrator's awareness of slavery, nineteenth-century slave narratives carried "frequent references to the partial nakedness" that resulted from an insufficient clothing allowance. Henry Bibb describes himself as "'a wretched slave, compelled to work under the lash without wages, and often without clothes enough to hide my nakedness.'"[79] Another slave narrator, William Wells Brown, also describes the inadequacies of the clothing allowed to slaves: "The clothing of the men consists of a pair of thin cotton pantaloons, and a shirt of the same material, two of each being allowed them every year. . . . They also have two suits allowed them every year. These, however, are not enough. They are made of the lowest quality of material, and get torn in the bush, so that the garments soon become useless, even for purposes of the barest decency."[80] Tubbee discusses his need for clothing over and over again, noting that every time he had saved up some money from his various odd jobs, he requested a suit of clothes. After being whipped by his mother, he remarks not on the harm to his psyche or body but on the damage to his clothes, "for which [he] had just paid $17."[81] As well as an issue of pride and self-esteem, the clothes would have enabled Tubbee to appear in public as a musician and to play and socialize at the parties the militia band attended, a key step in the process of regaining his freedom and sense of self.

After a recognition of their condition, slave narrators often present examples of the abuses suffered under slavery with an emphasis on the unjustness of the punishments. Frederick Douglass, for example, discusses the constant and "capricious punishment"[82] suffered at the hands of a slaveholder: "It would astonish one, unaccustomed to a slaveholding life, to see with what wonderful eyes a slaveholder can find things, of which to make occasion to whip a slave. A mere look, word, or motion,—a mistake, accident, or want of power,—all are matters for which a slave may be whipped at any time. Does a slave look dissatisfied? It is said, he has the devil in him, and it must be whipped out. Does he speak loudly when spoken to him by his master? Then he is getting high-minded, and should be taken down a button-hole lower."[83] Similarly, Tubbee describes years of whippings and other abuses from his mother. He is apprenticed to Mr. Russell, the blacksmith, and is surprised that the "unkind treatment" continues: "Some months had passed in this fearful manner, when at length one day Mr. Russell came to me, and ordered me to strip for the whip; in vain I begged to know what I had done to merit such usage; he only answered me with angry oaths, so loud that I was dead in silence, and obeyed, determining in my mind that this should be the last time I would do it."[84] Although Tubbee is determined from an early age that he shall be free, his vow that it would be the last time he would be whipped marks his first resolution to act on behalf of his freedom, another crucial stage in the slave narrative.[85] Tubbee was particularly outraged by his enslavement because of his unusual freedom to travel and play music. William Wells Brown also relates his yearnings for freedom, which were strengthened because of his travel on the steamboats: "'In passing from place to place, and seeing new faces every day, and knowing that they could go where they pleased, I soon became unhappy, and several times thought of leaving the boat at some landing place, and trying to make my escape to Canada.'"[86]

The whipping Tubbee receives from Mr. Russell would not be his last. Once more, at the hands of his own mother, he undergoes a whipping that fixes his resolve to escape slavery. He decides that it is time to act on his freedom, and he escapes, only to be caught and returned to Natchez. Frederick Douglass narrates the moment in his slavery when he resolves to escape. He describes his battle with the overseer Mr. Covey as a "turning-point," his step into manhood and identity: "but at this moment—from whence came the spirit I don't know—I resolved to fight; and, suiting my action to the resolution, I seized Covey hard by the throat. . . . He asked me if I meant to persist in my resistance. I told him I did, come what might; that he had used me like a brute for six months, and that I was determined to be used so no longer. . . . This battle with Mr. Covey was the turning-point in my career as a slave. It rekindled the few burning embers of freedom, and revived within me a sense of my own manhood."[87]

Tubbee describes a similar scene, although the beating is at the hands of his mother (and owner). He declares his resolve to fight for his manhood:

> She then saying, you are in my power, began to lay on the blows—now that I discovered my foe had tied me, and my senses had returned, the reality of my disgraceful situation was plain before me, together with the smart of the keen lash seemed to give me lion-like strength, and with a few desperate leaps I succeeded in tearing the bedstead into pieces, breaking the cord that bound my feet, tearing up a cloth pair of pants for which I had just paid $17, with the part to which my hands were fastened I felled the old woman, leaving her to pick up herself, while I rushed to the door where I soon gnawed my right hand loose, and seeing a friend of hers coming to her at a distance, I picked up a piece of brick and leveled him.[88]

Tubbee not only frees himself from the ropes, knocking down the aggressor in the melee, he asserts his control over the situation by briefly making himself the master in the house. His subsequent retrieval of the suit of clothes to replace his missing pants is a step toward the retrieval of his identity—his manhood symbolized by the pair of pants and his selfhood in the act of demanding decent clothes. Finally, although Tubbee had the option of purchasing himself from his family, he refused, and his reaction is similar to that of Linda Brent when she learns that Mrs. Bruce intends to purchase her in order to "free" her: "I felt grateful for the kindness that prompted this offer, but the idea was not so pleasant to me as might have been expected. The more my mind had become enlightened, the more difficult it was for me to consider myself an article of property; and to pay money to those who had so grievously oppressed me seemed like taking from my sufferings the glory of triumph. I wrote to Mrs. Bruce, thanking her, but saying that being sold from one owner to another seemed too much like slavery."[89] Tubbee is equally offended by the idea of purchasing himself and devotes a lengthy passage to his arguments, insisting that he would be degraded by such an act:

> My enemies said that I could make money fast, and could afford to buy myself of the woman, and thus settle the dispute. This mortified me very much; indeed my feelings I do not attempt to describe. . . . Could I stoop to this? I was exceedingly careful in my manners, and now that the boy was somewhat polished in the man, why should they persecute me still? I firmly refused them; not that I valued the money so much; no, to have

had them cease tormenting me, I would not have begrudged twice the amount, but to have it said that I had to buy my flesh and blood and this lofty spirit!—Oh! horrible thought! it stung my inmost soul, and almost maddened me into despair![90]

Another characteristic Tubbee's slave narrative shares with other nineteenth-century slave narratives is the use of Christianity as a political tool. African slaves (as well as Native Americans), upon learning to read, discovered that the Europeans had effectively masked particular portions of the Bible or had emphasized selective sections for their political ends. Sections that discussed equality, liberty (the U.S. Constitution was among the European American documents African Americans and Native Americans enlisted in their fight against oppression), and justice were particularly effective as a rhetorical tool against European American oppression. Since many slave narratives were Christian conversion, missionary, or spiritual narratives (or all three), many events were "interpreted as manifestations of God's power and grace."[91] Thus, the eighteenth-century African American slave narrative of James Albert Ukawsaw Gronniosaw discusses "'the interposition of Providence.'"[92] In nineteenth-century slave narratives, God's power not only to control all things but also to mete out justice was invoked. William Craft, for instance, acknowledges slaves' hope for "divine retribution" against their oppressors: "There is, however, great consolation in knowing that God is just, and will not let the oppressor of the weak, and the spoiler of the virtuous, escape unpunished here and hereafter."[93] After his whipping by Mr. Russell, Tubbee also invokes an instance of divine retribution: "He died a miserable death, being drowned in a ditch, in a fit of intoxication; making my prophesies true that God would punish him for his savage treatment of me. 'Though hand join in hand the wicked shall not go unpunished.'"[94] Finally, the authors of slave narratives developed many sophisticated arguments, the most powerful of which insisted that Christianity and slavery were simply incompatible. Tubbee's slave narrative invokes God again and again, effectively introducing him into the text as a witness to his sufferings, creating a authenticating documentation that carried a powerful weight among the European Americans.

Most slave narratives end in escape and the "freedom" of the North, but Tubbee's "escape" is never clear. There is a continuous argument over his legal status during which time he travels and plays his music, finding odd jobs along the way, until he meets Ceil. For several years he commutes between the North and the South, occasionally stopping in Natchez. Finally, he simply quits returning to Natchez, instead touring the North and Canada with Ceil and their family, constantly in fear for his freedom and their lives, particularly after the 1850 passage of the Fugitive Slave Act. The autobiography of Ceil and Tubbee begins as a slave narrative, but it develops into a Native American autobiography that focuses more intensely on Native American civil rights.

Toward the end of the autobiography, Tubbee introduces a self-created instrument that is representative of his and Ceil's efforts to portray Native Americans as peaceful, the musical tomahawk. While Black Hawk promised that the "tomahawk is buried forever," Tubbee and Ceil carry a potent symbol of such a promise with them at all times, having converted an instrument that represented Native American resistance to the European Americans into an instrument of peaceful performance.

Like their stage performance, the autobiography of Tubbee and Ceil ends in a burst of patriotic fervor that would have bested any Fourth of July display:

> The stars and stripes unfurled above their heads, waving gracefully to and fro in the gentle breeze, as if thus endeavoring to acknowledge the pleasure of gracing such an occasion; the gallant officers at their posts, warm hearted privates standing in unbroken ranks, yet forming no stronger line than the friendship of their brave and manly hearts; and then the worthy citizens of standing, a little way off, smilingly tipping the beaver in welcome recognition of their friends; and when the signal was given for taking up the line of march, then came the thrilling notes of the fife, brought forth with three fingers of one hand, while I ingeniously managed to wave my cap to both officers and privates, gentleman and ladies, while making my humble obeisance to all.[95]

As they do earlier, Tubbee and Ceil manage to write Tubbee into the midst of the narration; during their stage performances, he would actually play his fife one-handed while waving his cap, or perhaps while playing the castanets with the other hand,[96] embedding in both writing and performance their claim on American identity, citizenship, and justice. Tubbee and Ceil manage to bring together two divergent literary streams where their waters mingle most readily, creating a hybrid African–Native American autobiography that demonstrates in one text the development of cross-cultural literary influences in American literary history.

## Notes

1. Okah Tubbee was born into slavery in Natchez, Mississippi, in 1810 (or 1811) and was initially known as either Warner McCary or James Warner. His mother was Franky (or Frances); he had two older siblings, Robert and Kitty. In 1813, Franky, Robert, and Kitty were manumitted by their owner, James

McCary; Robert and Kitty subsequently received a substantial inheritance and "became known as Robert and Kitty McCary." Included in their inheritance was one slave, "the youngest child of Franky," and thus Warner McCary became a slave to his own family. Apprenticed at age eighteen to a blacksmith, Warner insisted on his release from slavery at age twenty-one. There was a great deal of discussion about his legal status, but never a resolution. Since Warner had joined the Natchez Cadets as a fife player, he traveled regularly. When he failed to receive his freedom, he simply continued traveling and playing, eventually developing his own repertoire. In this way he ignored the obligations of slavery. He began to assert that his father had been the Choctaw chief Moshulatubbee and that since he was really a Native American, he could not be a slave. He took the name Okah Tubbee and began to reclaim his Choctaw identity. See Daniel F. Littlefield Jr., Introduction to *The Life of Okah Tubbee,* by Okah Tubbee and Laah Ceil (Lincoln: University of Nebraska Press, 1988), 10, 13, 14.

2. Arnold Krupat, *For Those Who Come After: A Study in Native American Autobiography* (Berkeley: University of California Press, 1985), 53.

3. A. LaVonne Brown Ruoff, *American Indian Literatures: An Introduction, Bibliographic Review, and Selected Bibliography* (New York: Modern Language Association, 1990), 55.

4. Gretchen Bataille and Kathleen Mullen Sands, *American Indian Women: Telling Their Lives* (Lincoln: University of Nebraska Press, 1984), 53.

5. H. David Brumble, *American Indian Autobiography* (Berkeley: University of California Press, 1988), 254.

6. Littlefield, Introduction, xi.

7. H. David Brumble, *An Annotated Bibliography of American Indian and Eskimo Autobiographies* (Lincoln: University of Nebraska Press, 1981), 141.

8. Ibid.

9. In 1836 Okah Tubbee met Laah Ceil on the Delaware lands south of Fort Leavenworth. Born in New York in 1817, Ceil was of mixed Delaware and Mohawk descent. She arrived on the Delaware lands near Fort Leavenworth a number of years after the main body of the Delaware nation had been removed in 1829. They married and had four children. Together (and sometimes with their youngest child Mosholeh or Bruce) they would appear on stage. Laah Ceil would narrate portions of her autobiography and lecture on Native American land rights as well as temperance. Okah Tubbee would speak portions of his autobiography and play music. See Littlefield, Introduction, vii–xxxviii.

10. Ibid., ix.

11. Okah Tubbee and Laah Ceil, *The Life of Okah Tubbee,* ed. Daniel F. Littlefield Jr. (Lincoln: University of Nebraska Press, 1988), 91.

12. In the summer of 1848, after several years of performing, Ceil and Tubbee published the first of four editions of their autobiography. Narrated by Tubbee to Ceil, who subsequently sent it to the Reverend Lewis Leonidas Allen, a friend of Tubbee's, the initial autobiography included prefatory material by Allen. Ceil quickly followed this autobiography with another in late

1848, this one under her editorial control and greatly expanded. The third, also published in 1848, was an edited version of the second. The final autobiography was published in 1852 and included material from their lives from 1848 to 1852 as well as other substantial changes.

13. See Hertha D. Sweet Wong, *Sending My Heart Back across the Years* (New York: Oxford University Press, 1992), 6, 26, for a discussion of "communo-bio-oratory."

14. Mary Rowlandson, *The Soveraignty and Goodness of God*, in *American Captivity Narratives*, ed. Gordon M. Sayre (New York: Houghton Mifflin, 2000), 132–76.

15. Ruoff, *American Indian Literatures*, 62.

16. Krupat, *For Those Who Come After*, 35.

17. A. LaVonne Brown Ruoff, "Three Nineteenth-Century American Indian Autobiographers," in *Redefining American Literary History*, ed. A. LaVonne Brown Ruoff and Jerry W. Ward (New York: Modern Language Association, 1990), 252.

18. Wong, *Sending My Heart Back*, 44–87.

19. Krupat, *For Those Who Come After*, 30.

20. Ruoff, *American Indian Literatures*, 11.

21. James Dow McCallum, ed., *The Letters of Eleazar Wheelock's Indians* (Dartmouth College Manuscript Series No. 1) (Hanover, N.H.: Dartmouth College Publications, 1932).

22. Brumble, *Annotated Bibliography*, 16, 38, 61, 75.

23. Ibid., 16.

24. Krupat, *For Those Who Come After*, 31. Krupat refers to these texts as "bicultural compositions." The "bicultural element" or "bicultural composite composition" to which he refers appears always to indicate a collaboration or cultural exchange between the European American model and that of a specific Native American nation. I would imagine, though, that a bicultural exchange resulting in the alteration or creation of a bicultural Native American text is not limited to a European American–Native American contact but should incorporate as well the many cultural exchanges between any of the hundreds of Native American nations that must have resulted in significantly changed oral or written texts ("bicultural composite compositions") or perhaps even the availability of either entirely new forms or substantially new material from which to create new literatures.

25. Rosalind Cobb Wiggins, *Captain Paul Cuffe's Logs and Letters, 1808–1817: A Black Quaker's "Voice from within the Veil"* (Washington, D.C.: Howard University Press, 1996).

26. See Brumble, *Annotated Bibliography*, 47.

27. Rufus Anderson, *Memoir of Catharine Brown: A Christian Indian of the Cherokee Nation* (Boston: S. T. Armstrong/Crocker and Brewster, 1825).

28. Arnold Krupat, *The Voice in the Margin: Native American Literature and the Canon* (Berkeley: University of California Press, 1989), 147.

29. Ibid., 142.

30. Bataille and Sands, *American Indian Women*, 4.

31. If "publish" means the reproduction and distribution of a text, then perhaps Native Americans had published texts before European contact; in this case I mean a published text within a European American purview.

32. Ruoff, *American Indian Literatures*, 62; Samson Occom, *A Sermon Preached at the Execution of Moses Paul, an Indian* (Early American Imprints, Second Series, No. 9049) (Springfield, Ill.: Henry Brewer, 1805).

33. Hendrick Aupaumut, "A Narrative of an Embassy to the Western Indians, from the Original Manuscript of Hendrick Aupaumut, with Prefatory Remarks by Dr. B. H. Coates," ed. B. H. Coates, *Pennsylvania Historical Society Memoirs* 2, pt. 1 (1827): 61–131.

34. Brumble, *Annotated Bibliography*, 214.

35. Littlefield, Introduction, xxiv.

36. Ibid., xxvii.

37. Ibid., xxv.

38. Ruoff, "American Indian Autobiographers," 252.

39. Okah Tubbee and Laah Ceil, *A Thrilling Sketch of the Life of the Distinguished Chief Okah Tubbee Alias Wm. Chubbee, Son of the Head Chief, Mosholeh Tubbee, of the Choctaw Nation of Indians. By Rev. L. L. Allen* (New York: Cameron's Steam Power Presses, 1848), cover.

40. Ibid., 1.

41. Ibid., 3–5.

42. Tubbee and Ceil, *Life of Okah Tubbee*, 131.

43. Tubbee and Ceil, *Thrilling Sketch*, 11–12.

44. Ibid., 4.

45. Ibid., 12.

46. Ibid., 4.

47. Ibid., 15.

48. Frances Smith Foster, *Witnessing Slavery* (Westport, Conn.: Greenwood Press, 1979), x.

49. Littlefield notes that the identity of Pochongehala is unknown but that it may have been a reference to Buckongahelas (d.1805), a Delaware leader (Introduction, xiii).

50. Tubbee and Ceil, *Life of Okah Tubbee*, 54.

51. Littlefield notes that slaves and free blacks were not allowed to join the volunteer militia unit, particularly because one of the militia's duties was to put down slave rebellions, so this association also allows Tubbee and Ceil to further Tubbee's identity as a Choctaw rather than as an African American (Introduction, xiii).

52. Tubbee and Ceil, *Life of Okah Tubbee*, 52.

53. Ibid., 102–8.

54. Ibid., 111.

55. Ibid., 117.

56. Ibid., 120.

57. Ibid., 85–86.

58. Ruoff, "American Indian Autobiographers," 258.

59. Ibid., 254.

60. Ibid., 258–59.

61. Lawrence W. Levine, *Black Culture and Black Consciousness: Afro-American Folk Thought from Slavery to Freedom* (New York: Oxford University Press, 1977), 37.

62. Ibid., 61.

63. C. A. Weslager states that "discussions with Delaware traditionalists made . . . ethnologists aware that the most vital and intimate phase of Delaware religion was a belief in dreams and visions . . . the vision was the point of contact, a line of communication between the supernatural world and the sphere of everyday life" (*The Delaware Indians* [New Brunswick, N.J.: Rutgers University Press, 1972], 68).

64. Bataille and Sands, *American Indian Women*, 7.

65. Other African American writers did this as well. See Harriet E. Wilson, *Our Nig; or, Sketches from the Life of a Free Black, in a Two-Story White House, North—Showing That Slavery's Shadows . . .* (New York: Vintage Books, 1983).

66. Tubbee and Ceil, *Life of Okah Tubbee*, 15.

67. Ibid., 16.

68. Ibid., 58.

69. Ibid., 83.

70. Ibid., 87.

71. Foster, *Witnessing Slavery*, 45.

72. Ibid., 85.

73. Harriet Jacobs, *Incidents in the Life of a Slave Girl*, ed. Jean Yellin (Cambridge, Mass.: Harvard University Press, 1987), 5–6.

74. Foster, *Witnessing Slavery*, 116; Lunsford Lane, *The Narrative of Lunsford Lane*, 2d ed. (Boston: J. E. Torrey, 1842).

75. Frederick Douglass, *Narrative of the Life of Frederick Douglass* (New York: Signet, 1968), 25.

76. Tubbee and Ceil, *Life of Okah Tubbee*, 18.

77. As a result of his enslavement by his own family and the whipping he experienced at the hands of his mother, Tubbee carefully distances himself from his mother, calling her his "unnatural mother" or "the woman," a textual stance that allows him to distance himself further from African American (slave) identity as well as a pyschologically defensive stance that displays his deep anguish at his family's behavior and his resulting separation from them.

78. Tubbee and Ceil, *Life of Okah Tubbee*, 18.

79. Quoted in Foster, *Witnessing Slavery*, 100–101.

80. William Wells Brown, *Narrative of William Wells Brown, a Fugitive Slave* (Boston: Anti-Slavery Office, 1847), 31.

81. Tubbee and Ceil, *Life of Okah Tubbee*, 46.

82. Foster, *Witnessing Slavery*, 110.

83. Douglass, *Narrative of the Life*, 87–88.

84. Tubbee and Ceil, *Life of Okah Tubbee*, 36.

85. Foster, *Witnessing Slavery*, 115.

86. Quoted in ibid., 89.

87. Douglass, *Narrative of the Life*, 82.

88. Tubbee and Ceil, *Life of Okah Tubbee*, 46–47.

89. Jacobs, *Incidents in the Life of a Slave Girl*, 199.

90. Tubbee and Ceil, *Life of Okah Tubbee*, 41–42.

91. Foster, *Witnessing Slavery*, 48.

92. Quoted in ibid., 50.

93. Quoted in ibid., 119; William Craft and Ellen Craft, *Running a Thousand Miles for Freedom* (London: William Tweedie, 1860).

94. Tubbee and Ceil, *Life of Okah Tubbee*, 38.

95. Ibid., 100.

96. Littlefield, Introduction, vii.

# PART 3

# Mardi Gras Indian
# Performance

JASON BERRY,

JONATHAN FOOSE,

AND TAD JONES

6   *In Search of the*
*Mardi Gras Indians*

On Mardi Gras (French for Fat Tuesday), New Orleans teems
with parades and music and dancing. The streets fill with radiant maskers,
a flood of personas drawn from aging history books and television. But so
is Mardi Gras a season, more accurately called Carnival—several weeks
of society balls and parades, a rush of musical celebration culminating the
night before Ash Wednesday, which signals the beginning of Lent. The
parades are dazzling sights. Long floats, lavishly decorated and drawn by
tractors, course through the streets in rhythm with the marching bands.
In the night parades, black flambeau carriers strut between the bands and
the floats, raising poles studded with burning candles. Masked riders throw
beads, doubloons, dolls, and trinkets to the thousands jammed on sidewalks, tottering on ladders, yelling, "Throw me something, Mister!"

A long and lovely history of costume art is associated with Carnival; so is a growing film and documentary tradition and a body of lively
music, from jazz and rhythm and blues standards to more romantic lyrics played at the fancy balls. Parades and dances move to a distinct Carnival beat. Jukeboxes resonate with Professor Longhair's anthem "Go to
the Mardi Gras" and others, like Al Johnson's memorable "Carnival
Time." Carnival has spawned many traditions. The upper class enshrined
an ornate fictitious royalty: autumn debutantes as winter queens, big
businessmen as kings. Black New Orleans has its own society circuit, of
which Zulu is the most illustrious ball. But in the early 1970s a seemingly new tradition burst into popularity, the Mardi Gras Indians.

198 Jason Berry, Jonathan Foose, and Tad Jones

Before dawn broke on the Mardi Gras of 1979, a video crew set up outside of George Landry's shotgun house on Valence Street. Neighbors gathered, followed by red-eyed revelers from Tipitina's, where the Neville Brothers' last set had just ended. Momentarily, Art Neville arrived, joining the small group, waiting in the cold dawn for his uncle, affectionately called Jolley, who was still inside the house. For weeks, neighborhood kids had filed in and out of the room where the old man sewed rhinestones and sequins onto the patches and chest of the suit. Watching the costume emerge had become a ritual in itself, but when the house got too crowded, Jolley made everyone leave. He was Big Chief of the Wild Tchoupitoulas, founded in 1972.

Slowly, the dark sky washed blue. The cameraman waited with his sungun, a strong light encased in a metal sleeve. The first Indian arrived: Norman Bell, the portly Second Chief, wearing a pink-feathered suit with billowing ostrich plumes. Next came the Spy Boy, whose suit was vivid yellow. Then the door opened, and Big Chief Jolley stepped into the early light wearing a costume red as blood; he crashed the tambourine against his fist and yelled: "Whoaaa, Big Chief! Big Chief Jolleeeyyy!" People parted as he came down the steps, hitting the tambourine. He stopped and raised his tambourine toward the sun in a stunning red profile and cried: "Koochee mighty baum baum, nobody run this mawnin'! Koochee mighty baum baum, make blood chipahoona, make no bow!"

Word had spread that this would be Jolley's last Mardi Gras as Big Chief of the Thirteenth Ward tribe, named for the last uptown street bordering the river. Jolley was passing the mantle to Norman, but no one knew exactly when. Art Neville opened the door of someone's fender-bent convertible, and Uncle Jolley stepped in and plopped down on the top of the rear cushion. "I'm gonna ride this one, Norman. You take 'em down."

And it happened just like that. No grand ritual: the convertible chugged off, leaving the cameraman wondering who to follow—Jolley in the car or Norman on foot with the tribe. He stuck with the tribe on the streets. Spy Boy led the procession down Valence street, his yellow suit aglow in the dawn, while Norman Bell's costume took on a lush, rosy hue. People on porches and in yards waved to the black Indians. Their first stop was Dot's Patio Bar, a hole-in-the-wall on Tchoupitoulas where a hundred and fifty people, about half of them white, stood on the sidewalk and spilled into the street. Besides the Indians, pirates, cowboys, Zorro, and someone dressed as an ear of corn milled around cars, drinking early beers, while inside Dot's the sunguns and camera hit high gear as other Indians danced to the jukebox.

Maybe his majestic arrival was the gesture terminating Jolley's reign as Big Chief. The Indians marched, and Jolley stood in the open car, grinning like a winner at the track, red feathers radiant and his arms outstretched wide, bowing and smiling to cheers on the street. He went into Dot's for a few snorts, and when the tribe emerged, Norman Bell, a hefty former football player, was Big Chief. The weighty pink costume caused Norman's brow to glisten. The tribe formed a gauntlet in front of him; the crowd pressed in tight as Big Chief Norman raised his chin and sang deep from his chest: "Mightyyy Kooti Fiyooooo!" And the tribe, in African call-and-response tradition, handed down from slave ships to field chants into churches and early jazz, came back strong: "Eee Aie, Ayyy."

Norman sang, "Oh I got a Spyyy Boy . . . a Spy Boy," and up the gauntlet of Wild Tchoupitoulas Indians came the Spy Boy, yellow feathers dripping light, chanting "Koochee mallee, whoa Big Chief!" Big Chief Norman resumed: "The Spy Boy of the nation . . . the whole wide creation . . . oh how I love to hear them call my Indian Red." He introduced other members of the tribe in turn. Jolley sang each response with the chorus, and when the prayer of "Indian Red" was sung, Jolley got into the convertible and Norman led the Wild Tchoupitoulas along the street to the next bar. It was eight o'clock in the morning. Waves of second liners surrounded Big Chief Norman as he led the chant "Hey Pocky Way." No one knew it would be Norman's only Mardi Gras as Big Chief. He was in the hospital the following year and died before spring, so Jolley ended up leading the gang again in 1980.

Who are the Mardi Gras Indians and where did they come from? We are moving deeper now, beneath the contours of a popular culture, searching for a trail of chiefs embedded in the past. Indians and Africans were beaten people in colonial Louisiana: so much of what we know as history records the lives and deeds of winners. One notion is crucial to our journey. At root, the black tribes are a *spiritual* tradition in which the Indian persona is more than symbolism. The tradition carries a cultural language of sorts, representing what the historian Samuel Charters calls "a procession of spirit figures."[1]

In the 1720s, thousands of slaves were shipped from coastal West Africa to tropical colonies of the New World. Uprooted, these people underwent a massive dislocation under brutal conditions that effectively erased the language and most realities of daily life in Africa. But the disparate tribal peoples shared a primal bond rooted in the mother culture: communication with ancestral spirits.

A basic vision blanketed animist zones of the sub-Saharan map. When a leader died, his memory stayed alive through the enactment of ceremony, with masked dancers representing departed elders. Honoring these ancestors was the core of communal rites, and the attendant instruments—rattles, wooden horns, strings—melded with the singers and drum voices in a percussive stream to which people danced, often in long lines, forming a chain of human movement honoring the dead.

Such expressions varied greatly under the painful arch of New World slavery. North American plantation economies purposely divided slaves from remnants of their tribal family so as to facilitate subjugation. But in other regions tribal groupings were relocated somewhat intact. The Yoruba of what is now Nigeria retained specific deities and rituals in Cuba and Brazil. However much was taken from them, the Africans in many enslaved communities—of South America, of the Caribbean islands, of New Orleans—kept alive their primary belief in spirits. Even as the cosmology changed—the faces of African gods turning into visages of Christian saints—the ritual form endured: drums and dances to call the spirits.

"A characteristic of all African music," Francis Bebey writes, "is the fact that it is common property, a language that all members of any one group can understand."[2] In certain African cultures, the tonal vocabulary of drumming embraced real words. Word and tone were one, a drumvoice: "talking drums." Other instruments figured deeply in the African musical family, such as thumb pianos, shakers, gourds, unmetallic horns, and string instruments. As the African gods slowly died in the New World, so did the literal language of the drums.

But the spiritual sensibility lived on—more specifically, a *historical memory* in which music rituals gave voice to man's deepest religious yearnings. People summoned spirits and warded away others with rhythmic crossings: people sang and danced to the percussions.

Indians lived in the region near New Orleans long before the first slave ships came. Canadian woodsmen and French soldiers traded peacefully with some of them; Indian women, however, were often taken as concubines by the whites. The earliest slaves came from Senegambia. In 1730 a contingent of about two dozen runaway slaves found harbor with the Chickasaws and returned to slave quarters along the river to foment a rebellion. The plot was exposed, the leaders caught. Four of them were broken on wheels and their heads put on gates of the city. One woman was hanged. The following year an army of French soldiers, using Indian forces and black conscripts, slaughtered rebellious Indians with their own African allies at an upriver post, now named Natchez after the tribe.[3]

Although Indians took slaves in their own tribal wars, those passed on to colonists proved to be poor field workers. More ships arrived bearing slaves from Africa, and slaves continued fleeing plantations. By 1748, writes Carl Brasseaux, "lower river settlements had become a haven for a large, tightly knit and highly efficient band of maroon raiders."⁴ In May 1748 the governor of the colony sent troops to suppress them. Until that time, French fear of Indian attacks greatly shadowed concerns over slave uprisings. As the Indians around New Orleans dispersed, scattering seeds of their culture behind them, small groups lived on the fringes of the colony.

In such an environment, rebellion took on different forms. To Africans, religion served as an outlet for these rebellious thoughts. As early as the 1730s, slaves congregated at night to dance the *calinda*. Rural blacks rode their masters' horses to such drum gatherings, and thefts were reported by drunken slaves after *calinda* dances. In 1751 the government took actions to stop the dancing.⁵

A spiritualist sensibility was implicit in those gatherings. Living in quarters set back on the plantation estates, slaves kept alive the memory of animist worship. An earlier generation of scholars, including Harold Courlander, Robert Tallant, and Marshall Stearns, wrote about Haitian influences on New Orleans voodoo. The French imported slaves from various West African tribes to Haiti, but the strongest regional expression came from Dahomey (today the people's Republic of Benin). "It is the vodun of the Fon-speaking people," Melville Herskovits writes, "a word that is best translated as 'god.'"⁶ Other interpretations are "genius" and "protective spirit."⁷

The Fon monarchy was built on agriculture and used plantation slaves, though the slaves were more of a peasant class than chattel. Dahomean religion centered on a hierarchy of spirits whose literal human pasts lived in rituals of their tribal descendants. These *loa* were not necessarily good or bad deities, rather ones whose responses to the living hinged on the character of a given ceremony. The natural human urge for protection required appeasing worship, otherwise vexed *loa* might react accordingly. Dahomean kings sold two million ethnic peoples to Western slave merchants. In Haiti, the sprouting vodun ritual served both as a link to the mother culture and as a metaphysical impulse. What Western civilization saw as the dark side of voodoo—animal sacrifices, blood as a symbol of life—expressed rebellion via cultural preservation. Voodoo dances melded with the Catholic Mass, kindling the flames of African spiritualism.

But were the sacrifices only an African impulse? In 1730, five hundred Natchez Indians defeated by the French were sent as slaves to the island of Saint Domingue. Moreover, in a study of Haitian voodoo, Maya Deren argues that remnants of the Petro Indians, living in hills of the island in the sixteenth century, fired the African imagination with the rage of New World suffering. Indians and Africans shared compatible beliefs in spirits, in healing herbs and powers, and in a cosmic vision based on ancestral gods. New World Indians were driven by anger over the genocidal warfare of colonial conquerers. Deren writes: "The emphasis on Indian religious practice was aggressive, imperialistic and active, assertively dynamic, which met the New World need of the Negro in a way that his Dahomean religion—almost settled and passive with security— could not match. And finally, the American pattern was strongly colored by the severity of divinities; propitiation had the violent bloody character typical of the Aztecan, Mayan and Incan cultures."[8]

The 1804 liberation of Saint Domingue, which became the Republic of Haiti, triggered an exodus of planters, freedmen, and some slaves. Waves of them settled in New Orleans; the largest number (ten thousand) came after expulsion from Cuba in 1809. Amid the concentration of slaves descended from various African cultures, voodoo cults surfaced in New Orleans. Although voodoo did not exert a direct musical influence on the Mardi Gras Indians, it was a cornerstone of the cultural tradition out of which they eventually developed—a living link to the African spirit cults of the Caribbean. Whether of Dahomean origin, a reblending of other animist rituals, or as Deren argues, a fusion of Indian and African beliefs, the voodoo ritual as it became implanted in New Orleans fed a cultural consciousness: opposition to the master class.

Large drum-and-dance convocations by slaves surfaced about 1800 on a grassy field behind the French Quarter, now Louis Armstrong Park. In the late 1700s the area was called the Congo Plains. "No meaner name could be given the spot," George Washington Cable writes; "the Negro was the most despised of human creatures and the Congo was plebeian among Negroes."[9] Set behind the Vieux Carré, the area was surrounded by swamps and woods. Slave cabins were in the vicinity. Small clusters of Indians lived on the outskirts, too. On Sunday afternoons the Indian villagers played a ballgame called *raquette* with rough-and-tumble whites. Given the extraordinary overlay of ethnic folds in early New Orleans, it is safe to say that blacks, whether slaves or free, played sport with Indians.

The gathering site was called Place Congo—in later years, with English supplanting French as the local language, Congo Square. Drums boomed. Big wooden horns sent out notes. And from the shacks and shanties of the slave quarters came hundreds of men and women to the Sunday gatherings to dance, to make rhythm, to express freedom. However disparate the ethnic strands, however time-removed from the drumvoices and the praises and pleadings to African gods, Congo Square served a critical ceremonial function—a bridge, as it were, over which the inherited historical memory of the ancestral cults advanced in New Orleans.

Music came out of long, hollow drums that lay on the ground, then smaller ones, open at one end and covered by sheepskin at the other. Some were beaten with hands and fists, others were hit like tom-toms. The other instruments varied—triangles, animal jawbones, gourds filled with pebbles, primitive string instruments. No brass is known of, but Cable identifies a "Pan's pipe" made of cane. The kalinda and bamboula dances flourished, as they did in the West Indies.

Drums were the heartbeat of the African instrumental family. The river of percussions tumbling over the watershed of Congo Square and out of Reconstruction split into divergent tributaries; they flowed in years to come beneath the streams of jazz, rhythm and blues, and music by the Mardi Gras Indians. But that is to anticipate events. For the moment, it is the dancer who attracts our gaze; the dancer becomes the visible image of historical memory. Whether in secret voodoo gatherings or before thousands of onlookers at Congo Square, the dancer kept alive the cultural reality, the consciousness of spirits. The voodoo dancer is the first in our procession of spirit figures.

Congo Square separates New Orleans from the rest of the South by the more or less unbroken chain, the *form* if not the actual vocabulary of religious ceremony in the motherland. One wonders if Indians danced at Congo Square. The Choctaws made regular visits to the French Market. But it was "more than a market place," Maurice Martinez writes. "It was a social event, a moment when slaves and servants, sent to purchase foodstuffs for the white households, could talk with each other. They bought spices, filé, herbs and other products from the Indians. No doubt, such encounters developed into friendly relationships."[10] By 1890 the word *griffon*, which meant "black Indian," had entered the lexicon of the city's racial code. The Afro-Indian intermarriages formed a startlingly different sociocultural pool than the European-black miscegenation. One bond stemmed from two races thrown together by oppression; the other, infinitely less satisfying, from a guilty sexual imposition of master upon slave.

In many ways, the historical memory of Indians was markedly similar to that of the slaves. The Indian tribes referred to themselves as nations; in Africa, many tribes were called kingdoms. Both had hierarchical community structures, led by chiefs. They worshipped ancestral spirits, albeit different ones, and believed in spirits inhabiting the natural forces around them. Both lived close to the land, with their ceremonies steeped in percussive music.

As a spirit figure, the Indian would never have entered the folk streams of New Orleans music had it not been for Carnival. Congo Square was suppressed about 1835, though some gatherings probably occurred afterward. Voodoo ceremonies endured longer, but they were hardly a mass phenomenon nor particularly attractive to blacks, who by then attended Christian churches. Carnival thus became the stage for a ritual enacting of historical memory. In Old Italian *carnivale* means "taking away meat," or by other interpretations, "putting away the flesh." Carnival was a celebration common to Greek and Roman societies, a period of feast prior to spring planting. Early Christians changed the time to midwinter, the day before Lent. The French incorporated the tradition into their Catholic calendar. New Orleans had long since begun bidding the flesh farewell when the Krewe of Rex was founded in 1872. The movement of maskers through the streets goes back much farther; the city's early history is fraught with carnivalia. In 1762 the Spanish crown passed an edict permitting only Caucasians to mask. Masquerade balls were legally authorized in 1827. Errol L. Laborde writes that in 1841 "as many as four hundred citizens decked themselves out as bedouins (North African desert dwellers) and pranced through town . . . and by 1852, reportedly, they were able to organize a procession of 'thousands' on foot, on horseback, and in wagons."[11] Latin social custom, the French taste for music and fine things, Catholic seasonal feasts, the deep African energy, and the profound urge to dance were currents merging into Mardi Gras. Today, Rex is the king of Mardi Gras, a largely symbolic rule.

Carnival became ever more necessary for black New Orleans. It filled basic needs increasingly denied the people by allowing new identities to take shape. Creoles and the black bourgeois emulated the white aristocracy with society balls, but a network of social aid and pleasure clubs arose around Carnival. The costumes were another matter altogether. To whites, they were largely toy disguises, fancy fleetings reflecting one's humor or élan. To the black consciousness, masking often took on a heightened meaning. The mask became a cover, a new identity, a persona eluding the white policeman or soldier; the mask gave ephemeral freedom; the whole organic presence of the costume could scare people, delight them, it could satirize or do any number of things provided the person inside it fulfilled the role to the core of his imagination. In this way, Carnival became one linear extension of Congo Square. Out of the flickering memory of African spiritualism and percussive ceremony came a procession of spirit figures, an inherited cultural consciousness marching into Carnival.

Over the years, Claiborne Avenue became the meeting place for black Carnival. There were all kinds of costumes, but certain ones reflected primal urges of the mask, the transformation of self into a riveting new identity. Tribes of skeletons issued out of black neighborhoods, often in the most menacing of marches. There was a rivalry of sorts between Baby Dolls and Gold Diggers, women decked out in flashy garb, green bills stuffed in their garters, and a lot of flirting on the hoof. A satiric tradition arose with the Zulu parade, black men in blackface wearing grass skirts. In all of this, the Indian was a hybrid persona, a spirit figure anchored in the American sensibility. The traveling Wild West shows of the late nineteenth century popularized the Indian as an authentic culture figure, but the common struggle of Indians and Africans in Louisiana predates by many years the influences that such shows (particularly in the dress style of American Plains) probably had in New Orleans. In the final measure, the adaptation by blacks of the Indian persona was an act of ritual rebellion. The liberation inherent in masking required a cultural vocabulary: in chants and body language, in the collective imagery of Indian parades.[12]

But the phenomenon of black Indians sprouted in other carnivals, a wider geographic web of cultural memory. The Indian was a carnival fixture as early as 1847 in Trinidad and has long appeared in Haitian and Brazilian carnivals. These costumes bear some resemblance to those of many downtown Indians, particularly the "Mummy" crown style. Musical idioms arose, too. The calypso descended from the old kalinda dance, which was common to Congo Square and to Trinidad. In the relative isolation of Port-au-Spain, city blacks of Trinidad channeled great creativity into costumes. More than any other aspect of the culture, carnival masks drew praise as expressions of the inner self. There were Red Indians and Blue Indians and Black Indians of the Trinidad carnival. Yet the colors had symbolic meaning, too. The Reds were believed to have come from Venezuela, while the Blacks were thought of as African.[13]

Edward Kamau Brathwaite, the distinguished Caribbean scholar and poet, has observed that the mother culture, to survive the weight of New World domination, had to go through a submarine or tunneling stage to endure the imposed value system. Through this submersion period of generations, rituals of the mother culture underwent a permutation, surfacing in a visually different form but with the root sensibility, of dignity, intact. Voodoo conforms to this proposition, as do the spirit cults of Brazil and Cuba, which move to African drumming rhythms.[14]

Beginning in the 1880s, the Mardi Gras Indians started the slow rise out of submersion that the mother culture underwent with the disappearance of Congo Square and voodoo. The Indians' chants were not set to drums but to hand-percussion instruments such as tambourines. They did not worship spirits per se but through a slowly evolving body of coded lyrics established a tribal hierarchy that praised the Indian nations and celebrated the bravery of rebellion. The Mardi Gras Indians gave light to the memory of an African past but in a ritual fashion that embraced the Indian as an adopted spirit figure. It was the highest compliment the African could pay a race of the New World: it stemmed from common struggle, sociocultural intercourse, a shared vision of freedom—but most of all, from a profoundly African ritual retention. The Indian followed the procession of rebellious slaves, voodoo cultists, and Congo Square dancers as a spirit figure in the historical memory.

Not until the 1960s did serious scholarship address the Indians as a historical phenomenon. Subsequently, journalists and academics have advanced key themes, but the article bank is still thin. Where does it all begin? Written sources offer small assistance: no letters can be culled from dusty trunks. Timeworn memories, lodged in the minds of aging men, guide us down the path.

Our point of entry is the Seventh Ward, where the first black to mask as an Indian, Becate Batiste, founded the Creole Wild West Tribe in the early 1880s. The name suggests he may have borrowed a few ideas from traveling Wild West shows of the era. In any event, he was soon joined by his brother, Eugene, a plasterer. The Batistes were of Indian descent, though of how much is unknown. The story of Chief Becate has come down through three generations of a Seventh Ward Creole family. Today, the linear descendant of that tribe is called the Yellow Pocahontas, and its chief, Allison "Tuddy" Montana, began leading the tribe after World War II. Trim and sturdy, Tuddy is a folk hero to thousands of blacks in the neighborhood. Born on December 17, 1922, he learned of Chief Becate Batiste—his granduncle—from his grandmother, Jeanne Durrell, who was Becate's sister. Tuddy's father, Alfred Montana Sr., led the Pocahontas in the 1930s and 1940s: "Well my grandmother, she always said that we had Indian blood. If you'd seen her, you could tell. She always were bright as you could want. We had the Indian blood mixed in. Just like on my daddy's side. I have some cousins—my daddy's sister's children—man, they look just *like* an Indian. My grandmother died at ninety-eight. In those days they didn't keep birth records like they do now. French and Indian, in them days was all mixed up. Black folks registered as white. Things were all crossed up." Tuddy Montana states: "The Creole Wild West originated from that house on 1313 St. Anthony Street. That's where the Indians got their start, from my family."[15]

The earliest written reference comes from a slender memoir by Elise Kirsch about her childhood. She was born in 1876; the specific Mardi Gras mentioned in the following passage is apparently 1883: "At about 10:00

A.M. that day there was a band of men (about 60) disguised as Indians who wore the real Indian costumes and their chiefs had turkey feathers running down from around their heads way down in the back. They came along from St. Bernard Avenue on Robertson Street, shouting and screaming war whoops, and carried tomahawks—on their way back would stop and perform war dances, etc., and would run for a block and begin again. Though we were frightened when very young, we always waited for the passing of 'the Indians.'"[16]

Although the citation does not say a *black* "band of men," the street reference suggests they were coming from the Seventh Ward. More important, the size of the tribe indicates that the idea of masking as an Indian had caught on quickly.

Out of Chief Becate Batiste's tribe, the Creole Wild West, grew a fascinating hierarchy, a tribal structure that spread into different neighborhoods and, by the early twentieth century, formed the organizational patterns of later tribes. The Big Chief leads the tribe; his authority is supreme. He decides where his tribe will rehearse the chants and can admit or eject anyone from the tribe. Although the Indians are a preponderantly male tradition, many women have masked and marched with tribes over the years. They are known as Queens and usually occupy an ancillary slot by virtue of their relationship to the Big Chief.

Other chiefs occupy lower rungs beneath the leader—Councellor Chief, Second Chief, Third Chief, Trail Chief—titles that vary from tribe to tribe. These Indians back up the Big Chief in rehearsal sessions and on marches. "Their roles," one scholar writes, "are more or less to look good, initiate singing and dancing, etc."[17] One of the most memorable Yellow Pocahontas braves of the early years was the Wild Man. Sometimes called the Medicine Man, the Wild Man is the least restrained Indian: his outrageousness personifies the general liberation impulse. "Wild Man Rock," Tuddy Montana says, "was a cat who lived out by a junk heap, way down Elysian Fields where people dumped their garbage. He fished old cigarettes out the trash and strung them over the roof where he lived, let 'em dry in the sun, and rolled himself cigarettes. And let me tell you: he was *wild*. You never saw him so much until Carnival came. Then he'd come bargin' out with a ring in his nose, carryin' bones and a spear, whoopin' and carryin' on, used to throw that spear and scare all hell out of people."[18]

The most important Indian after the Big Chief is his Spy Boy, who scouts ahead to make sure the road is clear. When another tribe comes in sight, Spy Boy transmits the message back to the Flag Boy (who carries the tribal pennant), who in turn passes the word to the Big Chief. Jelly

Roll Morton described the workings of the Spy Boy: "They went armed with fictitious spears and tommyhawks and so forth and their main object was to make the enemy bow. They would send their Spy Boys two blocks on ahead. I happened to be a Spy Boy once myself so I know how this went, and when a Spy Boy would meet another Spy Boy from another tribe, he'd point his finger to the ground and say, 'Bow-wow!' And if they wouldn't bow, the Spy Boy would use the Indian call, woo-woo-woo-woo-woo, and that was the calling of the tribes, and many a time in these Indian things, there would be a killing and the next day there would be someone in the morgue."[19]

It is not certain that Morton was ever a Spy Boy, but his comment rings true in other respects. Killings and bloody clashes did occur among Indian tribes of early Carnivals. Although the cellular structure was rooted in African and Indian sensibilities, with dances of African derivation, the larger statement of solidarity and symbolic rebellion must be weighed against social factors. The underlying strength of the Indians was the articulation of a symbolic language, a cultural vocabulary based on pride and the self-image of a tradition.

To mask as an Indian meant that the poorest man could transcend the toil of daily life, however ephemerally, in open defiance of the role society imposed on him. The tribes drew from laborers, dock workers, street hustlers, and common criminals as well as from descendants of Indians and, in later years, from occasional musicians. Violence at the hands of whites provoked in some Indians a militant strain, suppressed through normal life yet freed in Carnival. In the 1850s Irish Channel whites openly terrorized blacks entering the area.[20] By the 1920s, in the same neighborhood, whites dressed as cavemen fought the Indians with spike-studded cypress clubs. Most of the Indians, especially the uptown tribes, came from impoverished households. Even in the Seventh Ward, with the "self-help" tradition of Creoles, Tuddy Montana recalls "men who'd walk the street here, real dangerous people. I'm talking about men who'd kill you with their fists. Stone killers. Today people run to the Indians. During them days, people would run away from the Indians."[21]

Near the end of the nineteenth century, for unknown reasons, the Creole Wild West moved uptown. A new tribe, the Yellow Pocahontas, formed in the Seventh Ward. Henri Marigny, who had marched with Becate Batiste, became Big Chief. The Creole Wild West was led by Robert Sam Tillman Jr., known as "Brother Timber." According to Paul Longpre, who marched with Tillman in the 1930s, he was "a desperado. He was a legend in his time. Never worked for nobody. When it came around Carnival time, he'd go in hiding. If the police knowed where he was, they would go after him, put him in jail till after Carnival. Because at Carnival, he was clean treacherous."

Longpre, who learned tribal lore from his uncle and stepbrother, claims that Tillman's father controlled the Creole Wild West; however, his interpretation of tribal origins is at variance with Tuddy Montana's. According to Longpre, the elder Tillman "had Louisiana blood in him, and also his wife. I think they was Choctaw." The elder Tillman and a man named Sam Tweed, he contends, founded the Yellow Pocahontas in 1896 in the Garden District, across town from the Seventh Ward. He says they took the name *Pocahontas* from a history book. The *Yellow* was supposedly added "when one guy had on a suit with this yellow fringe from an old-time lamp shade" and a white woman asked "Yellow Pocahontas?" Thus, says Longpre, the name stuck.[22]

Longpre contends that a split between the two men caused Tweed to take the Pocahontas downtown, while the elder Tillman, having seen the Hagenback Wallace Creole Wild West Show, took the latter name and stayed uptown. This version contradicts Montana's (and that of another source, Arthur "Creole" Williams) by placing the date of tribal origins some thirteen years after the reference in Kirsch's memoir. In fairness to Longpre, it must be said that stories that are passed down through the generations are often cloudy. The available information supports Montana: still, Longpre confirms the Creole Wild West's resurgence as an uptown tribe.

The younger Tillman, also called "Brother Timber," controlled the Creole Wild West in Longpre's youth and devised schemes to evade the law. In 1927 word of his death spread. Police attended his wake, says Longpre, where people wept and mourned: "They put him in the hearse, bringed him to Holt Cemetery. He got out of the casket inside the hearse. When they got to the cemetery, they buried the casket, brought him back. On Carnival morning he had on an Indian suit—returned from the dead!"

The emergence of Indian celebrations in early decades of this century was marked by a dichotomy similar to that between the first jazzmen. A cultural gulf divided the downtown Creole wards and the uptown black neighborhoods. The jazzmen bridged it peacefully. Although the Indians evolved out of family units, too, with Big Chiefs handing down leadership to sons or nephews, the uptown-downtown competition was hardly peaceful. Arthur "Creole" Williams, who was seventy-nine when interviewed, recalls the Mardi Gras of 1921:

> Henri Marigny was the chief of the Yellow Pocahontas for years: they didn't have but one gang down here this side of Canal. Uptown. Brother Timber. They used to fight. The Pocahontas hit Louisiana Avenue and St. Charles. The Creole Wild West and two divisions of the Red, White,

and Blues was coming up Louisiana, about three in the afternoon, foggy. Brother Tillman was leading Creole Wild West. But Henri Marigny wasn't leading the Pocahontas. He was too drunk: they left him around Parish Prison and Britt brought the gang up—him and Little Yam and all the rest of 'em. Most of the gang was with Henri. And then people started *shooting*! They had Wild Mans jumpin' in the cars, a woman got shot in the foot. It was something, man. I was there to the *last*.

Now Eugene Honore used to be Second Chief to Henri . . . big, tall, looked just like an Indian. Eugene is the one that mapped all them songs out—"Indian Red," "Take That Flag Down," he originated those songs.[23]

When the tribes met in neighborhood bars before Carnival, "Indian Red" was traditionally sung at the opening and closing of rehearsal sessions and again on Mardi Gras morning as the tribe set out. In earlier years it was called the "Indian Prayer Song." Longpre and Montana say it was often accompanied by recitation of the Our Father, and with some tribes it still is. Then the Big Chief slapped the tambourine and sang: "Ma-Day, Cootie-Fiyo." And the braves sang back in slow, rising unison: "Tee-Nah Aaayy." Unraveling the many chants requires a linguist's tools. The Creole dialect, heavily French, had Spanish influences and probably Indian ones, too. Of the Trinidad carnival Indians, Andrew Pearse writes: "One of the most popular song texts begins 'Indurubi,' which may be Spanish for 'Indo Rubi,' meaning 'Indian Red.'"[24] *Matar* in Spanish means "to kill," while *qui tu est fijo* can be translated as "who is immobile to you." Kill who is in your way. This is but one interpretation. More critical to our investigation is Eugene Honore, who "mapped all them songs out."

Vincent Trepagnier, another aging Creole, recalls his experiences with the Yellow Pocahontas in the 1930s. He says Eugene Honore was a Choctaw: "Eugene was seven-foot two-inches tall. He was a real Indian who came with his mama from up the country, somewhere the other side of Baton Rouge. They lived in tents. . . . And when they come in the city, they moved on Burgundy and Toulouse. Eugene was the tallest Indian I ever seen in my life. He had a high cheekbone, beautiful skin, olive complexion, and long black hair. People used to call his mama Miss Cherie, but that wasn't her name. Her name was Miss Choctaw."[25]

New tribes began masking in the 1970s. Brother Timber's shadow loomed over the groups, which had names like the Red, White, and Blues, the Hundred and Ones, and in the years after World War II, the Wild Magnolias, Black Eagles, and Wild Tchoupitoulas. Brother Timber, a street runner who became fiery during Carnival, was not prone to organization, drifting in and out of tribes, sometimes as Big Chief, other times as Spy Boy. Just before 1920, a new uptown tribe emerged, the Wild Squatoolas, led by Daniel "Dandy" Lambert, otherwise known as "Big Chief Copper-wire." "One year," Paul Longpre explains, "when he put his suit togeth-er it fell apart, and he hooked it up with this copper wire he got from a guy working on a telephone line. Everybody after that called him Big Chief Copperwire. He had one of the largest gangs of Queens of any In-dian on Carnival day."[26]

One attempt at tribal detente occurred when Lambert and Honore ended up in Parish Prison together. "Dandy Lambert was in jail for steal-ing a truckload of groceries at the French Market." Tuddy Montana con-tinues: "See, Dandy Lambert was from uptown, Eugene was from down-town, and by them bein' friends [in] jail, they got out of jail, the guys downtown allowed them to come from uptown."[27]

When tribes clashed, it was called a "humbug." The most memora-ble in Vincent Trepagnier's career locked the Yellow Pocahontas and Wild Squatoolas in battle. The Lambert-Honore truce had not held:

> We was going uptown to a place they called the Magnolia Bridge. I don't know if you ever heard talk of it. It's torn down now. The two Spy Boys from the Pocahontas and the Wild Squatoolas got into a humbug over the bridge and shooting took place. When that shooting took place, well, that draw the policemen, see?
>
> Now there was nowhere to go, so what we did, we jumped in the New Basin Canal with our clothes on. The policemen came and got some out, and some others they didn't. I stood right underneath the bridge till they left and then come on back home. I couldn't go uptown cause I was all wet.[28]

By the late 1920s the violent battles began to halt. According to Paul Longpre, "1932 was the last actual fight that the Indians had. They in-creased the number of policemens . . . they wasn't takin' no stuff off the Indians."[29]

*Gumbo Ya-Ya* contains a report on the Mardi Gras of 1940:

> Ten years ago the various tribes actually fought when they met. Some-times combatants were seriously injured. . . . Once a police officer was badly injured by an Indian's spear. After that occurrence a law was passed forbidding the tribe of maskers to carry weapons.
>
> Today the tribes are all friendly. The following song [probably from the Golden Blades tribe, whose 1940 march is recorded in the book] is a warning against tactics of other days.
> Shootin' don't make it, no no no no.
> Shootin' don't make it, no no no no.
> Shootin' don't make it, no no no no.
> If you see your man sittin' in the bush,

Knock him in the head and give him a push,
Cause shootin' don't make it, no no.
Shootin' don't make it, no no no no.[30]

The law and a heavier police presence were not the only forces behind the ebbing of open warfare among tribes. By the Depression, Indian
traditions were about half a century old. There was a purpose behind the
battles of old, a resolution of sorts, between the uptown and downtown
tribes, long divided by differences of caste. But as neighborhood and class
borders became less distinct, so did the tradition itself evolve; higher
values and a more positive self-image emerged. The violent clashes had
significance: they showed that the Indians were unafraid—of white police or of each other. It must be stressed that the Indians, at heart, were
not a violent tradition. Violence was but one manifestation of the early
years. But the phrase "ritual violence" has lasting resonance. Today Indian rehearsal sessions at local bars constitute a dance-and-music ceremony in which conflicts are symbolically enacted.[31] But challenges from
visiting tribes can on occasion cause grudges, and the Big Chief has to be
continually on his toes to quell challenges, or he will be shamed.

In the weeks leading up to Mardi Gras, the men crowd into bars. The
Big Chief pounds his tambourines; the braves bang percussive instruments of their own—sticks, bottles, shakers—and sing responses to the
Big Chief's chants. (Drums, notably congas, and at least one bass drum
are now becoming more popular. Even in parades, drums are becoming
common.) One brave challenges another: the confrontation is enacted by
dancing. The two men edge close, one drops a scarf or handkerchief on
the floor, the competitors veer close to it—the idea is to veer closer and
closer but not cross. A mock fight ensues around the symbolic line across
the floor. Territory is defended by the strength of the dance. The two men
move in the circle to the pounding rhythms of the clapping, chanting, and
rising energy of the tribe.[32] And resentments can develop if the challeng-
er crosses the "line."

Although the Indians symbolize violence to some blacks, to many
others their chants, marches, and dazzling costumes are a statement of
dignity, an articulation of protest, of rebellion, a masculine code of hon-
or that has come down through the years of Carnival in chants and cos-
tumed marches as a musical expression. A long tradition of costume art
has greatly influenced the evolution of the Mardi Gras Indians by
strengthening peaceful bonds among the tribes. As one brave told me
while passing by, "We used to fight with knives and guns. Now we compete by the beauty of our costumes."

Much of the Big Chief's prestige comes from the image he presents on Mardi Gras—how beautiful his suit is. The man becomes his art. In early years, these costumes were rough-hewn affairs, drawn from available materials: chicken and turkey feathers, Christmas ornaments, buckskin, ribbons, fringe and long beads stripped from lampshades, molds from egg cartons dipped in glitter and glued on the suit. The early crowns were stiff cardboard pasteups. In the 1920s the "drop crown" came into play, covered with feathers and extending from head to foot. Then came ostrich plumes, which gave the crowns a larger, billowing coloration when winds blew or the sun shone brightly. An old chief called Black Benny said, "'I went to Chicago and saw these plumes in the store window. They were dyed red, white, and blue. I bought the whole bunch of them, and that year I was the first to wear plumes in a crown.'"[33]

After World War II, as more tribes organized and disbanded, the art of costumery took on greater detail. Rhinestones, sequins, and recycled Mardi Gras beads began to fill out headbands, breastplates, and vests. "The costume is just made up out of your head," Tuddy Montana explains.[34]

The Indians traditionally marched on Mardi Gras and again on St. Joseph's Day, the Italian festival in the Catholic calendar. After the final appearance, the braves would take apart the costume and later begin work on next year's suit. It took long hours over many months, designing scenes for the knee pads, vests, and breastpads, sewing a thematic design in common with images affixed to the front and backside of the drop crown. As the tradition evolved, suits became more expensive to make. Big Chief Jolley of the Wild Tchoupitoulas remarked that a costume "can cost as less as three hundred dollars and as high as five thousand dollars, if you want to spend that kind of money."[35]

Emile "Bo" Dollis, Chief of the Wild Magnolias, draws a distinction between patterns of tribes from the two sides of town. "The difference in the uptown style and the downtown style is the pattern. So, the difference in the suits, if you compare the uptown and downtown, is the beadwork and the finishing work. Where they use sequins, we may use rhinestones. Where they may use feathers, we may use ostrich plumes. But they're totally the same thing: they're both beautiful."[36]

Tuddy Montana says, "In the Yellow Pocahontas we don't have no plumes. We all have feathers. They use the beaded designs, which they'll get from a book or somethin'. Maybe an Indian on horseback. A lot of them don't even know how to draw it themselves. They'll bring it to somebody and say, 'Look, man, I want you to draw this for me.' And they'll take it and trace it on canvas, and then they bead it, you see?"[37]

Costumes became a major theme in the songs, set to call-and-response chants. Paul Longpre says the Golden Blades got their name in 1935 at a rehearsal session in an uptown bar near Third and Rocheblave. From 1931 to 1935 they masked as the Creole Wild West with Brother Tillman:

> But then we had a split up, because Brother Tillman told us to be in one place and he was in another. We didn't meet him 'til four o'clock that evening. So, that next year we were going to mask as the Creole Wild West Juniors. We had a guy called Mice, one of the best at singing Indian songs because he could think fast. The idea of singing a Indian song is rhyming something, thinking fast to rhyme it. Mice was singing "My Big Chief Got a Diamond Crown"—
> Oh, the diamond crown,
>    The diamond crown,
> Two-day de-fey-hock,
>    Goo-make-who laun-day he,
> Big Chief got a diamond crown.
>
> Well one of the ladies happened to walk into practice, and Mice was singing "My Big Chief Got a Diamond Crown," and when he sang that, she say, "Oh, give it to the boys from Third and Rocheblave!" That made him chant and start singing "Third and Rocheblave," then later on he started singing, "Give it to the gang from the Golden Blades."
>
> Two-gay-de-hoc
>    Ma who-laun-day,
> Give it to the boy
>    From the Golden Blades.
> Oh, the Golden Blades, the Golden Blades.
>    We got some low-down ways![38]

Another 1930s chant by the Wild Squatoolas celebrated the act of costume-making: "Somebody got to sew, sew, sew." More recently, the Wild Magnolias have borrowed the identical rhythm: "Everybody's got soul, soul, soul."

The best-known and most widely sung chant is "Two-way Pocky Way," or as the Meters popularized it, "Hey Pocky Way." It is an old chant, with conflicting translations. In 1950 Alan Lomax translated the words in Creole dialect as *t'ouwais bas q'ouwais*. The refrain *on tendais* probably came from *entendez*, "to understand," or from *attendez*, "wait up" or "listen." But *t'ouwais bas q'ouwais* is more complicated. One possible meaning, which makes sense in the code of Indian concerns, depends on an etymological shift in the dialect enunciation; in standard French, *tu n'as pas couilles* means "you don't have balls" (testicles). But if we interpret *t'ouwais* as in derivation from the verb *tuer*, "to kill"—

followed by an abbreviation of the Creole phrase *a la bas,* meaning "over there"—we get *tuez bas qu'ou est,* or, "kill who is over there."[39]

Other interpretations have been made. Finn Wilhelmsen, a Norwegian scholar who wrote early articles on the Indians, states, "Allegorically, the expression means, 'I don't give a damn.'"[40] Tuddy Montana believes it is in reference to what the singer of a chant has just said before. "Like, 'That's what I say' or 'See what I mean.'"[41] Paul Longpre opines: "It means, 'You go disaway'—or 'You go dattaway.' Either one."[42] Unquestionably the chant has evolved into a series of popular interpretations quite different from its murky origins. But the *on tendais* refrain of old—which has since been dropped—was a tribal refrain, a warning: Stop! Wait! Listen! An educated guess suggests the meaning was close to "kill the one over there."

In the mid-seventies, Indian chants became popular in music recordings as the relative anonymity of the tribes began to peel away. As a cultural phenomenon, the Indians attracted producers, film and television people, oral historians, journalists, and nightclub owners. It was not always a smooth transition: some streets are hostile to white intrusion. But with the current acceleration of Indian tribal rhythms and verse as a new musical force, the tradition begun by Chief Becate Batiste in the early 1880s has come full circle, replicating the birth of jazz: from rooted urges of African consciousness into a spawning musical idiom, reflecting a performance style as African as it is visually native American.

## Notes

1. Samuel Charters, *The Roots of Blues: An African Search* (New York: Putnam, 1981), 68–69. On a research trip to the Gambia, Charters encountered a group of masked villagers, parading to music. "Where had I seen it before? It was in New Orleans, on a Mardi Gras morning in the 1950s. It was the first time I'd seen the 'Indians.' . . . What I saw in New Orleans was this same procession of a spirit figure, only in New Orleans the spirit had become an 'Indian,' through all the confusions of the new culture and new religion" (68–69).

2. Francis Bebey, *African Music: A People's Art* (Westport, Conn.: Greenwood, 1980), 116.

3. See *Negro Insurrections,* vol. 2 of *Louisiana,* ed. Alcee Fortier (Madison, Wis.: Century Historical Association, 1914), 213; Henry E. Chambers, *A History of Louisiana,* vol. 1 (Chicago: American Historical Society, 1925), 209–11.

4. Carl Brasseaux, "The Administration of Slave Regulations in French Louisiana, 1724–1766," *Louisiana History* 21.2 (Spring 1980): 155.

5. Ibid., 146.

6. Melville J. Herskovits, *Life in a Haitian Valley* (Garden City, N.Y.: Doubleday, 1971), 23.

7. Janheinz Jahn, *Muntu: An Outline of the New African Culture* (New York: Grove Press, 1961), 32–33.

8. Maya Deren, *Divine Horsemen: The Voodoo Gods of Haiti* (New York: Dell, 1970), 58–66.

9. George Washington Cable, "The Dance at Place Congo," in his *Creoles and Cajuns* (Gloucester, Mass.: P. Smith, 1959), 3.

10. Maurice M. Martinez, "Delight in Repetition: The Black Indians," *Wavelength* 16 (Feb. 1982): 21.

11. "The Carnival," *The WPA Guide to New Orleans* (New York: Pantheon Books, 1983), 175; Mitchell Osborne and Errol L. Laborde, *Mardi Gras! A Celebration* (New Orleans: Picayune Press, 1981), 42–44.

12. Martinez, "Delight in Repetition," 21.

13. See Andrew Pearse, "Carnival in the Nineteenth Century," *Caribbean Quarterly* 4.3–4 (1956): 175–93.

14. See Edward Kamau Brathwaite's "Caribbean Culture: Two Paradigms," in *Missile and Capsule*, ed. Jurgen Manini (Bremen, Germany: Bremen University, 1983), 28–54. Brathwaite's thematic observations in previous works are applied to New Orleans in an excellent article by Tom Dent, "A Critical Look at Mardi Gras," *Jackson (Miss.) Advocate*, Feb. 18, 1982, B1.

15. Interview with Allison "Tuddy" Montana, by Jason Berry, Mar. 13, 1982, New Orleans Ethnic Music Research Project (hereafter NOEMRP).

16. Elise Kirsch, *Downtown New Orleans in the Early Eighties: Customs and Characters of Old Robertson Street and Its Neighborhoods* (New Orleans: N.p., 1951), 9.

17. Finn Wilhelmsen, "Creativity in the Songs of the Mardi Gras Indians of New Orleans, Louisiana." The appendix to Wilhelmsen's manuscript, which he gratuitously sent after an initial correspondence, was published in part in *Louisiana Folklore Miscellany* 3 (1973): 56–74.

18. Montana interview.

19. Alan Lomax, *Mister Jelly Roll: The Fortunes of Jelly Roll Morton, New Orleans Creole and Inventor of Jazz* (Berkeley: University of California Press, 1973), 15.

20. Robert Tallant, *Mardi Gras* (New York: Doubleday, 1948), 107–8.

21. Montana interview.

22. Interview with Paul Longpre, by Jason Berry and Jonathan Foose, Feb. 13, 1982, NOEMRP.

23. Interview with Arthur "Creole" Williams and Allison Montana, by Jason Berry, Mar. 13, 1982, NOEMRP.

24. Pearse, "Carnival in the Nineteenth Century," 180.

25. Andrew Kaslow, "Folklore: Talking to Some Glorious Mardi Gras Indians," *Figaro*, Feb. 1, 1976, sec. 1, p. 19.

26. Longpre interview.

27. Williams and Montana interview.

28. Kaslow, "Folklore."

29. Longpre interview.

30. Lyle Saxon, Edward Dreyer, and Robert Tallant, *Gumbo Ya-Ya* (Boston: Houghton Mifflin, 1945), 20–21.

31. Alan Lomax, "The Power of New Orleans Music," lecture at the Louisiana State Museum, New Orleans, Mar. 10, 1984, sponsored by the Louisiana Committee for the Humanities. An enlightening study for comparative purposes is John Stewart's *Stickfighting: Ritual Violence in Trinidad* (Washington, D.C.: Smithsonian Institution, Research Institute on Immigration and Ethnic Studies, 1980).

32. See also Finn Wilhelmsen, "Verbal, Body and Territoriality Communications Concepts among the Mardi Gras Indians of New Orleans, Louisiana," seminar report for Professor H. Jause, Department of Anthropology, Tulane University, Mar. 1972, p. 33.

33. Qtd. in Martinez, "Delight in Repetition," 24.

34. Montana interview.

35. Jason Berry and Jonathan Foose, producers, *Up from the Cradle of Jazz*, documentary (New Orleans: WYES TV, 1980).

36. Interview with Emile "Bo" Dollis, by Shepherd Samuel, Feb. 20, 1978, broadcast on WTUL Radio, New Orleans.

37. Montana interview.

38. Longpre interview.

39. Lomax, *Mister Jelly Roll*, 14, 280. Jason Berry is indebted to George Reinecke, Department of English, University of New Orleans, for the interpretation of *q'ouwais* as possibly meaning *couilles.*

40. Wilhelmsen, "Creativity in the Songs of the Mardi Gras Indians."

41. Montana interview.

42. Paul Longpre, conversation with Jason Berry, Mar. 10, 1982.

## 7  Mardi Gras Indians: Carnival and Counternarrative in Black New Orleans

> It cannot be easy to move from oppression and its my-
> thologies to resistance in history; a detour through a no-
> man's land or threshold area of counter-myth and sym-
> bolisation is necessary.
> —Laura Mulvey, "Myth, Narrative, and Historical
>   Experience"

More than fifty years ago, alarmed by the rise of commercial culture and the attendant eclipse of literature and folklore, the great cultural critic Walter Benjamin envisioned a world without stories. Benjamin complained that in such a world, "It is as if something that seemed inalienable to us, the securest of our possessions, were taken from us; the ability to exchange experiences."[1] Certainly, subsequent events have more than justified Benjamin's pessimism. Social and economic changes have undermined the ascribed roles and inherited customs historically responsible for most storytelling traditions. A commodified mass-culture industry covers the globe, replacing traditional narratives with mass-produced spectacles, while the "ability to exchange experiences" often degenerates into the necessity to consume the same cultural commodities.

Yet storytelling persists, even inside the apparatuses of commercial mass culture. Indeed, commercial culture expressly depends upon the residues of local popular narratives for its determinate forms and themes.

Blues and reggae music form the unacknowledged subtext of most contemporary popular music. Suppressed ethnic, class, and gender rage un-
dergirds much of the comedy displayed on motion-picture screens around
the world, while vernacular art and popular oral traditions provide the
raw materials for much of mass culture's visual and aural stimuli.[2] Outside of popular culture, personal and collective memories of region, race,
class, gender, and ethnicity continue to provide the raw materials for
shared stories. But the pervasiveness of popular narrative forms and
themes is not just a matter of the sedimented residue of historical communities and cultures. Mass society and commercial culture provoke a
new popular narrative response, one that draws upon both old and new
forms of cultural creation. By circulating the stories of particular communities and cultures to a mass audience, the culture industry invites
comparison, interpretation, and elaboration. Culture consumers find
profound meaning in stories fashioned outside their own communities,
and they inevitably reexamine their own traditions in light of what they
discover about other cultures.

Sensitive and sympathetic cultural critics have vested great hopes in
the enduring emancipatory potential of popular narratives. In his extraordinary review essay, "Western Marxism and Folklore," José E. Limon
argues that popular self-generating cultural expressions and performances
can challenge the hegemony of the dominant commercial culture by presenting cultural creations as having an organic "use" value rather than
just a commercial "exchange" value. Limon quotes with approval Michel
de Certeau's contentions that these kinds of cultural performances contain political meaning and that they exist not only in the fading memories of marginalized groups but "in the strongholds of the contemporary
economy."[3] Fredric Jameson's germinal article "Reification and Utopia
in Mass Culture" insists that all popular-culture texts contain a radical
utopian kernel that contrasts the indignities of the present social order
with the possibilities for happiness conjured up by collective and individual imagination.[4] Similarly, in his persuasive discussion of "Folklore
and Fakelore," William Fox contends that even with a decline in identification with the traditional sources of popular narratives—region, occupation, race, ethnicity, and religion—contemporary society offers new
possibilities for sources of identity, possibilities likely to produce stories
underscoring the tensions between lived experience and the self-congrat-
ulatory propaganda for the status quo that is generated from within the
culture industry.[5]

The Mardi Gras Indians of New Orleans offer an important illustration of the persistence of popular narratives in the modern world, pro-

viding a useful case study about the emancipatory potential of grassroots cultural creation. Every Mardi Gras Day, "tribes" of anywhere from fifteen to thirty working-class black males dress as Plains Indians and take to the streets of New Orleans. They parade through black neighborhoods, displaying their costumes and flags, singing and chanting in a specialized argot, while treating themselves to the hospitality offered in neighborhood bars and private homes. The Indians work all year designing and sewing their costumes, but generally they show them in public only on Mardi Gras Day and St. Joseph's Day. Organized into a rigid status hierarchy of official positions (spy boy, flag boy, wild man, third chief, second chief, big chief, and council chief), the tribes celebrate their own worthiness in chants and songs while remaining vigilant for competing tribes who might challenge them with aggressive word play to compare costumes, dances, or singing and rhyming ability.[6] Although tribe members must be chosen directly by the group leader, the organizations represent entire neighborhoods. They practice all year in neighborhood bars, and they draw a group of neighborhood residents into the streets behind them, as a "second line" of supportive singers and dancers.[7]

On the surface, the core practices of the Mardi Gras Indians resemble quite conventional behaviors by other groups. Under the aegis of Carnival, they form secret societies, wear flamboyant costumes, speak a specialized language, and celebrate a fictive past. Carnival revelers all around the world engage in the same practices to release tension from the repressions and frustrations of everyday life. But what distinguishes the Mardi Gras Indians is their use of conventional forms for unconventional purposes. Drawing upon dominant icons and images, they invert them and subvert them. What for other groups might be a symbolic and temporary release from deep-seated repressions functions very differently for the Indian tribes. Rather than merely expressing utopian desires, the Indian spectacle gives coded expression to values and beliefs that operate every day in the lives of black workers in New Orleans. Although it takes place in response to the rituals and timetables of European carnival traditions, the Indian spectacle is not primarily European. It presents visual and narrative references to Native American Indians, but it bears little resemblance to genuine Indian celebrations and ceremonies. It draws its determinate modes of expression from African culture and philosophy, but it is not a purely African ritual. Instead, it projects a cultural indeterminacy, picking and choosing from many traditions to fashion performances and narratives suitable for arbitrating an extraordinarily complex identity.

The working-class blacks who create the Mardi Gras Indian tribes collectively author an important narrative about their own past, present, and future. Drawing upon the tools available to them—music, costumes, speech, and dance—they fashion a fictive identity that gives voice to their deepest values and beliefs. They replicate many traditional folk practices such as the aggressive festivity of Carnival, the ritualistic observance of holidays, and the celebration of a heroic lineage. They tap literary and oral traditions of storytelling through song lyrics, chants, word games, and names. But their collective narrative goes beyond literature and folklore. It draws upon a myriad of contradictory images and icons to fashion a syncretic identity. In the aesthetics of their performance, the Mardi Gras Indians balance the competing claims of commercial culture and folk culture, of America and Africa, of resistance and accomodation, and of spontaneity and calculation. Their art stems less from ancient storytelling traditions or aesthetic intentions than from the necessity imposed upon them by oppressive social conditions. Their utopian projections originate less from abstract images of an ideal future than from a determination to read the lessons of solidarity and struggle from the past and present into the future. If the practices of storytelling and the qualities of criticism and creativity embedded within them are to survive in the modern world, it will likely be through the multidimensional practices of artists and individuals like the Mardi Gras Indians.

The Mardi Gras Indian narrative does not always take the form of pure narrative—of a sequence of events taking place over time in a cause-and-effect relationship—but its central recurring theme is a story of heroic warriors resisting domination. The Indians tell about past Mardi Gras Days when challenges from other groups forced them to bring to the surface the bravery and solidarity they must repress in everyday life. Song lyrics, chants, and costumes celebrate brave tribes who "won't kneel, won't bow, and don't know how."[8] This Indian imagery draws upon many sources. In slavery times, Indian communities offered blacks a potential alternative to a society in which to be black was to be a slave and to be white was to be free. In New Orleans, black slaves mingled with Indians in local markets, and interactions between Native Americans and blacks gave many Louisiana blacks a historical claim to a joint Indian and African American heritage. In addition, more than twenty black spiritualist churches in New Orleans venerate the Native American Chief Black Hawk as a martyr, in keeping with the teachings of Leith Anderson, a half-Mohawk woman who preached the doctrine of "spirit returning." But the evidence tying the Mardi Gras Indians to direct Indian ancestry is slight.[9] New Orleans "tribes" wear the headdresses and costumes of Plains Indians, not of southeastern Indians, and with the exception of some styles of bead work, few of their practices replicate the crafts of local Native American tribes. South American and Caribbean Carnival traditions feature Indians prominently, and some of the New Orleans chants more closely resemble French and Spanish carnival phrases than they do any known Native American tongue.[10] As one Mardi Gras Indian told a researcher: "'We're not real Indians, we just masquerade as Indians really, and we just give our tribe a name, and different positions and things like that. But as for real Indians, like you'd have to go to Arizona or Texas or something like that to talk to a real Indian, and on a reservation or something like that, but he wouldn't tell you the things I'm telling you because what we're doing is just something that we copies behind the Indians really.'"[11]

In fact, the touring Wild West shows of Buffalo Bill Cody and other late nineteenth-century popular culture entrepreneurs were probably the real impetus for the creation of these mock Indian tribes. Carnival parades in New Orleans began in 1827, but blacks did not generally dress up as Indians until Becate Batiste founded the Creole Wild West tribe in the early 1880s.[12] Donning Indian headdresses and face paint enabled African Americans to circumvent the local laws that made it illegal for blacks to wear masks, but the Indian imagery held important symbolic meaning for them as well. One former chief of the Golden Blades tribe suggests that both blood ties and consumer tastes played a role in the formation of an early Indian tribe, telling a reporter, "'In 1895, Robert Sam Tillman got the idea to mask Injun by seeing a Wild West show that came through N'Awlins. Brother Tillman came from Indians himself, and in 1897 he started the [Yellow] Pocahontas tribe.'"[13] But to see the identification with Indian culture as more a matter of choice than a matter of blood lines hardly lessens its significance. While Carnival masking for all groups proclaims a generalized "right to be other" (as Bakhtin asserts), the Mardi Gras Indians adopt a very specific sense of otherness. Most other Carnival celebrants might dress as pirates or crows or cowboys in any given year to escape from their everyday identities, but the Indians are always Indians. Furthermore, the Indian image calls attention to the initial genocide upon which American "civilization" rests. It challenges the core dualism of American racism that defines people as either white or black. To perpetuate collective consciousness about Indians in this context is to perpetuate memories about runaway slaves seeking shelter. Other revelers may use Carnival masking to escape the repressions of their everyday existence, but the Indian tribes' disguise brings out into the open dimensions of repression that the dominant culture generally tries to render invisible. Of course, this kind of inversion runs the risk of being captured by the very forms it seeks to satirize. Native American viewers might not appreciate the Mardi Gras Indian appropriation of demeaning stereotypes; too many groups in American history have used the image of the Indian for their own purposes, and what comprises symbolic emancipation for one group might consequently oppress another. But images in negotiation with power are often ambiguous, complicated, and implicated in the crimes they seek to address.

In both content and form of presentation, the Mardi Gras Indian narratives and imagery revolve around self-affirmation and solidarity. Members of Indian tribes might be construction workers, dock hands, bakers, or porters oppressed by their race and class in everyday life, but in their rehearsals and performances as Indians they become part of a community of resistance and self-affirmation. They treat life as precious, celebrating its joys and pleasures, even while mourning the dead. Their song lyrics, costumes, speech, and dances all reinforce the same values— grace, strength, elegance, precision, happiness, composure, and dignity.[14] But the key to their collective story rests in more than specific words and images; it comes from the aesthetics of their performance. The Mardi Gras Indian narrative is eloquent and compelling because the forms used to convey it correspond to its basic message and because the daily lived experience of its adherents reinforces its core values.

In its aesthetics, the Mardi Gras Indian narrative resonates with the culture and philosophy of African music. Of course, they are African Americans and make distinctly African American music, but the Africanisms within Mardi Gras Indian music raise important ideological and artistic issues. The ethnomusicologist John Miller Chernoff identifies the definitive feature of the African musical sensibility as a "functional integration" of music and culture. In African communities, audience handclapping is seen as a vital part of a musical performance, not merely a response by the spectators. Similarly, during African rituals, music is joined with dance, drama, and visual representation to form a fused art made up of interdependent elements. These musical performances blend with lived experiences, accompanying day-to-day events rather than providing a break from them as a self-conscious form of leisure or enlightenment. Finally, music making in Africa is a functional group activity— a means for organizing and communicating tradition by giving different social groups rights and privileges connected to specific songs.[15]

The Mardi Gras Indian ritual draws upon these African sensibilities in significant ways. The neighborhood residents who attend weekly practice sessions and who follow the tribes into the streets as their "second line" function as active participants in the performance, not just as pas-

sive spectators. Second liners beat on bottles with sticks, shake tambourines attached to long poles, and dance to rhythmic chants in an interactive call and response with the singers and dancers in the tribe. Years ago,
the second line had an additional function—to protect the costumes and
persons of the Indians when the parade entered hostile neighborhoods.[16]
In addition, the tribes function as more than musical aggregations. While
they do offer opportunities for leisure, recreation, and creative expression,
they also serve as mutual-aid societies providing burial insurance, bail
money, and other forms of assistance.[17] Most important, the Indians use
artistic expressions as a means of reinforcing desired behaviors within
their community. As Chernoff says about African music, "the practice
of art is an explicitly moral activity because African art functions dynam-
ically to create a context of values where criticism is translated into social action. The meaning of the music is externalized through an event
in which participation parallels the musician's artistic purpose: an artist's coolness lends security to intimacy, and the rhythms of an ensem-
ble become the movement of an event when people dance."[18] In New
Orleans, as in Africa, this translation of criticism to action takes place
through a fusion of music, dress, speech, and dance.

Fewer than twenty songs make up the basic corpus of Mardi Gras
Indian music, although each song has many variants. New songs have
become popular, and old songs have disappeared, but year in and year out,
on Mardi Gras Day and in rehearsals throughout the year, the Indians
rework familiar words and melodies.[19] All the tribes sing all of the songs,
changing the words to insert the distinctive histories and features of their
own group. Musical traditions from around the globe appear in Mardi Gras
Indian music. Songs like "Handa Wanda" and "Get Out the Way" involve
an interaction between leader and chorus by means of antiphony, or call
and response, a form that originated in West Africa but has become a basic
feature of African American and European American popular music. In
"Don't Like That Song," the leader and chorus exchange groups of phrases
in the manner of Anglo-American Protestant hymns. "Indian Red," the
song used to end all rehearsals and to begin the Mardi Gras Day procession, contains Caribbean phrases and styles.[20]

The structural forms of Mardi Gras Indian songs relate directly to
their functions. The limited corpus of songs ensures a great deal of repetition, but it also places a premium on subtlety and improvisation. As
Chernoff points out about African music,

> People can hear the music for years and always find it fresh and lively
> because of the extent to which an African musical performance is inte-
> grated into its specific social situation. In traditional African music-

making situations, the music is basically familiar, and people can follow with informed interest the efforts of the musicians to add an additional dimension of excitement or depth to a performance. Relatively minor variations stand out clearly and assume increased importance in making the occasion successful.[21]

These musical principles reflect philosophical and moral stances. Unlike the Euro-American musical tradition, which places a premium on individual authorship of finite texts, the African tradition manifest in Mardi Gras Indian music values dialogue and conversation between artists and audiences to adapt old texts to new situations. The "audience" participates in the creation of this music by singing responses to the leader, by handclapping, and by dancing or chanting in a way that acknowledges the creativity of the musicians. As Chernoff explains, "The music works more by encouraging social interaction and participation at each performance than by affirming a fixed set of sanctioned concepts and beliefs."[22]

But it is not merely an abstract philosophy that emerges from the Indian music; the musical forms employed by the tribes reflect concrete social relations. Thus the call and response between the leader and tribe in "Handa Wanda" represents the symbiotic relationship between the individual and the group. The chiefs have certain concrete responsibilities—in life and in songs—and when appropriate they take the lead both musically and socially. But each individual plays an important role in the tribe, replete with occasions to show off individual skills and attributes for the benefit of the entire group. Similarly, the form of "Indian Red" mirrors the social organization of Indian tribes. Only the chief can sing lead on this song, but his responsibility is to call forth the other members of the tribe by naming their roles—spy boy, flag boy, trail chief, etc. In most tribes, each "rank" has three people in it, and appropriately enough, "Indian Red" employs a triple meter.[23] The song "Big Chief Wants Plenty of Fire Water" tells a story about a chief who likes to drink, but the Indian tribes and the audiences know that it is used to take up a collection to buy wine for the Indians.[24] Obviously reflective of Anglo and mass-media stereotypes about Indians and alcohol, this song is one of the places where the metaphor employed undermines the culture of antiracism intended by the Mardi Gras Indian ritual. Yet the act that accompanies it—hospitality and treating within the community—affirms self-worth and solidarity at the same time.

Like their music, the Mardi Gras Indians' costumes and insignia serve both expressive and functional purposes. Most generally, their beads, feathers, designs, and colors celebrate the bounty of life. Plumes and feathers extend outward magnificently, laying claim to dominion all over the space around them, just as bright colors and rhinestones command spectators' fields of vision. This sartorial display draws upon both the Euro-American sensibility of Carnival as a time of pleasure before the deprivations of Lent as well as the celebration of life's pleasures ritualized in African American funerals in New Orleans. But it is impossible to understand the full meaning of the Indian suits from their appearances alone. To the Indians these costumes have meaning only as coded reflections of a complex social process.

Designing and sewing Indian suits is a year-round endeavor; as soon as one Carnival ends, the Indians begin to prepare for the next. No one wears the same suit two years in a row; indeed, no one wears the same color suit two years in a row. Each member of the tribe selects his own colors and designs his own suit, although tribes generally adopt at least one theme color that appears in all of the costumes.[25] While specialized craftspersons may be asked to assist others with drawing or other particular tasks, Indians are responsible for their own beading and sewing. The sense of craft is so strong among them that using sewing machines risks unqualified disapproval. Individual expression is encouraged and prized, but most of the sewing takes place in collective work sessions involving the sharing of skills, advice, and opinions.[26] Like music rehearsals, these sewing sessions bring the group closer together and provide an opportunity for passing along skills, attitudes, and traditions.

The costumes and insignia also serve as part of the tribe's communications system. Flags display the names of treasured symbols of each group, but they are also used by the flag boys to signal directions along the line of march, to warn of the approach of other tribes, and even to encourage changes in rhythms for the chants, songs, and dances.[27] The Indians also send a message to the community via the costume of their chief, whose prestige rests largely on the beauty of his suit. One of the stock songs of the Indians boasts, "My big chief got a golden crown." The entire tribe takes pride in the chief's appearance as well as responsibility for his protection. Many tribes have bodyguards in plain clothes accompanying the line of march, and most have a "wild man" whose sole job is to clear the path for the chief and to make sure that no one attacks his costume.[28]

The same calculated playfulness that informs Mardi Gras Indian music and dress makes itself felt in its language as well. Les Blank captures the logic of this speech beautifully in his 1978 documentary film *Always for Pleasure,* in which he has an informant reel off a dazzling set of rhymes in "Indian talk." When asked how he knows what to say, the man replies, "It's no script, no set language; you say what you feel."[29] Of course, most viewers of Blank's film (like most readers of this essay) could say what they feel all day and never come up with "Wild Tchoupitoula, uptown ruler, blood shiff ahoona, won't kneel, won't bow, don't know how." Such words come "spontaneously" only to those whose preparation is so thorough that the language has become completely internalized. But the seeming inaccessibility of "Indian talk" plays an important role within the subculture, drawing lines between insiders and outsiders and cultivating an active sense of ambiguity capable of serving many purposes.

For years, ethnomusicologists have attempted to decode the language of the Mardi Gras Indians. Some phrases contain a direct meaning, when chanted or sung during parades. For example, "Two Way Pockaway" conveys a warning to get out of the way, while "on tendais" denotes approval of the previous phrase.[30] The folklorist Alan Lomax believed that the phrase "Two Way Pockaway" came from Louisiana dialect French *t'ouwais bas q'ouwais*, which he surmised came either from *tu na's pas couilles* (you don't have testicles) or from *tuez bas qu'ou est* (kill who is over there). Lomax believed that "on tendais" also came from the French *entendez* (understand) or *attendez* (wait up or listen).[31] Similarly, the song "Indian Red" has been traced by Andrew Pearse to a Carnival song from Trinidad, "Indurubi," which he felt came from the Spanish *Indo Rubi* (Indian Red). In New Orleans, "Indian Red" is generally preceded by the chant "Ma Day Cootie Fiyo." Jason Berry, Jonathan Foose, and Tad Jones point out that *matar* in Spanish means "to kill," while *qui tu est fijo* can mean "who is immobile to you," giving "Ma Day Cootie Fiyo" the possible meaning of "kill who is in your way."[32]

But to search for a static and literal meaning for each Mardi Gras Indian phrase is to gravely misread their playful and deliberately ambiguous language. Word play provides an important facet of many expressions of Indian identity. As one former chief explained, "The idea of singing a Indian song is rhyming something, thinking fast to rhyme it."[33] When tribes meet on the streets, part of their competition involves "talking" by the chiefs who rhyme praise for themselves and insults for their enemies in the manner of the popular African American folk game "playing the dozens."[34]

Just as the Mardi Gras Indian music features variation and improvisation on traditional forms, tribal speech reflects a similarly creative dynamism. For example, the Golden Blades tribe used to be known as Creole Wild West but changed their name because of a verbal interchange between one of their singers and someone from their "second line." In 1935, during a rehearsal at a bar near Third and Rocheblave streets, this tribe member started singing about his big chief's "diamond crown." When a woman in the crowd responded, "Give it to the boys from Third and Rocheblave," the singer picked up on her phrase but soon changed "Third and Rocheblave" to "give it to the gang from the Golden Blades."[35] Similarly, the 1930s chant by the Wild Squatoolas, "Somebody got to sew, sew, sew," became transformed in the 1960s by the Wild Magnolias to "Everybody's got soul, soul, soul."[36]

The imprecision of "Indian talk" might not engender confidence in the idea of language as a central feature of the Mardi Gras Indian ritual. After all, if the origins of words remain obscure, and if the words themselves change over time, how can we be sure that speakers know the significance of what they are saying? It is likely that the tribes and their followers are not always exactly aware of the denotative meaning of every word they use. But in another sense, the use of this language in collective rituals conveys a greater meaning than can be found in the individual words themselves. Another African example might help illumine the consciousness behind this approach to language. Chernoff interviewed a famous Ghanaian musician known as "The Entertainer" about the meaning of his songs:

> When I asked him what the songs he sang were about, he said that he did not really understand some of them and that he would have to go ask the old men who had given him the proverbs which he had set to music. People from various walks of life told me that The Entertainer's songs were in "deep Dagbani," which they could not "hear." They did not have to understand the songs to be moved, but nevertheless, they valued the songs' expression of their deepest traditional sentiments. What was important to them was that the songs had a depth which they enjoyed trying to interpret even while they acknowledged that the songs were often beyond them. In effect, the music does and does not rely on a specific traditional meaning.[37]

Just as African audiences value the traditions conveyed by The Entertainer, Mardi Gras Indians and their audiences profit from the cultural legacies of the past, even while adapting them to the present. Mardi Gras Indian traditions are not a matter of establishing precise origins or maintaining authentic folk forms; rather, they seek to unite the present with the past in a dynamic, yet continuous process. Words and names often play key roles in building that unity. When new tribes form, they often connect themselves to the past by using the name of a disbanded group. Yet they only do so if they can locate the disbanded tribe's chief and secure his permission.[38]

Song lyrics also connect contemporary heroism to traditional figures. Thus the Wild Tchoupitoulas' "Brother John" pays tribute to John "Scarface" Williams (a rhythm-and-blues singer and Mardi Gras Indian who died from a knifing shortly after Carnival in 1972) by comparing him to "Cora" who "died on the battlefield." An earlier song by Willie Turbinton of the Wild Magnolias (based on a chant by the Magnolias' chief Bo Dollis), told the story of a rebellious slave named Corey. In the 1920s, the jazz musician Danny Barker recorded a song, "Corrine Died on the Battlefield," that Paul Longpre of the Golden Blades claims told the story of a woman named Cora Anne who masked as Queen of the Battlefield Hunters and died of gunshot wounds incurred when she got caught in a crossfire between the Hunters and the Wild Squatoolas.[39] "Cora" thus refers to at least four people living more than one hundred years apart, three of them male and one female. The story touches on the histories of at least five tribes and has appeared in four separate songs. There is no one authentic Corey; the purpose of all this borrowing is precisely to fashion a collective narrative embracing a wide range of actual events and individuals. No one lyricist or storyteller can control the narrative about Corey; it filters though the community, undergoing significant changes, yet retaining important continuities.

Language, costumes, and music combine to shape the fused art of Mardi Gras Indian pageantry, but it is largely through dancing that each of these separate forms becomes part of a larger totality. Indians who chant "two way pockaway" ("get out of the way") will dance differently from those chanting "handa wanda" ("we're not looking for trouble"). Dancing offers an opportunity to display the beauty of one's costume; conversely, costume design anticipates the movements of street dancing. Musical selections not only have their own lyrics, melodies, and rhythms, they also have specific dance steps that acccentuate their other meanings.

In recent years, dancing has taken on an even greater importance among the Mardi Gras Indian tribes as a symbolic form of combat. At one time the tribes carried real hatchets and spears and used the aggressive festivity of Carnival as a cover for gang warfare. After a day of drinking and marching, they would meet to settle grudges and rivalries on the "battlefield"—an empty lot at the intersection of Claiborne and Poydras Streets. But when urban renewal destroyed the basis for neighborhood competitions, and when police vigilance made violent acts on Carnival day more difficult, a new spirit began to emerge. Aesthetic rivalries took the place of street fighting, and dancing became a key way of demonstrating one's superiority over others. When Indians challenge each other in the streets, they draw an imaginary line between them and compete by dancing as close as possible to it without crossing. Their dance enacts a mock fight replete with attacks on territory and each other's bodies. The dancers capable of giving the appearance of fighting without resorting to actual combat win the highest esteem from their tribe and from other spectators.[40]

The transformation of actual violence into symbolic aesthetic competition has many precedents and parallels in African American communities all across the nation, but it has a special history in New Orleans. Art Neville, a rhythm-and-blues musician who has played with the Hawketts, the Meters, and the Neville Brothers (and whose "Uncle Jolly" formed the Wild Tchoupitoulas tribe in 1972), remembers music as a viable alternative to gang fighting in the public housing project where he grew up in the 1940s and 1950s. "We used to do the doo-wop thing," Neville recalls, referring to the close harmonies and scat singing favored by his friends and relatives at that time. "There were gangs from different neighborhoods and some would fight. I was with a gang that did the singing, so I didn't have nothing to worry about."[41]

Yet dancing means much more to the Indian tribes than the mere displacement of aggressive tendencies. Dancing is a communication system in its own right. In parade situations, certain steps by the spy boys and flag boys alert the rest of the tribe to the presence of hostility ahead.[42] Second liners and tribe members create the rhythms for chants and songs with their dancing every bit as much as the beating of tambourines and sticks conveys a beat for the dancers. Willie Turbinton of the Wild Magnolias remembers that it was the dancing of the Indians that attracted him to them in the first place. When he was eleven years old he saw his first Indian tribe and remembers, "'It just always intrigued me. There were certain steps and certain moves they'd make that were synonymous with the kind of rhythm they played.'"[43] Turbinton liked the Indian costumes and language, and he was fascinated by the rituals that gave each member of the tribe a particular significance. But he felt drawn into the spectacle most strongly by the ways that the rhythms made him want to dance. "'It was the kind of groove that you couldn't resist,'" he recalls. "'The pulse affected you. You find yourself patting your foot, and if you're shy, you just feel it inside yourself.'"[44]

The centrality of dancing to the Mardi Gras Indian ritual reveals yet another layer of African cultural retentions among New Orleans blacks. In his research on African music, Chernoff discovered villagers who identified pieces of music by the dances that accompanied them, and he found over and over again that the musicians expected their audiences and dancers to demonstrate active involvement with the music by providing a beat for the musicians to follow. Unlike the concert and dance traditions of European American popular music, the audience in Africa is part of the performance through their dancing, handclapping, and singing. In addition, dancing in African cultures is a form of public worship, a visual demonstration of belief, just as the dance itself is a visual expression of the music.[45] Like their African counterparts (and forebears), Mardi Gras Indians in New Orleans manifest their values about art and life through performance of a "danced faith."[46] Chernoff's analysis of public dancing by African village chiefs applies equally to the chiefs of Mardi Gras Indian tribes:

> In his dance, the chief combines aesthetic command and moral command, and the satisfying beauty of his dance is a visible display of his closeness to his ancestors and his fitness for authority. The chief asserts the community through a dance in which gracefulness implies the tranquility of mature strength, elegance implies the bounty of life, precision implies dedication of purpose, happiness implies the accessibility of compassion, composure implies the discretion of power and dignity implies destiny.[47]

Much of the power of the Mardi Gras Indian ritual stems from its force as a counternarrative challenging the hegemony of New Orleans's social elite. During Mardi Gras, New Orleans "high society" celebrates its bloodlines and mythologizes itself as the heir to a powerful tradition of mysticism and magic. The elite mask themselves in expensive costumes and ride motorized floats along the city's main thoroughfares, throwing beaded necklaces and souvenir doubloons to crowds of spectators. The Indians subvert this spectacle by declaring a powerful lineage of their own, one that challenges the legitimacy of Anglo-European domination. Their costumes are made, not bought. They avoid the main thoroughfares and walk through black neighborhoods. They define the crowds along their route as participants, not only as spectators. Their fusion of music, costumes, speech, and dance undermines the atomized European view of each of these activities as distinct and autonomous endeavors, while it foregrounds an African sensibility about the interconnectedness of art and the interconnectedness of human beings.

Yet the degree to which this counternarrative actually threatens the hegemony of the dominant culture is open to dispute. One can well imagine how easily those in power might dismiss black workers in outlandish costumes drinking and dancing in the streets on Mardi Gras Day. Certainly within the black community, the ambiguities and multilayered symbolism of the Indian ritual might well obscure the historical and social power realities behind its genesis, as the traditional internal rivalries it has provoked have demonstrated. The dominance of males and the peripheral role allotted to females within the Indian ritual reinforces the sexist hierarchies of the dominant culture. Furthermore, even if one were to claim that the Indian ritual served an oppositional purpose within black New Orleans, there would be no guarantee that this particular counternarrative could transcend specific experiences of race, region, and class to speak to people with different values and histories. The forms and styles fashioned by the Indians seem so rooted in the specific history and culture of New Orleans that it is difficult to imagine how their practice could be representative of counternarratives generated under different conditions.

Indeed, even the cultural critics most sympathetic to the emancipatory potential of popular narratives express reservations about them that are relevant to an evaluation of the ultimate significance of the practices of the Mardi Gras Indians. Limon warns that ostensibly oppositional behaviors sometimes simply reflect unequal opportunities and resources. Thus, rather than parodying or undermining dominant narratives, these behaviors might instead be imitating them, albeit with inadequate resources. Limon emphasizes that traditional folklore best retains a critical edge in the modern world when it represents self-generated and relatively autonomous cultural practices that contrast radically with the "largely imposed character of mass media culture."[48] In a similar vein, Fox points to the ways in which modern society undermines the kinds of communities and cultures traditionally oriented toward the creation and preservation of folklore. Fox notes that folk practices often draw their critical content from an essentially conservative function-preserving group cohesion and conformity in traditional societies under attack by modernization. He points out that such societies are increasingly rare and increasingly anomalous in the modern world and that they constitute an inadequate basis for cultural and political contestation.[49] Jameson contends that the truly "popular" art has all but disappeared under the assault of commercial mass culture, surviving only in isolated pockets removed from the main channels of communication and commerce.[50]

The concerns raised by Limon, Fox, and Jameson offer useful cautions about analyzing the Mardi Gras Indian ritual as an example of counternarrative. Like all subordinated groups, the Indians lack access to significant power and resources, and their organizations do serve purposes of mutual aid and self-affirmation denied them in other spheres. Their ritual may have started in relative isolation from the "largely imposed character of mass media culture," but their present-day and future audiences have been saturated with competing images and sounds from other cultures through the mass media. They seem to exemplify Jameson's contention that truly "popular" art exists only in specialized and marginalized circumstances, far removed from the centers of mainstream commerce and culture.

Yet the same forms of commercial culture that destroy the organic basis for traditional folklore enable people to escape the prejudices and parochialisms of their own communities. The same forces that relegate ethnic, linguistic, and subcultural minorities to the margins of contemporary culture also transmit the oppositional sensibilities of marginal groups to a mass audience. The same feelings that motivate people to fashion autonomous signs and symbols within folkloric traditions impel them to put the stamp of their own experience on the ideas and images circulated within commercial culture. Most important, the internal properties of the electronic mass media favor precisely the kinds of dynamic cultural creation basic to the entire Mardi Gras Indian activity. Commercial culture destroys the sense of "origins" and "authenticity" prized by European American music and folklore, but its biases toward repetition, nonlinear reasoning, and immediacy make it a viable conduit for oppositional narratives like those created by the Mardi Gras Indians. Nothing illustrates this tendency more convincingly than the way in which New Orleans musicians have inserted Mardi Gras Indian music into American and international popular music.

As early as the 1920s, jazz musicians from New Orleans recorded Mardi Gras Indian songs. Danny Barker and His Creole Cats did "My Indian Red" and "Chocko Mo Fendo Hando" on the King Zulu label, while Louis Dumaine and His Jazzola Eight performed "To Wa Bac a Wa" for Vic Records.[51] In 1954, Sugar Boy Crawford inserted Indian music into mainstream popular culture when his song "Jock-A-Mo" became a big regional hit. Although not an Indian himself, Crawford created "Jock-A-Mo" by combining two songs he remembered hearing them sing when he was growing up near the "battlefield" on Claiborne and Poydras streets.[52] Dave Bartholomew's 1957 "Can't Take It No More" begins with chanting evocative of Indian call and response.[53] In 1965, the Dixie Cups, a female trio from New Orleans, reached the national top-twenty list with "Iko Iko," which like "Jock-A-Mo" originated with the Mardi Gras Indians. In a story that illustrates how commercial and folk cultures can intersect, Barbara Hawkins of the Dixie Cups relates how "Iko Iko" became a record: "We were clowning around the studio, while the musicians were on break, it was just the three of us using drumsticks on ashtrays and glasses singing 'Iko Iko.' We didn't realize that producers Jerry and Mike (Leiber and Stoller) were in the control room with the tape rolling. They came out and said that's great, they had never heard it before, all they added was a calypso box. We had never planned on recording it."[54] Hawkins described the song as "the type of thing the Indians have always used, inventing new words as they march along."[55] In the late 1970s, Hawkins herself came full circle with the Indians, marching as Queen of the Wild Magnolias on Mardi Gras Day.

Other Indian songs that have been recorded successfully include versions of "Iko Iko" by Doctor John and by the Neville Brothers, "Handa Wanda" by the Wild Magnolias, and compilations of Carnival songs by the Wild Tchoupitoulas and the Wild Magnolias.[56] In addition, songs about parts of the Mardi Gras Indian ritual have been recorded by Professor Longhair, Huey Smith and the Clowns, and Earl King. Some of the influence of the Indians on New Orleans pop music has been indirect. Cyril Neville of the Neville Brothers attributes his skill on percussion instruments to the lessons he learned from the tambourine playing of his "Uncle Jolly" (George Landry), who founded the Wild Tchoupitoulas tribe in 1972. Those lessons involved the kind of interactions with African music characteristic of the Mardi Gras Indian aesthetic. As Neville explains: "The drum comes to me as a symbol of what I, or we, used to be. I can't speak on the drums, but I try to convey my feelings. . . . I think about Africa when I play. To me, right now, my Africa is the drums cause when I feel like going back to Africa, I play my drums."[57] Evidently, Cyril Neville learned his lessons well; when the Neville Brothers played on a bill in Chicago with the Nigerian Juju band, King Sunny Ade and His African Beats, a reporter for the *Chicago Sun Times* noted, "Many of the African players were enchanted with the funk and soul of the Neville Brothers, most notably the West African persuasions of percussionist Cyril Neville."[58]

But to trace only the direct links between the Indians and popular artists and songs underestimates their true influence on New Orleans, American, and world popular music. An amazing variety of recorded music from New Orleans resonates with the values, aesthetics, and musical traditions of the Indians. Their jubilant celebration of the bounty of life informs Shirley and Lee's 1956 "Let the Good Times Roll," Aaron Neville's 1966 "Tell It Like It Is," and The Meters' 1972 "They All Axed for You." Indian-style call and response dominated Huey Smith and the Clowns' 1958 "Don't You Just Know It," while "second line" rhythms permeated The Meters' 1970 "Handclapping Song."

The great New Orleans rhythm-and-blues pianist Professor Longhair replicated Mardi Gras Indian music in his polyrhythmic compositions, demonstrating a philosophical commitment to the unity among percussion, dance, and melody by refusing to play the grand pianos and insisting on uprights so that he could kick the base boards rhythmically at the appropriate moments. Alfred Roberts, who played conga drums behind Professor Longhair, once described what the two of them tried to do musically in words that serve as a capsule introduction to African musical sensibilities:

> I try and answer whatever he's doin' and try and lay out a basic pattern that he could listen to and build off. Cause this is what he made me think of the role he wanted me to play. If the drummer is playing a certain rhythm with his foot, and Fess [Professor Longhair] got somethin' happenin' with his hands, syncopatin', it's best for you to play in a space where nothin' is happenin' and kind of blend in with the drummer and the bass player. It's just backwards and forwards your hand and your brain, your eyes, your ears, and it's just flowin' like that into a rhythm.[59]

Just as Alfred Roberts and Professor Longhair reproduced African musical forms in New Orleans, musicians from all over the world knowingly and unknowingly absorbed Mardi Gras Indian music into the basic vocabulary of rock and roll. The New Orleans drummer Earl Palmer laid a solid "parade beat" beneath the rhythm-and-blues hits of Little Richard and Sam Cooke, while the melody and chord progressions from the parade song "Second Line" predate their appearance in Bill Haley and His Comets' "Rock around the Clock."[60] The New Orleans rhythm-and-blues artist Ernie K-Doe exaggerated only slightly when he said in 1979, "'I'm not sure, but I'm almost positive, that all music came from New Orleans.'"[61]

In 1986, the rock singer Cyndi Lauper delayed the release of her *True Colors* album in order to include "Iko Iko" on it. Lauper had been listening to playbacks of her rendition of Marvin Gaye's 1960s antiwar, antiracist "What's Going On," and she began to be reminded of another song. Eventually, she realized that the rhythms she had been using in "What's Going On" fit perfectly into "Iko Iko," which came to Lauper through listening to the Neville Brothers, Doctor John, and the Dixie Cups.[62] On the surface, her connection might seem absurd. The profound political lyrics of "What's Going On" bear little resemblance to the nonsense rhymes of "Iko Iko." The life experience of a white woman rock star from New York seems to have little in common with the historical struggle against racial and class domination waged by the Mardi Gras Indians. Yet Lauper's intuition led her to the right place. "What's Going On" and "Iko Iko" are both about fighting racism and exploitation. The magnificent plumes and bright colors of the Mardi Gras Indians express in their way what the multicolored hair and self-parodying costumes of Cyndi Lauper represent in another way. The protofeminist blend of adolescent female voices and adult sexual desires in the Dixie Cups' "Iko Iko" serves as a legitimate progenitor to Lauper's own breakthrough hit in 1985, "Girls Just Wanna Have Fun."

That Lauper came to "Iko Iko" through the apparatuses of commercial culture raises intriguing questions about the supposedly diminishing power of popular narratives. It illustrates how marginalized cultures can insinuate their oppositional values into the texts of popular culture and create allies among people with similar though not identical experiences. It is no more ridiculous for Cyndi Lauper to appropriate "Iko Iko" than it was for nineteenth-century working-class blacks to use the Wild West show, Mardi Gras, and gang fighting as a basis for an oppositional subculture. As part of the history of rock and roll, as part of the historic opposition to hierarchy and exploitation in America, "Iko Iko" offered a logical source of inspiration and celebration for Lauper. The critics may be right when they talk about the decline of traditional narratives, the marginalization of "popular" art, and the "largely imposed character of mass media culture." But people fight with the resources at their disposal, and frequently their pain leads them to quite innovative means of struggle. They do not all have the same story, and they often fail to understand the stories of others. They often suffer terrible oppression and anguish as they search for a narrative capable of making sense out of their existence. But storytelling survives, even when the storytellers develop coded and secret ways of communicating with one another, inside and outside of commercial culture. For all of his pessimism, even Walter Benjamin understood this. In the same essay in which he fretted about the demise of storytelling, Benjamin offered a phrase that he meant figuratively, but which has a literal meaning as well. "Indeed," Benjamin observed, "each sphere of life has, as it were, produced its own tribe of storytellers."[63]

## Notes

1. Walter Benjamin, *Illuminations* (New York: Schocken Books, 1969), 83.

2. See Paul Buhle, *Popular Culture in America* (Minneapolis: University of Minnesota Press, 1987).

3. José E. Limon, "Western Marxism and Folklore," *Journal of American Folklore* 96.379 (1983): 49.

4. Fredric Jameson, "Reification and Utopia in Mass Culture," *Social Text* 1.1 (1979): 130–48.

5. William Fox, "Folklore and Fakelore: Some Sociological Considerations," *Journal of the Folklore Institute* 17.2–3 (May–Dec. 1980): 249.

6. David Elliot Draper, "The Mardi Gras Indians: The Ethnomusicology of Black Associations in New Orleans" (Ph.D. diss., Tulane University, 1973), 7, 27, 38, 40.

7. Ibid., 35, 54.

8. Les Blank, director, *Always for Pleasure* (Flower Films, 1978).

9. See Jason Berry, "Controversy Swirls around Mardi Gras Indian Origins," *New Orleans Times-Picayune*, Feb. 17, 1984, sec. 1, p. 6.

10. Jason Berry, Jonathan Foose, and Tad Jones, *Up from the Cradle of Jazz* (Athens: University of Georgia Press, 1986), 210, 218.

11. Quoted in Helen Joy Mayhew, "New Orleans Black Musical Culture: Tradition and the Individual Talent" (M.A. thesis, University of Exeter, 1986), 187–88.

12. Berry et al., *Up from the Cradle of Jazz*, 210.

13. Quoted in Jason Berry, "Pomp and Circumstance of the Mardi Gras Indians," *Dynamic Years* 16 (Mar. 1981): 1–3.

14. Draper, "Mardi Gras Indians," 42. John Miller Chernoff identifies grace, strength, elegance, precision, happiness, composure, and dignity as key elements in performances by African chiefs in his wonderful book *African Rhythms and African Sensibility* (Chicago: University of Chicago Press, 1979), 150.

15. Chernoff, *African Rhythms and African Sensibility*, 33–34.

16. Draper, "Mardi Gras Indians," 54. See also Alan Lomax, *Mister Jelly Roll: The Fortunes of Jelly Roll Morton, New Orleans Creole and Inventor of Jazz* (1950; rpt., Berkeley: University of California Press, 1973), 12.

17. Draper, "Mardi Gras Indians," 23. See also John Blassingame, *Black New Orleans, 1860–1880* (Chicago: University of Chicago Press, 1973).

18. Chernoff, *African Rhythms and African Sensibility*, 143.

19. Draper, "Mardi Gras Indians," 218, 360.

20. Ibid., 227, 276, 286; Berry et al., *Up from the Cradle of Jazz*, 213.

21. Chernoff, *African Rhythms and African Sensibility*, 61.

22. Ibid., 125.

23. Draper, "Mardi Gras Indians," 362, 363.

24. Finn Wilhelmsen, "Creativity in the Songs of the Mardi Gras Indians of New Orleans, Lousiana," *Louisiana Folklore Miscellany* 3 (1973): 58.

25. Draper, "Mardi Gras Indians," 130, 166, 167.

26. Ibid., 122, 166, 167.

27. Ibid., 103.

28. Ibid., 51, 53, 54.

29. Blank, *Always for Pleasure.*

30. Draper, "Mardi Gras Indians," 115; Berry et al., *Up from the Cradle of Jazz*, 221.

31. Berry et al., *Up from the Cradle of Jazz*, 218.

32. Ibid., 213.

33. Ibid., 218.

34. Draper, "Mardi Gras Indians," 117, 118.

35. Berry et al., *Up from the Cradle of Jazz*, 218.

36. Ibid.

37. Chernoff, *African Rhythms and African Sensibility*, 124, 125.

38. Draper, "Mardi Gras Indians," 69, 70.

39. Berry et al., *Up from the Cradle of Jazz*, 224, 235.

40. Ibid., 216; Draper, "Mardi Gras Indians," 36, 38.

41. Don Palmer, "Gumbo Variations," *The Soho News,* Aug. 11, 1981, 23.

42. Draper, "Mardi Gras Indians," 103.

43. Quoted in Berry et al., *Up from the Cradle of Jazz,* 220.

44. Ibid.

45. Chernoff, *African Rhythms and African Sensibility,* 50, 144, 150.

46. The phrase "danced faith" is Robert F. Thompson's (see ibid., 144).

47. Ibid., 150.

48. Limon, "Western Marxism and Folklore," 39.

49. Fox, "Folklore and Fakelore," 249, 255, 256.

50. Jameson, "Reification and Utopia," 134, 137, 138.

51. Draper, "Mardi Gras Indians," 389.

52. Jeff Hannusch, *I Hear You Knockin'* (Ville Platte, La.: Swallow, 1985), 262.

53. Mayhew, "New Orleans Black Musical Culture," 215.

54. Shepard Samuels, "The Dixie Cups," *Wavelength* 19 (May 1982): 18. For a description of Leiber and Stoller's role in disseminating other popular narratives, see George Lipsitz, "Land of a Thousand Dances: Youth, Minorities, and Rock and Roll," in *Recasting America,* ed. Larry May (Chicago: University of Chicago Press, 1988), 302–12.

55. Samuels, "Dixie Cups," 18.

56. See Hannusch, *I Hear You Knockin',* 359–73.

57. Berry et al., *Up from the Cradle of Jazz,* 232.

58. Dave Hoekstra, "King Sunny Brightens Sound of Juju Music," *Chicago Sun-Times,* May 10, 1987, 10.

59. Jason Berry, "The Caribbean Connection," *New Orleans* 19 (May 1985): 67.

60. See also Hal Singer's song "Cornbread" and Hank Williams's "Move It on Over."

61. Quoted in *Wavelength* 19 (May 1982): 3.

62. Jon Bream, "Cyndi Lauper," *Minnesota Star and Tribune,* Dec. 7, 1986, G1. A 1982 recording of "Iko Iko" by the Belle Stars appeared in the 1988 film *Rain Man* and subsequently made the best-seller charts in 1989.

63. Benjamin, *Illuminations,* 85.

# PART 4

*Contemporary
African–Native American
Subjectivity*

PATRICIA RILEY

# 8 Wrapped in the Serpent's Tail: Alice Walker's African–Native American Subjectivity

> In regard to the contact between the two races . . . it is not commonly known that in all the southern colonies Indian slaves were bought and sold and kept in servitude and worked in the fields side by side with negroes up to the time of the Revolution. . . . [W]e find the Cherokee as early as 1693 complaining that their people were being kidnapped by slave hunters. . . . Furthermore, as the coast tribes dwindled they were compelled to intermarry with the negroes until they finally lost their identity and were classed with that race, so that a considerable proportion of the blood of the southern negroes is unquestionably Indian.
>
> —James Mooney, *Myths of the Cherokee and Sacred Formulas of the Cherokee*

In *Africans and Native Americans: The Language of Race and the Evolution of Red-Black Peoples,* Jack D. Forbes notes that in spite of the often complex ancestry of contemporary Americans "of 'black' or 'Indian' appearance . . . many such persons have been forced by racism into arbitrary categories which tend to render their ethnic heritage simple rather than complex," and he calls upon scholars to remedy this situation by "replac[ing] shallow one-dimensional portraits of non-whites with more accurate multi-dimensional portraits."[1] Alice Walker's novel *Meridian* (1977) and the dedicatory poem in *Horses Make a Landscape*

241

*More Beautiful* (1984) are two works that are well-suited for the kind of project that Forbes had in mind in that both function as vehicles for the expression of Walker's own mixed-race identity as a woman of African American and Cherokee ancestry, and both illustrate her "acceptance of [her] actual as opposed to [her] mythical sel[f]."[2] That is, both works celebrate her identification of herself as a multicultural and multiracial person as opposed to the monoracial identification assigned to her by the dominant society.[3]

In *Meridian*, Walker relates the story of a young southern black woman, Meridian Hill, a civil rights activist who continues to work for the fruition of Martin Luther King's dream years after his assassination and in spite of the fact that the people she is working to help view her as eccentric. As Barbara Christian observes in *Black Feminist Criticism: Perspectives on Black Women Writers*, Walker's "use of Native American culture as well as Afro-American culture emphasizes the need for a point of view that values *all* life rather than some life" and, by extension, all heritages rather than some heritages.[4] In *Meridian*, Walker writes within an African–Native American subjectivity that not only includes cultural elements from her Cherokee and African American heritage but, additionally inspired by Lakota (Sioux) culture and the heroic endeavor of the Lakota people to retain their autonomy, firmly links together the collective struggle for freedom undertaken historically by Native American and African American peoples.

To illustrate this connection between the two peoples, Walker fashions a narrative that speaks to the continuing struggle for the African American dream that was shattered at the time of King's assassination. She then ties this struggle to that of America's indigenous peoples by choosing for her epigraph a quote from the conclusion of *Black Elk Speaks*, as told to John G. Neihardt, that recollects the dream of the Lakota people that was shattered at the Massacre of Wounded Knee. Black Elk reflects upon the massacre by U.S. troops of almost three hundred Lakota people, including women and children,[5] and describes the impact of this tragic event upon the spirit and the lives of his people, an impact that has much in common with the pain and despair felt by many following the King assassination: "I did not know then how much was ended. When I look back now . . . I can still see the butchered women and children lying heaped and scattered all along the gulch as plain as when I saw them with eyes still young. And I can see that something else died there in the bloody mud, and was buried in the blizzard. A people's dream died there. It was a beautiful dream . . . the nation's hoop is broken and scattered. There is no center any longer, and the sacred tree is dead."[6]

The horrifying event that took place at Wounded Knee, South Dakota, on the morning of December 29, 1890, was in direct response to the Lakotas' participation in the Ghost Dance. This pantribal religious movement, with Christian elements, was visionary in nature and was founded by the Paiute prophet Wovoka, a "holy m[a]n who arose to meet [his] people's needs"[7] in desperate and oppressive times, much in the same way as Martin Luther King, also a "holy man," would later rise to meet the needs of his own desperately oppressed people. Wovoka's visions were communicated to him while he was in a death-like trance.[8] His teachings centered around a belief that "the ghosts of dead Indians were on hand to help living Indians in their hour of extremity"[9] and "that there would be a natural catastrophe which would result in the extinction of the white men and the return of all the ancestors of the Indians."[10] While waiting for the cataclysm that would bring about a new world free from European American oppression, Wovoka preached a kind of nonviolent resistance and counseled people not to "'hurt anybody or do harm to anyone. You must not fight. Do right always. It will give you satisfaction in life.'"[11] Impressed with Wovoka's teachings, the Lakota took up the Ghost Dance religion and began to dance and "to make special 'Ghost shirts' which according to their teaching could stop bullets." Fearful of an "Indian uprising," the Indian agent "called for soldiers. They came and, misinterpreting Indian actions, massacred a whole encampment of Sioux at Wounded Knee Creek."[12] Like the Ghost Dance movement, the civil rights movement was visionary, based on a man's dream of peace and rooted in the principle of nonviolence. And, as with the Ghost Dance movement, that nonviolence was too often plagued by a violent response on the part of a fearful Euro-America that misinterpreted and misunderstood what the movement was all about or, in some cases, understood all too well and moved to prevent its success.

Walker further strengthens the association between the struggles of African American and Native American peoples through *Meridian's* sudden recall of a dream she had about Indians the night before the bombing of a house occupied by a group of black voter registration workers in which three small children and one adult were killed:

> This struck her, that they had had a guard. Why did they need a guard. . . . How had they *known* they would need a guard? Did they know something she did not know? She had lived in this town all her life, but could not have foreseen that the house would be bombed. Perhaps because nothing like this had ever happened before. Not in this town. Or *had* it? She recalled that the night before she had dreamed of Indians. She thought she had forgotten them.

And so it was that . . . Meridian Hill became aware of the past and present of the larger world.[13]

By linking the bombing to Meridian's dream of Indians, Walker reminds readers of the frequently forgotten historical violence that was perpetrated against America's indigenous peoples and asks them to consider this event as a continuation of an American tradition of violence against people of color that has simply risen up in a new form.

In addition to comparing the historical struggles of indigenous and African American peoples, Walker also utilizes Lakota cultural traditions to present the character of Meridian as one who functions as a kind of sacred clown for her people. As the novel opens, we find Meridian embroiled in what initially appears to be a "contrary-wise,"[14] seriocomic episode straight out of a theater of the absurd. Seen through the eyes of Truman Held and an elderly black man whom Walker refers to as "the sweeper," the reader follows Meridian as she fearlessly confronts a tank and armed policemen to lead a group of mostly black children in a civil rights action to demand entrance to a circus wagon where the phony mummified remains of Marilene O'Shay, a so-called good woman "gone wrong," lay on display.[15] They have been barred from admittance by the white proprietor and the one-time spouse of the deceased on the grounds that they smell bad through association with their family members who work in a guano plant. The sweeper tells Truman how Meridian came to be involved:

> "That mummy lady's husband, he got on the good side of the upper crust real quick: When the plant workers' children come round trying to get a peek at his old salty broad while some of *them* was over there, he called 'em dirty little bastards and shoo' em away. That's when this weird gal that strolled into town last year come in. She started to round up every one of the po' kids she could get her hands on. She look so burnt out and weird in that old cap she wear you'd think they'd be afraid of her—they too young to 'member when black folks marched alot—but they not."[16]

Having challenged the tank and won, Meridian leaves its occupants bewildered as she continues to make her way to her objective. As Truman watches her kick down the door of the forbidden circus wagon, he exclaims to the sweeper, "'God! . . . How can you not love somebody like that!'" to which the sweeper replies, "'Because she thinks *she's* God, . . . or else she just ain't all there. I think she ain't all there myself.'"[17]

Truman's heartfelt exclamation can be construed as a kind of variation of the old saying that "all the world loves a clown," for Walker has deliberately drawn the character of Meridian as someone who appears outwardly as backward, clownish, and crazy. She wears a silly cap, does seemingly crazy things, behaves outrageously in public, and is the object of much derision among the members of a revolutionary group in New York who perceive her adherence to a civil rights consciousness, tied as it is to a past they are ashamed of, as "decidedly unrevolutionary."[18] When she is unable to make a firm commitment to "kill for the Revolution,"[19] the group "turn[s] away" from her, equally unable to take seriously her decision to return "to the people" and "live among them, like Civil Rights workers used to do."[20]

However, Meridian's actions are revolutionary in spite of the fact that her critics fail to recognize them as such. Her extraordinary behavior ties her closely to Lakota and other Native American traditions regarding the figure of the sacred clown that is an inherently revolutionary role. Sacred clowns play an integral part in many Native American cultures, and Walker's against-the-grain portrayal of Meridian, her deliberate inversion of chronology, and the context in which Meridian acts out her role bear a strong resemblance to the sacred clown of the Lakota, the *heyoka*. According to John (Fire) Lame Deer, a "*heyoka* is somebody sacred, funny, powerful, ridiculous, holy, shameful, visionary . . . an upside-down, backward-forward, yes-and-no man, a contrary-wise."[21] He further states that, although it is not often the case, "a *heyoka* could also be a woman."[22] One becomes a *heyoka* by having a "dream about the lightning, the thunderbirds," and although a *heyoka* has "a power," it is a power that has a price.[23] Part of that price is related to having "to act out his [or her] dream in public"[24] and to risk humiliation, misunderstanding, or derision. Barbara Tedlock observes that "[t]hese actions, while they expose him [or her] to the ridicule of the unthinking, have important meaning," for it is through the medium of laughter that "the people are opened to immediate experience."[25]

Although most of these outward signs relate Walker's protagonist to this *heyoka* tradition, Lame Deer clearly states that there must be a thunder dream of some sort before one can become *heyoka*. While Meridian does experience a number of recurring dreams, none of them contains the required thunder and lightning. However, she comes into a relationship with these elements through her vision in the Cherokee Sacred Serpent Mound on her father's farm in Georgia. And it is through this serpent that, in true *heyoka* fashion, Walker merges Lakota and Cherokee elements in an affirmation of a belief that Native American spiritual traditions are rooted in a common conviction, a belief that Lame Deer shares: "Different but the same—that is real *heyoka* business. I think when it comes right down to it, all the Indian religions somehow are part of the same belief, the same mystery. Our unity, it's in there."[26]

In *Myths of the Cherokee and Sacred Formulas of the Cherokee,* James Mooney points out that in Cherokee tradition, "They [snakes] are all regarded as *anida'wehi,* 'supernaturals,' having an intimate connection with the rain and thunder gods."[27] Charles M. Hudson also indicates that Cherokees closely associated snakes with thunder and lightning and that they referred to the rattlesnake as "Thunder's necklace." Furthermore, he asserts that Cherokees affiliate all snakes with the Underworld, "which was a source of danger, but it was also a source of water, fertility, and a means for coping with evil."[28] Thus Meridian, provided with a vision that enables her to cope with evil, behaves in a Lakota *heyoka* manner, which dictates that she translate "the knowledge of another reality"[29] to her people while having received this responsibility from her experience at the Cherokee Serpent Mound.

It is also important to note that there is a kind of *heyoka* or shamanistic tradition running through Meridian's family that is directly related to descending into the well of the coiled serpent's tail and experiencing an altered state of consciousness that carries the individual past the boundaries of this world and into contact with the infinite. Meridian's great-grandmother, Feather Mae, a character most likely fashioned in homage to Walker's great-grandmother Tallulah, who was part Cherokee,[30] apparently was the first to have gone down inside the coil of the serpent's tail. Significantly, Feather Mae is alerted to its existence by "some squirrels playing up and down the Serpent's sides."[31] The Cherokee myth concerning the "Origin of Disease and Medicine," which could be construed as a forerunner of a civil rights movement of sorts, recounts how a council was called among all the animals, birds, fish, and insects to discuss their mistreatment at the hands of mankind and "to consult upon measures for their common safety." Of all the creatures who spoke at the council, "the Ground-squirrel alone ventured to say a good word for Man, who seldom hurt him because he was so small."[32] Walker's use of the squirrel signifies on this sympathetic association in that the squirrel leads Feather Mae not only into the hidden recesses of "a pit forty feet deep" but into contact with a visionary experience that is beneficial to her and results in her spiritual rebirth: "When she stood in the center of the pit, with the sun blazing down directly over her, something extraordinary happened to her. She felt as if she had stepped into another world, into a different kind of air. The green walls began to spin and her feeling rose to such a high pitch the next thing she knew she was getting up off the ground. She knew she had fainted but she felt neither weakened nor ill. She felt renewed, as from some strange spiritual intoxication. Her blood made warm explosions through her body, and her eyelids stung and tingled."[33]

Enlightened and imbued with a new vision, Feather Mae emerges from that place forever changed. From Walker's description of her behavior afterward and the way in which she alters her lifestyle following the experience, she appears to have become completely and irrevocably immersed in the life of the spirit. Later, Feather Mae renounces all religion that is not based on the experience of physical ecstasy—thereby shocking her Baptist church and its unsympathetic congregation—and near the end of her life she loves walking nude about her yard and worshipping only the sun.[34]

Meridian's experience while wrapped in the serpent's tail is similar to her great-grandmother's and is indicative of some type of communion with Grandmother Sun, "the most sacred . . . deity" of the Cherokee people.[35] She is lifted up and outside of herself, drawn upward through the many-leveled heavens, "And when she came back to her body—and she felt sure she had left it—her eyes were stretched wide open, and they were dry because she found herself staring directly into the sun."[36]

Meridian's father also experiences the power of being wrapped in the serpent's tail. No doubt it is there that he learns compassion "for people dead centuries before he was born."[37] This compassion shapes his life as what Meridian calls "a mourner"[38] and enables him to understand, when his wife could not, how Native American and African American peoples have been unwittingly manipulated and pitted against one another by the dominant culture: "'We were part of it, you know,' her father said. 'Part of what?' 'Their disappearance.' 'Hah,' said her mother. 'You might have been, but I wasn't even born. Besides, you told me how surprised you were to find that some of them had the nerve to fight for the South in the Civil War. That ought to make up for those few black soldiers who rode against Indians in the Western cavalry.' Her father sighed. 'I never said either side was innocent or guilty, just ignorant.'"[39]

Meridian tells of seeing him sitting in a tiny room he had "built himself," which is wallpapered with the photographs of long-dead Indians. Surrounded by numerous "books on Indians, on their land rights, reservations, and their wars," he intensely studies an old disintegrating map "that showed the ancient settlements of Indians in North America."[40]

As a girl, Meridian often watches her father emerge from the Serpent Mound transfigured, bathed in radiant light; a light much like that which was later seen to glow as a kind of halo around Meridian's own head during her illness at Saxon College. This phenomenon is described by her friend, Anne Marion, as a "full soft light, as if her head, the spikes of her natural, had learned to glow."[41]

The nature of Meridian's illness at Saxon and the way in which it manifests itself later in Chicokema (paralysis, falling down, and ecstasy) is part of many Native American and African tribal shamanistic traditions. In *The Sacred: Ways of Knowledge, Sources of Life,* Peggy V. Beck and Anna L. Walters describe what happens when one is called to be a shaman. The following description is reminiscent of Meridian's experiences:

> A typical situation is that the shaman-to-be suddenly gets very sick, falls unconscious, or begins to "act crazy." Perhaps the man or woman "hears things," complains of voices speaking at night, or perhaps he/she runs away and won't speak to anyone for a period of time. Sometimes these things keep happening to an individual on and off for a number of years. At first the individual does not understand what is happening. Later when the individual is older and has a greater understanding of sacred ways and practices he/she may see that these afflictions and pains, the voices and the strange dreams, are trying to tell him/her something.[42]

In *Black Elk Speaks,* Neihardt relates the story of how Black Elk became very ill as a young man, during which time he lost the use of his legs, went into a trance state, and experienced visions.[43] This experience is similar to Meridian's. Following the episode with the tank and the circus wagon in Chicokema, Meridian walks away from the crowd, out of sight of the children, and collapses. She tells Truman that certain townsmen make a practice of following her and carrying her home: "It doesn't bother them. They have a saying for people who fall down as I do: If a person is hit hard enough, even if she stands, she falls."[44]

Later, during her stay in the community of Chicokema, Meridian functions in yet another shamanistic capacity that Beck and Walters describe as being one of the "servants to the people."[45] They further explain this aspect of shamanism as the desire "to help the people" and state that the sincerity of this desire is of the utmost importance in maintaining the trust of the community.[46] The townspeople see Meridian in this capacity and repay her selflessness with gifts of food and livestock. Meridian recognizes herself in this role as well and tells Truman, "They're grateful people, . . . They *appreciate* it when someone volunteers to suffer."[47]

Walker's depiction of the Wild Child and Meridian's interaction with her while attending Saxon College introduce a theme of abandonment and responsibility that signifies on the well-known African proverb, "it takes a whole village to raise a child," and the Cherokee story, "Kanati and Selu: The Origin of Game and Corn," in which a character called the Wild Boy, or "He-who-grew-up-wild," plays a prominent role.[48] Hudson explains: "In the story, Selu [Corn Woman] washes in the river game killed by Kanati [the Lucky Hunter], thus mixing blood with water. As a consequence, from the blood a boy called Wild Boy comes into existence claiming to be Se-lu's son and claiming to be the elder brother of her own son."[49]

The Wild Boy tells his younger brother that "his mother was cruel to him and threw him into the river."[50] When Selu and Kanati become aware of the Wild Boy's existence, Kanati tells his son to "hold on to him and call for us"[51] so that they could bring him home and raise him. During the ensuing struggle, the Wild Boy again chides his family for abandoning him: "'Let me go; You threw me away!' but his brother held on until the parents reached the spot, when they seized the Wild Boy and took him home with them. They kept him in the house until they had tamed him, but he was wild and artful in his disposition."[52]

In Walker's novel, the Cherokee mythological figure of the Wild Boy is feminized and reconfigured as "The Wild Child . . . a young girl who had managed to live without parents, relatives, or friends for all of her thirteen years."[53] Walker then situates this hybrid creation within an African American community that has neglected its responsibilities as set down in the African proverb. To underscore the community's negligence, Walker gives her Wild Child a younger brother whose disappearance fails to elicit an active response from those who should have undertaken the responsibility: "Wile Chile, as the people of the neighborhood called her . . . had appeared one day in the slum that surrounded Saxon College when she was already five or six years old. At that time there were two of them, Wile Chile and a smaller boy. The boy soon disappeared. It was rumored that he was stolen by the local hospital for use in experiments, but this was never looked into."[54]

True to her status as one who has been thrown away, the Wild Child rummages "through garbage cans . . . her ashy black arms straining at the task" in search of such necessities as "cigarette butts . . . rancid food" and "cast offs." And like her mythic predecessor, the Wild Child also mistrusts the adults who have abandoned her. When spoken to, she "bolted . . . when called to, she would run."[55]

Walker further illustrates the failure of the community to rally together and raise its child by pointing out that no immediate effort is made to rescue her or take her in when it is discovered that she is pregnant. Although the neighborhood was "critical of the anonymous 'low-down dirty dog' who had done the impregnating," they "could not imagine what to do." When "a home for her lying-in" is finally offered, the community only makes one feeble attempt to "capture her" before it gives up, citing Wild Child's slipperiness and "odor" as the rationale behind abandoning her yet again.[56]

After hearing about the Wild Child "while she was canvassing vot-ers in the neighborhood," Meridian returns "to her room in the honors house" and immediately falls into one of her paralytic trances. When she eventually awakens from her visionary state, her determination to shoul-der the responsibility that the community has abdicated is immediately put into action: "With bits of cake and colored beads and unblemished cigarettes she tempted Wile Chile and finally captured her."[57]

Traditionally, the figure of the Wild Boy is associated with "disorder" and rule breaking.[58] Walker continues this tradition by having the Wild Child scandalize the prim and proper campus community as she shouts "loud obscenities," drinks "from the tea pitcher and puts ashes in her cup." These actions, coupled with the fact that she farts "as if to music" while "raising a thigh," are intolerable social atrocities to the "house mother," who tries to "persuade Meridian that the Wild Child [is] not her responsibility."[59] Undaunted, Meridian tries to find an alternative home for her. However, while she is attempting to do so, the Wild Child escapes, darts into traffic, and is killed.

During the riot that follows the college president's refusal to allow the Wild Child's funeral to be held in the college chapel, the shielding Sojourner tree, that had often provided shelter for the oppressed in the past, is destroyed. This tree, made sacred by having been nourished on the flesh of a slave woman who buried her own severed tongue beneath its fledgling branches centuries before and further sacralized by Meridi-an's association of it "with the same sense of minuteness and hugeness, of past and present, of sorrow and ecstasy that she had known at the Sa-cred Serpent,"[60] is cut down by the students "in their fury and frustra-tion."[61] The destruction of the sacred Sojourner tree further tightens and strengthens the African–Native American connection within the narra-tive as it calls our attention once more to the words from *Black Elk Speaks* that are quoted in the epigraph: "There is no center any more, and the sacred tree is dead."[62]

By accepting her "heyoka" vision and working it out within her cho-sen community, Meridian is healed and able finally to leave Chicokema, taking with her Anne Marion's words: "Who would be happier than you that The Sojourner did not die." This revelation, that "[a] tiny branch, no longer than [a] finger, was growing out of one side"[63] of the Sojourn-er's stump, interjects a hopeful final note into the conclusion of the novel that carries the promise of future regeneration for the people and echoes the hope expressed at the close of *Black Elk Speaks:* "I recall the great vision you sent me. It may be that some little root of the sacred tree still lives. Nourish it then, that it may leaf and bloom and fill with singing birds. Hear me, not for myself, but for my people. . . . Hear me that they may once more go back into the sacred hoop and find the good red road, the shielding tree."[64]

Walker's novel clearly expresses her African–Native American subjectivity. As a writer, Walker performs before the people in her own "heyoka" way. She does a literary "backward-forward," "contrary-wise" dance across the pages of *Meridian* to embrace her own diverse ancestors as she reminds the people of themselves and cautions them to remember what and who has gone before them. In doing so, she repeatedly challenges herself and the politically correct as she questions whether or not the price for that correctness is too high.

Throughout her literary career, Alice Walker has embraced and reclaimed the lives of those who have been expediently cast aside in the interest of furthering and developing divisive political and racial ideologies. Within this project of reclamation, as *Meridian* illustrates, she has consistently made a point of expressing her own African–Native American identity and subjectivity by addressing the forgotten or ignored fact that African Americans share a history as well as bloodlines with the indigenous peoples of the South. While Walker's efforts to acknowledge this historical tie have largely been ignored by literary critics, it is interesting to note that, at least on one occasion when the issue was critically examined, the reaction was extremely negative.

Walker's essay, "In the Closet of the Soul," from *Living by the Word* (1988), highlights the violent reaction of the black male poet and critic K. T. H. Cheatwood to the poetic dedication to *Horses Make a Landscape More Beautiful.* Much to Cheatwood's perturbation, while dedicating the work to her ancestors, Walker includes a few that he would have preferred to have remained quietly stuffed away in the genealogical closet:

> for two who
> slipped away
> almost
> entirely:
> my "part" Cherokee
> great-grandmother
> Tallulah
> (Grandmama Lula)
> on my mother's side
> about whom
> only one
> agreed-upon
> thing
> is known:

> her hair was so long
> she could sit on it;
>
> and my white (Anglo-Irish?)
> great-great grandfather
> on my father's side;
> nameless
> (Walker, perhaps?)
> whose only remembered act
> is that he raped
> a child;
> my great-great grandmother,
> who bore his son,
> my great-grandfather,
> when she was eleven.[65]

Cheatwood's review, which appeared in the *Richmond News Leader* in the winter of 1984,[66] expresses his "disdain" for Walker's work, which he describes as "'whimpering, half-balanced neurosis,'" while rabidly attacking the poetic dedication by accusing Walker of mumbling what he refers to as "'the old Negro refrain of: me ain't really a nigger . . . no, no . . . me really a Injin; and let me point out the rapist in my bloodline to you.'"[67] Apparently it is "incorrect," in Cheatwood's jaundiced view, to acknowledge the presence of white rapists and Indian women in one's lineage, in spite of the fact that it was through them that one came to be. It appears that he would have Walker remember his memories rather than her own. He would have her disavow these parts of her uncomfortable lineage that smack of miscegenation of any kind or that delve too deeply, too personally as they reveal the brutal life of one of her own enslaved female ancestors.

Cheatwood's inability to face reality is not unlike the ostrich who sticks his head in the sand. Fortunately for herself and her readers, Walker has chosen to deal in reality, muddled and brutal as it often is, in the hopes that by facing the skeletons in our collective closets a healing may begin for us all.

Cheatwood goes on to warn the reading public that these matters must not be taken lightly "'because Alice Walker is being pushed by the Liberal mainstream as *the* black writer in season.'"[68] He cites the "Liberal mainstream" as seeking to extricate Toni Morrison from a position of recognition in favor of Walker, who, according to Cheatwood, seems to have fallen for "'the bone of divide and conquer'"[69] in her own quest for literary recognition. He further accuses Walker of hating her blackness and having "bourgeois" affectations.[70]

It is ironic that Cheatwood, in the enthusiastic throes of self-styled Walker bashing, has picked up the very "bone" that he has accused Walker of having taken home for dinner. Not only has he pitted himself against a member of his own race, compared two black women authors in a negative way that depicts them as pawns in a kind of bizarre competition over which is better suited to represent the black race, he has also chosen to put another brick in the wall that separates African Americans from Native Americans, a wall that was intentionally erected during slavery to prevent blacks and Indians from uniting and successfully overcoming their mutual oppressors. It was the frequent and calculated practice to employ black slaves as soldiers against Indians and to use Indians on slave-catching expeditions as a means of stirring up antagonism between the two races.[71]

Unfortunately, Cheatwood remains caught in the grip of a tactic that was employed by slaveholders centuries ago. His deep-seated dismay that Walker chooses to acknowledge her Cherokee great-grandmother and his shocking stereotypical use of a manufactured Hollywood Indian dialect to express that dismay breathes new life into old wounds instead of opening the doors of restoration and reconciliation as Walker's poem intended.

Cheatwood's failure to recognize and honor Walker's reclamation of all that she is as her own honest "search for truth and healing in black life"[72] speaks of a kind of rigid patriarchal thinking that demands that one cut off the hand that offends to the detriment of the body as a whole. Obviously, Cheatwood has taken this biblical prescription a step further and would cut off the African–Native American voice as well.

In spite of any negative criticism that she has received, Walker continues to insist on remembering her ancestral past with all its twists and turns. Remembering (re-membering) implies an adding on to something that has been taken away from. In much the same way as the tiny new finger sprouted from the dismembered stump of Meridian's Sojourner tree in an effort to re-member itself, Walker writes to re-member her multiple lineages. She re-fleshes all those skeletons in her family closet and re-peoples the landscape of her heritage.

This re-membering is not an attempt to disidentify with blackness, as Cheatwood would have his readers believe; rather, it is an attempt to own all the shades of the race and all the ancestors who brought these shades into being. Walker knows that wholeness cannot be bought in the house of denial.

By refusing to disown those diverse parts of her genetic and spiritual self, Walker has chosen once again to walk the path of the contrary *hey-*

*oka* and ally herself with the so-called politically incorrect in the cause of cultural reclamation and integration of self and community. By taking this road, she has set herself staunchly against those racist thought-ways that were created hundreds of years ago to insure separation, fear, and confusion; thoughtways that, as Forbes notes, attempt to force African-Native Americans like Walker "into arbitrary categories which tend to render [her] ethnic heritage simple rather than complex."[73] By owning all that she is, Walker enriches what it means to be African American and Native American, and she extends a hand of reconciliation across the centuries. It is up to all of us, red, black, and white, to grasp that hand in the spirit in which it is offered.

## Notes

This chapter was written with support from the University of Idaho Research Office.

1. Jack D. Forbes, *Africans and Native Americans: The Language of Race and the Evolution of Red-Black Peoples,* 2d ed. (Urbana: University of Illinois Press, 1993), 271.

2. Alice Walker, *Living by the Word* (San Diego: Harcourt Brace Jovanovich, 1988), 82.

3. Alice Walker, *Meridian* (New York: Pocket, 1977), and *Horses Make a Landscape Look More Beautiful* (San Diego: Harcourt Brace Jovanovich, 1984).

4. Barbara Christian, *Black Feminist Criticism: Perspectives on Black Women Writers* (New York: Pergamon Press, 1986), 247.

5. Alvin M. Josephy Jr., *Now That the Buffalo's Gone: A Study of Today's American Indians* (Norman: University of Oklahoma Press, 1982), 215.

6. John G. Neihardt, *Black Elk Speaks* (New York: Pocket Books, 1972), 230.

7. R. David Edmunds, "National Expansion from the Indian Perspective," in *Indians in American History,* ed. Frederick E. Hoxie (Arlington Heights, Ill.: Harlan Davidson, 1988), 162.

8. Edward H. Spicer, *A Short History of the Indians of the United States* (Malabar, Fla.: Robert E. Krieger, 1983), 90.

9. William Brandon, *Indians* (Boston: Houghton Mifflin, 1987), 318.

10. Spicer, *Short History of the Indians,* 90.

11. Quoted in James Mooney, "The Doctrine of the Ghost Dance," in *Teachings from the American Earth: Indian Religion and Philosophy,* ed. Dennis Tedlock and Barbara Tedlock (New York: Liveright, 1975), 82.

12. Spicer, *Short History of the Indians,* 92.

13. Walker, *Meridian,* 73.

14. John (Fire) Lame Deer and Richard Erdoes, *Lame Deer: Seeker of Visions* (New York: Pocket Books, 1976), 225.

15. Walker, *Meridian,* 19.

16. Ibid., 20–21.

17. Ibid., 22.

18. Ibid., 30.

19. Ibid., 27.

20. Ibid., 31.

21. Lame Deer and Erdoes, *Lame Deer*, 225.

22. Ibid., 232.

23. Ibid., 225.

24. Ibid., 230.

25. Barbara Tedlock, "The Clown's Way," in *Teachings from the American Earth*, ed. Tedlock and Tedlock, 106.

26. Lame Deer and Erdoes, *Lame Deer*, 235.

27. James Mooney, *Myths of the Cherokee and Sacred Formulas of the Cherokee* (Nashville: Charles and Randy Elder, 1982), 294.

28. Charles M. Hudson, *The Southeastern Indians* (Knoxville: University of Tennessee Press, 1987), 166.

29. Tedlock, "Clown's Way," 106.

30. Walker, *Horses Make a Landscape*, viii.

31. Walker, *Meridian*, 57.

32. Mooney, *Myths of the Cherokee*, 250–51.

33. Walker, *Meridian*, 57.

34. Ibid.

35. Hudson, *Southeastern Indians*, 145.

36. Walker, *Meridian*, 58.

37. Ibid.

38. Ibid., 54.

39. Ibid., 55.

40. Ibid., 53.

41. Ibid., 120.

42. Peggy V. Beck and Anna L. Walters, *The Sacred: Ways of Knowledge, Sources of Life* (Tsaile, Ariz.: Navajo Community College Press, 1977), 100.

43. Neihardt, *Black Elk Speaks*, 17–39.

44. Walker, *Meridian*, 26.

45. Beck and Walters, *The Sacred*, 115.

46. Ibid.

47. Walker, *Meridian*, 25.

48. Mooney, *Myths of the Cherokee*, 242–49.

49. Hudson, *Southeastern Indians*, 148.

50. Mooney, *Myths of the Cherokee*, 242.

51. Ibid.

52. Ibid.

53. Walker, *Meridian*, 35.

54. Ibid.

55. Ibid.

56. Ibid., 36.

57. Ibid.

58. Hudson, *Southeastern Indians,* 148.

59. Walker, *Meridian,* 36–37.

60. Ibid., 93.

61. Ibid., 48.

62. Ibid., 11.

63. Ibid., 217.

64. Neihardt, *Black Elk Speaks,* 233.

65. Walker, *Horses Make a Landscape,* viii.

66. Walker, *Living by the Word,* 88.

67. Quoted in ibid., 86–87.

68. Quoted in ibid., 87.

69. Quoted in ibid.

70. Quoted in ibid., 88.

71. William S. Willis Jr., "Divide and Rule: Red, White, and Black in the Southeast," in *Red, White, and Black,* ed. Charles M. Hudson (Athens, Ga.: Southern Anthropological Society, 1971), 106.

72. Walker, *Living by the Word,* 87.

73. Forbes, *Africans and Native Americans,* 271.

SHARON P. HOLLAND

# 9 *"If You Know I Have a History, You Will Respect Me": A Perspective on African– Native American Literature*

... the life of American realism exists, perhaps, either everywhere or nowhere; like "the real" itself, it resists containment, and for the very good reason that "the real" in America, like the country itself, has always had a notoriously short life.

—Eric J. Sundquist, "The Country of the Blue"

When Black Americans have pursued their genealogy, they have focused on their African roots and sought a meaningful black heritage. Children of black awareness of the 1960s have rarely cared to mention an Indian ancestry because this might be seen as a denial of their African origins and the value of blackness. All this is part of the racial nightmare we have inherited.

—William Loren Katz, *Black Indians*

... due to the untouched nature of its landscape, its ontology, the Faustian presence of the Indian and the Black, the revelation inherent in the continent's recent discovery and the fruitful cross-breeding this discovery engendered, America is still very far from exhausting its wealth of mythologies. Indeed, what is the history of America if not the chronicle of the marvelous of the real?

—Alejo Carpentier, *The Kingdom of This World*

Quintessentially, to be African American is to be a conglomeration of selves and experiences, at once changeable and circumscribed by laws and regulations that attempt to control rather than speak to the difference that constructs, empowers, and sustains communities. The efficacy and creation of literary canons can be described in much the same way; establishing what is "real" and "American" runs parallel with attempts to master borders (perceived and unperceived), to discipline people whose imaginations consistently resist and/or subvert attempts to establish recognizable hegemony, and to impose normalcy through notions of reality defined, for lack of a better word, as tradition. We only have to look at the "family values" platform campaign of the 1992 presidential election for proof of the manic workings of "American"[1] hegemony. In an introduction to the rise of realism in the American novel, the noted Americanist Eric J. Sundquist observes that "[t]o escape the 'paralysis of tradition' is, of course, the typifying American gesture—in religion, in politics, in business, in literature, in life."[2] If we follow Sundquist's formulation, what makes us American—or at least what makes us act like Americans—is this insistence upon decentralizing the primacy of tradition, or American patterns of reality. While this can be seen as a universal paradigm, I would argue that the penalty for feeling this most "American" of emotions—for subjectivities both black and Native—is most severe for those who not only move against tradition but attempt to define themselves against its consistent hegemony, not only challenging "tradition" per se but the superstructure it presents itself upon.

Hence, I begin framing the perimeters of this discussion with words like "tradition," "real," and "American" because each not only speaks to the particulars of a discursive tradition but also facilitates a discussion of African-Native literatures that mediates and problematizes our understanding of varying fields of inquiry. As a graduate student at the University of Michigan, I was drawn to the "tradition" debates in African American studies that challenged not only essentialist analyses of "black" experience but also pushed the edges of the field to more rigorous examinations of "blackness" as agency rather than "blackness" as aesthetics.[3] In responding to an interview question about the making of African American studies, Houston A. Baker Jr. notes, "not only did we envision ourselves in fatigues, but I think we envisioned ourselves as exclusively black, whatever that may mean. And to find that one is in an arena that is multiethnic, multiracial, and international now is quite stunning."[4] What Baker "find[s]" is the changing demographics of America and along with this physical shift an accompanying ideological breakdown of the white/black dichotomy that informed the political movements that created African American studies programs across the country as well as provided the founding critical work of the field. It was the continuing politicization of identity within the field that ultimately led me to seek a definition of otherness that was linked not only with what has been typified as black struggle but also to other struggles for agency and self-determination in this country. After my work with Lorraine Canoe and Jake Swamp at Akwesasne during my undergraduate years and my too-brief trip to Pine Ridge and Turtle Mountain as part of a dissertation research grant, I quickly recognized the similarity between urban and rural "reservations" in this country, and it took even less time for me to see that my physical presence on campus was emblematic of a connection steeped in blood struggle.[5]

In discovering through my family's limited oral tradition a personal heritage that is African, Native American, and Irish, I still struggle with a crossblood identity with the full realization that I might well understand my bloodlines, but I can neither access nor lay claim to them as my own—the economies of slavery, western frontierism, and famine shut the door on any existing "records" of origin that I could trace. In defining myself, I use the term "crossblood"[6] rather than "mixed blood" because I want to make a point about language and terminology; to be a mixed-blood African American is to be counted among the hundreds of thousands of African Americans who have the *knowledge* of some European and/or Native American ancestry, but to be a crossblood is to *identify* as such, to read the "racial" categories on the U.S. census as bogus and to consistently cross the borders of ideological containment. In her preface to *Borderlands/La Frontera: The New Mestiza*, Gloria Anzaldúa remarks that "the Borderlands are physically present wherever two or more cultures edge each other, where people of different races occupy the same territory, where under, lower, middle and upper classes touch, where the space between two individuals shrinks with intimacy."[7] This border—ideological at times, but always an omnipresent political encounter—is a margin that is both dangerous and empowering. Furthermore, the familiarity and proximity that Anzaldúa stresses is a potentially problematic locality in the field of African American studies; while the discourse is intent upon interrogating ideas and ideals of purity in the canon and imploding antiquated notions of an essentialized "blackness," these issues remain nonetheless problematized by literary examinations that move "otherness" outside the limits of essential discourses and seek to extrapolate that existence from the vantage point of an interior rather than exterior landscape. The present tenor of the field is to ask questions along the margin between discourses that could constitute a dangerous yet empowering act of dismantling the very categories of identification that led to its creation.

Moreover, in espousing a "new direction" or field of study within American literature, it is appropriate to outline both the problematics and beauty of such cross-pollination. I do not seek a notion of African–Native American agency through the written text that ultimately reconfigures the territory that is now the United States, or what I would call "occupied America," as a blank slate—a space devoid of any active presence or peopled with European Americans always in control of the standards and means of discourse.[8] Such attention to Eurocentric models of literary self-determination ignores the dynamics of precolonial and postcolonial interactions. The most appropriate way to establish personal legitimacy or to develop agency through literature in the American formula is to set oneself apart from and above any peoples not representative of the mainstream body; such postulating borders on Euro-American uses of supremacy and denies agency to all by catheterizing legitimate connections between peoples. In naming my departure from an all-too-popular way of reading, I am attempting to locate a danger in canon formation already exposed in the work and queries of scholars such as Hazel V. Carby, Michael Awkward, and Toni Morrison.[9] In "Unspeakable Things Unspoken: The Afro-American Presence in American Literature," Morrison notes: "Looking at the scope of American literature, I can't help thinking that the question should never have been 'Why am I, an Afro-American, absent from it?' It is not a particularly interesting query anyway. The spectacularly interesting question is 'What intellectual feats had to be performed by the author or his critic to erase me from a society seething with my presence, and what effect has that performance had on the work? What are the strategies of escape from knowledge? Of willful oblivion?'"[10] Morrison outlines a strategy of literally emancipating traditional canonical literature from the bondage of critical discourse in order to discover a disguised or suppressed presence. In terms of this study of African-Native presence in literature, I do not feel that this is a legacy suppressed so much as one taken for granted. However, finding a space, let alone a subjectivity, that embraces both African and Native identity is also an endeavor to develop an understanding of literature as a process of both *emancipation* and *sovereignty,* as we are seeking the history and lives of a people whose experience crossed the barriers of enslaved bodies and lands. In recovering a concept of Native American sovereignty through Indian intellectual traditions, Robert Warrior surmises,

> Though we have been good at proclaiming our inclusion among the oppressed of the world, we have remained by and large still caught in the

death dance of dependence between abandoning ourselves to the intellectual strategies and categories of white, European thought or declaring that we need nothing outside of ourselves and our cultures in order
to understand the world and our place in it. . . . When we remove ourselves from this unfortunate dichotomy, many things become possible.
We see first that the struggle for sovereignty is not a struggle to be free
from the influence of anything outside of ourselves, but a process of as-
serting the power we possess as communities and individuals to make
decisions that affect our lives.[11]

Warrior speaks of the move toward sovereignty as a conscious rectifying
of energy displaced onto a threat perceived as outside the community, to
a sense of self positioned within the community—a reversal that is ultimately an empowering act. Using Morrison's and Warrior's assessments,
it is possible to move into the space of African-Native literatures with
both emancipation and sovereignty in mind. In tracing the Seminole
maroons, the historian Kevin Mulroy observes a unique move from freedom to agency: "at first freedom meant simply an escape from bondage
but ultimately it would come to embody the larger notion of self-determination."[12] It is this moment and the dynamic between both subject
positions that this work finds most engaging.

Numerous historical accounts have been written on the subject of
an African-Native presence in the Americas, and scholars in the field are
always indebted to the work of Kenneth Wiggins Porter, the late historian who collected material on African and Native American peoples and
developed not only a new field of inquiry but also set the tone for future
scholarship; his research is collected at the Schomburg Center for Research in Black Culture in New York. In the 1980s, two early studies of
African-Native peoples and contacts emerged—William Loren Katz's
*Black Indians: A Hidden Heritage,* originally "designed for schools and
young adult readers" (according to the preface to the eighth printing) and
the Native scholar Jack D. Forbes's *Africans and Native Americans: The
Language of Race and the Evolution of of Red-Black Peoples.* Each is in
its own right a classic in the field of African-Native History, but Katz's
book is especially problematic in places—where Forbes tends to pay attention to the politics of identity and naming, Katz is more apt to hap-
hazardly employ terms like "race" and "wilderness," and he often falls
into romantic (always already supremacist) notions of Native peoples as
folk "who worshipped Nature." Forbes asserts the "hope that [his] study
of interethnic contact and racial classifying will lead to progress in the
field of human rights by highlighting and clarifying a major area of abuse:
the arbitrary and often racist practice of defining the identities of other
human beings by powerful outsiders, as well as by governments and in-

stitutions."[13] Despite the flaws of *Black Indians*, Katz does move to answer the serious query of how these peoples and their history have remained so shrouded with a hypothesis that in the quest for freedom from slavery or self-determination as a people, many African-Native peoples fell between the cracks in settlement discourse and community narrative. In many cases, entitled to neither land nor freedom, African-Native Americans suffered under a dual disenfranchisement, and it is only in this century that we find accounts in literature that begin to match the varied experiences told in oral and written history.

With no separate nation status, African-Native peoples have emerged as subjects in and topics of contemporary literature. Among the few are Michael Dorris's *A Yellow Raft in Blue Water*, which details the growth of a fifteen-year-old African-Native character named Rayona, and Alice Walker's *Temple of My Familiar*, which outlines the obsession of one character, Fanny, with the Seminole chief John Horse.[14] Of those novels whose characters deal with African-Native presence, I would like to focus the remainder of this study on Nettie Jones's *Mischief Makers*, which chronicles four generations of an African-Native family in Michigan from 1920 to 1950, and a section of Leslie Marmon Silko's *Almanac of the Dead*, an epic tale of colonization and the forces that can bring about its reversal. Both novels attempt to explore the complexity of the dual task of representing a people fallen between the cracks of the often competing discourses of emancipation and sovereignty. Questioned about the America revealed in *Mischief Makers*, Jones replies that she attempts to portray this country as "a true ethnic melting pot whose temperature is perpetually near the boiling point because most Americans refuse to recognize the beauty in the beast," and reviews in the *New York Times* and the *Chicago Tribune* have wavered between citing Jones as failing to develop prose and characters that exist "in a solid, convincing world"[15] and praising her for managing "to tell a very complicated story with calculated simplicity and . . . characters [who] are never stereotypes."[16] However, what reviewers and to a certain extent Jones herself fail to acknowledge is that in *Mischief Makers* is the first sustained fictional account of African-Native subjectivity, and that "firsts," no matter how honest, never fail to move into the metalevels of stereotype and dysfunction often recorded in the society at large. After close examination of *Mischief Makers*, it is clear that what is most fascinating about her text is its reliance upon and navigation of categories of "beauty" and "beast," "Indianness" and "blackness," to tell a story of crossbloods and commingling.

Sending her only daughter, Raphael, off to Lake Leelanau, Michigan, to prevent her from marrying into a skin color that they thought they'd passed out of, Asil De Baptiste warns her daughter, "'If you hear every-thing, Peaches, you'll hear a lot you won't understand. I don't want you wasting your life hearing things that you do not like or that you cannot change.'"[17] The efficacy of using silence as a mode of protection becomes cross-examined as the novel progresses. What is ironic about this state-ment is that Raphael remembers these words and recalls them to block out the racist discourse of her new employer, who appears to believe that his new nurse *is* in fact white. Several chapters later it is casually revealed that Dr. Wilhelm Olkers is well aware that Raphael is passing: "He'd never told her or anyone that the instructor she'd used as a reference had felt compelled to tell him she looked white but wasn't, not completely. Willi had told the instructor he was looking for a nurse, not a wife."[18] The secret of Raphael's blackness is exposed as not a private transaction be-tween mother and daughter but a public secret of sorts, hidden from dis-course to allow these characters to cohabitate and, later in the novel, to procreate. But the secrets here are mutually owned, as Raphael is sub-jected to some community truths via her maid, Jeanine, who inquires, "Did she know, for example, that the doctor never married because some said he and another boy carved their initials inside a heart shape all over the forest years ago? Raphael had pretended she didn't hear that one."[19] Like her refusal to name her own blackness, Raphael pretends that she is not witness to the details of Willi's life. But a later scene demonstrates that both secrets are neither life-affirming nor nurturing. In a brief scene, Raphael dies giving birth to a stillborn son who was to be named Francis "after [Dr. Olkers's] first love, the one who'd gone marching off to save democracy and never returned." The irony of the lover's death and the birthing—"There was no sound, only the putrid smell of death"[20]—sym-bolically weds the effect of generational silence that permeates the nov-el's beginnings as the secret of blackness is paralleled with the secret of "homosexuality." Although it appears that this silence is balanced, it still works to the advantage of the doctor more than Raphael, who must be bombarded with Willi's racist remarks about "squaws" and "pickers." Despite the delegitimizing fact of Willi's homosexuality, it is clear that he is empowered to have agency in the society regardless of his public secret; in truth, Raphael has no agency when it comes to the "fact" of her bloodline. She is semi-emancipated only because the fact of Willi's homosexuality prevents him from bartering the word "nurse" in ex-change for a "wife."

If blackness is a public secret and figuratively a beast of burden in *Mischief Makers*, then "Indianness" is defined in contradistinction to blackness as the "beauty" of the text. The relationship between Raphael and Mishe, a full-blood Chippewa from northeastern Michigan, is weighted with sensuality and tension. Jones's Mishe is an embarrassing caricature, whose body is so often oversexualized that he becomes almost mythic and at one point in Raphael's dream appears as a centaur rather than as human. What is also unbelievable is that Raphael, a talented nurse and a self-assured woman, after marrying Mishe becomes figuratively tied to their bed—birthing children, raising them, and sleeping with her husband. But between Mishe and Raphael the tension is most prominently placed in their evaluations of history, and it is evident that in this exchange Jones is searching for the right vocabulary to explicate this cross-blood identity. Unlike the public secret of her blackness, Raphael's African-Native roots exist solely in the domain of her private consciousness—she will share her Native heritage with Mishe but keep what is "black" to herself. During what Jones labels Mishe's "Chippewa's version of history," Raphael muses:

> She loved her husband's history lessons almost as much as she loved her daddy's version. She promised herself that one day she was going to tell them about aunt Rosebud, who went to Alaska during the gold rush days. It was her strike that provided the money for her only nephew, Raphael's father, to receive medical training. Aunt Rosebud's money bought a lot of land for him too. Some of the land he sold to build the Lynne Cheryl. Good he did that too. Otherwise a lot of Detroit Negroes would not have use of a hospital. She'd save all of that. For later.[21]

Imparted to Raphael earlier in the text is her father's account of his Potawatomie and Pawnee blood, his service in the Spanish-American War, and the thievery of robber barons accused of swindling Native peoples in Michigan's Upper Peninsula to secure the land's resource of lumber; and here Raphael equates Mishe's story with her "daddy's version," creating a continuity between the histories, implying that each is a strand from the same lock. Raphael gives breath to this part of her legacy but chooses to omit her private story; the issue at stake here is who has access to this private viewing, and access is a matter of gender relationships and encoded notions of "race" practiced in postcolonial America.

Jones makes it clear that Raphael has access to parts of a family story that her father approves of and considers worth repeating, but as a woman Raphael is silenced about her "blackness" by a father who administers the truth in small doses and a husband who controls the makings of the family's history. However, Raphael begins to bristle when Mishe's story speaks to the materiality of land allotment among the Chippewa of his father's generation. Raphael responds to this capture of lands with:

"The Indians got their forty acres and more. The poor Negroes didn't get their forty acres or the mule they were promised. Haven't gotten it 'til this day. None of the homesteaders that settled around here on the land they were practically given were Negroes either." She was surprised at the bitterness in her voice.

"Niggers are dumb. Dumb niggers and flies I do despise." He looked down at the two sleeping children in his arms. "As much as I do dumb Indians."[22]

In this quick retort Raphael attempts to test the waters with Mishe—to see if he can see himself in solidarity with other disenfranchised peoples. Mishe's gaze directed toward his children confirms for him, figuratively, the *fact* that there is no "dumb Indian" or "nigger" blood in his progeny, and the *knowledge* that this fallacy and private secret stares him in the face is both ironic and an effort to crack open his somewhat self-contained family history. By striving to keep blackness out of the blood, out of reach or out of family discourse, Mishe and Raphael demonstrate that they have the same "use" for blackness in their lives. Disgusted by his language but unable to bring herself to speak the truth about her own blackness that would give him a glimpse into her reality, Raphael resorts to the rhetoric of white abolitionists of the late 1800s with the query, "'Aren't they children of God like us?'" Mishe responds with a "'yes'" but still intones that he now calls them "pickers"—an interesting lyrical change from "niggers" but still in keeping with the economics of slavery, which sees "blackness" as resource rather than source. The major flaw of this scene is that Mishe's tale of history is not given a parallel at any point in the novel with his sister Suk's version of history—its making is sheerly a male enterprise. And enterprise it is, as not only is Mishe's acquisition of land born from a capitalist rather than tribal viewpoint, his language also mirrors Willi's handling of African American presence in Lake Leelanau with reference to migrant workers as "pickers" and the statement, "We need their labor. Not their kind."[23]

In reverse of her mother's journey, Lilly, one of three of Raphael and Mishe's children, moves in with her grandparents in Detroit to attend a preparatory high school. Unlike her other sisters, who do not seem to struggle with their identities, Lilly is made conscious of hers during a previous trip to the house "above Grand Boulevard" where she eavesdrops on the De Baptistes' housekeeper, Dorothy, in conversation with friends. Jones writes, "Lilly overheard one of them refer to the doctors [Asil and David De Baptiste] as 'hankdie niggers.'"[24] In the ensuing conversation Jones tries to hurriedly sketch the dynamics of class always implicit in any claim to African-Native identity in an African American community: "'Are you a Negro?' she asked, sounding as innocent as baby Jesus. Her cousin, Amir, had put her into colored-consciousness training an hour after they'd met. Dorothy, who was black, was almost a pure Negro. Amir didn't know that Dorothy was as much Seminole-Creek-Choctaw as she was African. As a child in the South, Dorothy had learned not to talk about her Indian heritage. Possessing that blood made you a 'hankie nigger' too."[25] For African Americans aspiring to bourgeois positions in American society, to possess Indian blood is literally a "red" badge of success, while for those in the working class possession of Indian blood is liable to make an individual subject to criticism within the community. As the scene continues, Lilly's grandfather responds that he is a "Negro" "by definition of this country," and when she asks about herself and discovers that she is "[p]artly Negro, partly white, partly Indian," she enjoins: "I like being parts of all those people. Makes me a part of everyone—American." At the close of this discussion she observes, "I've got to tell my sisters. For their sakes. And for my father's sake. . . . He's rather proud of having been married to a 'white' woman. He isn't nice to a lot of the pickers, especially the Negro ones. This news ought to help him become a better guy." Lilly's quest to educate her father is so flatly and unrealistically portrayed that we are almost thankful as readers that Jones decides not to incorporate this moment of revelation into the narrative. However, Lilly's own subjectivity is explored further, and she discovers that although being a crossblood might make her feel "American," she does not have access to the privilege of citizenship in America of the 1940s, and she is eventually killed in a "race" riot by a "gang of Negro boys" who mistakenly think that she and her companions are white.[26] Lilly literally pays the price for giving words to a self that her mother never could bring herself to verbalize. Ironically, she is mistakenly killed by folk who cannot see through a cultivated disguise nurtured by her foreparents—her mother's mask of whiteness becomes a burial shroud. Moreover, Lilly's older sister, Blossom Rose, literally blinded by a bullet and figuratively blinded by Christianity, is also confined to her mother's secret self; "As a very small girl, she'd listened when her mother told her not to see or hear everything that went on around her. If you saw it or heard it, perhaps you'd be forced to do something about it."[27]

This parallel of healing and change is, perhaps, the kernel upon which much of the thematics of the novel work. If Jones's African-Native characters can speak their heritage *and* derive a sense of agency through the emancipation of language, then they have carved a place for themselves that might be distinctly American. In a review of *Mischief Makers*, Itabari

Njeri surmises: "Increasingly, . . . 'black' writers are portraying the multiracial reality of their heritage as a source of pride rather than shame, an affirmation of their Americanness. For in what other country have so many of the planet's people merged? Among what other American ethnic group has the blood of so many others blended?"[28] While I agree with Njeri that Jones is suggesting a definition of the term "American" that is not bound by borders or racialized discourses, I would maintain that she is also advocating, specifically through Mishe's narrative, that the politics of what it is to be "American" be seriously scrutinized. In a scene examined earlier, Mishe asks Raphael, "'How'd you feel if someone forced you to give up your tribe to become an American?'" Jones has Raphael continue a pattern of subconscious musings: "She wanted to blurt out that she knew exactly how it felt. She'd done it to become a full American."[29] For both of them the process of becoming "American" is one of negation, as the characters have to dissolve an essential self in order to assume the mask of a nebulous American identity. Even though characters in *Mischief Makers* strive for an identity that is not specified through the delusion of racial purity, it is clear to the reader that finding a place in America as an "American" is still a matter of vistas to be crossed outside the self and in the highly charged space of a politics of multivocal discourses. *Mischief Makers* proves that freedom without agency is neither.

Contesting the site of America by dissolving the efficacy of borders and univocal identities with the publication of *Almanac of the Dead*, the Native American writer Leslie Marmon Silko reaches beyond Laguna Pueblo and back again with an epic novel wherein death is the principle *character* of a violent popular culture—one that thrives on the grotesque and the macabre. If we can view, to use José Saldívar's words, "Postmodern realism as a space of affinities and alliances among diverse histories" and agree that "[p]ostmodern realist invention thus by way of its very speculation becomes the figure of a larger politics of the possible and of resistance,"[30] then Silko's text is a prime candidate for its method of moving across continents to dissolve the disparity of historical tradition and for its myriad of possible sites for resistance to a forced occupation. *Almanac* centers itself both within and without various communities, as technocrats and corrupt officials meander through a succession of gross actions, and the "people" who wish to "take back the land" also experience and wander through a maze of grotesque circumstances, couplings, and terrains, so that the categories of "self" and "other," "inside" and "outside" become blurred in the telling of this story. Inverting the hierarchy of civilized/primitive, Silko explores the depravity and utter disconnectedness of a contemporary society wherein what is irrational and what is potentially alternative are posited as the dominant reality; she maintains that within the terrain of *Almanac* is both the story of witchery[31] and slavery and of revolution and freedom. For Silko, the grotesque functions as a landscape where the trickster plays a game of conflating opposites, subverting reality and surviving the effects of living in the margins of several often competing discourses. Spanning the southwestern part of the United States, *Almanac* moves from northwestern Mexico to Central America, with many of its characters living permanently or for periods of time in Tucson, Arizona. A text that is both universal and specific, it is a story that the many contribute to, but only those who view the *days* as cyclical can understand the meaning embedded in them.[32] The novel is Silko's attempt to deconstruct Western notions of binary oppositions and to create a space of simultaneity—a process supported by both the way events are told in the text and by Silko's narrative structure, where each story is not a "new" beginning but is meant to be laid beside the others in the text.

Reading *Almanac* requires a considerable suspension of disbelief with regards to its inherent reliance upon the discourses of "spirits"—living and dead—that occupy the pages of the novel. Here, "spirits" are both "alive" in language and "heard," as the voices of the dead speak to the living. Writing about the complex epistemology of Native American literature, Kenneth Lincoln finds: "Crossings of breath: every 'word' translates the world we experience by aural or visual signs. Words embody reality. When language works, in flesh or print, our known world comes alive in words, animate and experiential. With more than one epistemological complex in this metamorphic process, any translator must look two ways at once—to carry over, as much as possible, the experiential integrity of the original; to *re*generate the spirit of the source in a recreated text."[33] Because the stories in *Almanac* are created as links in a revolutionary chain, Silko's characters are as diverse as her landscape, and in this difference emerges an African-Native narrative in a section of the novel entitled "Africa." This text appears not as a departure from the other voices in the novel so much as a disruption of the categories of "blackness" and "Indianness." In these chapters, the notion of "self" and "history" as static and contained is shattered; moreover, as the narrative progresses, we see the issues of emancipation and sovereignty conflated and questioned as not only eminent but already present.

During the five chapters of Silko's African-Native text, she declares, "No outsider knows where Africa ends or America begins."[34] Working from the principle that the destinies of the Americas are intricately linked in the history of the people, Silko creates a metalevel where history and illusion blend and our worst fears become our most potent strengths. On the border between illusion and truth is a space of uncertainty, paranoia, and brilliance—it is out of this discourse that the narrative of African-Native subjectivity is born. In the preceding quote, Silko's allusion to an "outsider" is forked, as she refers to European Americans *and* people of color as folk who remain ignorant of the several identities that cross and overlap to create a space prime for use as a location for revolutionary change. She reminds us, "[the] powers who controlled the United States didn't want the people to know their history. If the people knew their history, they would realize they must rise up."[35] This serves as an echo to the title of this study and moves us into the narrative of Clinton, a homeless Vietnam veteran who appears in a chapter entitled "First Black Indian." The opening of this chapter gives us a hint of the prose style of Silko's vast novel as well as an adequate characterization of Clinton himself:

> Clinton didn't bow and scrape for no Arizona honkietrash crackers. Clinton had grown up outside Houston where the cops and Texas Rangers really hated African-American folks. Clinton lives alone in a Sears garden shed he bought for himself. Roy hears rumors Clinton has relatives in Tucson, but Roy doesn't ask questions because that sets something off in Clinton's head. . . . Roy is not afraid of Clint's bad days; on Clint's bad days, Roy is free to talk wild-talk right back at that crazy black fucker. They don't talk to one another; they talk *at* each other, and neither of them bothers to listen to the other. What is important is Clinton's outrage—Clinton's pure, pure contempt for any authority but his own.[36]

As with other parts of *Almanac,* a character's first words provide a guideline for her or his actions throughout the text. Here we are reminded that what matters is Clinton's "outrage" and his "pure contempt for any authority but his own." Unlike characters in *Mischief Makers,* who appear tangible, many of Silko's characters are figures for larger issues and concerns, and Clinton is no exception. This technique allows Silko to throw away much of the baggage of romanticization that surrounds characters of color; it also allows her to transgress the borders between "races" and cultures—in this excerpt, Clinton stands in for the "First Black Indian," and his outrage is both a sign of the times and a manifestation of five hundred years of colonial invasion and intrusion. Clinton's friendship with Roy, a white Veteran of the same war, and their subsequent conversations allude to both the impossibility and necessity of dialogue between representations of colonizer and colonized. It is also ironic and hilarious that the two men "talk *at* each other" but do not bother to listen, their conversations constructed as a tacit miming of their relationship, as Silko later observes: "Roy and Clinton get along because neither man tries to argue good or bad, right or wrong, only what is necessary."[37] As counterparts, Roy and Clinton represent two sides of the same coin.

If we are to understand Clinton's particular generational "outrage," then we have to view his diatribes against history as attempts not only to rewrite parts of the fallacy that is "American" history but also to give voice to a crossblood existence denied to most in the retelling of colonial rule. Recalling the impetus behind the Vietnam War, "Clinton had seen how many dark American faces had been in the Asian war. Clinton had seen the white toads, Lyndon Johnson, and his generals, smacking their lips at all the splattered brains and guts of black and brown men. Forces sent to destroy indigenous populations were themselves composed of 'expendables.'"[38] As if to recall the infamous Buffalo Soldiers sent to "protect" land in Oklahoma's Indian Territory from invasion by greedy settlers,[39] Silko merges Clinton's knowledge of the expendability of soldiers of color in the Vietnam War with an insatiable greed on the part of those in power; this insatiable hunger is an aspect of the grotesque that continually presents itself in the pages of *Almanac*. Clinton achieves agency and a move toward sovereignty because he can see himself in solidarity with other oppressed peoples. With his revision of history he is able to create a landscape and a sense of place from a reconfigured geography and historical record of the Americas. The landscape of reality that Clinton builds serves as a temporary repository of his sovereign narrative. And this reality lives because it is constantly in flux.

In preparing for a revolutionary moment, Clinton stores tapes of potential radio broadcasts to be aired after their "Army of the Homeless" seizes the airwaves. At the opening of a chapter entitled "Spirit Power," Silko begins: "Clinton's first broadcast in the reborn United States was going to be dedicated to the children born to escaped African Slaves who married Carib Indian survivors. The first broadcast would be dedicated to them—the first African-Native Americans."[40] In the next chapter, his philosophy about radio broadcasting is substantiated: "The white man had had the radio waves all to himself; but funny thing was, white men didn't have nothing alive left to say."[41] If we are to view—as the characters in *Almanac* certainly do—revolutionary change as present rather than lodged in a static future, then the moment Clinton constructs is very real with possibility. And, returning to Kenneth Lincoln's discussion of language as living and the "translator's" task as one of "*regenerat*[ing] the spirit of the source," we can observe a model for an understanding of the colonizer's word as deceased and Clinton's potential broadcast as living. Clinton intends to move a degenerate language from the airwaves and allow folks to access a discourse that can be potentially liberating. This revolutionary site is consciously linked in Clinton's version of history to a belief that "it was important for the people to understand that all around them lay human slavery, although most recently it had been called by other names. Everyone was or had been a slave to some other person or to something that was controlled by another. Most people were not free."[42] During Clinton's narrative there is a unique parallel drawn between the absolute dysfunction of "American" discourse and the efficacy of a living language propelled by a hidden history that, once revealed, can end the continent's enslavement by a dead language.

Much of this goal is accomplished through a way of rewriting history that begins with Clinton himself. Listening to his "old grannies" as a child, Clinton remembers the news of his Indian ancestry:

> Clinton had not got over the shock and wonder of it. He and the rest of his family had been direct descendants of wealthy, slave-owning Cherokee Indians. That had been before Georgia white trash and President Andrew Jackson had defied the U.S. Supreme Court to round up all the Indians and herd them west. Clinton had liked to imagine these Cherokee ancestors of his, puffed up with their wealth of mansions, expensive educations, and white and black slaves. Oh, how "good" they thought they were! No ignorant, grimy cracker-men dare touch them! So pride had gone before their fall. That was why a people had to know their history, even the embarrassments when bad judgment had got them slaughtered by the millions.[43]

Obviously self-emancipated by the knowledge of his own history, Clinton is obsessed with viewing that history in its full manifestation—both its tangible and intangible elements. Because of this, Clinton's personal history is not to be seen as isolated from the collectivity of "minority" experience in this country; what Silko describes as "bad judgment" is also the effect of the dead language of whiteness that permeates communities of color so that living connections between individuals are severed and replaced by those that are nurtured by an economics of slavery imposed on both subject and overseer. Throughout *Almanac,* people of color who subscribe to a dead view of themselves and history are continually reminded, as are the Cherokee slaveholders in this scenario, that they have access to this barren language, but ownership is still maintained by its creators and for their benefit. For people of color, *Almanac* is a landscape of virtual reality.

Clinton's broadcasts are meant to disrupt this aging dichotomy with a form of empowerment fostered generations before the appearance of Europeans on the continents of the Americas. Creating a philosophy of agency that is steeped in the intangible,

Clinton wanted his radio broadcasts to emphasize the African people's earliest history in the Americas because slave masters had tried to strip the Africans of everything. . . . The slave masters thought Africans would be isolated from their African gods in the Americas because the slave masters themselves had left behind their god, Jesus, in Europe. . . . Of course the Europeans were terrified, but did not admit the truth. . . . The white man had sprinkled holy water and had prayed for almost five hundred years in the Americas, and still the Christian God was absent. Now Clinton understood why European philosophers had told their people God was dead: the white man's God had died about the time the Europeans had started sailing around the world. Clinton found himself smiling.[44]

Clinton's interpretation of history seems to stand in complete contradiction to Western methodologies employed by scholars in the various fields; his discourse is not confined to "departments" of knowledge but constitutes a hodgepodge of information reflective of his own multifaceted heritage. Clinton's history refuses to be enshrouded—understanding American history as always already lifeless, he replaces it with something uncontainable and more alive than traditional viewpoints, suggesting that the bifurcation of selves and histories in contemporary America constitutes the ultimate crime against people of color and humanity in general. Adhering to a view of "religion" that is eclectic and is not circumscribed by the colonizing religious discourses of Christianity or Islam, Clinton "wasn't trying to scare anyone with his radio broadcasts; scared fuckers would kill you faster than any cocky son of a bitch. Clinton simply wanted people to know the truth. Clinton's only regret was not listening more to the old granny women talking."[45] This view of "ancestor spirits" is not necessarily attributed to the machinations of Clinton's own library of information but to an oral tradition, a living tradition, passed on by the keepers of oral tradition in his family—women. These living words stand to change the face of a disconnected historical record and to emancipate what is dead in us and create a viewpoint that is sovereign by its inclusivity. Rejecting a material reading of this discourse that would obfuscate its meaning, Silko strives for a revolutionary moment that does not necessarily require resistance to a master narrative but undermines its primacy by exposing it as a fallacy—as pieces of the truth parceled out and hidden in tomes erroneously labeled as "American history."

Throughout Clinton's narrative is a constant allusion to hunger, greed, and bloodshed; this connection is often sutured in sexual violence. In his "Slavery Broadcast," Clinton lists thirteen hypotheses about slavery, one of which is that "[t]errorism takes many forms, but most often the violence is sexual, to convince victims suffering is part of their very identity, as unchangeable as their sex or skin color."[46] In this world of "spirits" that he imagines as empowering for people of the Americas is also a story of spirit hunger and greed, as Clinton observes, "European overseers fell victim to terrible vices urged on by the spirits. Overseers no longer concerned themselves with business; instead, [they] lost themselves for hours in savage sexual pleasures. . . . Each day the colonials had retired more and more into their private world, a world that shut out their terror because each instant had celebrated their personal power with the flesh of their slaves . . . nowhere except in the Americas had the colonial slave masters suddenly been without their own people and culture to help control the terrible compulsions and hungers aroused by owning human slaves."[47] Believing that ancestral spirits from West Africa "[o]n American soil . . . had been nurtured on bitterness and blood spilled,"[48] Clinton's particular take on slavery critiques the notion of American enterprise and determination as a false category of national consciousness; instead, we are given a view of Europeans as having been abandoned by their own spirit-life and subsequently urged toward destruction by the power of spiritual discourse. In effect, Silko creates another discursive metalevel altogether, one that, to borrow Hortense J. Spillers's words, "does not escape concealment under the brush of discourse" but begs for recognition and response.[49] Occasioning a new direction for discourse about slavery, Spillers insists upon "a distinction . . . between 'body' and flesh and [would] impose that distinction as the central one between captive and liberated subject-positions. In that sense, before the 'body' there is the 'flesh,' that zero degree of social conceptualization that does not escape concealment under the brush of discourse. . . . If we think of the 'flesh' as primary narrative, then we mean its seared, divided, ripped-apartness, riveted to the ship's hole, fallen, or 'escaped' overboard."[50] Spillers argues that the psychic damage of slavery has yet to be explored as a significant aspect of the slave experience in critical discourse. Focusing too much attention on the body as both metaphor and means of slavery, critics have forgotten about the "flesh" and its discourse, intangible to us today but still very real, nonetheless. Silko's text seems to seek the kind of reading that Spillers insists upon: "Back in the United States, the spirits seemed to be angry and whirling around and around themselves and the people to cause anger and fear . . . people everywhere had forgotten the spirits, the spirits of all their ancestors who had preceded them on these vast continents. Yes, the Americas were full of furious, bitter spirits, five hundred years of slaughter had left the continents swarming with millions of spirits that never rested and would never stop until justice had been done."[51]

Overall, Clinton's narrative stands as an affirmation of every conspiracy theory we've ever heard of, but an affirmation with a twist, providing himself and his audience with a sense that history can be a self-determining factor in a people's emancipation. Most importantly, Clinton is portrayed as no grand revolutionary hero, as his own discourse is marred by misogyny, homophobia, and hatred of a "whiteness" he views as outside of himself. About *Almanac,* Silko says, "it's about time, and what's called history, and story, and who makes the story, and who remembers. . . . But this time I have purposely . . . taken Indian characters . . . and I've dumped [them] off the reservation."[52] Without a connection to a community story or a concrete sense of self-determination, many of Silko's characters are forced to piece together subjectivity taken from diverse narratives offered in the novel as the reality that constitutes contemporary America.

If we are to take Spillers's framework seriously, then the move to discuss African American subjectivity should be a simultaneous motion to unpack the ideology of "captive" and "liberated" subjectivities—the discourse of African-Native peoples provides a space wherein to challenge a highly creative and discursive energy, and both Jones and Silko attempt to use African-Native experience to demonstrate a means of subverting American appeals to normalcy and reality. In no way has this study exhausted all of the parameters of African-Native subjectivity explored in either Jones's or Silko's texts, but sustained here is the hope that this beginning comes close to the spirit of the literature as the struggle to name a new discourse is also a clash with language and its myriad inadequacies. In contemporary African-Native subjectivities we see "blackness," "Indianness," and "whiteness" as categories, commingling and constantly in states of contestation; it is a subject position infused with the ideology of America and the reality, or virtual reality, it utilizes to sustain itself as primary narrative and primary myth.

## Notes

The title of this chapter is borrowed from a chapter title in William Loren Katz, *Black Indians: A Hidden Heritage* (New York: Atheneum, 1986).

1. The word "American" is set in quotes because I want to make it clear that the political space known as the United States, but sustained in quotidian usage as "America," is indeed a superficial site that does not take into consideration that there are two Americas, North and South, and that boundaries between them are always disputed and open to fluidity. For the remainder of this study, my use of the word "American" is always subject to the kind of double-edged meaning ascribed to it in this endnote.

2. Eric J. Sundquist, "Introduction: The Country of the Blue," in his *American Realism* (Baltimore: Johns Hopkins University Press, 1982), 6–7.

3. I am referring in particular to the debates between Joyce A. Joyce, Henry Louis Gates Jr., and Houston A. Baker Jr. in *New Literary History* 18.2 (1987): 335–69. See also articles by Toni Morrison, Eric Foner, and Hazel V. Carby in *Michigan Quarterly Review* 28.1 (Winter 1989): 1–49, and Michael Awkward in "Afro-American Literary Studies and the Politics of Identity," *Voices of the African Diaspora* 8.1 (Spring 1982): 3–8.

4. Michael Bérubé, "Hybridity in the Center: An Interview with Houston A. Baker Jr.," *African American Review* 26:4 (Winter 1992): 550.

5. As an undergraduate at Princeton I had the privilege of working with the Tree of Peace Society in conjunction with the Mohawk Nation and the Friends Society. As a graduate student at the University of Michigan I received a Ford Foundation Research Grant through the Center for African and Afro-American Studies for a trip to North and South Dakota to gather materials for a dissertation project entitled "Qualifying Margins: The Discourse of Death in Native and African American Women's Fiction."

6. Defining crossblood identity, Gerald Vizenor writes: "Crossbloods are a postmodern tribal bloodline, an encounter with racialism, colonial duplicities, sentimental monogenism, and generic cultures. The encounters are comic and communal, rather than tragic and sacrificial; comedies and trickster signatures are liberations; tragedies are simulations, an invented cultural isolation. Crossbloods are communal, and their stories are splendid considerations of survivance" (*Crossbloods: Bone Courts, Bingo, and Other Reports* [Minneapolis: University of Minnesota Press, 1990], vii).

7. Gloria Anzaldúa, Preface to *Borderlands/La Frontera: The New Mestiza* (San Francisco: Aunt Lute, 1987).

8. In "'There Is No More Beautiful Way': Theory and the Poetics of Afro-American Women's Writing" (in *Afro-American Literary Study in the 1990s*, ed. Houston A. Baker Jr. and Patricia Redmond [Chicago: University of Chicago Press, 1989], 135–63), Baker moves dangerously close to this methodology. While arguing for the formulation of an African American women's theory of spiritual discourse, he locates part of this task on a palimpsest, a metaphor that locates a theory of African American women's agency as a process of inscribing their experience on the blank slate of "America," figuratively negating all other presences on this continent.

9. For discussions about literary canon formation, see Hazel V. Carby, "The Canon: Civil War and Reconstruction," *Michigan Quarterly Review* 28.1 (Winter 1989): 35–43; and Michael Awkward, "Afro-American Literary Studies and the Politics of Identity," *Voices of the African Diaspora: The CAAS Research Review* 7.1 (Spring 1992): 3–8.

10. Toni Morrison, "Unspeakable Things Unspoken: The Afro-American Presence in American Literature," *Michigan Quarterly Review* 28.1 (Winter 1989): 11–12.

11. Robert Warrior, "Intellectual Sovereignty and the Struggle for an American Indian Future," *Wicazo Sa* 8.1 (Spring 1992): 18–19.

12. Kevin Mulroy, *Freedom on the Border: The Seminole Maroons in Florida, the Indian Territory, Coahuila, and Texas* (Lubbock: Texas Tech University Press, 1993), 1. I am indebted to Professor Melinda Micco for pointing me toward this contemporary study. Micco also works with African-Native peoples and is completing a project on the Seminole Nation.

13. Jack D. Forbes, *Africans and Native Americans: The Language of Race and the Evolution of Red-Black Peoples* (Urbana: University of Illinois Press, 1993), 5.

14. Michael Dorris, *A Yellow Raft in Blue Water* (New York: Warner Books, 1988); Alice Walker, *The Temple of My Familiar* (San Diego: Harcourt Brace Jovanovich, 1989).

15. Caryn James, "Mischievous Women and Skin-Deep Relationships," review of *Mischief Makers,* by Nettie Jones, *New York Times,* Mar. 1, 1989, C-23.

16. William O'Rourke, "Disturbing Picture of Color and Class," review of *Mischief Makers,* by Nettie Jones, *Chicago Tribune,* May 15, 1989, sec. 3, p. 5.

17. Nettie Jones, *Mischief Makers* (New York: Weidenfeld and Nicolson, 1989), 15.

18. Ibid., 59.

19. Ibid., 22.

20. Ibid., 47–48.

21. Ibid., 32.

22. Ibid., 34.

23. Ibid., 14–15.

24. Ibid., 69.

25. Ibid., 69–70.

26. Ibid., 87.

27. Ibid., 137.

28. Itabari Njeri, "The Mind of Mestizo America," review of *Mischief Makers,* by Nettie Jones, *Los Angeles Times,* Feb. 5, 1989.

29. Jones, *Mischief Makers,* 33.

30. José Saldivar, "Postmodern Realism," in *The Columbia History of the American Novel: New Views,* ed. Emory Elliott (New York: Columbia University Press, 1991), 522, 535.

31. In an earlier work, *Storyteller,* Silko repeats a Laguna story about how "witchery," or sorcery, brought about the coming of the "alien invaders." In this story, the presence of Europeans is cited as caused by the telling of a story that, in the end, cannot be recalled by the "witch" who birthed it with the words, "as I tell the story / it will begin to happen." See *Storyteller* (New York: Little, 1981), 132–37.

32. The events that unfold in this Indian epic are a simultaneous fulfillment and inscribing of the prophecies of the Mayan Books of Chilam Balam, twelve of which have survived and remain as almanacs/manuscripts of the Mayan priests and as the four codices of Mayan hieroglyphs housed in Dresden, Madrid, Paris, and Grolier. In an interview, Silko explains: "The Mayan people . . . believed that a day was a kind of being and it had a . . . we would

maybe say a personality, but that it would return. It might not return again for five thousand or eight thousand years, but they believed that a day exactly as it had appeared before would appear again. It's a view that basically denies a lot of western European notions about linear time, death, simultaneous planes of experience, and so on" (Kim Barnes, interview with Leslie Marmon Silko, *Journal of Ethnic Studies* 13.4 [Winter 1986]: 104).

33. Kenneth Lincoln, *Native American Renaissance* (Berkeley: University of California Press, 1983), 24–25.

34. Leslie Marmon Silko, *Almanac of the Dead* (New York: Simon and Schuster, 1991), 421.

35. Ibid., 431.

36. Ibid., 404.

37. Ibid., 406.

38. Ibid., 407.

39. William Loren Katz, *The Black West,* 3d ed. (Seattle: Open Hand Publishing, 1987), 202. Katz chronicles the work of African American soldiers, named by their Indian adversaries "Buffalo Soldiers," who were enlisted to do the most dangerous job of bringing about white law, order, and settlement to the tribal lands known to Americans as the "frontier."

40. Silko, *Almanac of the Dead,* 410.

41. Ibid., 416.

42. Ibid., 411–12.

43. Ibid., 415.

44. Ibid., 417.

45. Ibid.

46. Ibid., 427.

47. Ibid., 425.

48. Ibid., 417.

49. Hortense J. Spillers, "Mama's Baby, Papa's Maybe: An American Grammar Book," *Diacritics* 17.2 (Summer 1987): 67.

50. Ibid.

51. Silko, *Almanac of the Dead,* 424.

52. Laura Coltelli, *Winged Words: American Indian Writers Speak* (Lincoln: University of Nebraska Press, 1990), 151.

PAUL PASQUARETTA

10  *African–Native American*
*Subjectivity and the Blues Voice*
*in the Writings of Toni Morrison*
*and Sherman Alexie*

One of the most obscured connections in American history involves the shared experiences of Native American and African American peoples. Only recently the focus of critical inquiry, these experiences have been traced to the earliest Spanish expeditions to the Americas and possibly may have earlier origins.[1] As some observers point out, this intercultural connection is characterized by a commonality of interest, attitude, and culture. bell hooks, a writer of mixed African American and Native American descent, celebrates red-black peoples' mutual "reverence for nature, for life, [and] for ancestors. . . . Let us remember," she writes, "that in the beginning of their meeting, Native Americans and Africans were different, but One, among the same world family."[2] Jack D. Forbes notes that these interconnections have had a profound influence on the development of American folklore, music, and literature.[3]

While the convergences of Native Americans and Africans in the Americas have been sources of nurturing and collaboration, a variety of historical factors have caused relations between these groups to be fraught with tension and misgiving. As several writers have pointed out, while shared cultural attitudes and common experiences have contributed to the development of intercultural connections among black and Indian peoples, the racist attitudes and policies of the dominant white community have served to alienate these groups from each other and to prevent them from recognizing the similarities of their experiences. This paradox is evident in the writings of Toni Morrison and Sherman Alexie, two contemporary writers who figure musical invention and the blues as the site of red-black convergence. For both writers, music in general and the blues in particular function as signs that call attention to the historical alliances of Africans and Indians as well as to the silences and omissions that have sometimes resulted from a shared history of dispossession, slavery, and oppression.

Although rarely the subject of critical commentary, the interrelationships between black and Indian communities are central, if subtle, elements of the writings of Toni Morrison. In *Beloved*, her Pulitzer Prize–winning novel, the mountain hideout of Cherokee who managed to avoid removal to Indian Territory provides a safe resting place for a band of escaped slaves on their journey north. In *Paradise*, Reconstruction converges with federal allotment policies in the establishment of a town of Oklahoma freedmen. In *Song of Solomon*, the protagonist's journey into the Pennsylvania and Virginia woods to discover the truth of his mixed cultural identity bears similarities to the roots journey of African American stories and the vision quests of Native American tradition.[4]

While the use of Indian materials is a common practice among American writers, Morrison's is unique in its emphasis on the aural and tactile bonds that unite black and Indian peoples.[5] For Macon Dead Jr., a.k.a. Milkman, the character in *Song of Solomon* who undertakes the vision quest/roots journey, these bonds are made through sound and touch. His first insights into his red-black ancestry occur on a hunting expedition undertaken at night. In the darkened woods, where his eyes are useless, he hears the "long moan" and "sobbing" of a woman's voice mixed in with the yelping dogs and shouting men.[6] The woman's voice, the hunters say, is produced by the wind blowing through a rock formation known as Ryna's Gulch. Ryna, as Milkman later learns, is the name of the woman Solomon left behind, making her possibly the mother of Milkman's grandfather Jake. In hearing the earth speak, Milkman literally hears the voice of his own people. As he becomes attuned to the sounds of the woods, he realizes that the dogs and men are not just signaling location but are talking to each other in "distinctive voices," saying "distinctive, complicated things." Milkman conceives of this dialogue as a protolanguage that existed before "things were written down" and from a time when "man and animals did talk to one another."[7] Given Milkman's entrenchment in the materialistic values of middle-class white culture, as well as his experience as an urban black man, these connections represent a profound shift in his consciousness.

Auditory sensations soon lead to the development of Milkman's tactile senses. Following the example of the experienced hunters, he sinks his fingers into the grass "to hear what, if anything, the earth had to say."[8] What he hears literally saves his life, as it alerts him to the ambush by Guitar, his best friend turned arch enemy, and prevents him from being strangled from behind.

Having survived the hunt, Milkman begins to comprehend a link between his experience in the woods and his tribal ancestry. The key to the ancestral puzzle is provided to him by Susan Byrd, a Native American woman who turns out to be his cousin. According to Susan, Milkman's grandfather's wife, Sing Byrd, was American Indian. Decoding her name to read "Singing Bird," Milkman recognizes the importance of words in keeping alive one's connections to the past. On his return trip north he contemplates the Indian place names, "Ohio," "Indiana," and "Michigan." Dressed in the colors of fall, the states appear to him in the fashion of Indian warriors "from whom their names came." Reading the road signs with interest and wonder, he considers "what lay beneath the names. . . . The Algonquins had named the territory he lived in Great Water, *michi game.* How many dead lives and fading memories were buried in and beneath the names of the places in this country. . . . Under recorded names [that] hid from view the real names of people, places, and things. Names that had meaning. . . . Names they got from yearnings, gestures, flaws, events, mistakes, weaknesses. Names that bore witness." Among the names that Milkman imagines are several with musical associations, among them Muddy Waters, Pinetop, Jelly Roll, Fats, Leadbelly, Bo Diddley, Gatemouth, and Cleanhead.[9] While such names are normally associated with African American musicians, their placement in the text after a discussion of Indian place names emphasizes the indigeneity of the blues tradition, its existence as an African American art form influenced by connections to the culture and traditions of American Indians. With this detail, the text emphasizes the shared history, language, and music of red and black peoples.

Although it has generally been ignored by critics, Milkman's most significant discovery on his journey to Virginia is the identity of his Native American grandmother. As he learns from Susan, Sing's niece, Macon's grandfather Jake was raised by Sing's mother, Heddy Byrd, an Indian woman. According to Susan, the Byrds were never slaves, a detail that raises important questions: Was Jake, the son of Solomon, the legendary flying African, raised as a slave or a free person of color? Did Heddy raise him, along with her daughter Sing, as her own child? These questions are begged but never answered. Milkman, assuming that Jake was a slave, asks Susan if Jake registered with the Freedmen's Bureau before he left Virginia. Susan's ambiguous response leaves the question open: "'everybody who had been slaves [did]. . . . But we were never slaves, so—.'"[10] Her uncompleted sentence, ending with a dash, leaves the reader to ponder yet another mystery. The implication is that Jake and Sing were raised as brother and sister and that their running off and getting married was a family scandal as well as a violation of the incest taboo.

The ambiguity of Jake's status combined with Susan's reticence to speak about the mixing of blacks and Indians point to the complexities of black-Indian relations. Dominated by and often reflecting the racist, Eurocentric attitudes of whites, these relations are fraught with ambivalence. As Susan comments, "'colored people and Indians mixed a lot, but sometimes . . . some Indians didn't like . . the marrying.'"[11] Her hesitant betrayal of a Native bias against blacks as well as her reluctance to speak before her gossipy friend Grace Long suggests her own unwillingness to recognize publicly her African relatives; she only tells Milkman what she knows about their shared ancestors because she expects never to see him again. Susan's racial feelings are immediately recognized by Milkman, who has the "distinct impression" that she "did not like the color of his skin."[12]

Susan's responses are balanced by those of Grace. A teacher at the normal school, Grace is welcoming and encouraging to Milkman. Her emphatic response to the revelation of Milkman and Susan's ancestral ties, "'Relatives! You are all relatives!'"[13] demonstrates her own impulse to recognize and celebrate the African-Indian connection. Her open-mindedness is reinforced when she invites Milkman to visit her class, presumably to share with the children his discoveries. Taken as a pair, the women represent two sides of the historical coin. On the one side, inflicted divisions between black and Indian subjects result in tension and misgiving  between the groups; on the other side, alliances and shared experiences reveal relations of nurturing and kinship.

The interactions of these characters suggest many of the historical and social realities that have complicated black-Indian relations. Emphasizing the inflicted divisions between the two groups, some historians have shown how colonial policies and practices have had the effect of creating an Indian bias against blacks. In *Slavery and the Evolution of Cherokee Society,* Theda Perdue argues that this bias developed as a response to a variety of social and political pressures related to the colonial enterprises of Europeans and European Americans. According to her analysis, Indians initially regarded the darker-skinned people as simply other human beings who, along with the Europeans they accompanied, were either traversing or invading their territory. It was soon apparent to them that Europeans considered blacks inferior, kept them as slaves and servants, and that they were in danger of receiving the same treatment.[14] Thus, while the Indians may have had more in common with Africans than Europeans, the racial hierarchy introduced by Europeans provided powerful incentives for Indians to disassociate themselves from blacks.

Despite their efforts to remain free, Native Americans were enslaved alongside Africans. Indians thus became acquainted with blacks through the experience of common bondage. Despite Susan Byrd's assertion that her family was never enslaved, the practice was common enough to produce the apparent anxiety she expresses over the legal status of her ancestors. Indian slavery did not diminish until the late seventeenth century, when some colonial governments were interested in pacifying bordering nations. According to Perdue, the presence of Indian slaves made it difficult to establish rapport with other indigenous nations, and because Indian slaves could more easily escape into the interior, African slaves were perceived as a better investment.[15]

Capitalizing on the Indians' fear of being enslaved, and fearful themselves of black-Indian alliances, the English colonists helped to contribute to the fiction that Africans and Indians were distinct and unrelated people. This notion of racial difference is preserved in the writings of Thomas Jefferson, who found the Indians' eagerness for hunting and games of chance evidence that their "vivacity" and "activity" of mind were equal to that of whites. Jefferson describes blacks, however, as physically, intellectually, and morally inferior to both whites and Indians.[16] As whites became concerned that blacks would run away and be absorbed into indigenous communities, possibly joining Indians in wars against whites, they made treaties that required Indians to return all runaway slaves. In *Red over Black*, R. Halliburton Jr. observes that these provisions were assiduously kept. Among the Cherokee "Slave Catcher" became a common name.[17] Along with earning rewards for returning escaped slaves, Indians profited from stealing slaves who were later sold or ransomed. Traffic in black slaves thus served as an important aspect of the tribal economy. Eventually, southern nations such as the Cherokee, Creek, and Choctaw developed plantation economies and slave codes as restrictive as those found among the whites. While most slaveholders were of mixed descent (the so-called white Indians), many others were full-bloods.[18]

Despite these policies of separation, the historical associations of blacks and Indians were often characterized by acceptance and sharing.

Many peoples of African descent, slave and free alike, spoke indigenous languages, sang indigenous songs, wore indigenous styles of clothing, and married indigenous people. For many blacks, Indian territory represented a possible safe haven from racism and slavery. In some cases, as with the Seminole in Florida, escaped slaves were fully integrated into the nation as coequal members. During slavery, a colored person could achieve a greater degree of liberty if he or she could pass for an American Indian. After Emancipation, freedmen from Indian nations were allotted land, something that former slaves of whites were never granted.

The cross-acculturation of blacks and Indians is represented in the life of Warner McCary, a.k.a. Okah Tubbee, one of the most gifted American musicians of the mid-nineteenth century. As reported by Daniel F. Littlefield Jr., Tubbee played many instruments, including flute, flageolet, and fife as well as several of his own invention, including a musical tomahawk.[19] Originally from Natchez, Mississippi, he is believed to have been the child of a slave woman named Frankie who was owned by James McCary, a Philadelphia cabinet maker then living in Natchez. While Warner's mother and her two other children were manumitted at McCary's death, Warner and his progeny, according to the will, were to be held as slaves during "all and each of their lives." Littlefield theorizes that the inequality of Warner's condition relative to that of his siblings led the young man to strip himself of a "hated identity and replace it with another more desirable one" that could help him get along in the world.[20] For Warner McCary, the more desirable identity was that of a Native American. Littlefield suggests that it was with this intention in mind that Warner began to pass for Okah Tubbee, the son of Moshulatubbee, a well-known Choctaw chief. In a biography dictated to his Native American wife, Laah Ceil, Warner describes himself as Moshulatubbee's long lost son. As Okah Tubbee, he dedicated his life to bringing peace to the Indians through his music. It would be as an itinerant Choctaw musician, missionary, and herb doctor that Okah Tubbee would enjoy opportunities and freedoms generally unavailable to persons of color living in the United States at that time.

Okah Tubbee's life provides a point of departure for examining the convergences of African and Native American musical traditions. As *Song of Solomon* indicates, music, singing, and the blues are associated with the black-Indian experience. This becomes evident to Milkman, who in the singing game played by the children of Shalimar first hears the story of his red-black ancestors. In another part of the novel, Jake's daughter Pilate hears her father's spirit crying out "sing," which she understands as an exhortation to sing; she sings the blues. As her nephew later learns,

Sing is also the name of Jake's Indian wife. Thus, "sing" figures as a sign that connects the blues tradition with black America's experience vis-à-vis the Indians.

The influence of Native Americans on the development of the blues is evident in a white missionary's description of a Cherokee dance in the early nineteenth century. The writer describes lines of men and women dancing all night, "laughing," "hallooing," and "yelling," as the leader sings extemporaneously about his exploits in a manner the missionary finds "disagreeable" and "monotonous."[21] Whites often described black music in similarly pejorative language, and, when we read beyond the racial biases of the missionary's statement, we see that many of the things described in the report, including the steady rhythm, the call and response between audience and leader, and the improvised lyrics are also features of African American musical traditions. It is certain that African Americans, slave and free alike, attended such dances and came away with impressions of their own. It is likely that they incorporated the new sounds into existing musical repertoires. According to Mixashawn Rozie, an African Algonquian jazz artist and music educator from the Connecticut River valley, there are striking similarities between blues shuffle patterns and the two-step rhythms found in some Indian dance music.[22] While many of the rhythms associated with African American music can be traced to Africa, he suggests the possibility that blues rhythms are indigenous to North America and informed by the shared experiences of African and Native American peoples. Music historians and musicologists have likewise argued that spirituals, jazz, rhythm and blues, and other forms primarily associated with black musical invention are similarly inflected by a Native Americanist presence.[23] This connection is evident in New Orleans's Mardi Gras traditions as well as in the biographies of such well-known singers and musicians as Paul Robeson, Josephine Baker, Lena Horn, Pearl Bailey, Lead-belly, Tina Turner, and Charles Mingus, all of whom claim partial Native American ancestry.[24]

Among the American writers most influenced by the shared musical heritage of red and black peoples is Sherman Alexie. In poems such as "Red Blues" and "John Coltrane Blowing," the speaker describes "drum[s] that sound . . . like the blues," Robert Johnson and Crazy Horse playing slide guitar, and John Coltrane blowing a "tender tenor pain" for the Indian boys.[25] In the short story "Because My Father Always Said He Was the Only Indian Who Saw Jimi Hendrix Play 'The Star Spangled Banner' at Woodstock," the narrator Victor Joseph comments that "the first time [he] heard Robert Johnson sing [he] understood what it meant to be Indian on the edge of the twenty-first century, even if [Johnson] was black at the beginning of the twentieth."[26] These references are central to the form, style, and politics of Alexie's writing. In "Rock and Roll, Redskins, and Blues in Sherman Alexie's Work," P. Jane Hafen writes that Alexie reinscribes the blues trope for the purpose of presenting an American Indian cultural and political view of subversion and resistance.[27]

In "My Father Always Said," Jimi Hendrix, a blues guitarist of partial Cherokee descent, is celebrated as an iconic symbol of a distinct black Indian presence that subverts and resists the homogenizing influences of mainstream white culture. The historical Hendrix made a point of emphasizing his black-Indian roots. In songs like "I Don't Live Today" and "Castles Made of Sand," he kept alive the cultural connection to his Indian past and even politicized the contemporary plight of Native American people by linking their struggle to African American civil rights.[28] In *Reservation Blues,* Alexie celebrates Hendrix's music by linking it to the lives of his Indian characters and narrators. In "My Father Always Said," Hendrix's version of "The Star Spangled Banner" provides a moment of reconciliation for an Indian boy and his alcoholic father.[29]

The references to Coltrane, Johnson, and Hendrix suggest more than a casual connection between Alexie's art and black musical invention. While Alexie also celebrates the music of iconic white musicians like Elvis Presley and Janis Joplin, the speakers of his poems and the narrators of his stories gravitate toward black musical icons. Describing the relationship between black music and contemporary Native American writing, Rebecca Tsosie describes the story of Indian survival as a "coyote story, with a trickster-figure singing the blues, laughing and crying (often simultaneously), and beating incredible odds."[30] As Indian writers "track past hurts and wrongs," they "transcend the pain through song, prayer and unity, much as the black people have done through the spirituals and the blues."[31] This transcendence is particularly apparent in Alexie's writing. As Jennifer Gillan notes, blues, jazz, gospel, rock, and folk, along with Native American pow-wow music and drumming, provide Alexie with the materials to explore the possibilities of cross-cultural articulation. Blues is one of the most important of these elements. Citing Ralph Ellison's description of the blues as "'an impulse to keep the painful details and episodes of a brutal experience alive in one's aching consciousness, to finger its jagged grain, and to transcend it, not by the consolation of philosophy but by squeezing from it a near-tragic, near-comic lyricism,'" she points out that Alexie adapts the blues to express his own joy and loss.[32]

These musical connections are even more evident in *Reservation Blues.*[33] In this 1995 novel, the Spokane Indian Reservation is the crossroads where the blues legacy is renewed by a Native American band named Coyote Springs. For Robert Johnson, the legendary blues player, the reservation is a place of sanctuary and healing. The historical Johnson is a tragic figure whose death in the 1930s is shrouded in mystery. According to the legend that grew up around his name, Johnson sold his soul to the devil in exchange for extraordinary abilities on guitar. In the novel, a resurrected Johnson accompanied by his magical guitar arrives on the Spokane Indian Reservation in search of Big Mom, a tribal healer and music teacher. Wishing to be free of the instrument, Johnson seeks sanctuary on Big Mom's mountain. While the guitar has made Johnson famous, it has cost him his freedom. Having the powers both to create and destroy, it rules its possessor like a drug rules the addict. In the course of the novel Johnson is restored to spiritual health, but only after he learns to deny the guitar's seductive power and be content with a humbler instrument, a cedar harmonica fashioned by Big Mom, who explains that this was the instrument he was supposed to be playing all along.[34] Through this retelling of the blues legend, Alexie makes the tragic trope comic. Like the characters in Toni Morrison's fiction, or like real-life figures such as Okah Tubbee, Johnson finds freedom and possibility in tribal culture.

Big Mom provides the ritual site where music and healing are combined. Each morning she plays a new flute song to remind the people that "music created and recreated the world daily."[35] The flute is made from the rib bone of a horse killed by U.S. soldiers. She also plays a guitar made from the body of a '65 Chevy Malibu and the blood of a child killed at Wounded Knee. These materials suggest the connection between history and music found in Morrison's writing as well as in such artifacts as Okah Tubbee's legendary musical tomahawk. The surreal combination of iconic American symbols allows Big Mom to play a chord invented especially for Indians, the "loneliest" chord that Coyote Springs had ever heard.[36] In order to develop as musicians, the band must memorize its effects upon their bodies. Big Mom's music, like the voice that echoes through Ryna's Gulch or the song sung by the children of Shalimar, allows the band an auditory route to the past. While this music recalls a painful history, it does so in order to begin the curative process.

If music is essential to the survival and well-being of Alexie's characters, it is by no means the cure for what ails them. As the-man-who-was-probably-Lakota comments early in the novel, "Music is a dangerous thing" that can both heal and hurt.[37] This paradox is evident to Thomas Builds-the-Fire, the band's leader, who wonders if Coyote Springs deserves to succeed.[38] Like players in the tribal stick game to which Alexie's narrator makes reference, Thomas and his cohorts must choose among the options presented to them.[39] According to the narrator, "If an Indian chose the correct hand, he won everything, he won all the sticks. If an Indian chose wrong, he never got to play again. Coyote Springs had only one dream, one chance to choose the correct hand."[40] For Thomas, who wants his songs and stories to "save everybody," these choices have a moral dimension.[41] While he desires fame and fortune, the rights of the successful musician, he wishes to avoid the proverbial deal with the devil. Choosing the correct hand therefore involves making moral choices that resist the forces that corrupt and literally capitalize on the healing powers of music. On the ill-fated trip to the New York City studios of Cavalry Records, the band learns just how dangerous it is to deal with these forces, which, in this case, are embodied in the voice of Robert Johnson's guitar and the record company executives named for two nineteenth-century Indian fighters, George Wright and Phil Sheridan. When the recording session degenerates into a fist fight, it would seem that the band has made the wrong choice. Upon their return home, one member commits suicide and another turns to alcoholism. Three others move to Spokane. Wiser for their experience, they are optimistic about their chances in the city. As in *Song of Solomon*, music provides the vehicle through which characters come to a truer recognition of themselves and their history. By itself, however, it can offer no solution to their problems.

As well as celebrating the shared political, social, and artistic sensibilities of black and Indian peoples, Alexie's writings call attention to the forces that have contributed to what bell hooks calls the "historical erasure and suppression of documents and information affirming the depth of [black-Indian] ties."[42] The fear and misunderstanding behind this erasure is the subject of Alexie's found poem, "Harmful Jazz." A rearrangement of a 1921 newspaper article, it reflects traditional attitudes among whites to separate and control black and Indian peoples:

> Jazz music is proving too much
> for the American Indian
> says Dr. Henry Beets, secretary of the
> Christian Reform Church Missions.
> He declares that jazz and the shimmy
> are driving the redskin back to the war dance.[43]

In the first half of the poem the speaker expresses fear that jazz is stimulating a revival of traditional Indian culture ("driving" the Indians back to the "war dance"), thereby imperiling white, Christian culture. Later in the poem, however, "modern steps" constitute a threat to traditional Indian culture as well:

> [Dr. Beets] suggests that the Interior Department stop
> Indian maids and youths dancing modern steps
> in order to save their morals and bring them back
> to the paths of their fathers.[44]

In this passage the speaker describes the contradictory impulses of whites to control the supposedly subversive aspects of Native culture while at the same time working to save "pure" Indians from contamination with blacks. It would seem never to have occurred to the ironically named Dr. Beets that the modern steps of jazz include, rather than exclude, indigenous musical traditions.

By suppressing the so-called harmful effects of shared musical traditions, church and government officials cut off Native Americans and African Americans from their historical ties to each other. In *Reservation Blues,* Alexie calls attention to the alienation that results from this process of cultural separation by examining its effects upon the reservation community. As the narrator comments throughout the novel, the isolation of the Spokanes and the influence of church and government officials has made them closed-minded and insular. In one episode the reservation priest instructs tribal members to burn books and records believed to be the devil's tools.[45] By introducing new people and ideas to the community, Coyote Springs is likewise the focus of violence and scapegoating. While Thomas is sensitive to the "ancient, aboriginal, and indigenous" character of the blues, the Spokanes in general are unable to connect it with their own lives: "Those blues created memories for the Spokanes, but they refused to claim them. Those blues lit up a new road, but the Spokanes pulled out their old maps. . . . Thomas listened closely, but the other Spokanes . . . would not speak about any of it. They buried all of their pain and anger deep inside, and it festered, then blossomed, and the bloom grew quickly."[46] In this passage, Alexie reflects upon the ambiguities and tensions foregrounded in Morrison's treatment of the red-black connection. While both writers bring to their texts the shared experiences of African American and Native American peoples, they find those experiences to be both divisive and binding. On the one hand, they indicate alliances and shared cultural traditions; on the other hand, they call attention to common misfortunes and sufferings that have contributed to the alienation of these groups from each other. While song provides a means for both writers to "track past hurts and wrongs," it has only a limited power to bridge the gaps and silences that foster alienation. Nonetheless, while it may not heal by itself, music is necessary to the process of healing. As James Baldwin writes in "Sonny's Blues," while the tale of suffering, delight, and triumph conveyed by the blues is never new, it must be heard. "There isn't any other tale to tell, it's the only light . . . in all this darkness."[47]

## Notes

1. Jack D. Forbes, *Africans and Native Americans: The Language of Race and the Evolution of Red-Black Peoples,* 2d ed. (Urbana: University of Illinois Press, 1993), 6–25.

2. bell hooks, *Black Looks: Race and Representation* (Boston: South End Press, 1992), 180. The antiquity of this intercultural link is preserved in a Guyanese story reported by Forbes. It describes an ancient meeting between the spirit powers of Africa and the Americas. Present for the Africans are Nyan, an African sky-spirit, Anancy, the spider-trickster, and their companions, the African earth-mother and river-mother; the Native Americans are represented by the Great Spirit, the Father Sun, and other spirit powers. According to the story, this was the first time that the ebony people made themselves heard to the Americans. After this encounter, the powers agree to share each other's domains and establish a close cooperative relationship (Forbes, *Africans and Native Americans,* 6).

3. Forbes, *Africans and Native Americans,* 190.

4. Toni Morrison, *Beloved: A Novel* (New York: Knopf, 1987), *Paradise* (New York: Knopf, 1998), and *Song of Solomon* (New York: Signet, 1977). *Song of Solomon* bears many similarities to Leslie Marmon Silko's *Ceremony* (New York: Viking Press, 1977). Both novels chart the spiritual journey and development of a man dislocated from his people and culture.

5. A comparison to Faulkner's well-known use of Native American materials in "The Bear" will serve to demonstrate this point. In both "The Bear" and *Song of Solomon,* the hunt for an animal provides the vehicle for the protagonist to connect metaphysically with the land, the ancestors, and the past. Lucinda MacKethan describes the shared theme of both texts as the "making and reading of texts centered on the past, in which grandfathers represent how the past is passed on" ("The Grandfather Clause: Reading the Legacy from 'The Bear' to *Song of Solomon*," in *Unflinching Gaze: Morrison and Faulkner Re-Envisioned,* ed. Carol A. Kolmerten, Stephen M. Ross, and Judith Bryant Wittenberg [Jackson: University Press of Mississippi, 1997], 99). To make this connection both characters must relinquish materialism and the trappings of civilization. A native of rural Mississippi, Ike leaves behind his watch and compass. A northerner raised in an urban, middle-class environment, Milkman foregoes his money, reputation, and fine clothes. In Faulkner's text, it is the black Indian guide, Sam Fathers, who leads the white protagonist; in Morrison's novel, the black protagonist is led to an Indian household, where he discovers his ancestral ties not only to the land but to the indigenous peoples to whom he is related. An important difference between Faulkner's white Indian and Morrison's black Indian is suggested by each character's dominant sense. Ike's dominant sense is sight; his object is to see the bear. For Milkman, the dominant senses are hearing and touch.

William Faulkner, "The Bear," in *The Portable William Faulkner*, ed. Malcolm Cowley (New York: Penguin Books, 1977), 197–320.

6. Morrison, *Song of Solomon*, 276.

7. Ibid., 281.

8. Ibid., 282.

9. Ibid., 333–34.

10. Ibid., 328.

11. Ibid., 325.

12. Ibid., 291.

13. Ibid., 293.

14. Theda Perdue, *Slavery and the Evolution of Cherokee Society, 1540–1866* (Knoxville: University of Tennessee Press, 1979), 36.

15. Ibid., 37. Others have shown that the institution of Indian slavery made it quite difficult for Indians to escape into the interior. Enslaved far from their own nations and surrounded by other Indian nations hostile to them who captured and sold escaped slaves, Indians received treatment similar to that of their black counterparts. See Almon Lauber, "Indian Slavery in Colonial Times within the Present Limits of the United States," *Studies in History, Economics, and Public Law* 54.3 (1913): 1–352.

16. Merrill D. Peterson, ed., *The Portable Thomas Jefferson* (New York: Penguin Books, 1977), 186–93.

17. R. Halliburton Jr., *Red over Black: Black Slavery among the Cherokee Indians* (Westport, Conn.: Greenwood Press, 1977), 8.

18. Ibid., 11.

19. Daniel F. Littlefield Jr., Introduction to *The Life of Okah Tubbee*, ed. Daniel F. Littlefield Jr. (Lincoln: University of Nebraska Press, 1988), vii.

20. Ibid., viii–ix.

21. Quoted in John Ehle, *Trail of Tears: The Rise and Fall of the Cherokee Nation* (New York: Anchor Books, 1988), 139.

22. Mixashawn's own recordings demonstrate this shared musical legacy: *The Maheekanew View of Mixashawn*, audiocassette, 1991; *Word, Out . . . Music for the Next Century*, compact disc, 1993; *Live at Schemitzun '93*, audiocassette, 1993. Recordings are available through Indian Ruins Studio in Minneapolis, Minn., or by calling 1-800-949-MIXA.

23. The influence of Native American music on jazz is discussed by Burton W. Peretti in *The Creation of Jazz: Music, Race, and Culture in Urban America* (Urbana: University of Illinois Press, 1994), 42.

24. Forbes, *Africans and Native Americans*, 190; Charles Mingus, *Beneath the Underdog: His World as Composed by Mingus* (New York: Vintage Books, 1973), 66.

25. Sherman Alexie, *Old Shirts and New Skins* (Los Angeles: UCLA American Indian Studies Center, 1993), 85–87, and "John Coltrane Blowing," in *Hanging Loose 61* (Brooklyn, N.Y.: Hanging Loose Press, 1992), 12.

26. Sherman Alexie, "Because My Father Always Said He Was the Only Indian Who Saw Jimi Hendrix Play 'The Star-Spangled Banner' at Woodstock," in *The Lone Ranger and Tonto Fistfight in Heaven* (New York: Harper Perennial, 1994), 35.

27. P. Jane Hafen, "Rock and Roll, Redskins, and Blues in Sherman Alexie's Work," *Studies in American Indian Literatures* 9.4 (Winter 1997): 71.

28. See Harry Shapiro and Caesar Glebbeek, *Jimi Hendrix: Electric Gypsy* (New York: St. Martin's Press, 1990); The Jimi Hendrix Experience, *Are You Experienced?* compact disc, MCA, 1993, liner notes by Michael Fairchild, 22.

29. Hafen, "Rock and Roll, Redskins, and Blues," 73.

30. Rebecca Tsosie, "Surviving the War by Singing the Blues: The Contemporary Ethos of American Indian Political Poetry," *American Indian Culture and Research Journal* 10.3 (1986): 27.

31. Ibid., 49.

32. Jennifer Gillan, "Reservation Home Movies: Sherman Alexie's Poetry," *American Literature* 68.1 (Mar. 1996): 109.

33. Sherman Alexie, *Reservation Blues* (New York: Warner Books, 1995).

34. Ibid., 278.

35. Ibid., 10.

36. Ibid., 207.

37. Ibid., 12.

38. Ibid., 72.

39. Gambling metaphors are common in Native American literature. Some of the best examples are found in these contemporary writings: Leslie Marmon Silko, *Ceremony* and *Storyteller* (New York: Little, Brown, 1981); Gerald Vizenor, *Bearheart: The Heirship Chronicles* (Minneapolis: University of Minnesota Press, 1990) and *The Heirs of Columbus* (Middletown, Conn.: Wesleyan University Press, 1991); and Louise Erdrich, *Love Medicine* (New York: Harper Perennial, 1993), *Tracks* (New York: Henry Holt, 1988), and *The Bingo Palace* (New York: Harper Collins, 1994). One of the earliest and best examples of gambling metaphors in American Indian fiction is found in the 1927 novel *Cogewea, the Half Blood* (Lincoln: University of Nebraska Press, 1981), by Christal Quintasket under the pen name Mourning Dove. In common with Alexie, Mourning Dove lived and wrote in Washington state. As in *Reservation Blues,* the tribal gaming metaphors in *Cogewea* provide cultural, ideological, and ethical touchstones for characters working through their own set of choices.

40. Alexie, *Reservation Blues,* 220.

41. Ibid., 101.

42. hooks, *Black Looks,* 182.

43. Sherman Alexie, "Harmful Jazz," in *Summer of Black Widows* (Brooklyn, N.Y.: Hanging Loose Press, 1997), 77.

44. Ibid.

45. Alexie, *Reservation Blues,* 146.

46. Ibid., 174–75.

47. James Baldwin, "Sonny's Blues," in *Early Novels and Stories* (New York: Penguin Putnam, 1998), 862.

# CONTRIBUTORS

Sandra K. Baringer is a lecturer at the University of California at Riverside. She has published essays in the *American Indian Culture and Research Journal*, *Studies in American Indian Literature*, and other journals and anthologies. Her research focuses on the intersection of race theory and the construction of criminality.

Jason Berry, a New Orleans writer and jazz critic, is the author of *Amazing Grace: With Charles Evers in Mississippi* (Saturday Review Press, 1973), *Lead Us Not into Temptation: Catholic Priests and the Sexual Abuse of Children* (Doubleday, 1992; rpt., University of Illinois Press, 2000), and *Spirit of Black Hawk: A Mystery of Africans and Indians* (University Press of Mississippi, 1995). He is also a coauthor with Jonathan Foose and Tad Jones of *Up from the Cradle of Jazz: New Orleans Music since World War II* (University of Georgia Press, 1986).

Jonathan Brennan teaches African American and Native American literature at Mission College in Santa Clara, California. He is the editor of *Mixed Race Literature* (Stanford University Press, 2002), and his published essays include "African–Native American Literature" in the *Oxford Companion to African American Literature* (Oxford University Press, 1997).

Jonathan Foose is a producer of blues recordings and an independent writer and folklorist in Austin, Texas. He conducted many oral interviews with New Orleans musicians in the 1970s and coproduced, with Jason Berry, the video documentary *Up from the Cradle of Jazz*.

David Elton Gay teaches folklore in the School of Continuing Studies at Indiana University. His published essays include "The Creation of the Kalevala, 1833–1849" (in *Jahrbuch fur Volksliedforschung* [1997]), "The Supernatural World of Christian Folk Religion in Twentieth-Century America" (in *Papers Given at the Symposium "Christian Folk Religion"* [1999], vol. 2 of the serial publication *Studies in Folklore and Popular Religion*), and "Inventing the Text: Scholarly Editing as a Creative Act" (in *Rethinking Ethnology and Folkloristics*, ed. Pille Runnel [2001]). He has also contributed reviews on Native American, European, and Jewish folk religion and mythology to various publications.

Sharon P. Holland is the director of graduate studies in the Department of English and an associate professor of English and African American studies at the University of Illinois at Chicago. She is the author of *Raising the Dead: Readings of Death and (Black) Subjectivity* (Duke University Press, 2000), which was awarded the Lora Romero First Book Prize by the Association of American Studies. Her interests include the fields of African and Native American studies and feminist and queer studies. She is at work on a number of projects, including a second monograph (with the working title "Between Fabrication and Generation: Telling the Story of a Woman"), a novel, and a play.

Tad Jones is an independent scholar and music historian in New Orleans. He has written for *Living Blues* and other journals and has taught at the University of New Orleans. He is an authority on the city's musical history and is at work on a biography of Louis Armstrong's early years. He has been a consultant on many projects for WYES-TV and the video documentary *Up from the Cradle of Jazz.*

George Lipsitz is a professor of ethnic studies at the University of California at San Diego. He is the author of *Time Passages: Collective Memory and American Popular Culture* (University of Minnesota Press, 1990), *The Sidewalks of St. Louis: Places, People, and Politics in an American City* (University of Missouri Press, 1991), *Rainbow at Midnight: Labor and Culture in the 1940s*, rev. ed. (University of Illinois Press, 1994), *Dangerous Crossroads: Popular Music, Postmodernism, and the Poetics of Place* (Verso, 1994), and *A Life in the Struggle: Ivory Perry and the Culture of Opposition*, rev. ed. (Temple University Press, 1995).

Benilde Montgomery, an assistant professor and chair of the drama and dance department at Dowling College in Oakdale, New York, is a member of the Franciscan Order. While his earliest published essays appeared in journals devoted to religion and American literature (*Renascence, Journal of the American Academy of Religions, Concerning Poetry*), his most recent published essays have been in the field of dramatic criticism (in *Modern Drama, Eighteenth Century Studies, Twentieth Century Literature*).

Paul Pasquaretta teaches American studies, literature, and writing at SUNY Empire State College. He has written widely on literary and cultural texts involving gambling, music, ethnicity, and the environment and is the author of *Gambling and Survival in Native American History, Politics, and Literature* (University of Arizona Press, 2003).

Patricia Riley, a poet and writer of Cherokee and Irish descent, is an assistant professor of English at the University of Idaho, where she teaches courses in Native American and other ethnic literatures. She is the editor of *Growing Up Native American* (Morrow, 1993), an anthology of fiction and nonfiction, and has published articles in *Fiction International* and essays in the anthologies *Understanding Others: Cultural and Cross-Cultural Studies and the Teaching of Literature* (National Council of Teachers of English, 1992) and *Our Voices: Essays in Culture, Ethnicity, and Communication* (Roxbury, 1994, 1997, 2000). Her poetry has appeared in *Northeast Indian Quarterly: Akwe:kon* and *Studies in American Indian Literature,* and her short fiction has been included in *Earth Song, Sky Spirit: Short Stories of the Contemporary Native American Experience* (Anchor Books, 1993) and *Blue Dawn, Red Earth: New Native American Storytellers* (Anchor Books, 1996).

The late John Sekora was a professor of English at North Carolina Central University. He coedited, with Darwin T. Turner, *The Art of Slave Narrative: Original Essays in Criticism and Theory* (Western Illinois University, 1982) and authored *Luxury: The Concept in Western Thought, Eden to Smollett* (Johns Hopkins University Press, 1977), as well as essays on African American literature.

# INDEX

*The University of Illinois Press*
*is a founding member of the*
*Association of American University Presses.*

_____

*Composed in 9.5/12.5 Trump Mediaeval*
*by Jim Proefrock*
*at the University of Illinois Press*
*Manufactured by Thomson-Shore, Inc.*

*University of Illinois Press*
*1325 South Oak Street*
*Champaign, IL 61820-6903*
*www.press.uillinois.edu*